Four-Step Watercolour

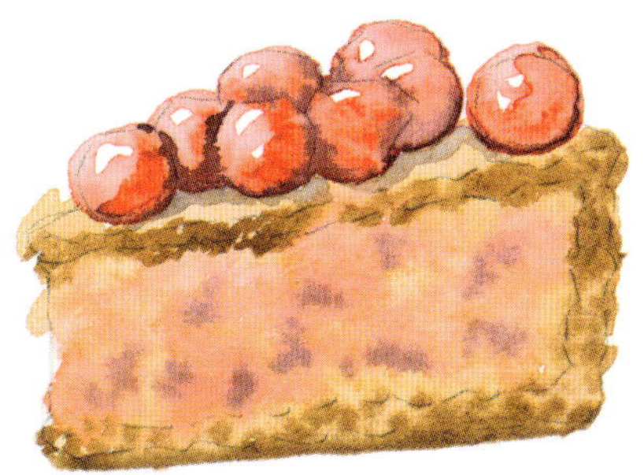

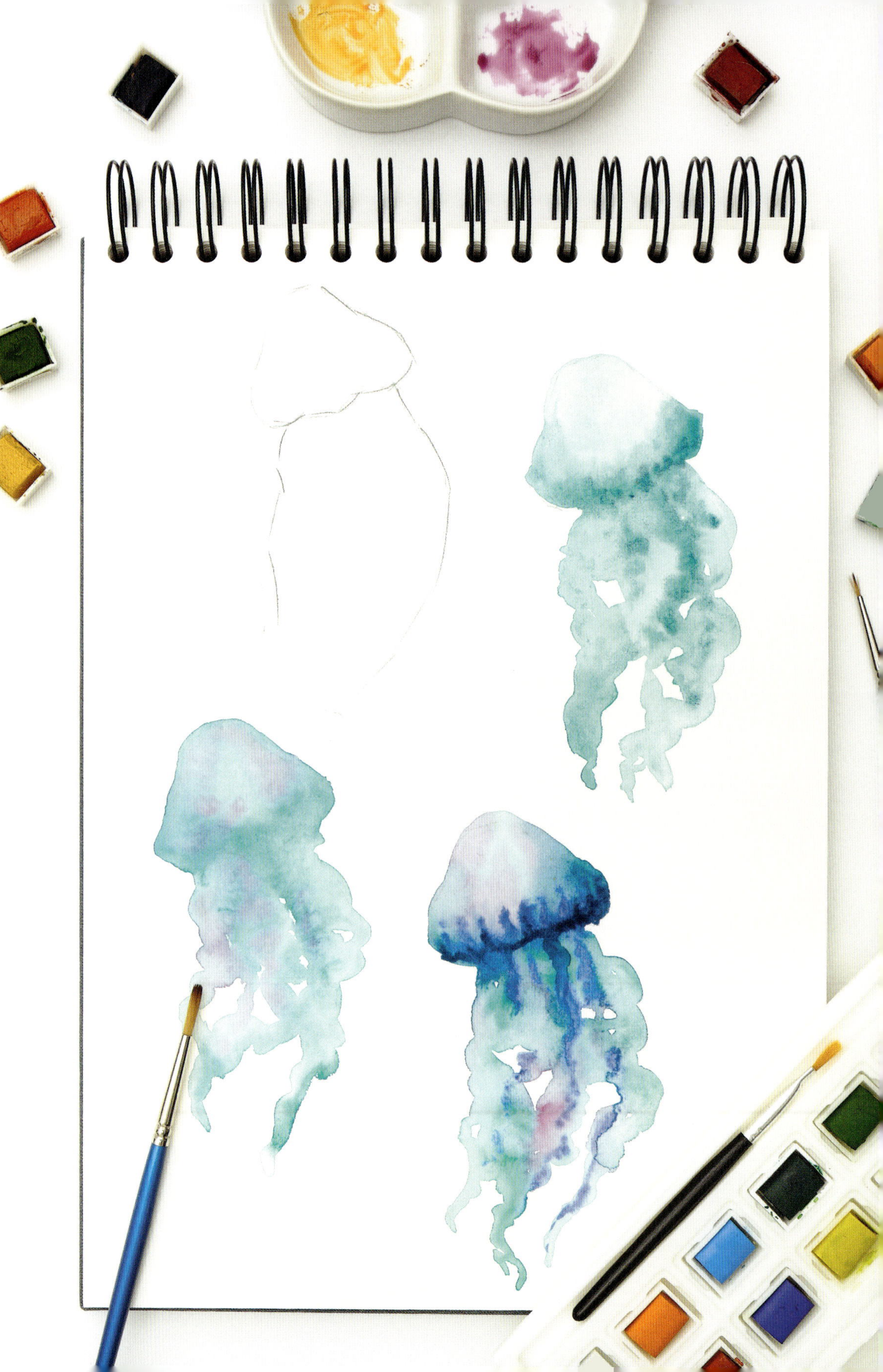

Four-Step Watercolour

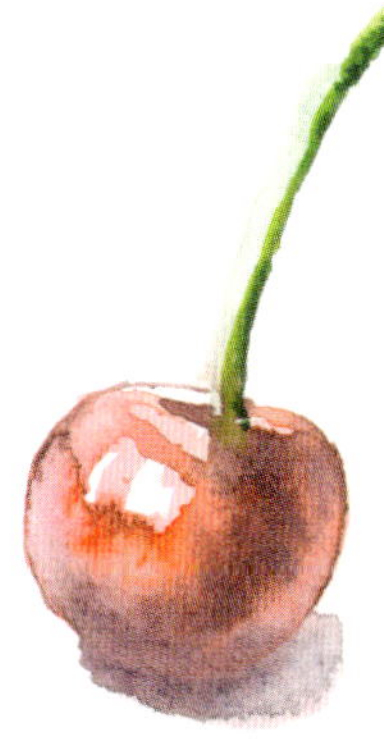

Marina Bakasova

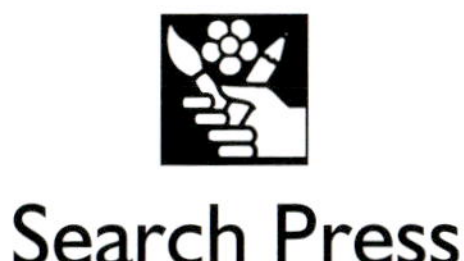

Search Press

A QUARTO BOOK

This edition published in 2020 by
Search Press
Wellwood
North Farm Road
Tunbridge Wells
Kent TN2 3DR

Reprinted 2021, 2022, 2023, 2024, 2026

GPSR information can be found at
www.searchpress.com

ISBN: 978-1-78221-850-0

Conceived, edited and designed by
Quarto Publishing plc
an imprint of The Quarto Group
1 Triptych Place,
London, SE1 9SH,
United Kingdom
www.quarto.com

QUAR: 325424

Editor & designer: Michelle Pickering
Digital illustrations: Olya Kamieshkova
Photographer: Phil Wilkins
Editorial assistant: Charlene Fernandes
Art director: Gemma Wilson
Publisher: Samantha Warrington

Printed in China TT032026

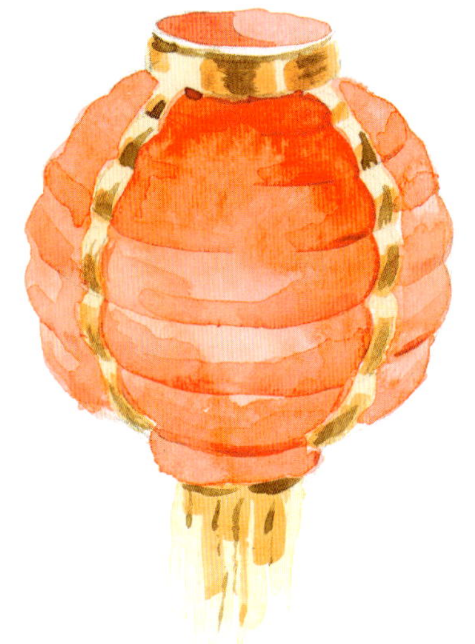

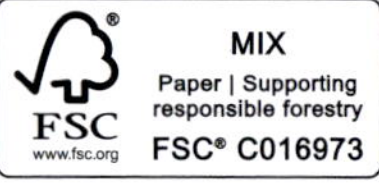

Contents

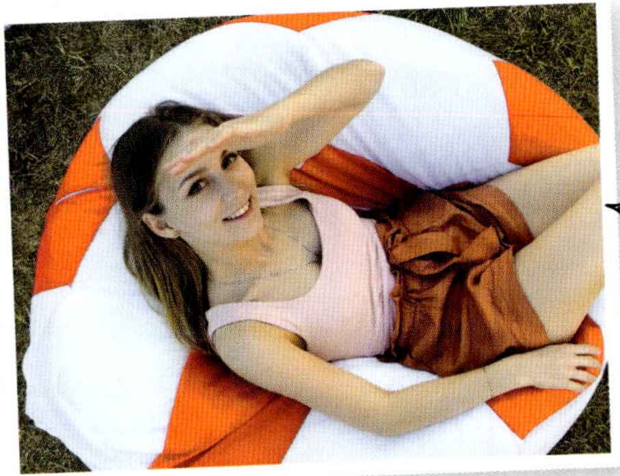

Project Selector

Go to pages 16–25 to see all of the projects pictured together, to help you choose which one to paint next.

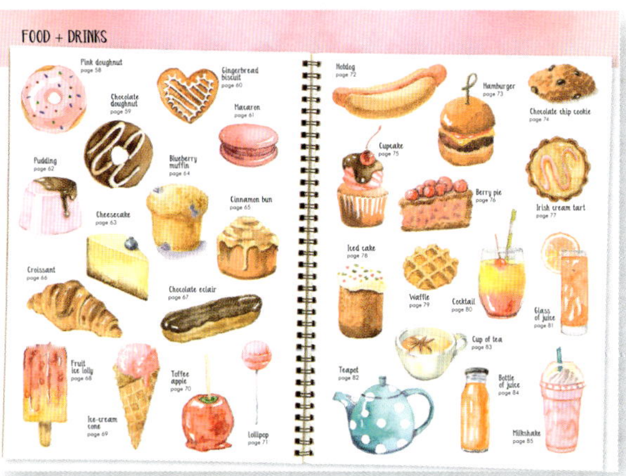

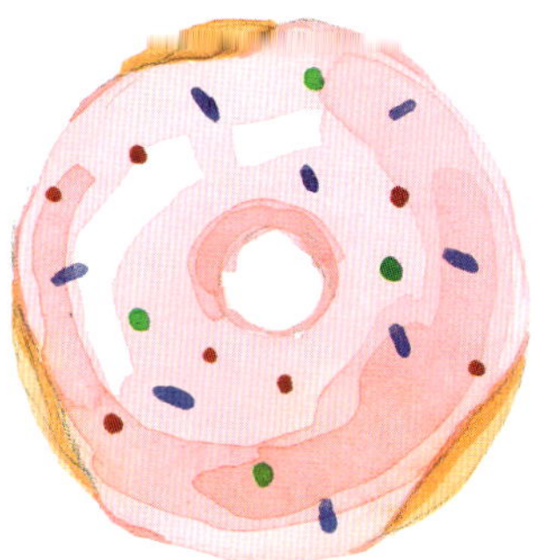

Projects

Meet Marina

My name is Marina Bakasova. I was born in Bryansk, Russia, and have been fond of drawing and painting from early childhood. After graduating from Moscow State Stroganov Art University, I began working as a freelance illustrator. I am obsessed with art and painting.

Nature is my inspiration and I also like to paint food and different desserts. In this book I want to teach people watercolour painting in an easy way. All of the projects are based on my own experience – and mistakes. I have been improving my painting skills for more than ten years, four of them at an art academy in Moscow. During all that time I was trying to devise some kind of formula or sequence for creating a successful artwork. I tried working with different materials and techniques, and found out which of them were best for me. And now I am ready to share my knowledge with everyone in four steps.

I hope this book will help not only the professional artist, but also every person who wants to learn watercolour painting but doesn't know what to start with. I have tried to include many art topics and objects, so you will get the chance to experiment with different pigments, techniques and subjects, and learn the combinations that you like best and that produce the effects you want. After learning them, I think it is highly likely that the desire to create will fill your heart, as it does mine. Maybe one day you will start making celebration cards or something else with your own illustrations – and I hope this book will inspire it.

◉ @marinabksv
I would love to see your artworks inspired by this book.

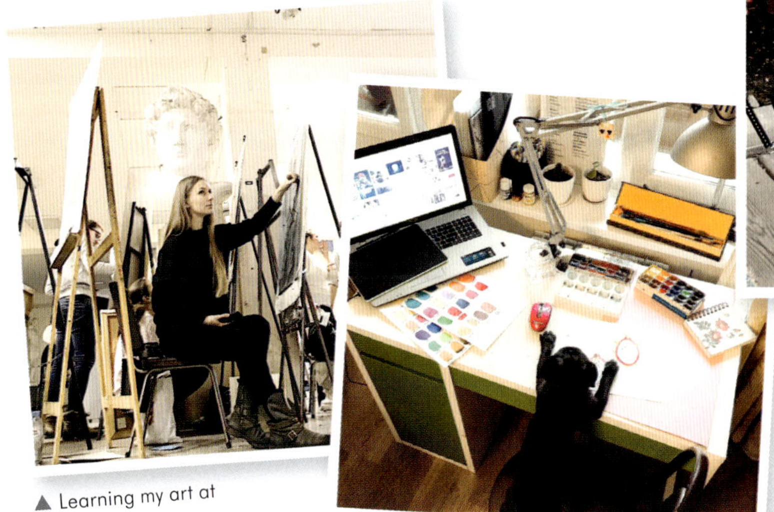

▲ Learning my art at the academy.

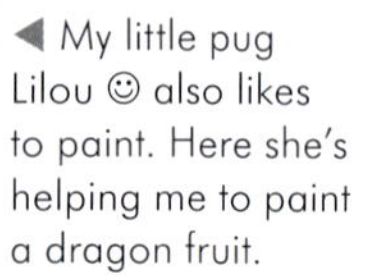

◄ My little pug Lilou ☺ also likes to paint. Here she's helping me to paint a dragon fruit.

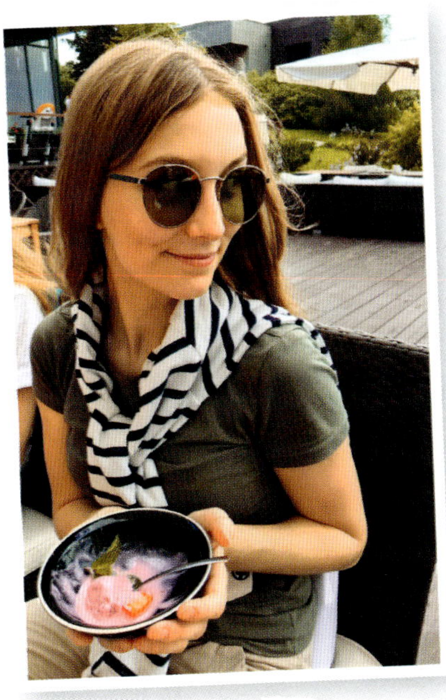

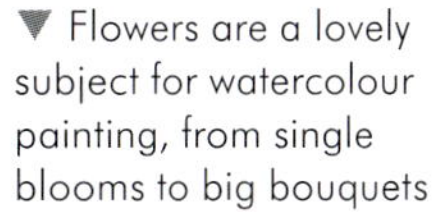

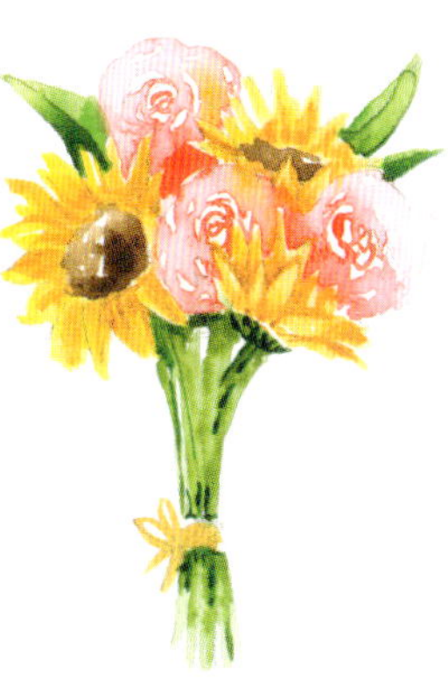

▼ Flowers are a lovely subject for watercolour painting, from single blooms to big bouquets.

◀ I love painting food, but especially delicious desserts!

▼ I painted the little sailboat after spending a lovely day on the water

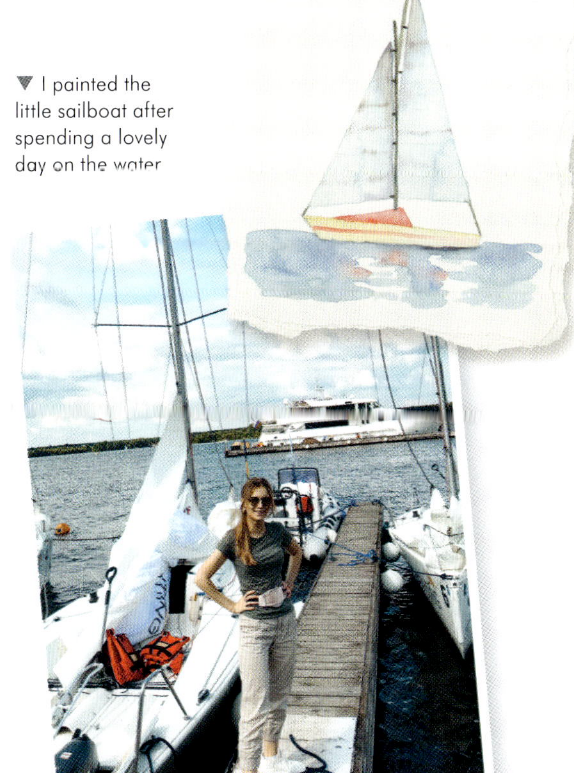

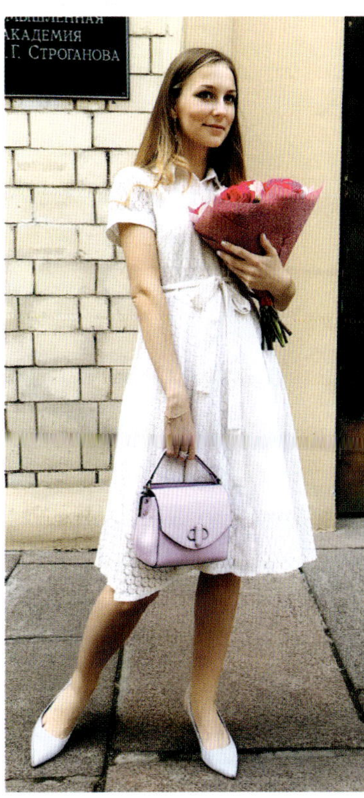

Tools and Materials

Apart from paints, brushes and paper, you will only require a few additional bits and pieces, many of which you will probably have around the house already, such as jars for water.

Watercolour paints

Watercolour paints are made from pigment suspended in a binding agent. There are two main types available: dry (in pans, or cuvettes) and liquid (in tubes). Tubes of paint are good for large-scale work, but many artists find pans more convenient, as they fit within a paintbox and can be carried around easily. Watercolours also come in two qualities: professional (or artist's) colours, which contain richer pigment but are more expensive, and student's colours.

Good-quality watercolour paints contain bright pigments and don't lose this brightness very much after drying. Be aware that all pigments are different. They have different levels of transparency, and some granulate (produce a grainy effect) while others do not. You will find information about each paint on its package or the manufacturer's website.

It is best to build up your colour palette gradually, buying new colours to suit the subject. Remember also that you can mix pigments to create new colours.

Paper

Ordinary paper will buckle if you apply wet paint to it. Special watercolour paper is designed to absorb water well, so that you can apply multiple layers of paint. It is available in both sheet and pad form, in a wide range of sizes. If using loose sheets of paper, you will need a drawing board for support – a piece of plywood cut to size will do.

Watercolour paper is made in three different surfaces: smooth (or hot-pressed), medium (or cold-pressed, also known as Not, meaning not hot-pressed) and rough. Cold-pressed is the most commonly used, as it has sufficient texture to hold the paint but is smooth enough to enable you to paint fine detail. Watercolour paper also comes in different thicknesses, or weights. In general, any paper lighter than about 300gsm (140lb) will buckle unless it has been pre-stretched (there are instructional videos online). The paper used in most watercolour pads is 250gsm (168lb).

There are also different colours of paper available, which can be useful – beige paper can act as the first layer of colour when painting light skintones, for example.

Setting up your workspace

Set up your workspace with everything you need close by – paints, water jars, palettes, brushes and so on. Watercolour paints dry quickly, so you need everything to hand before you start painting. Keep your water jars next to your mixing palette to prevent water from dripping on to your painting.

However, most artists paint on white paper, because it reflects through the transparent paint to give the painting a luminous quality. You can also leave areas of white paper free from paint to act as highlights.

Drawing pencil

Pencils have different levels of hardness: B – soft, HB – medium and H – hard. I recommend using a hard pencil, at least H, but take care to use a light touch when drawing to avoid indenting the paper. I use a mechanical pencil (because I hate to sharpen them) with 2H lead. Sometimes I draw with a watercolour pencil, so that the pencil lines blend in with the wet paint. If you need to remove pencil marks, use a putty eraser that won't scuff the paper.

Paintbrushes

Brushes come in a range of shapes (round, flat, etc), fibres (natural sable, synthetic, etc) and sizes (the lower the number, the smaller the brush tip). The traditional choice for watercolour painting are natural fibre brushes, because they can hold a large amount of water and paint while retaining their shape. I prefer round squirrel-hair brushes with a pointed tip, and use sizes 8, 4 and 2 most often.

If you are a beginner, start with round brushes with sharp tips in these sizes:
• Size 00/01 – thin brush for small details
• Size 2/3 – medium brush
• Size 8–20 – big brush for big spaces
A 6mm (¼in) flat brush is also useful for painting straight-edged shapes.

Mixing palette

You will need a mixing palette, ideally with multiple recessed slots, for preparing paints and mixing colours. There are two types: plastic and ceramic. Plastic palettes are cheaper and lighter to carry around, but will absorb pigment and stain. Ceramic palettes are easy to clean and allow paints to stay wet for longer, but they are heavier to carry if you want to work outside. If you store your paints in a paintbox, many of them have a lid designed for use as a palette.

Water jars

It is a good idea to start collecting glass jars at every opportunity – you will need them for rinsing brushes so you don't contaminate colours on the page. Most artists use transparent glass jars at home and transparent plastic containers outside. You can also buy a non-spill water pot if you wish. The most important thing is not the jar but the water in it: don't forget to change dirty water.

Extras

• Masking fluid can be used to retain an area of white on the paper for highlights, since white is difficult to replicate in watercolour. Coloured masking fluid is easier to see on the white paper. Keep an old, thin brush for use with masking fluid, because you will not be able to clean it completely.
• White ink can be used to add highlights after you have finished painting. I use a pen with white ink that will produce thin, smooth lines.
• Cotton buds are useful for lifting out paint and softening edges.
• Salt can be used to achieve some beautiful texture effects. Ordinary kitchen table salt or sea salt will do.

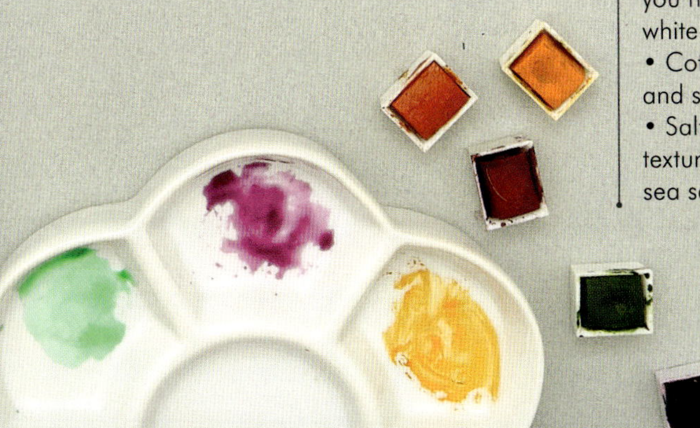

Techniques

Watercolour painting is rich and unpredictable, and there is no single method for painting a particular object. Most watercolour paintings use a combination of techniques.

Drawing a pencil sketch

Start by making a pencil drawing of the project. A simple outline is all you need. You can sketch it freehand or trace the drawing provided, using tracing paper or a lightbox. Your drawing should be light and easy to erase, because watercolour paint is transparent.

Locating the light source

Decide from which direction the light is falling on the object you are painting. All highlights should be placed where the light hits the object. The most common method of creating a highlight is to leave areas of the paper free from paint. A shadow will fall on the opposite side. All highlights and shadows should be consistent on the same artwork.

Choosing the right brush

Flat brushes are designed to make flat marks. Round brushes are more versatile; you can make broader marks by applying more pressure, or paint a fine line using the point of the brush. With practice, you will learn how much pressure to apply to make thicker, thinner, lighter or darker marks.

I recommend a size 8 brush for covering larger areas and adding large drops of colour; a size 2 or 3 brush for smaller areas and drops; and a size 00 or 01 brush for fine details.

Preparing your paints

Prepare separate dilutions (or washes) of each of the colours required for your project. Start by putting some water into a slot in your palette, then begin to add pigment, making sure that it dissolves completely. The ratio of pigment to water determines the strength and transparency of the colour. You need to use enough water to make a puddle of wet paint, while the colour remains vibrant.

Note that colours always look darker in the palette than on paper, and they will dry lighter too, so test different dilutions on scrap paper until you achieve the strength of colour you want. You are aiming for clear colour, with the white of the paper shining through.

What is a wash?

The term 'wash' simply means watercolour pigment diluted with water to achieve the desired intensity of tone – the more water you use, the paler the wash will be. A single colour laid evenly so that it dries to the same overall tone is known as a 'flat' wash. A single colour applied so that it graduates from dark to light is known as a 'graduated' or 'graded' wash. A 'variegated' wash involves two or more colours that bleed softly into each other.

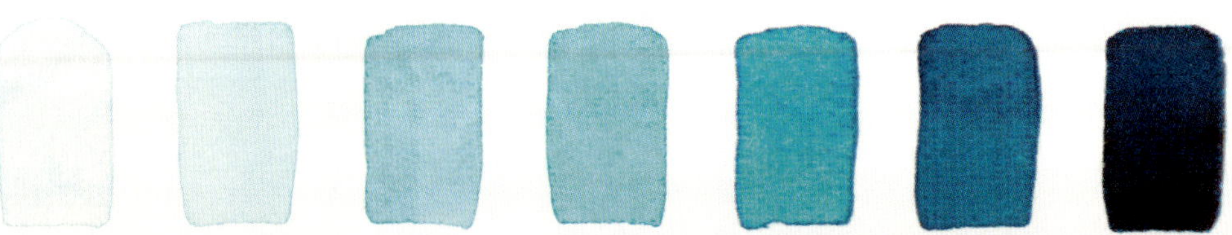

The same pigment at different dilutions. The more layers you intend to use, the more dilute the pigment should be in order to preserve the colour's transparency.

Applying the first wash

To apply a flat, even wash of colour, dip your brush into the prepared colour and spread it on the shape. Don't try to cover the shape in one go; start with a medium-sized drop of paint, then while the paint is still wet, add more until you have covered the shape. For a softer outline, brush clean water over the shape and then apply the paint, starting in the centre and working outwards to the edges. With both methods, if you don't finish before some areas have dried, wait until everything is dry, then carefully cover the shape with clean water. You can then add more colour as needed.

To apply a graduated or variegated wash, simply apply different dilutions of pigment (or different colours) so that they just touch each other, working quickly while everything is still wet. The colours will blend softly where they meet. Another method is to paint the whole shape with the lighter tone or colour, and then, working on wet, apply the darker tone or colour over the areas that you want to be darker. You can also lighten areas by adding drops of water.

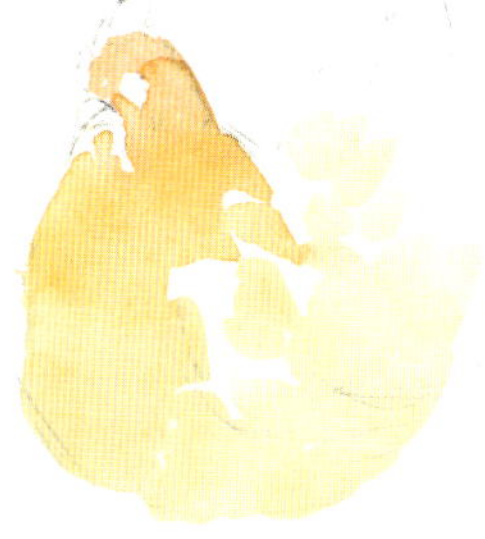

◀ The chicken begins with a graduated wash of sienna, with the strongest pigment at the head graduating to very dilute sienna near the tail.

◀ The first stage for painting the candle is to apply a flat, even wash of pink.

▶ The flat peach begins with a variegated wash of orange, yellow and green, with all three colours bleeding softly into each other.

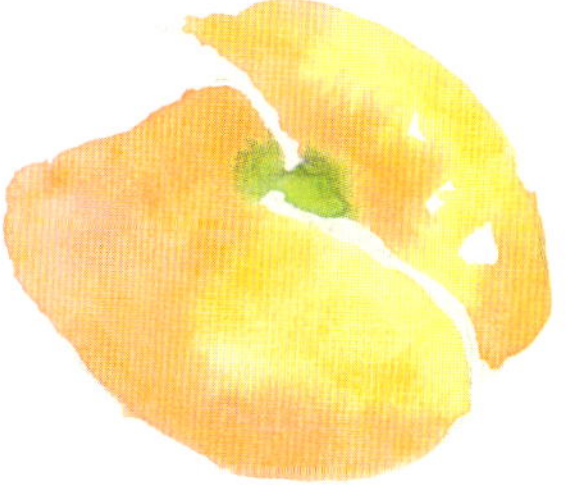

▼ The sheep is painted with a single colour, but not as an even wash. Drops of water are used to lighten the sheep's rear, and stronger pigment is applied to create shaded areas on the head, neck, chest and belly.

▲ The first layer of the dolphin is a variegated wash of indigo and blue, fading to areas of white paper. The paper is dampened with clean water before applying the paint in order to achieve a very soft, diffuse edge where the colours fade to white.

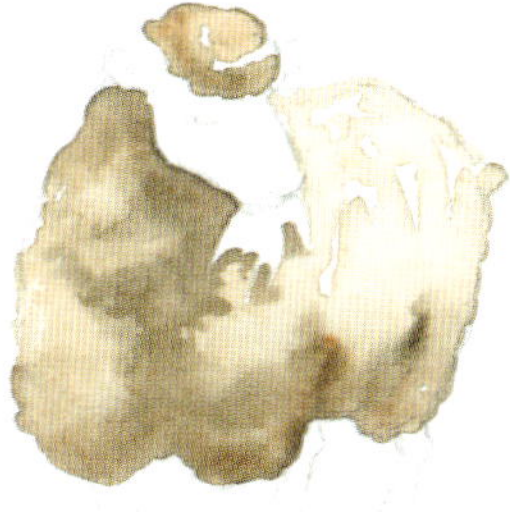

Building up the picture

A damp base allows watercolour to spread; a dry base contains it. If you work on wet, either on damp paper or a damp wash, the wetness of the underlying surface allows the paint to bleed outwards and to dry with a soft, blurry edge. If you work on dry, either on dry paper or a dry wash, the paint will be contained within the area to which it has been applied, so that it dries with a hard edge. Note that different pigments have different qualities and thus behave in different ways – some are opaque, some more translucent, for example. When painting fine details and edges, you can work on wet, half-wet or dry. Just choose the method that suits your artwork best.

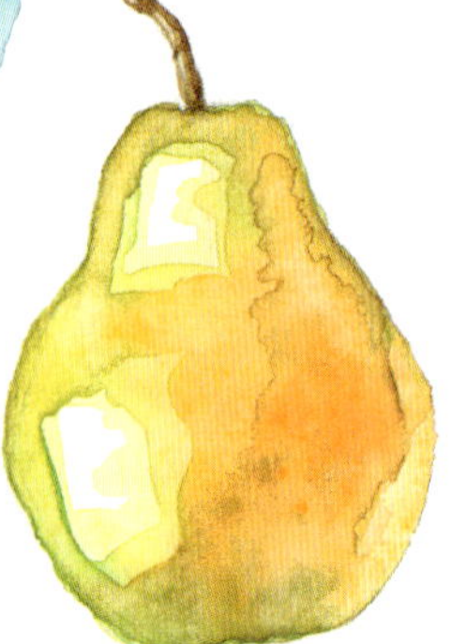

► The jellyfish is worked entirely on wet, starting with a flat blue wash on to which various colours are dropped to mimic the anatomy of the creature.

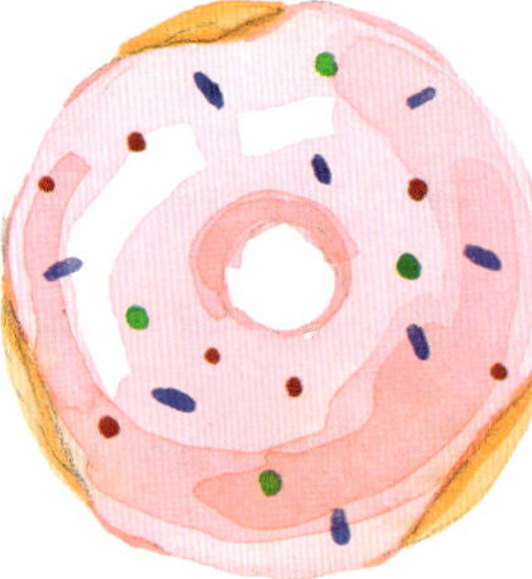

► The pink doughnut is worked entirely on dry, using glazes of flat colour to build up volume.

◄ Like the doughnut, the pear also uses glazes to build up volume, but with layers of variegated washes. Notice how in both the doughnut and pear, the edges of each dried layer remain visible, helping to enhance the illusion of a three-dimensional object.

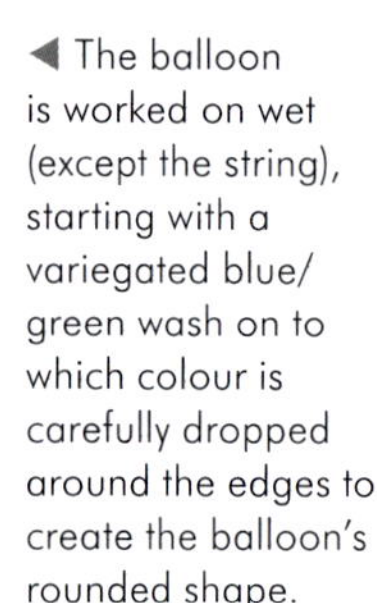

◄ The balloon is worked on wet (except the string), starting with a variegated blue/green wash on to which colour is carefully dropped around the edges to create the balloon's rounded shape.

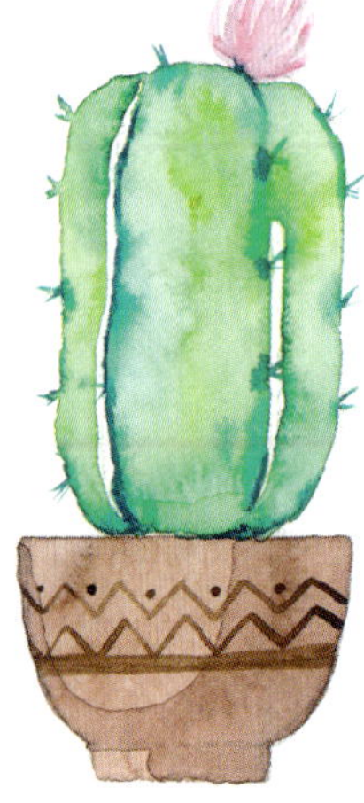

► Like the balloon, the contours of the cactus plant are painted on wet to create softly diffused shading, but then stronger pigment is overlaid on dry for finer, more defined edges. Working on dry is also used to paint the crisp geometric pattern on the plant pot.

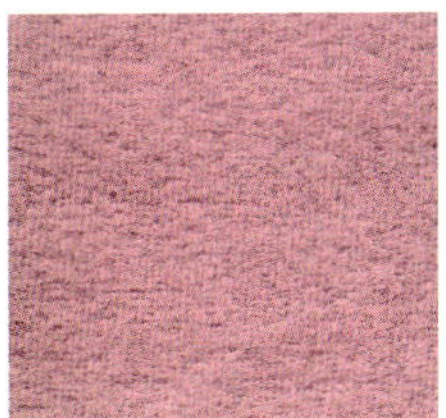

Light pink and blue mixed in the palette.

Overlaid glazes of light pink and blue.

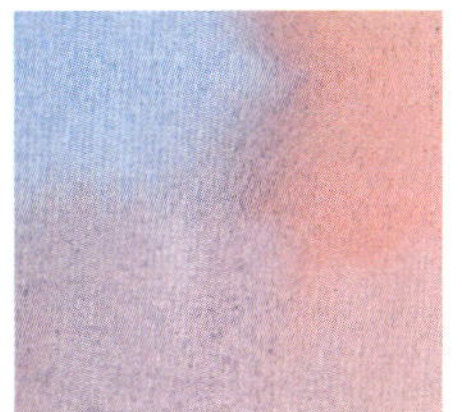

The same colours mixed by working on wet.

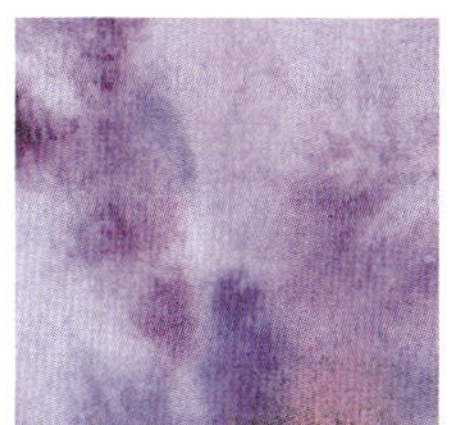

Colours dropped on to a wet wash.

Mixing colours in the palette

Whenever a project requires colours to be mixed in the palette prior to painting, the instructions refer to this as a 'mix' – for example, 'pink + blue mix'. I have used just two colours in each mix, because mixing too many colours together can produce a muddy result.

To make a colour mix, prepare separate dilutions of each colour in your palette. Then, in a clean slot, blend the two colours to make a third. Test your colour mixes on scrap paper.

Working on wet or on half-wet

Working on wet means applying colour to a wet surface, which can be either dampened plain paper or a previous wash that is not fully dry. Working on wet produces soft edges and allows adjacent colours to blend softly into each other. The wetter the paper, the more the colours will flow into each other in an unpredictable way. Wait until the paper has lost its sheen and is only slightly damp (half-wet) for a subtler effect.

Working on wet means that you must work fast. However, even if the underlying wash has already dried, you can just re-wet the surface with clean water and then continue working on wet. If you find that a colour runs too much or bleeds into an area where you don't want it, you can gently lift out the excess colour with a dry brush, cotton bud or tissue.

Dropping in colour

Dropping spots of colour on to a wet wash is a way of creating surface texture. The drops will spread and feather out on their edges, and the colours will blend. The brush can be touched to the surface for more control, or droplets can be allowed to fall from above. Larger droplets are made by using more paint, smaller ones by using less. Experiment first on scrap paper.

Working on dry

Working on dry means applying colour to a dry surface, which can be either plain paper or a previous wash that has fully dried. Working on dry produces crisp, clean edges and allows you to build up depth of colour and tone by glazing (see below). Working on dry allows you greater control than working on wet, because the layer beneath will not move and colours won't bleed.

Glazing

Glazing is the technique of layering a wash (or glaze) of transparent watercolour over another that has fully dried. The underlying colour will alter the one you place on top, and vice versa. Always work from light to dark, and the more layers you are going to apply, the more water you should mix with the pigment to preserve transparency.

Edges painted on dry.

Edges painted on half-wet.

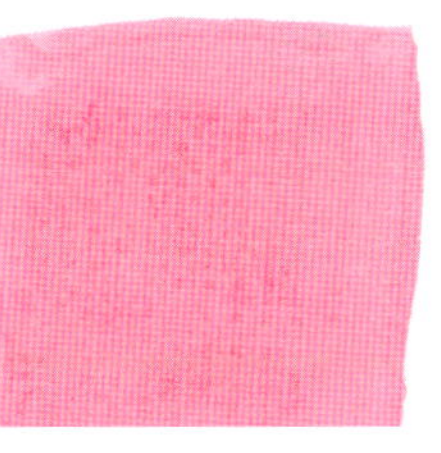

Dry paint re-wetted with clean water.

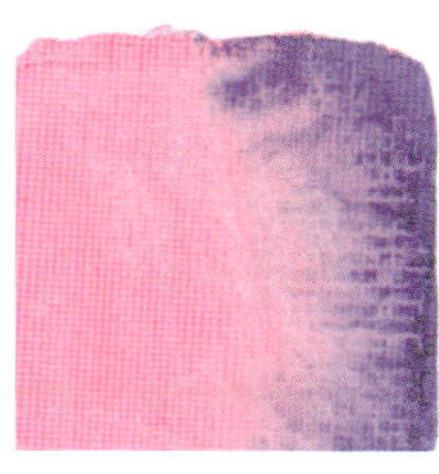

Edges painted on wet.

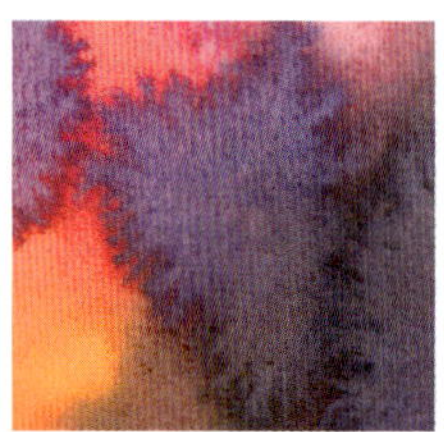

Backruns made by dropping in colour.

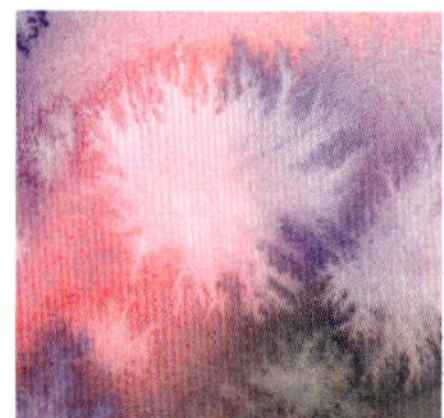

Backruns made by dropping in water.

Backruns

If you apply a brush loaded with a more watery colour to a damp wash, the first colour will 'run away' from the water in the new colour, causing intriguing shapes with jagged edges. The shape will be lighter in the centre (where the brush was placed) and surrounded by a fringe of concentrated pigment. You can create similar effects by dropping clean water on to a damp wash. Note that if the initial wash is too wet, the colors will blend together. For a backrun, the wash needs to have started to dry. The water content of the dropped-in colour must also be higher than that of the previous colour.

Granulation

Some pigments dissolve entirely in water, while others tend to granulate – that is, the particles (or grains) of pigment separate from the water, producing a speckled finish. Granulation can also occur when a wet wash is laid over a dry one. Another way to create granulation is to fill a shape with colour and then, while still wet, add a drop of water.

Masking fluid and white ink

Masking fluid is a way of reserving areas of the paper as highlights. It forms a waterproof seal that protects the paper underneath, and you can then paint washes over the dried masking

Five simple – but important! – rules

1) To avoid muddy-looking colours, don't mix more than three colours in the palette.
2) Try not to use more than four layers of colour for the same reason.
3) Before you start, decide where the light is located so that you can paint the highlights and shadows correctly.
4) There are lots of techniques for painting with watercolours; just choose the ones you like most of all.
5) Don't forget to change your water. It should always be at least transparent. Dirty water creates dirty pictures.

fluid without having to carefully leave areas unpainted. Use an old brush to apply the fluid. Putting the brush in some soapy water before dipping it in the fluid will help stop the fluid from clinging to the bristles. When the paint is dry, remove the mask by gently rubbing with a finger or an eraser.

If you want to add extra highlights to a finished painting, simply draw them with a white ink pen.

Salt

Dropping table or sea salt on to wet paint can produce some interesting textures. The grains of salt soak up the wetness of the paint from the immediate area, speeding up the drying process there. As the paint dries, little star shapes appear as the water floods out of the crystals and pushes the colour away to create feathered edges. Larger salt grains produce distinct star shapes; smaller salt grains produce a finer texture. You can also experiment with using sea water to dilute your pigments.

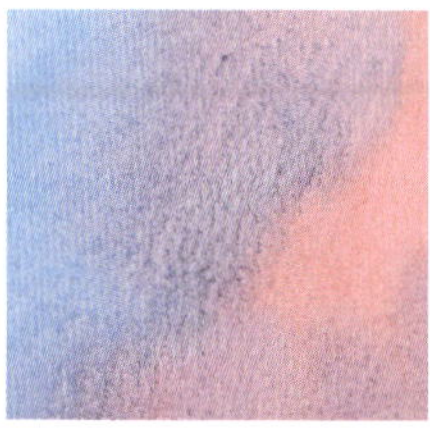

Granulation where the two colours overlap.

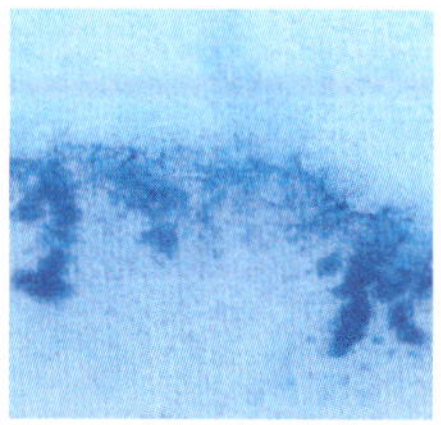

Adding drops of water to cause granulation.

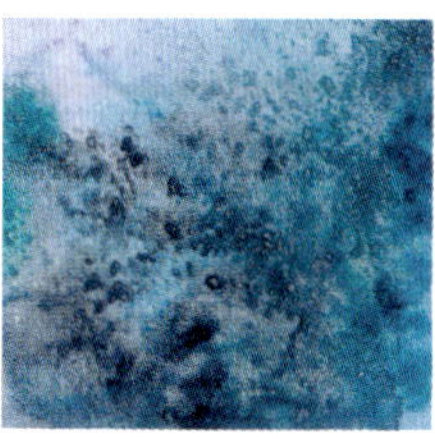

Sea salt dropped on to a wet wash.

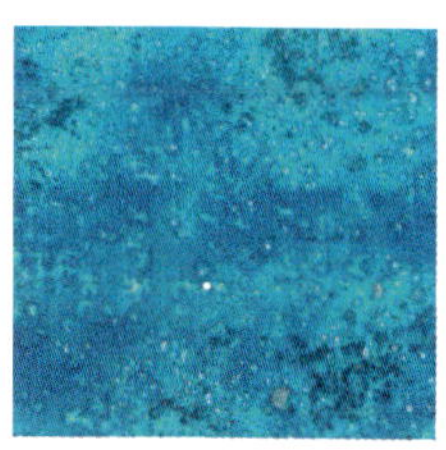

Paint diluted with sea water.

Following the four steps

Watercolours are unpredictable, and you will never get the same result each time. For this reason I have painted each project three times, starting from a freehand sketch and stopping at the end of step 2, then step 3 and finally step 4. You will see how the paint acts slightly differently each time. This is part of the fun and excitement of working with watercolour – enjoy!

SKILL LEVEL * MEDIUM •——— A skill level – easy, medium or high – is indicated at the top of each project page, so you know which ones might take a bit more practice.

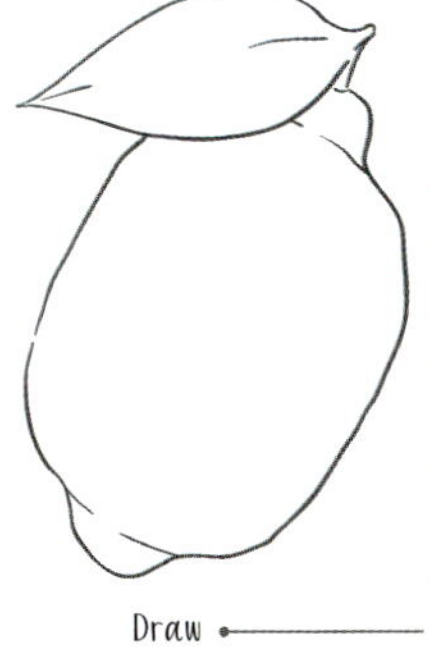

Sketch or trace the outline of the project. Use a lighter line than shown here; this line drawing has a heavier line to make it easy to see clearly.

Draw •———

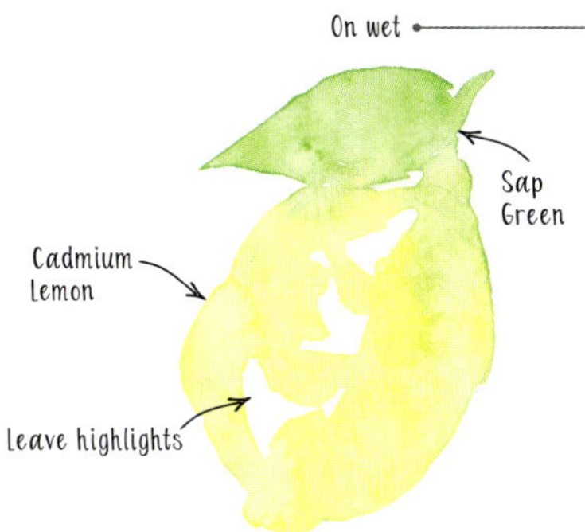

On wet •——— If there is a general instruction 'On wet' next to a step painting, then you should apply each colour in that step while any adjacent or underlying colours are still wet unless instructed otherwise. Apply the same principle for 'On dry' and 'On half-wet'.

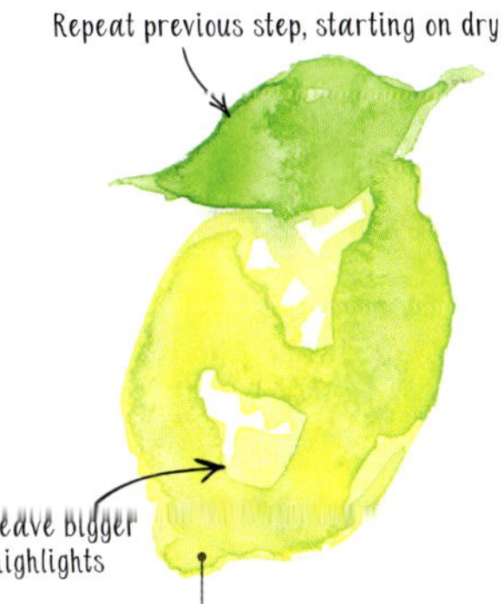

Some step instructions are labelled a), b), c) and so on. This indicates my recommended order for applying the colours in that step, usually because some are applied on wet and some on dry. If the order doesn't matter, then there are no a), b), c) labels.

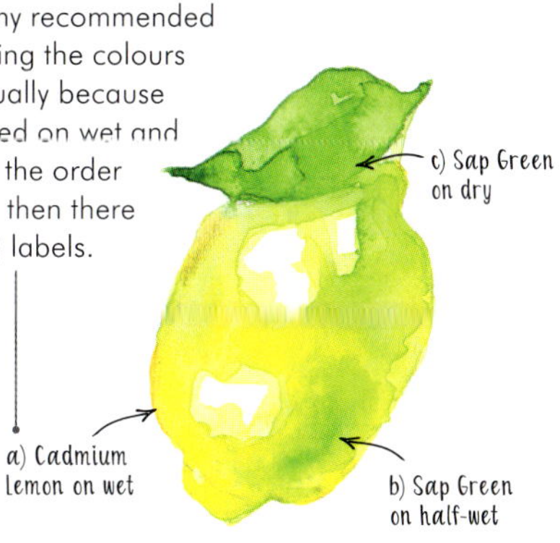

Read through the whole project before you start, noting where you will need to work quickly when working on wet or half-wet. Here, for example, you need to move on to the final step while the paint is still wet.

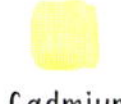
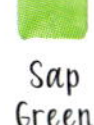

Cadmium Lemon   Sap Green

Swatches of all the colours in the project are shown at the bottom of the page, in the order I used them. Prepare your paint dilutions to match what you see in the step-by-step pictures. Some are strong, while others are dilute. If you don't have the same colours in your paintbox, just choose something similar, or mix something similar. For many projects, you can use completely different colours if you prefer.

FRUIT + VEGETABLES

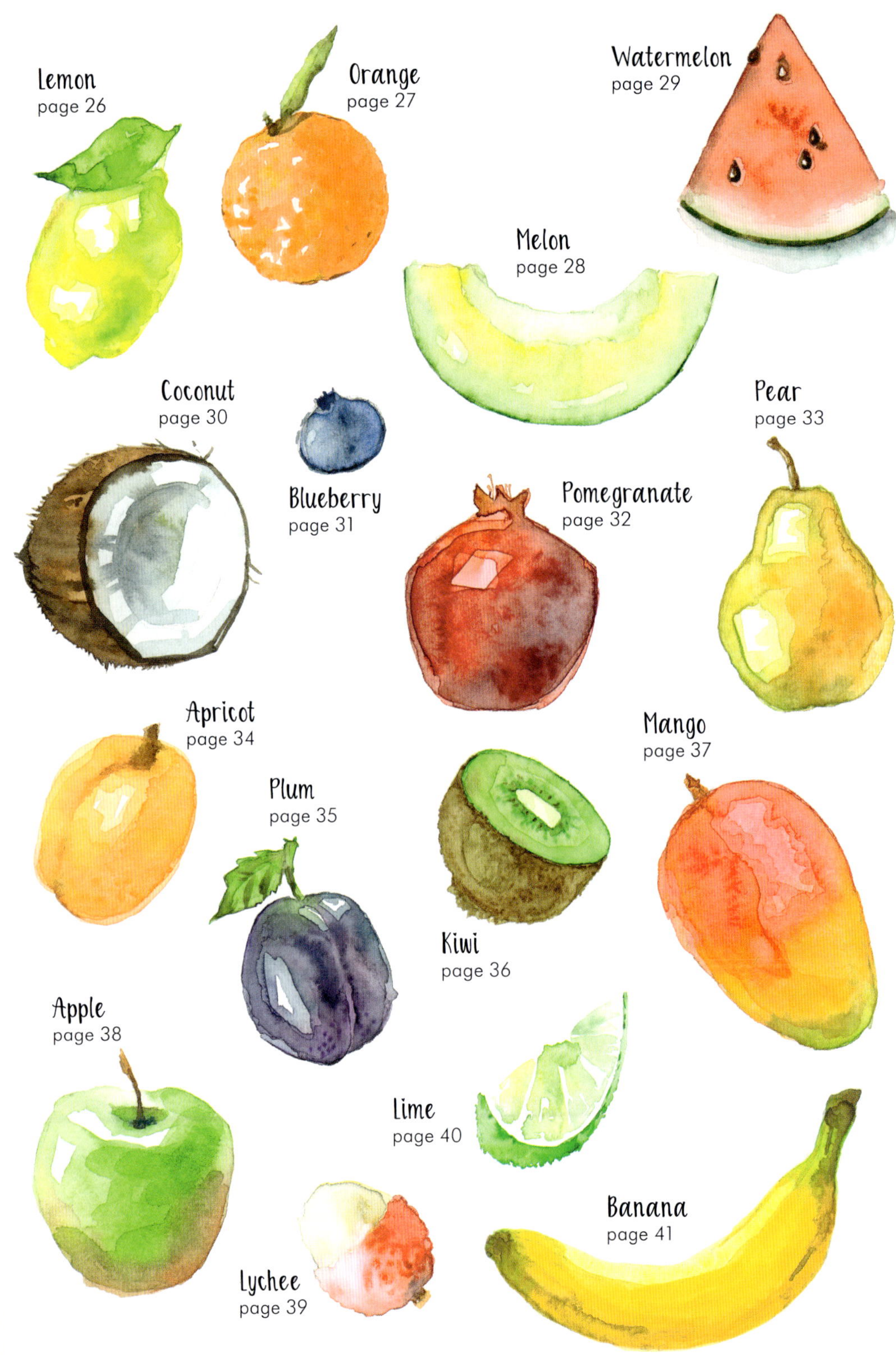

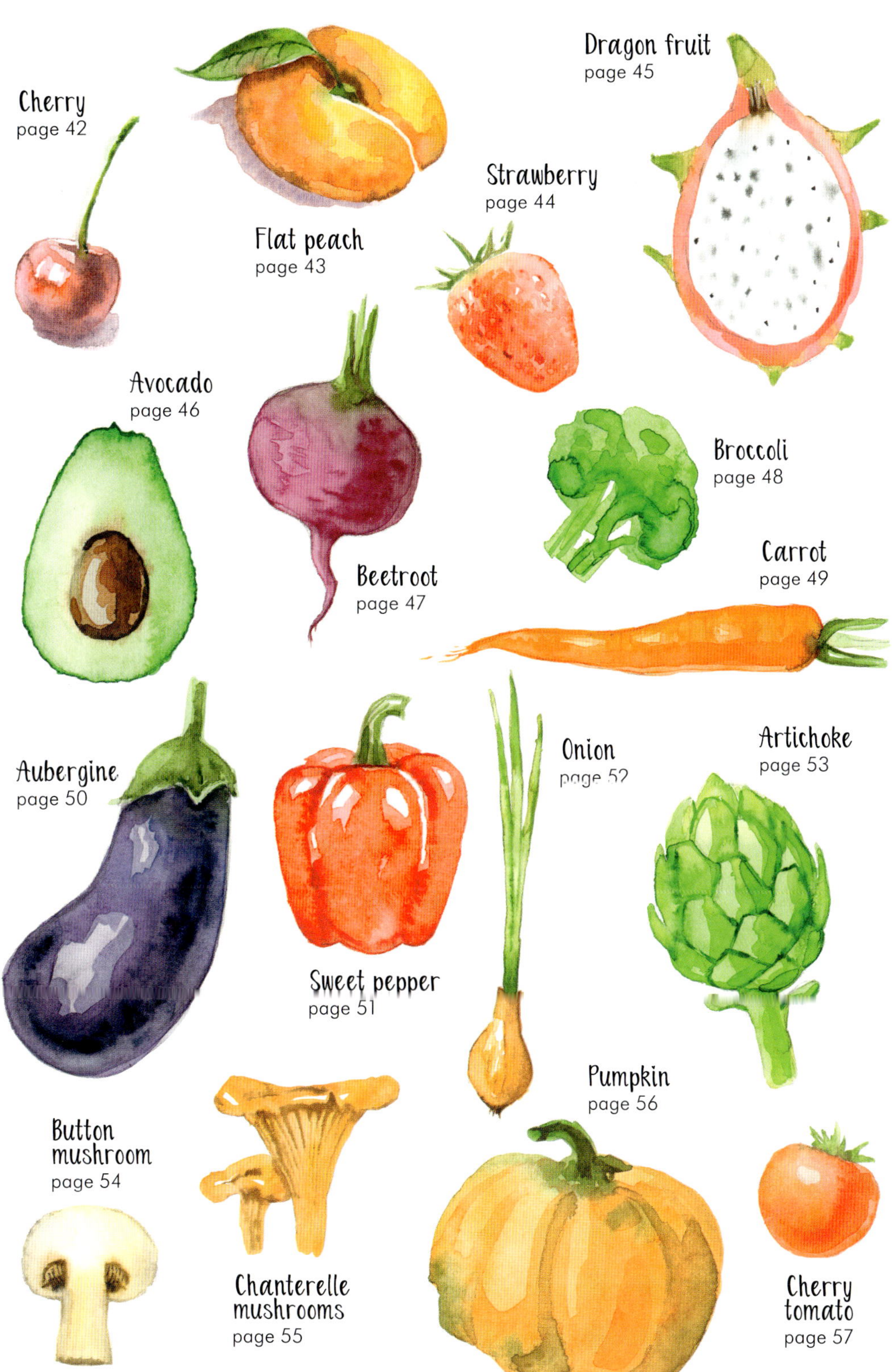

Cherry
page 42
Flat peach
page 43
Dragon fruit
page 45
Strawberry
page 44
Avocado
page 46
Beetroot
page 47
Broccoli
page 48
Carrot
page 49
Aubergine
page 50
Sweet pepper
page 51
Onion
page 52
Artichoke
page 53
Pumpkin
page 56
Button
mushroom
page 54
Chanterelle
mushrooms
page 55
Cherry
tomato
page 57

FOOD + DRINKS

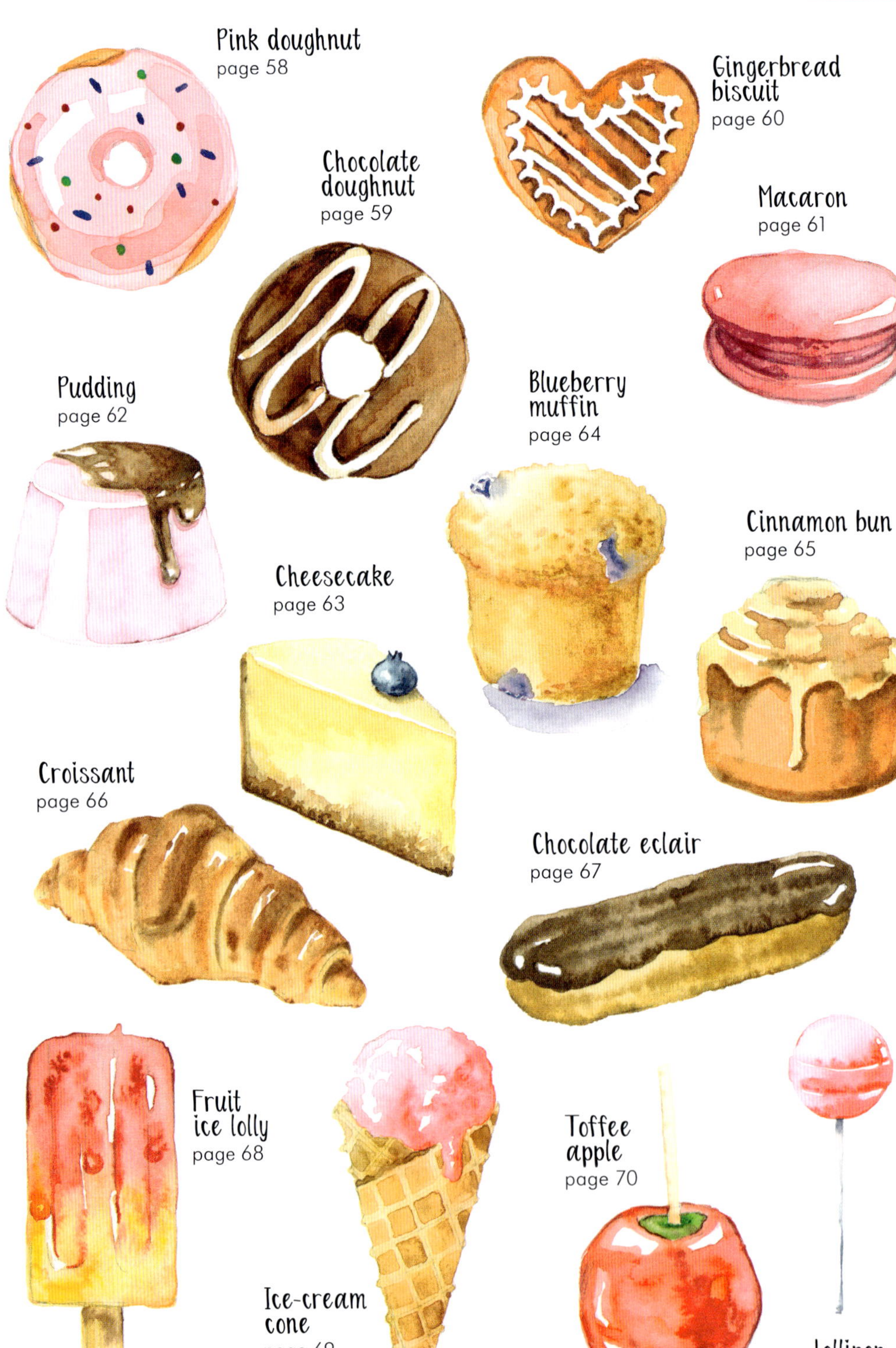

Pink doughnut
page 58

Chocolate
doughnut
page 59

Gingerbread
biscuit
page 60

Macaron
page 61

Pudding
page 62

Blueberry
muffin
page 64

Cinnamon bun
page 65

Cheesecake
page 63

Croissant
page 66

Chocolate eclair
page 67

Fruit
ice lolly
page 68

Toffee
apple
page 70

Ice-cream
cone
page 69

Lollipop
page 71

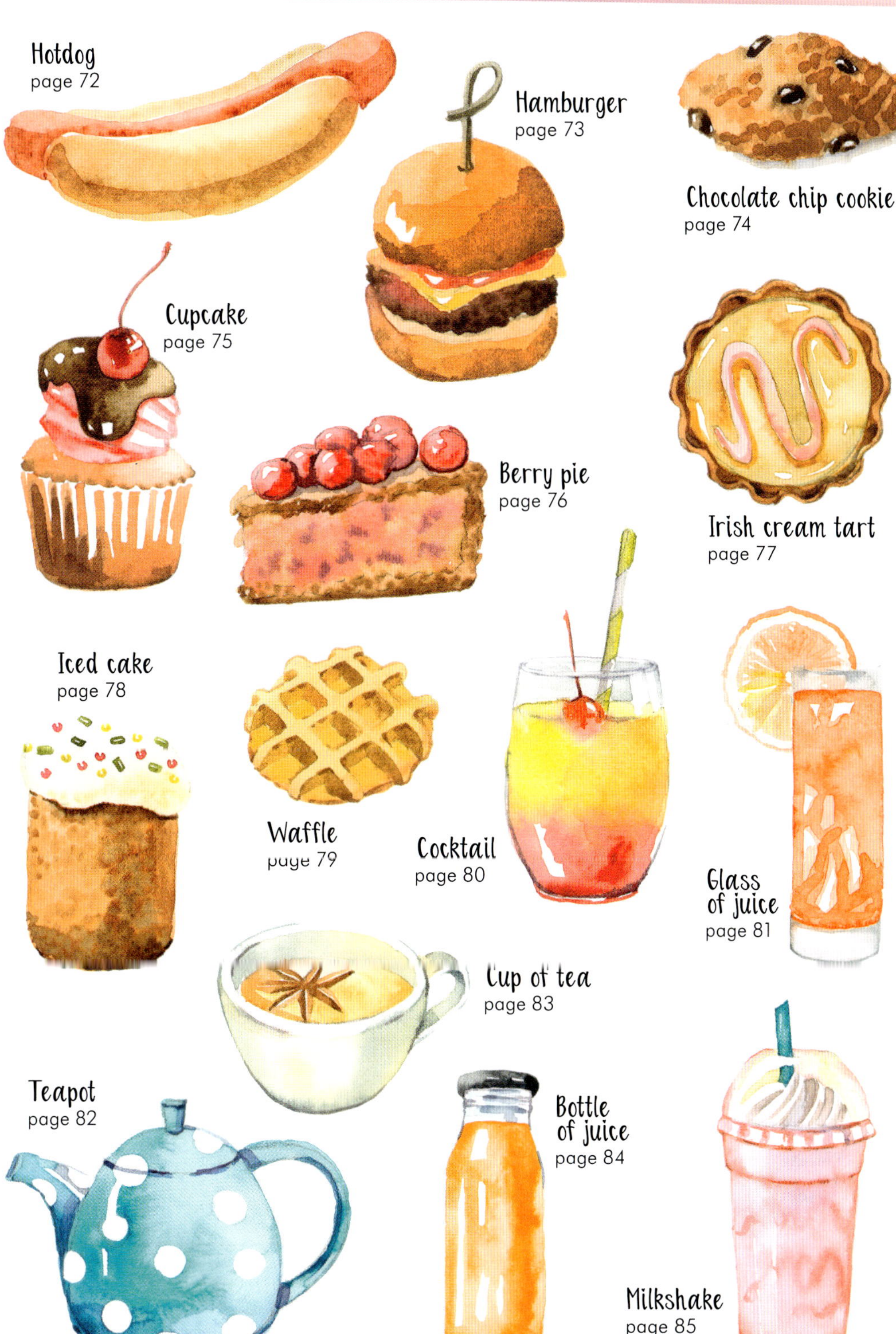

Hotdog
page 72
Hamburger
page 73
Chocolate chip cookie
page 74
Cupcake
page 75
Berry pie
page 76
Irish cream tart
page 77
Iced cake
page 78
Waffle
page 79
Cocktail
page 80
Glass
of juice
page 81
Cup of tea
page 83
Teapot
page 82
Bottle
of juice
page 84
Milkshake
page 85

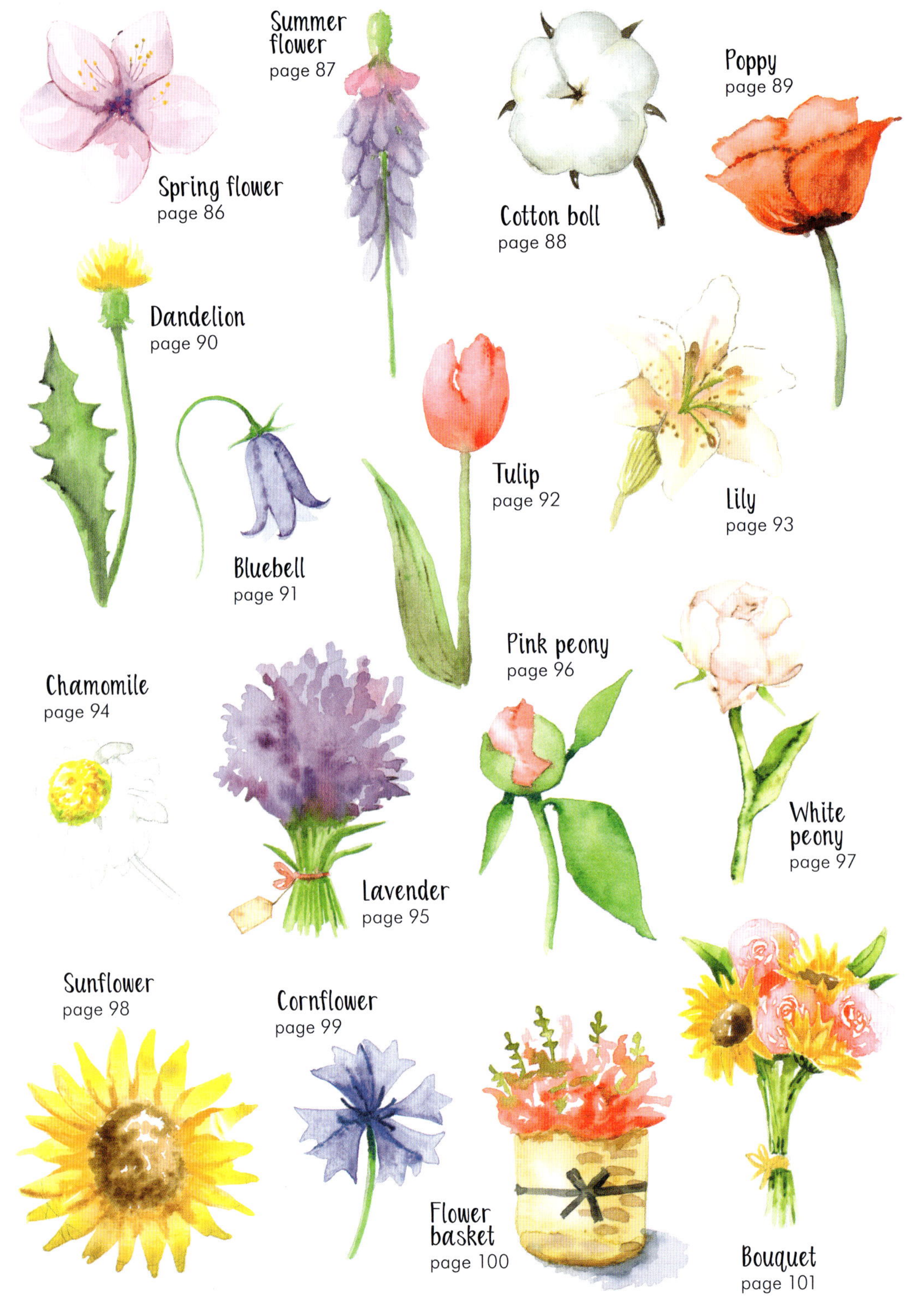
Spring flower
page 86
Summer flower
page 87
Cotton boll
page 88
Poppy
page 89
Dandelion
page 90
Bluebell
page 91
Tulip
page 92
Lily
page 93
Chamomile
page 94
Lavender
page 95
Pink peony
page 96
White peony
page 97
Sunflower
page 98
Cornflower
page 99
Flower basket
page 100
Bouquet
page 101

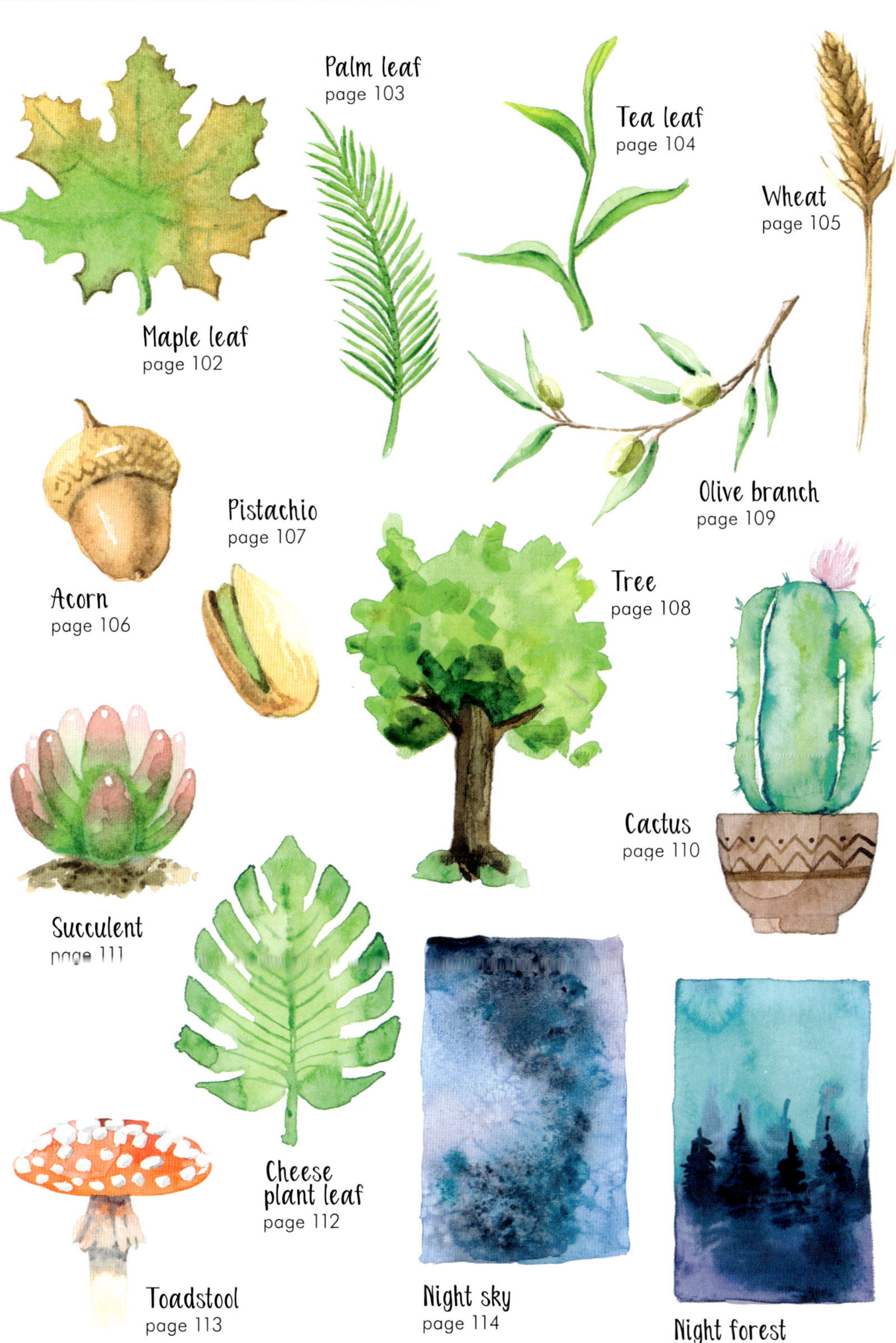

Palm leaf
page 103
Tea leaf
page 104
Wheat
page 105
Maple leaf
page 102
Olive branch
page 109
Acorn
page 106
Pistachio
page 107
Tree
page 108
Cactus
page 110
Succulent
page 111
Cheese
plant leaf
page 112
Toadstool
page 113
Night sky
page 114
Night forest
page 115

INSECTS, ANIMALS, BIRDS + SEA LIFE

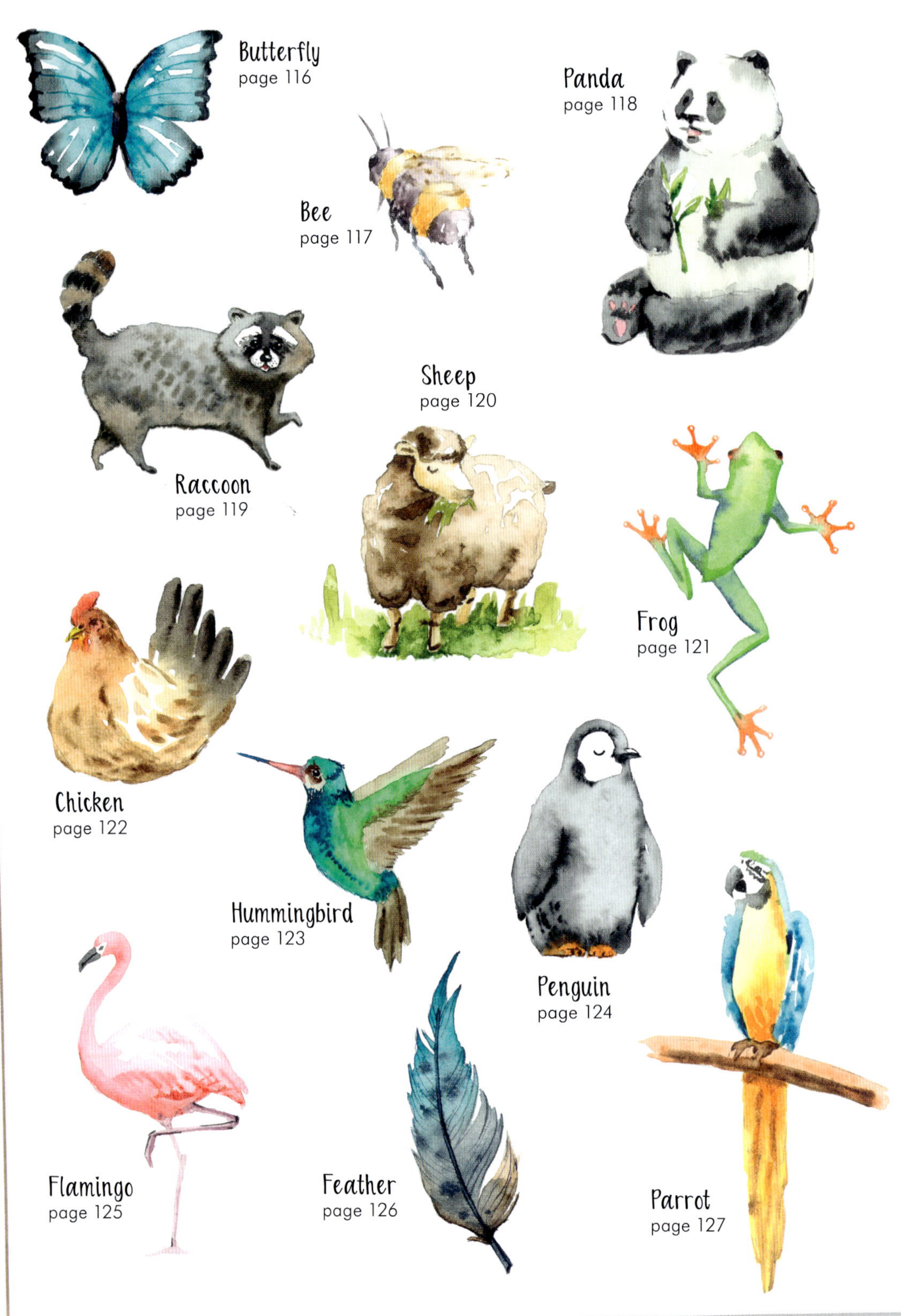

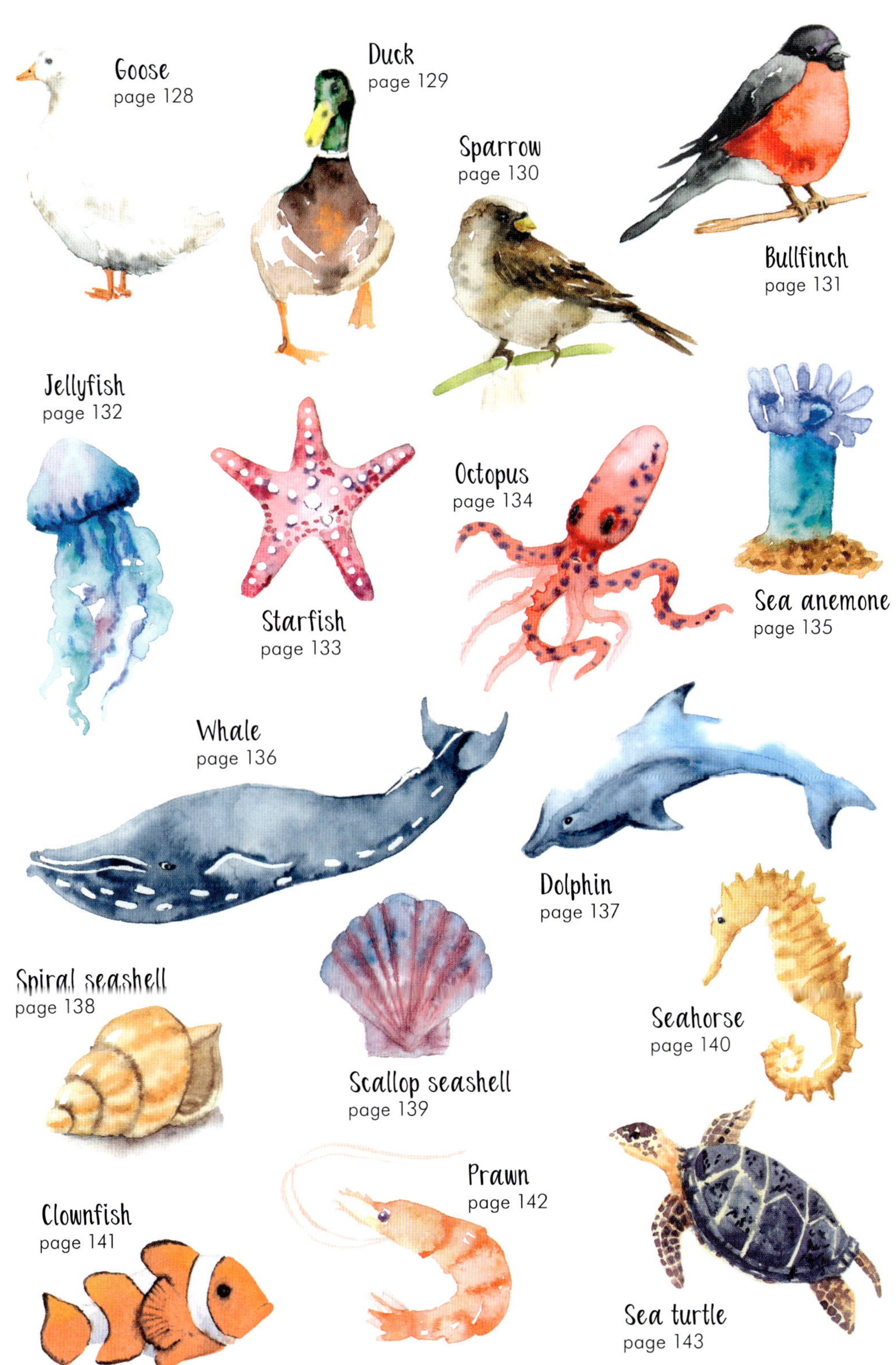

Goose
page 128
Duck
page 129
Sparrow
page 130
Bullfinch
page 131
Jellyfish
page 132
Starfish
page 133
Octopus
page 134
Sea anemone
page 135
Whale
page 136
Dolphin
page 137
Seahorse
page 140
Spiral seashell
page 138
Scallop seashell
page 139
Clownfish
page 141
Prawn
page 142
Sea turtle
page 143

OBJECTS, TRAVEL + CELEBRATIONS

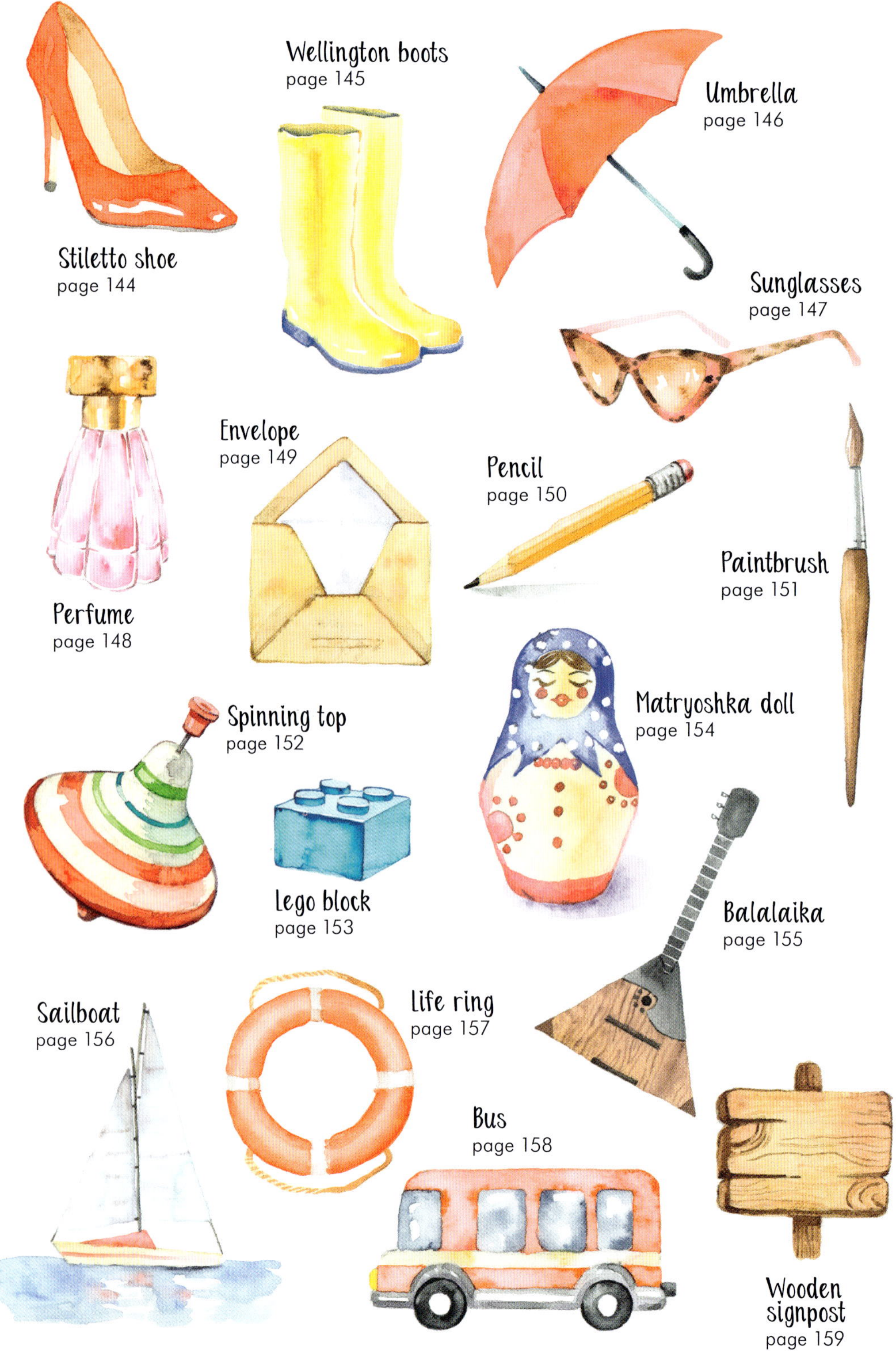

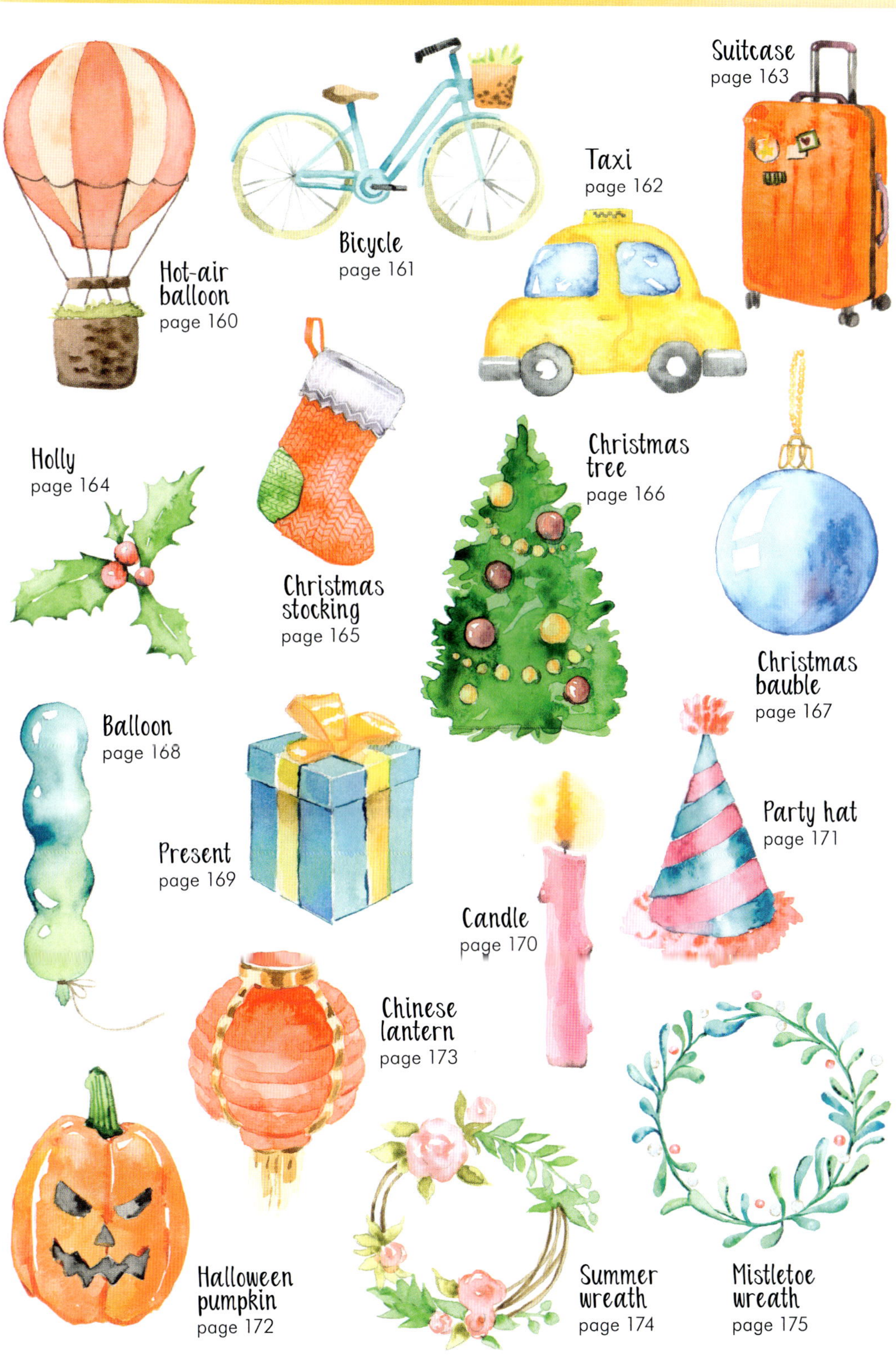

Suitcase
page 163
Taxi
page 162
Bicycle
page 161
Hot-air
balloon
page 160
Holly
page 164
Christmas
stocking
page 165
Christmas
tree
page 166
Christmas
bauble
page 167
Balloon
page 168
Present
page 169
Candle
page 170
Party hat
page 171
Chinese
lantern
page 173
Halloween
pumpkin
page 172
Summer
wreath
page 174
Mistletoe
wreath
page 175

1

Draw
On wet
Sap Green
Cadmium Lemon
leave highlights

Repeat previous step, starting on dry
leave bigger highlights
c) Sap Green on dry
a) Cadmium Lemon on wet
b) Sap Green on half-wet

Cadmium Lemon

Sap Green

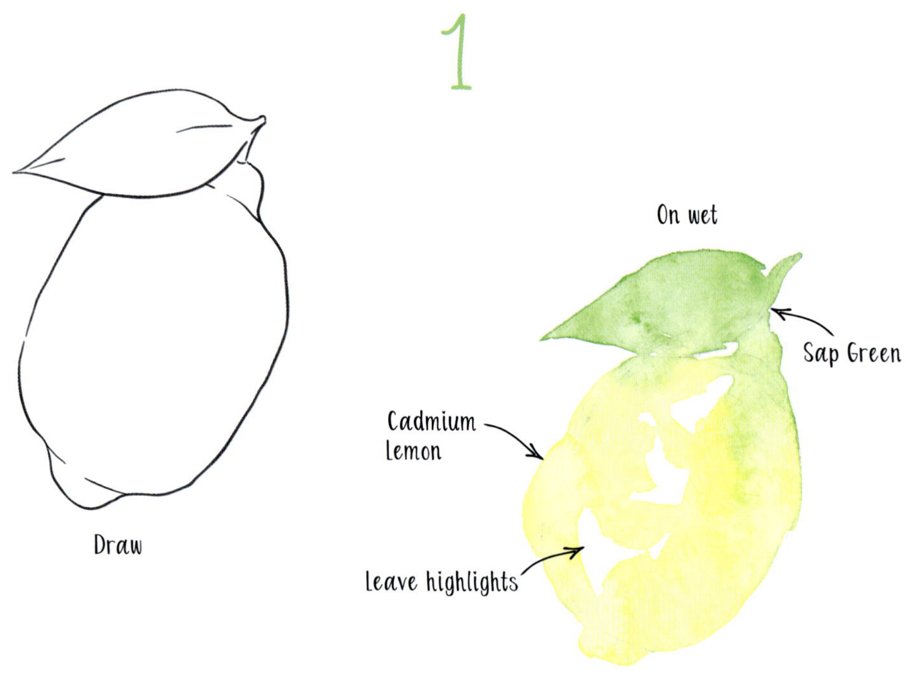

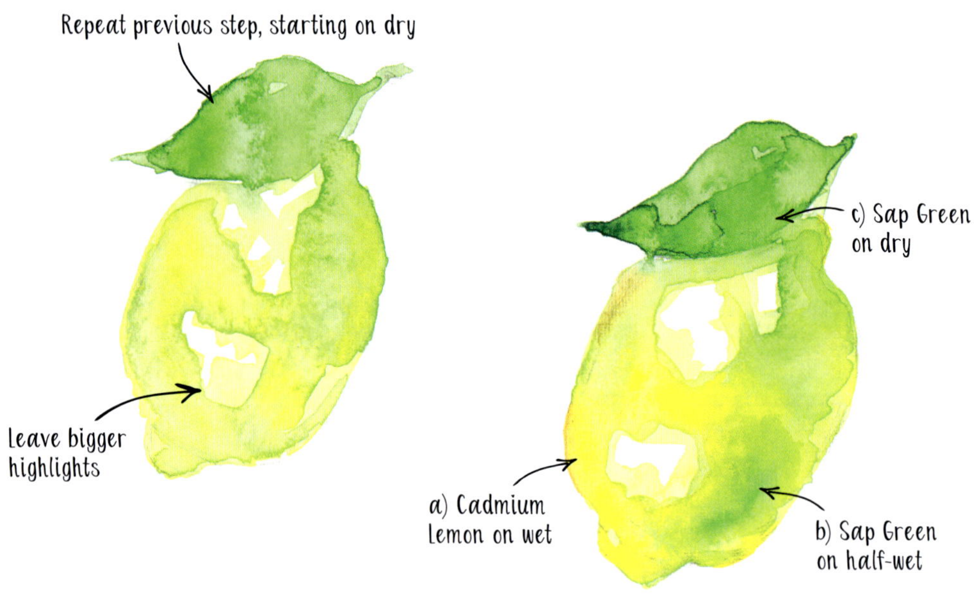

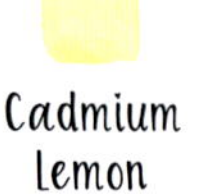

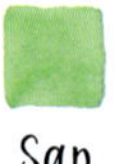

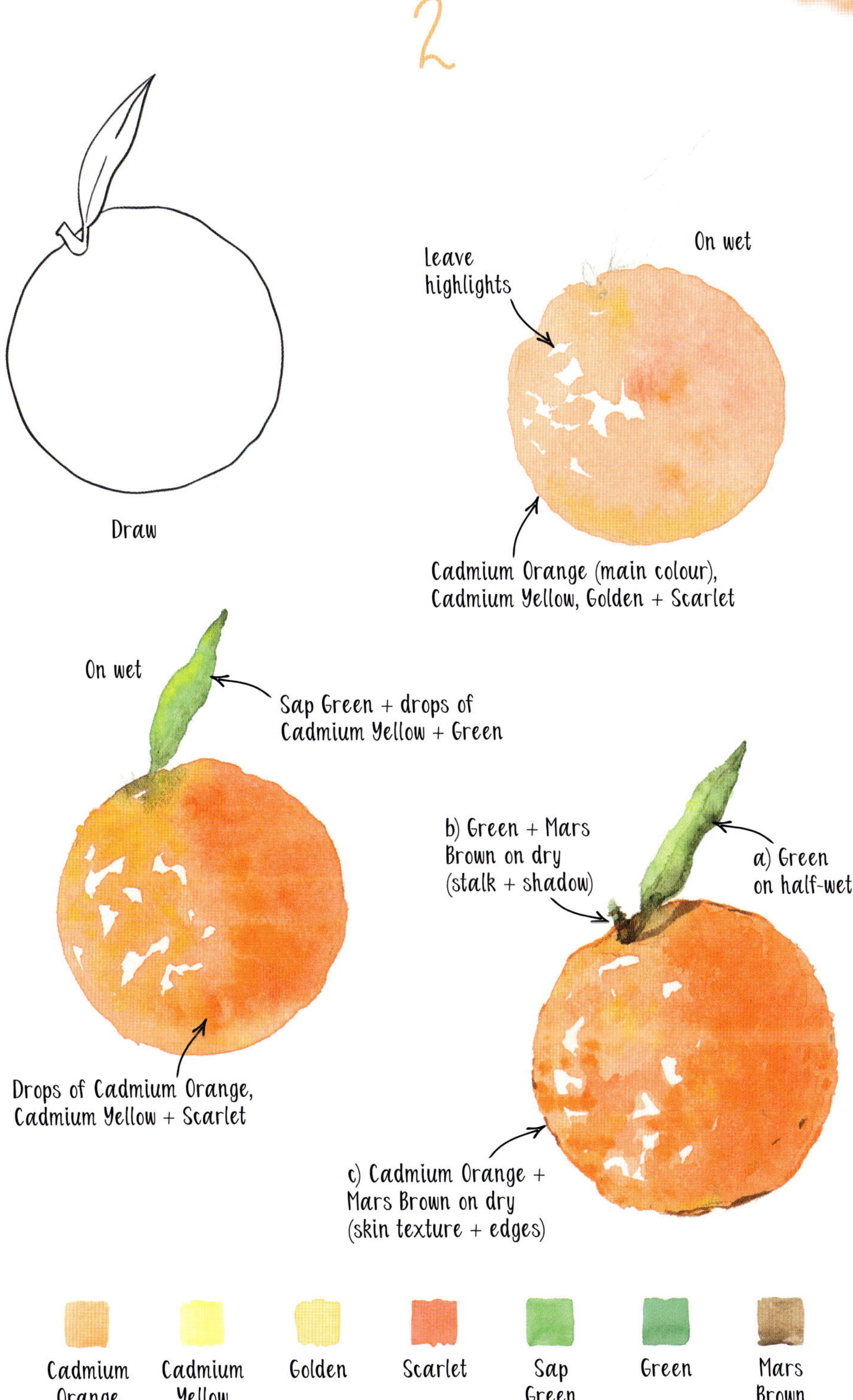
2

Draw

leave
highlights

On wet

Cadmium Orange (main colour),
Cadmium Yellow, Golden + Scarlet

On wet

Sap Green + drops of
Cadmium Yellow + Green

Drops of Cadmium Orange,
Cadmium Yellow + Scarlet

b) Green + Mars
Brown on dry
(stalk + shadow)

a) Green
on half-wet

c) Cadmium Orange +
Mars Brown on dry
(skin texture + edges)

Cadmium
Orange

Cadmium
Yellow

Golden

Scarlet

Sap
Green

Green

Mars
Brown

3

Draw

Cadmium Yellow
Sap Green
On wet

a) Starting on dry, Sap Green
+ drops of water
b) Repeat previous step,
starting on dry
leave highlights

Cadmium Yellow
Drops of Sap Green + Green
On wet

Cadmium
Yellow
Sap
Green
Green

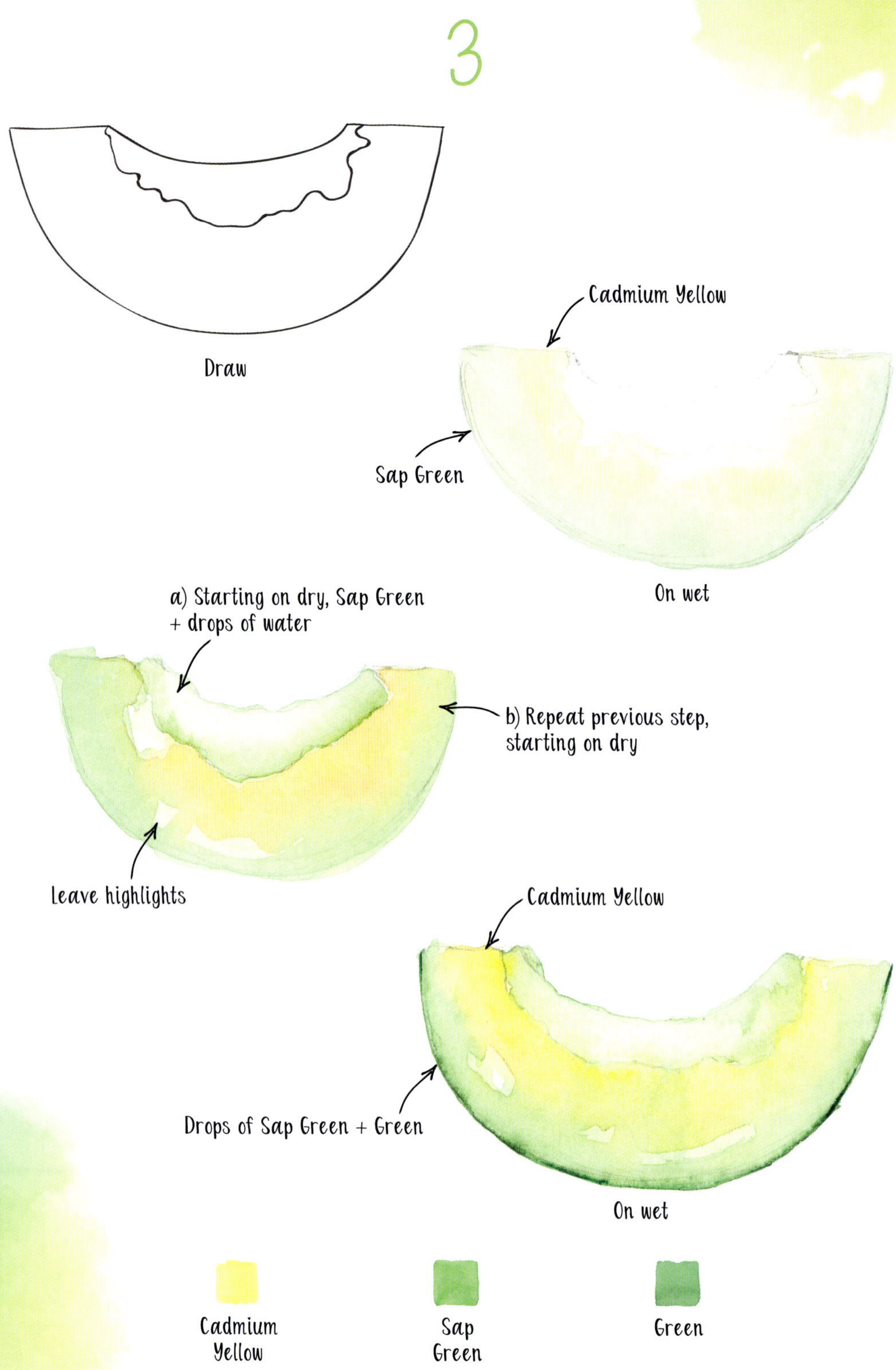

4

Draw

On wet
leave highlights
a) Madder Lake
Red Light
b) Sap Green
c) Water

On dry
a) Madder
Lake Red
Light
c) Sepia
leave wider
space here
b) Sap Green

On dry
a) Sap Green +
Indigo mix
b) Indigo

Madder Lake
Red Light
Sap
Green
Sepia
Indigo

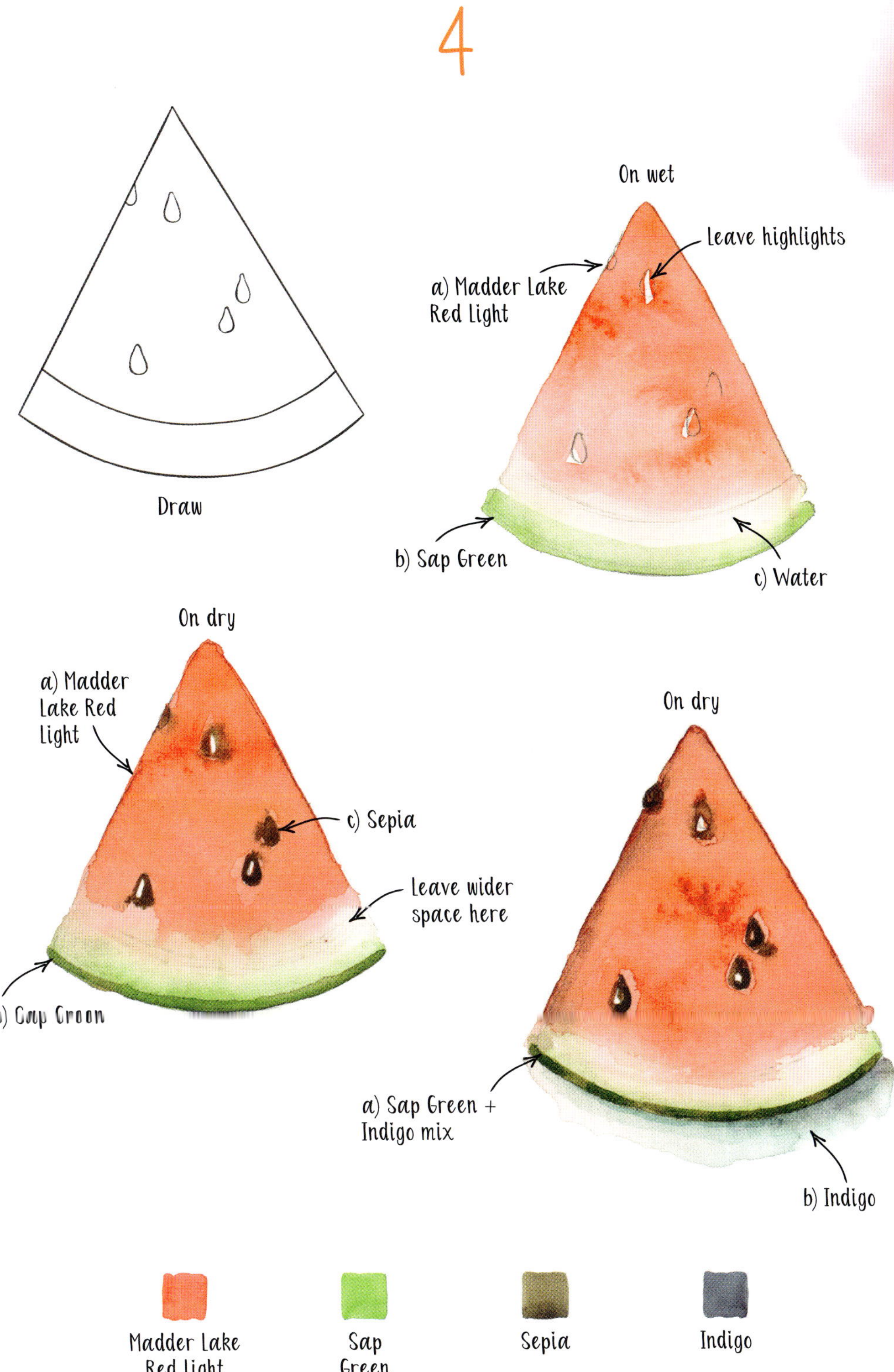

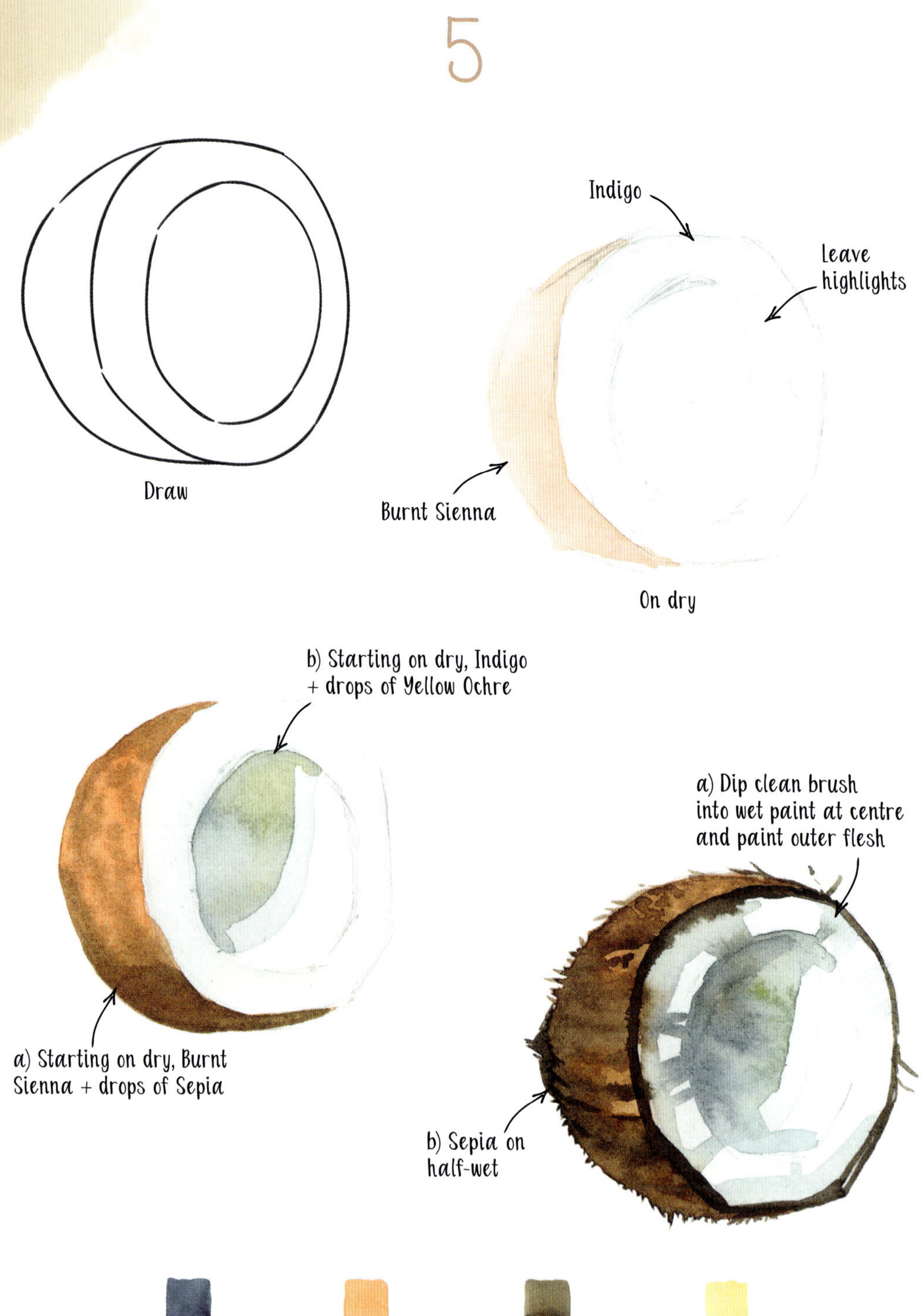

5

Draw

Indigo

leave highlights

Burnt Sienna

On dry

b) Starting on dry, Indigo + drops of Yellow Ochre

a) Dip clean brush into wet paint at centre and paint outer flesh

a) Starting on dry, Burnt Sienna + drops of Sepia

b) Sepia on half-wet

Indigo

Burnt Sienna

Sepia

Yellow Ochre

6

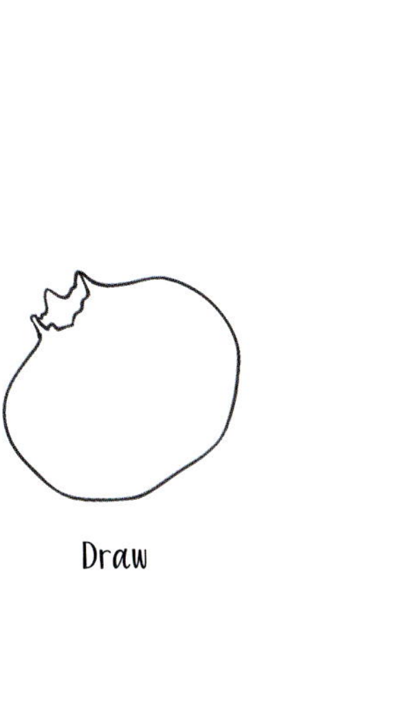

Draw

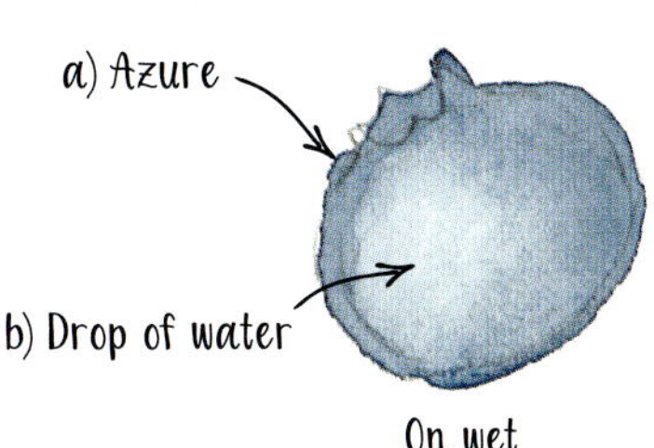

On wet

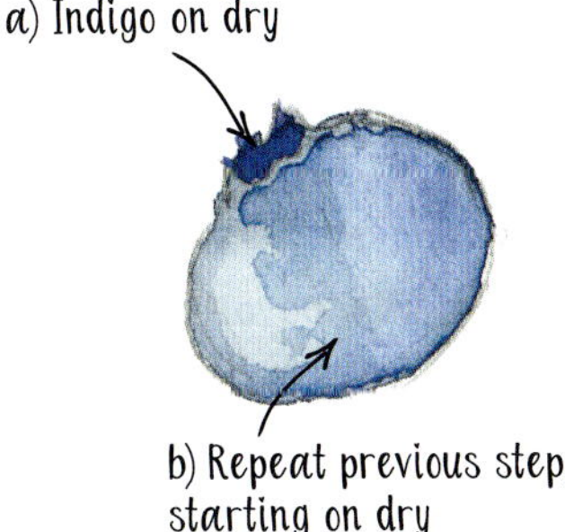

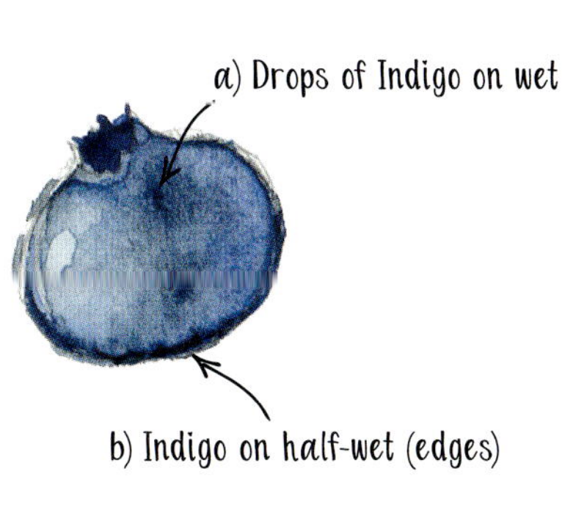

Azure

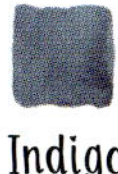

Indigo

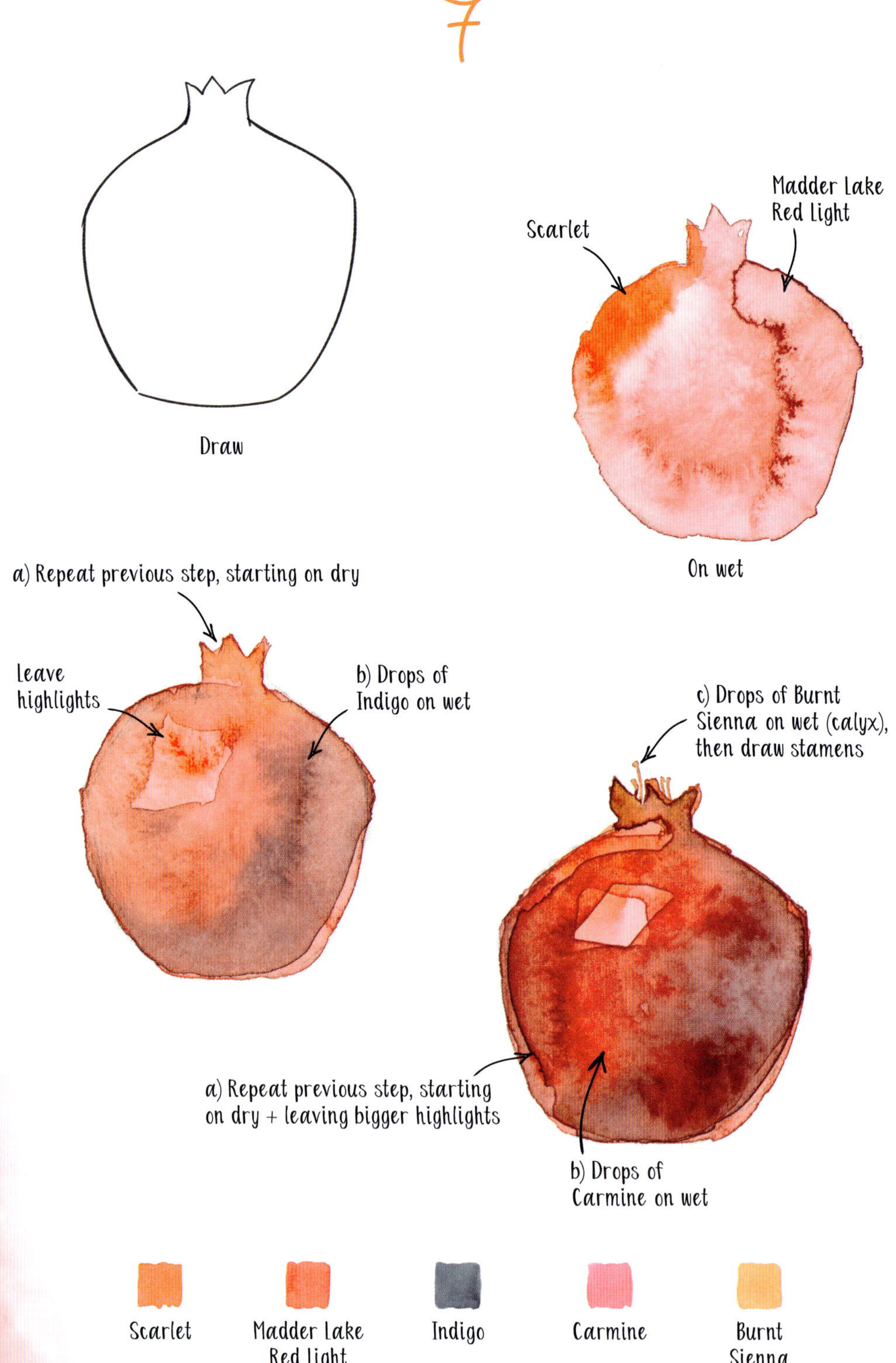
7
Draw
Scarlet
Madder Lake
Red light
On wet
a) Repeat previous step, starting on dry
leave
highlights
b) Drops of
Indigo on wet
c) Drops of Burnt
Sienna on wet (calyx),
then draw stamens
a) Repeat previous step, starting
on dry + leaving bigger highlights
b) Drops of
Carmine on wet
Scarlet
Madder Lake
Red light
Indigo
Carmine
Burnt
Sienna

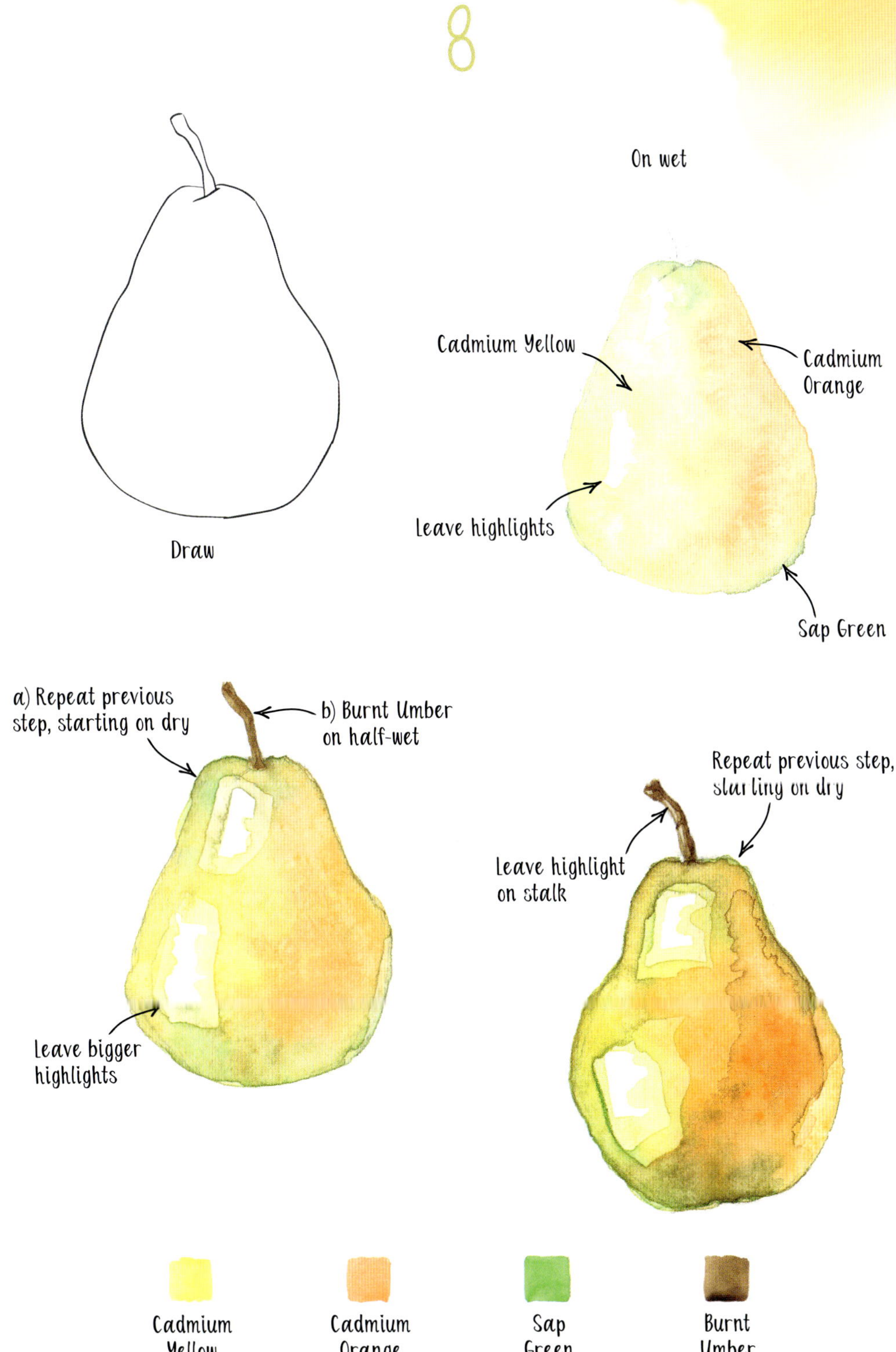
8

Draw

On wet

Cadmium Yellow

Cadmium Orange

Leave highlights

Sap Green

a) Repeat previous step, starting on dry

b) Burnt Umber on half-wet

Leave bigger highlights

Repeat previous step, starting on dry

leave highlight on stalk

Cadmium Yellow

Cadmium Orange

Sap Green

Burnt Umber

q

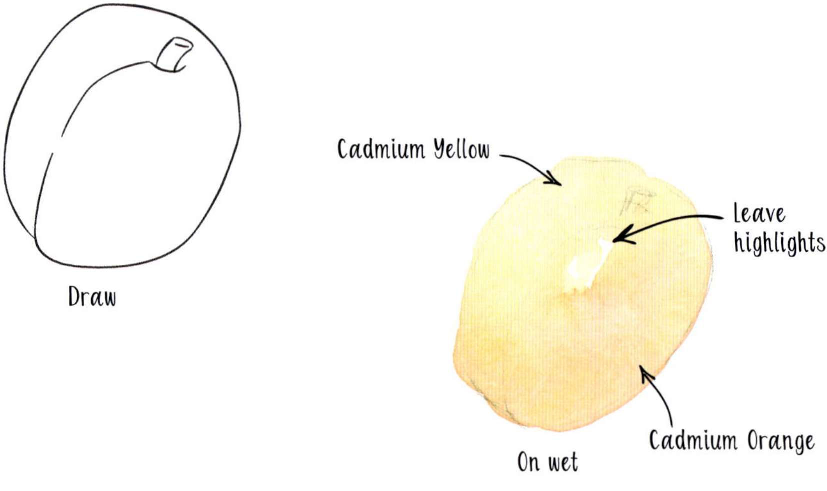

Draw

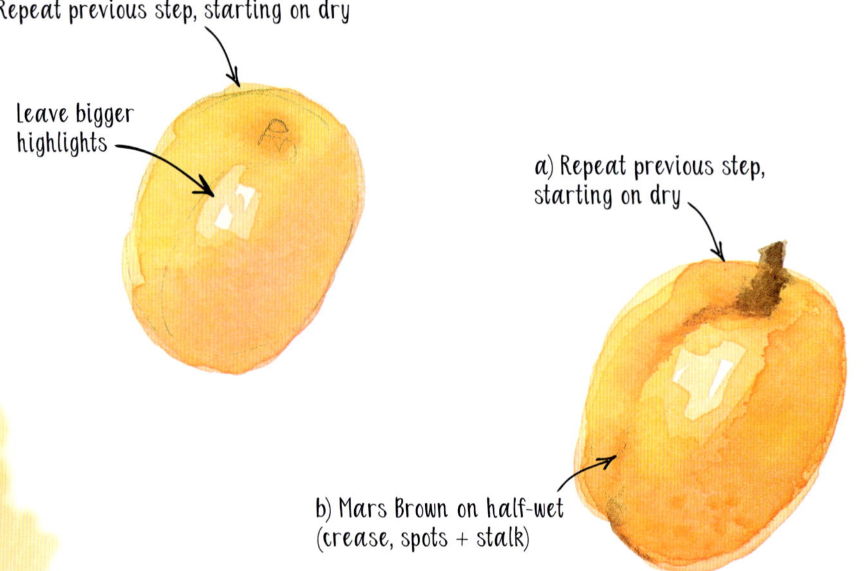

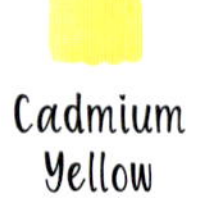

Cadmium
Yellow

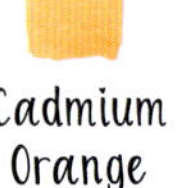

Cadmium
Orange

Mars
Brown

10

Draw
On wet
Sap Green + Green Light mix
Leave highlights
Ultramarine
Drops of Quinacridone Lilac

Repeat previous step, starting on dry
Leave bigger highlights
c) Green on dry
a) Repeat previous step, starting on dry
b) Drops of Ultramarine on wet (spots + each side of crease)
Ultramarine
Quinacridone Lilac
Sap Green
Green Light
Green

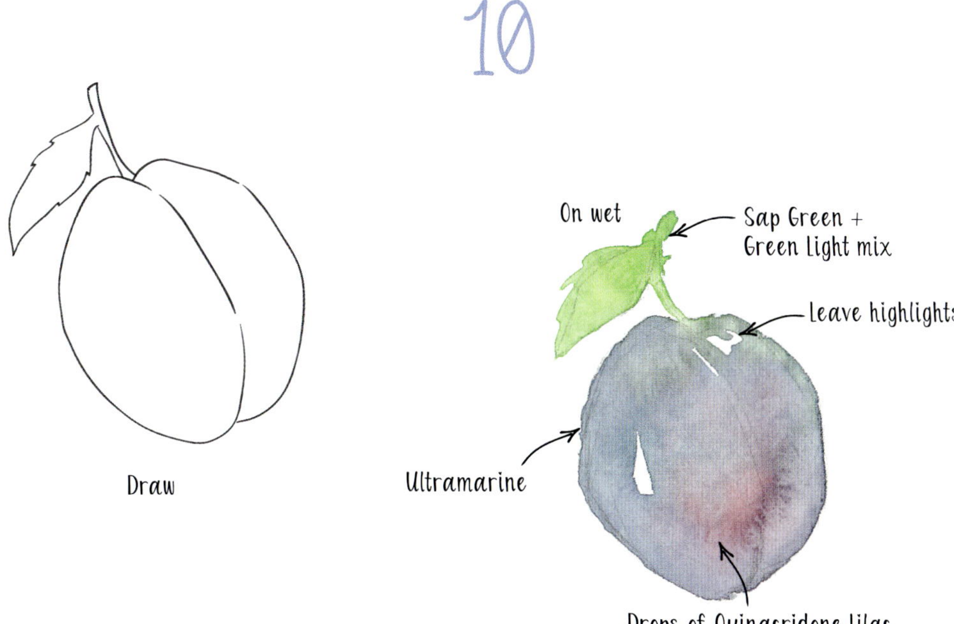

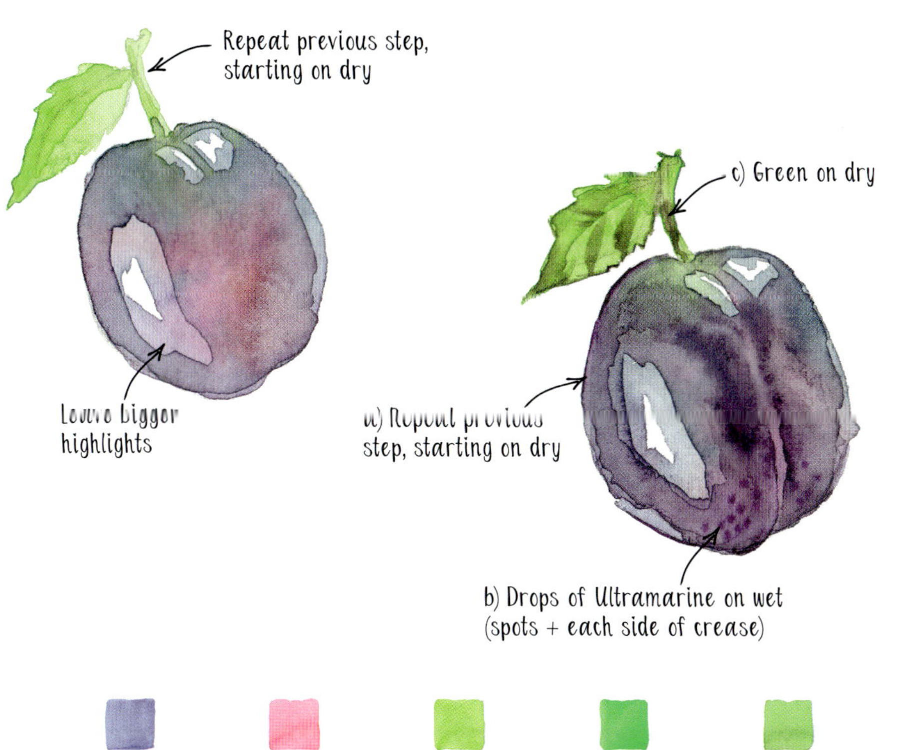

11

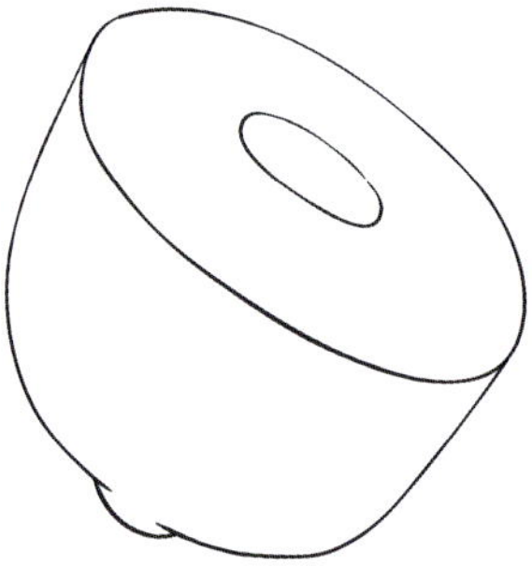

Draw

a) Cadmium Lemon
(whole fruit)

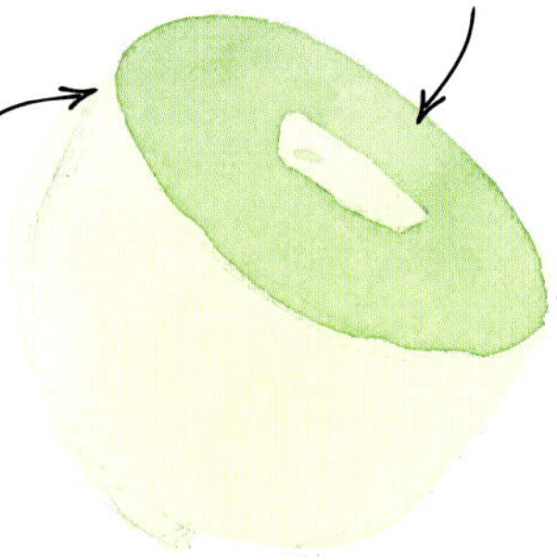

b) Sap Green +
Yellowish Green mix

On dry

a) Drops of Green on wet
(around outer + inner edges)

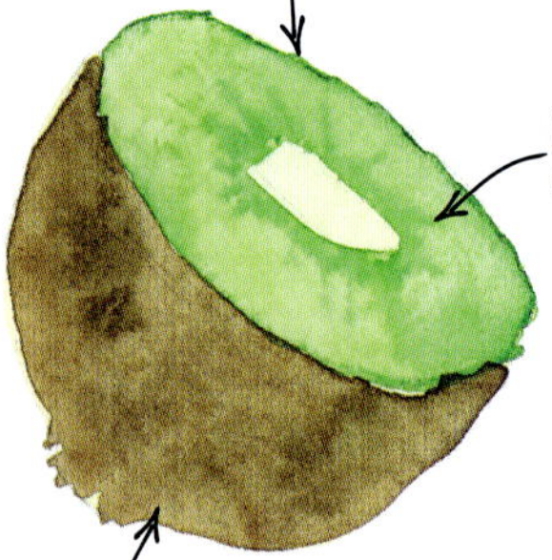

b) Draw lines outwards
from inner drops

c) Umber on dry

c) Umber on
half-wet (seeds)

b) Sap Green + Yellowish
Green mix on dry (around
outer + inner edges)

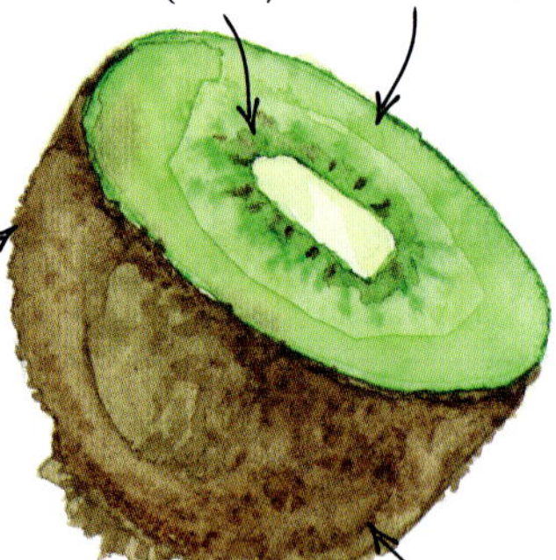

a) While wet, use brush
to create rough edge

d) Umber on dry, leaving highlight +
using brush to create skin texture

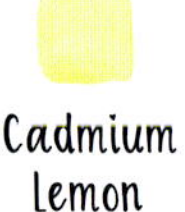
Cadmium
Lemon

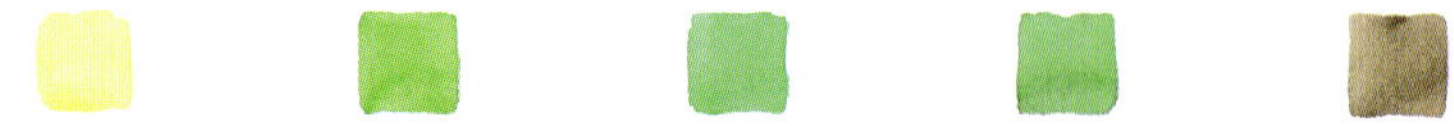

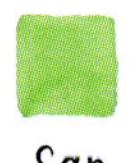
Sap
Green

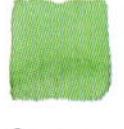
Yellowish
Green

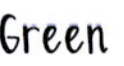
Green

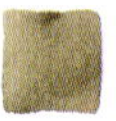
Umber

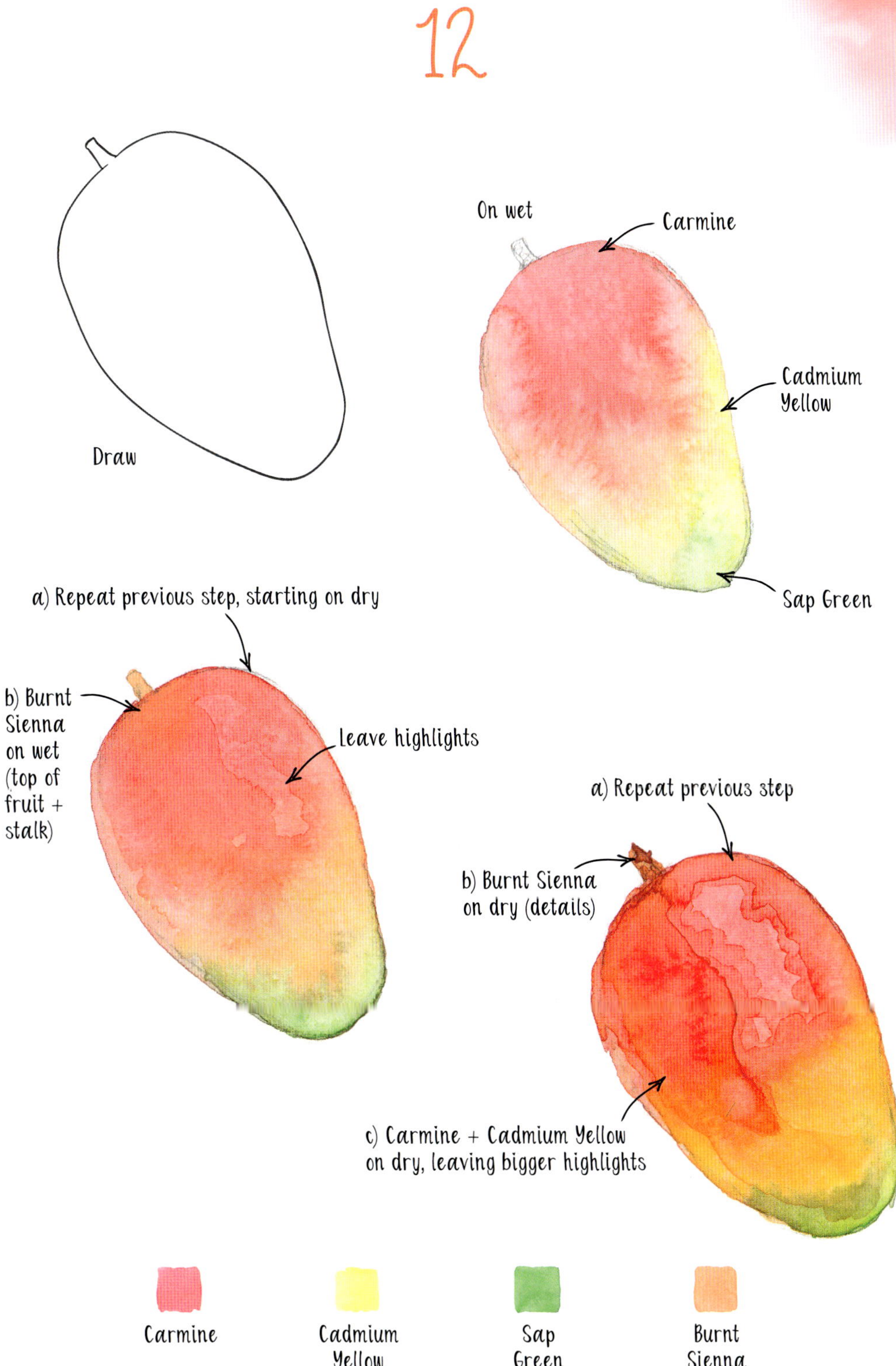
12
Draw
On wet
Carmine
Cadmium Yellow
Sap Green
a) Repeat previous step, starting on dry
b) Burnt Sienna on wet (top of fruit + stalk)
Leave highlights
a) Repeat previous step
b) Burnt Sienna on dry (details)
c) Carmine + Cadmium Yellow on dry, leaving bigger highlights
Carmine
Cadmium Yellow
Sap Green
Burnt Sienna

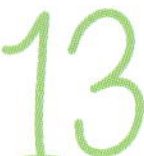

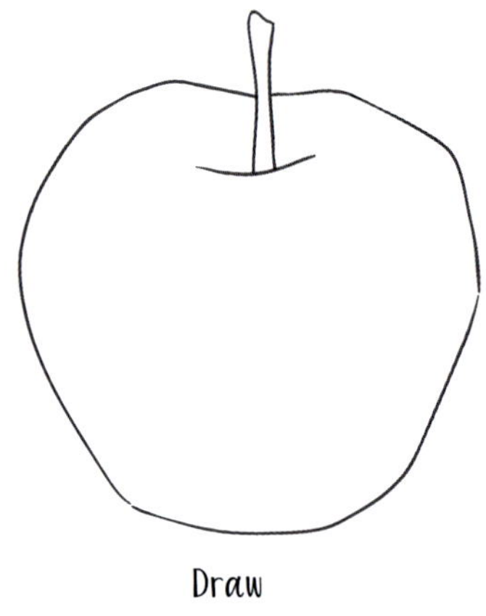

Draw

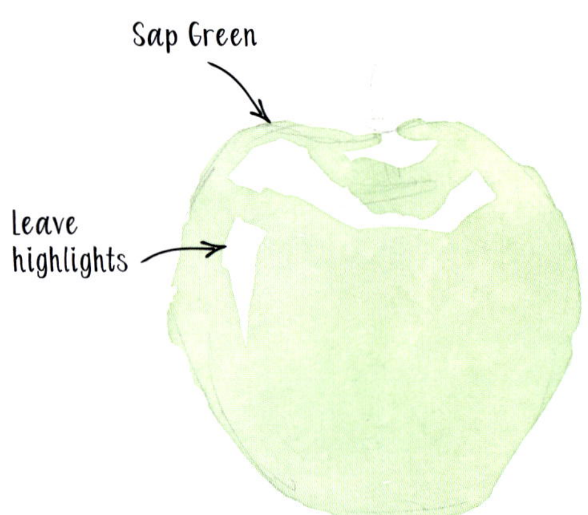

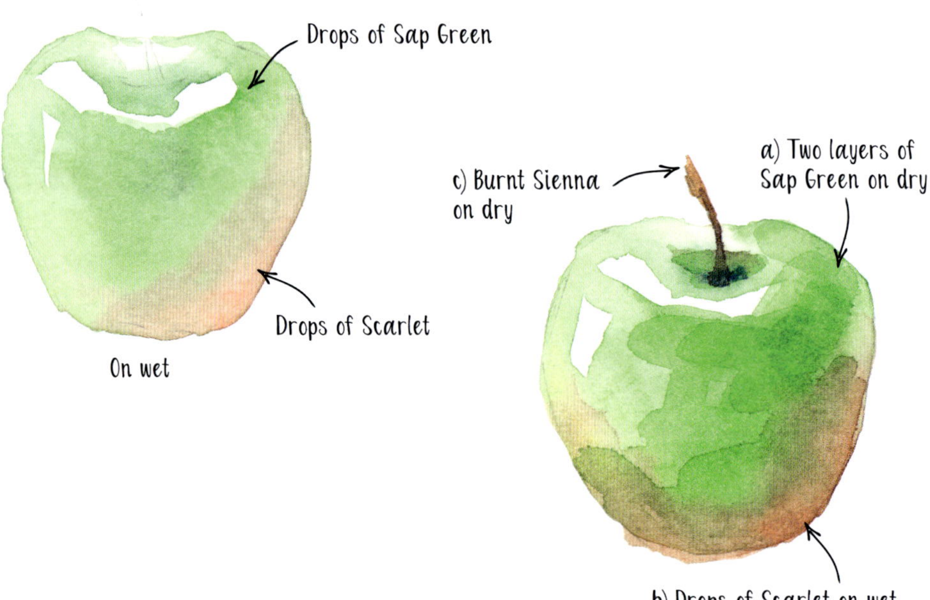

On wet

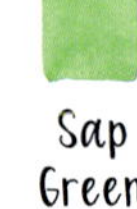

Sap Green

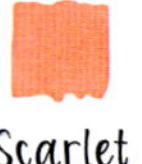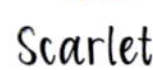

Scarlet

Burnt Sienna

14

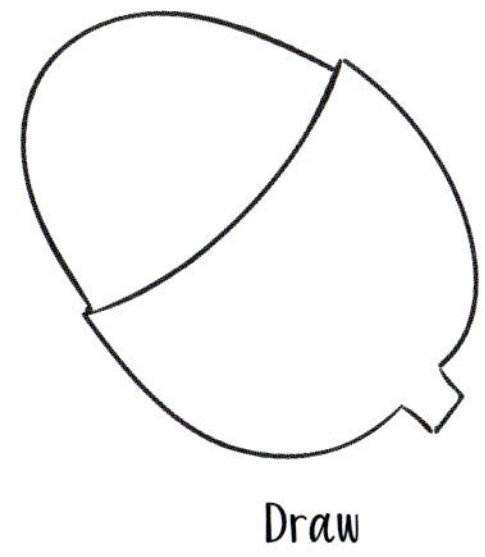

Draw

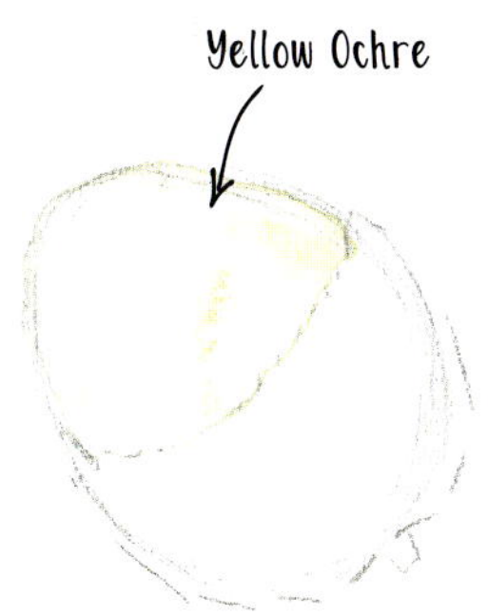

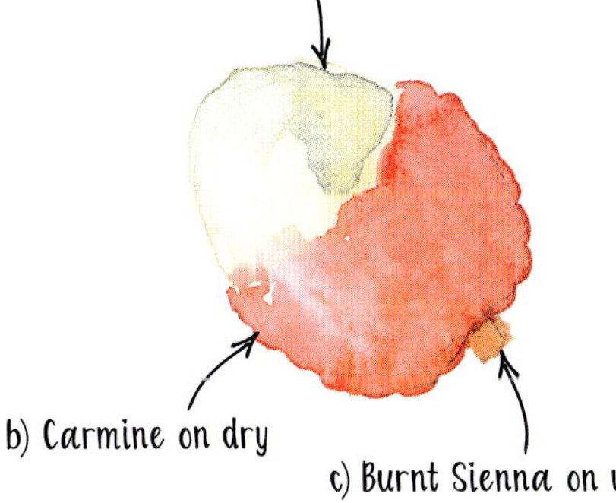

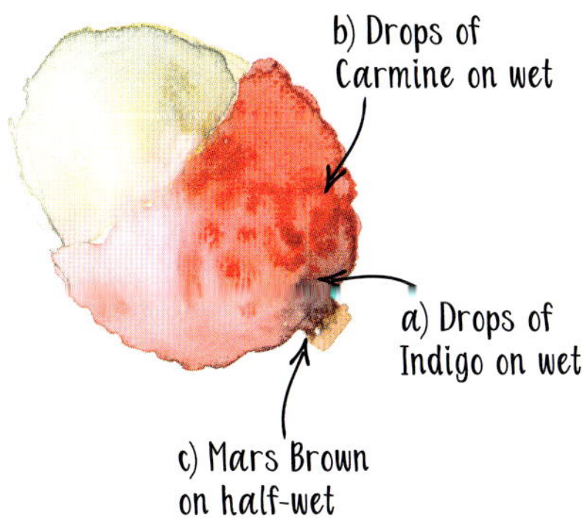

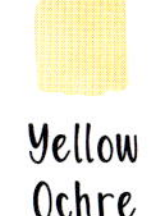

Yellow
Ochre

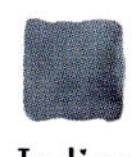

Indigo

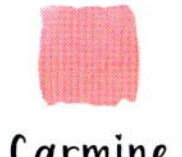

Carmine

Burnt
Sienna

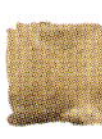

Mars
Brown

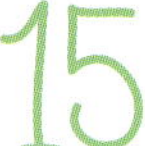

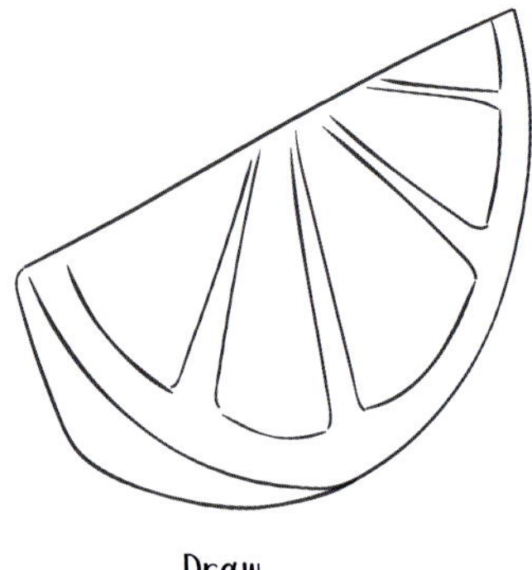

Draw

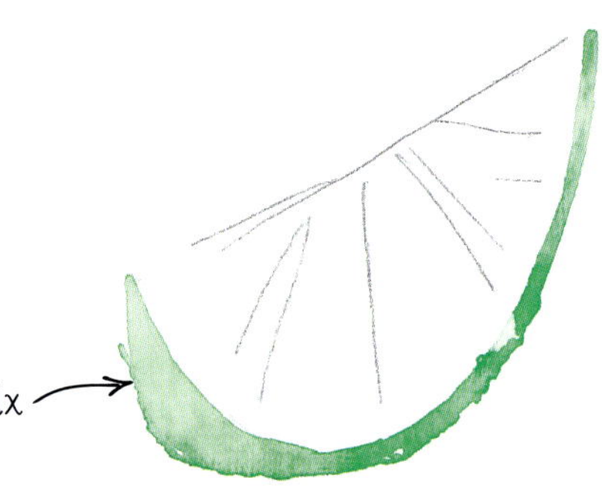

Emerald Green +
Yellowish Green mix

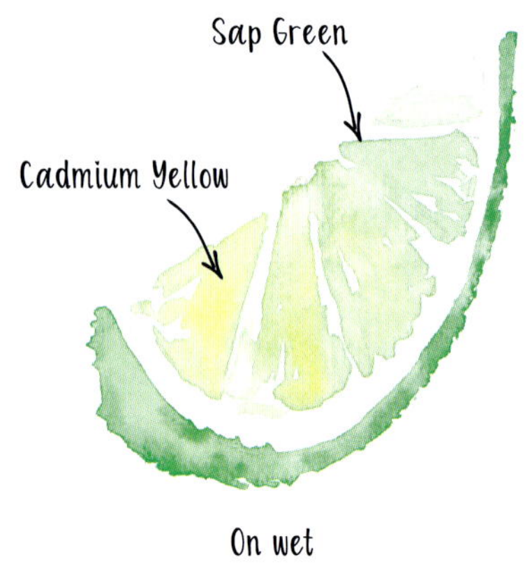

Sap Green

Cadmium Yellow

On wet

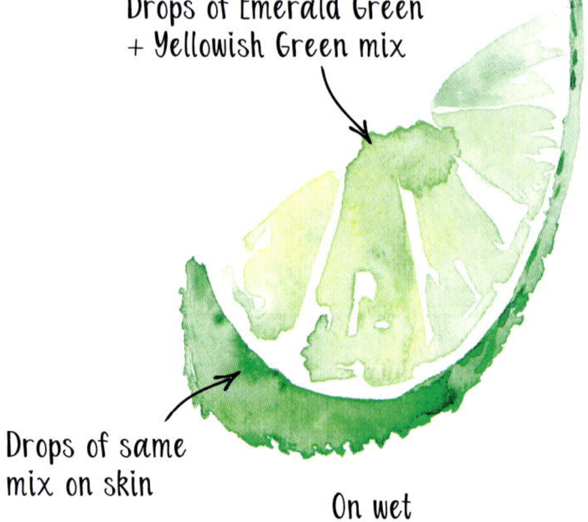

Drops of Emerald Green
+ Yellowish Green mix

Drops of same
mix on skin

On wet

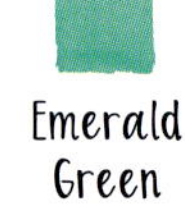

Emerald
Green

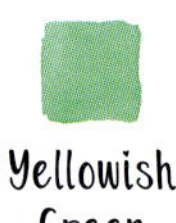

Yellowish
Green

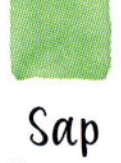

Sap
Green

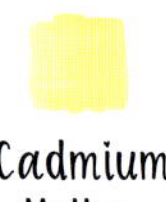

Cadmium
Yellow

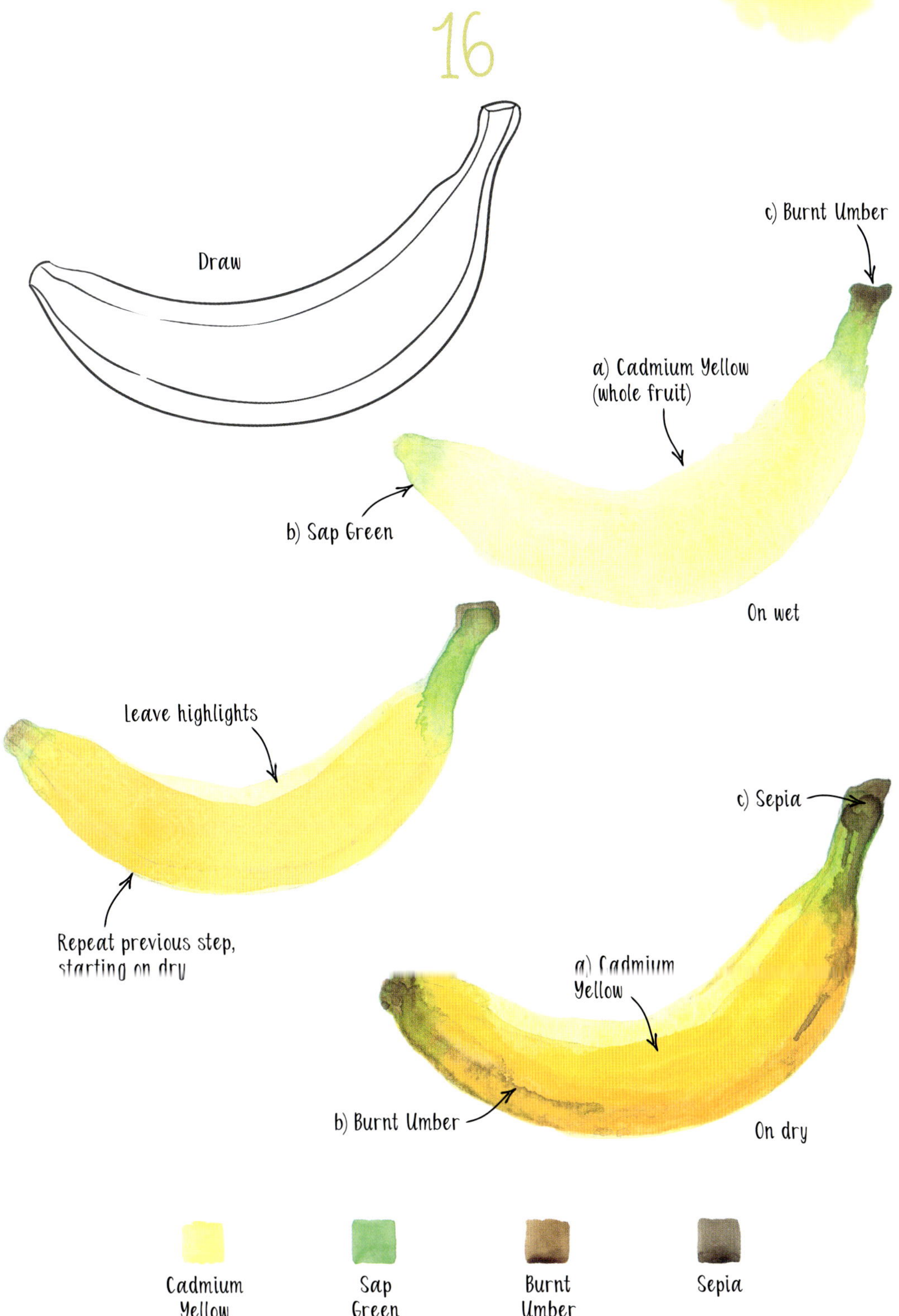
16
Draw
c) Burnt Umber
a) Cadmium Yellow
(whole fruit)
b) Sap Green
On wet
Leave highlights
Repeat previous step,
starting on dry
c) Sepia
a) Cadmium
Yellow
b) Burnt Umber
On dry
Cadmium
Yellow
Sap
Green
Burnt
Umber
Sepia

17

Draw

a) Madder
Lake Red light
(whole cherry)

Leave highlights

c) Cadmium Yellow
+ Green mix

b) Scarlet

On wet

Repeat previous step,
starting on dry +
omitting Scarlet

leave bigger
highlights

Remove some colour
around outer edges
with cotton bud
(to create volume)

Add shadow

a) Green + Cadmium Yellow mix

Remove colour with
wet cotton bud to
make stalk thinner
if necessary

c) Green

b) Claret + Cobalt Blue mix

On dry

Madder Lake
Red light

Scarlet

Cadmium
Yellow

Green

Claret

Cobalt
Blue

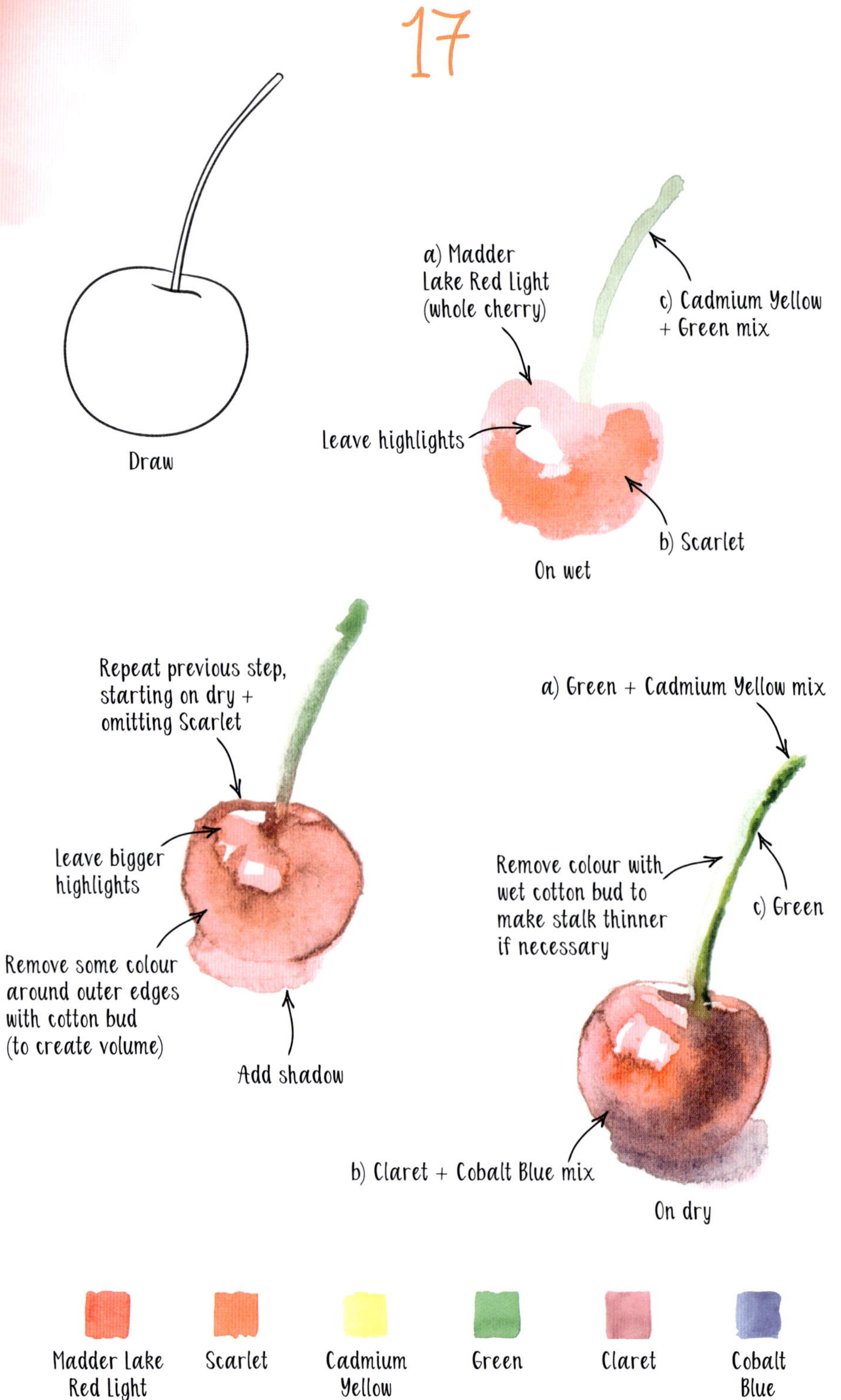

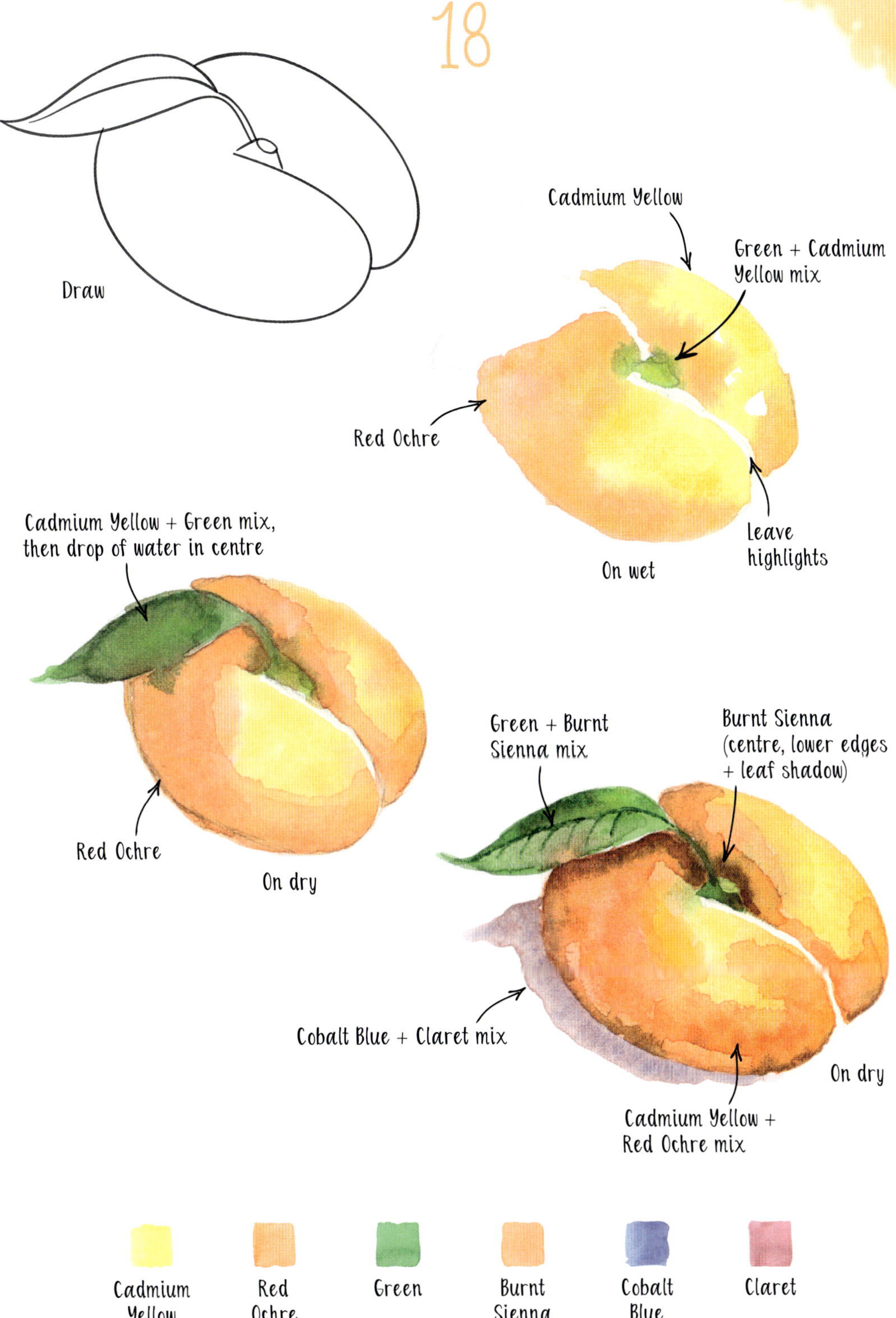
18

Draw

Cadmium Yellow

Green + Cadmium
Yellow mix

Red Ochre

leave
highlights

On wet

Cadmium Yellow + Green mix,
then drop of water in centre

Red Ochre

On dry

Green + Burnt
Sienna mix

Burnt Sienna
(centre, lower edges
+ leaf shadow)

Cobalt Blue + Claret mix

On dry

Cadmium Yellow +
Red Ochre mix

Cadmium
Yellow

Red
Ochre

Green

Burnt
Sienna

Cobalt
Blue

Claret

19

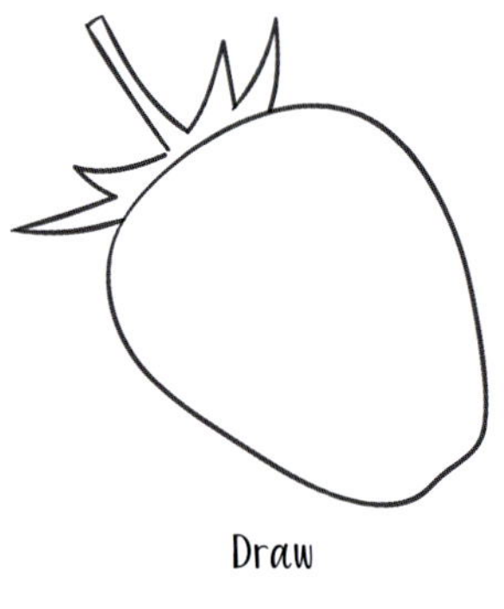

Draw

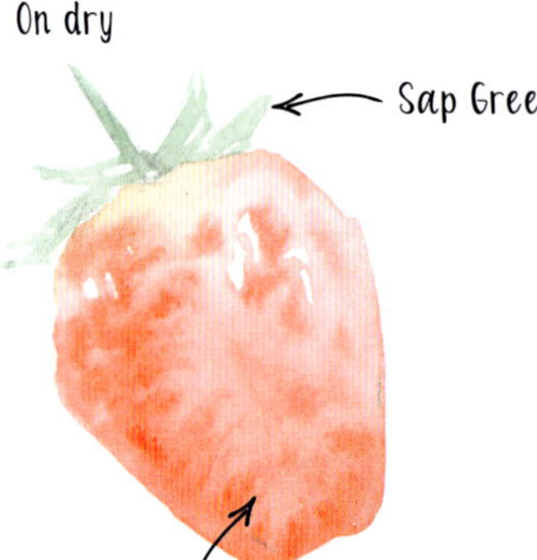

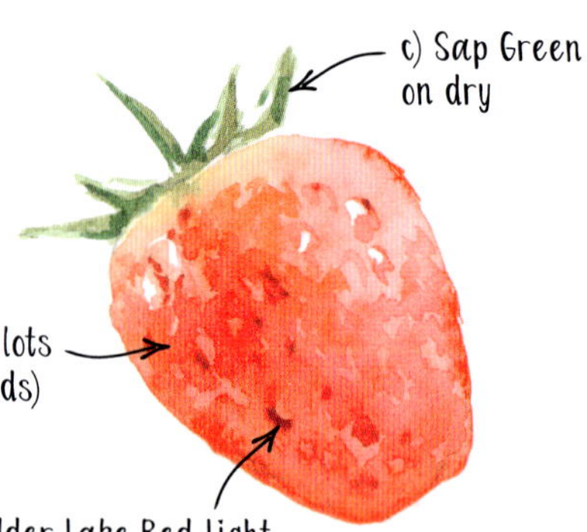

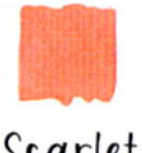

Scarlet

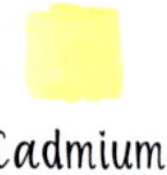

Cadmium
Yellow

Sap
Green

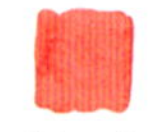

Madder Lake
Red light

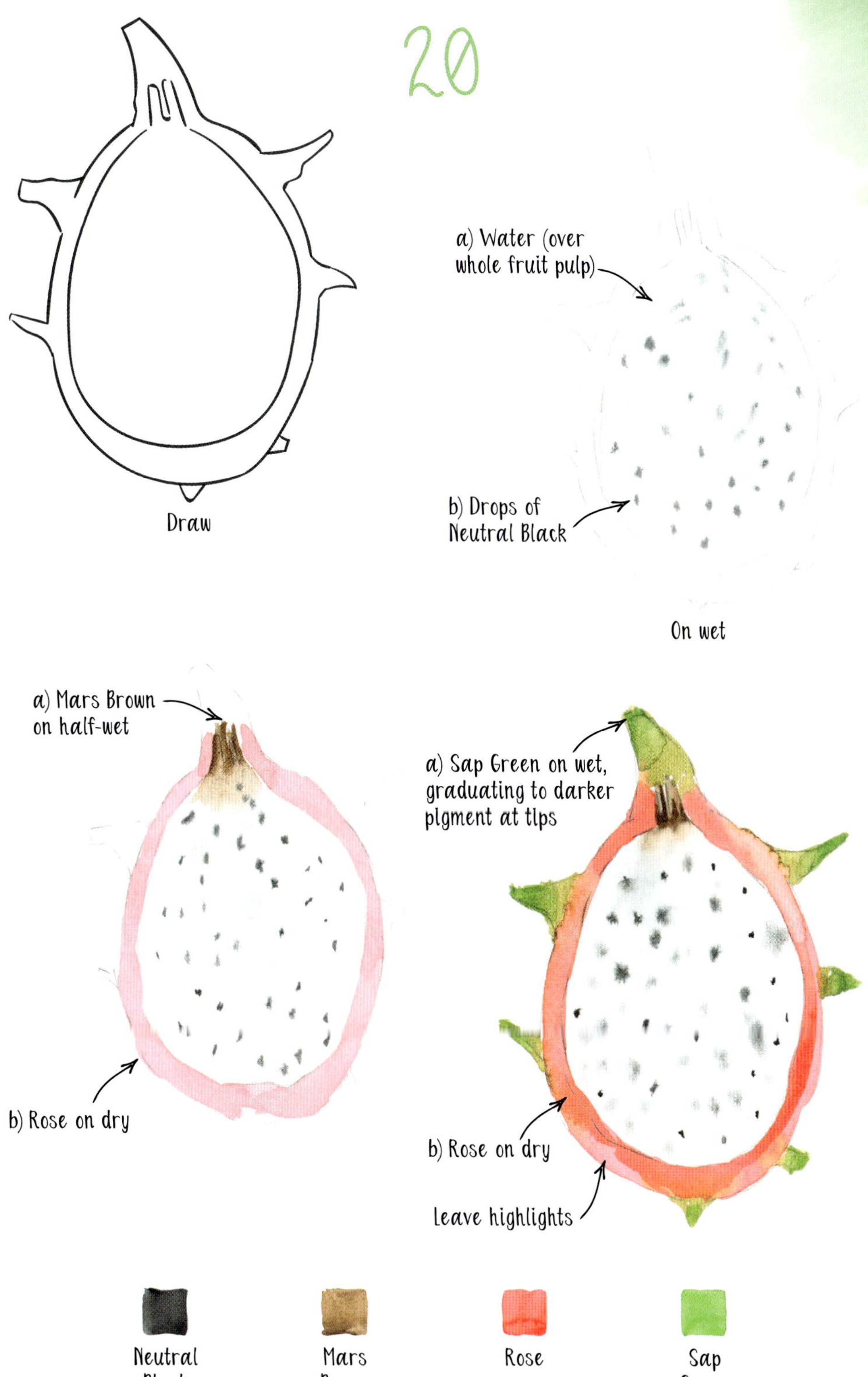
20

Draw

a) Water (over whole fruit pulp)

b) Drops of Neutral Black

On wet

a) Mars Brown on half-wet

b) Rose on dry

a) Sap Green on wet, graduating to darker pigment at tips

b) Rose on dry

Leave highlights

Neutral Black

Mars Brown

Rose

Sap Green

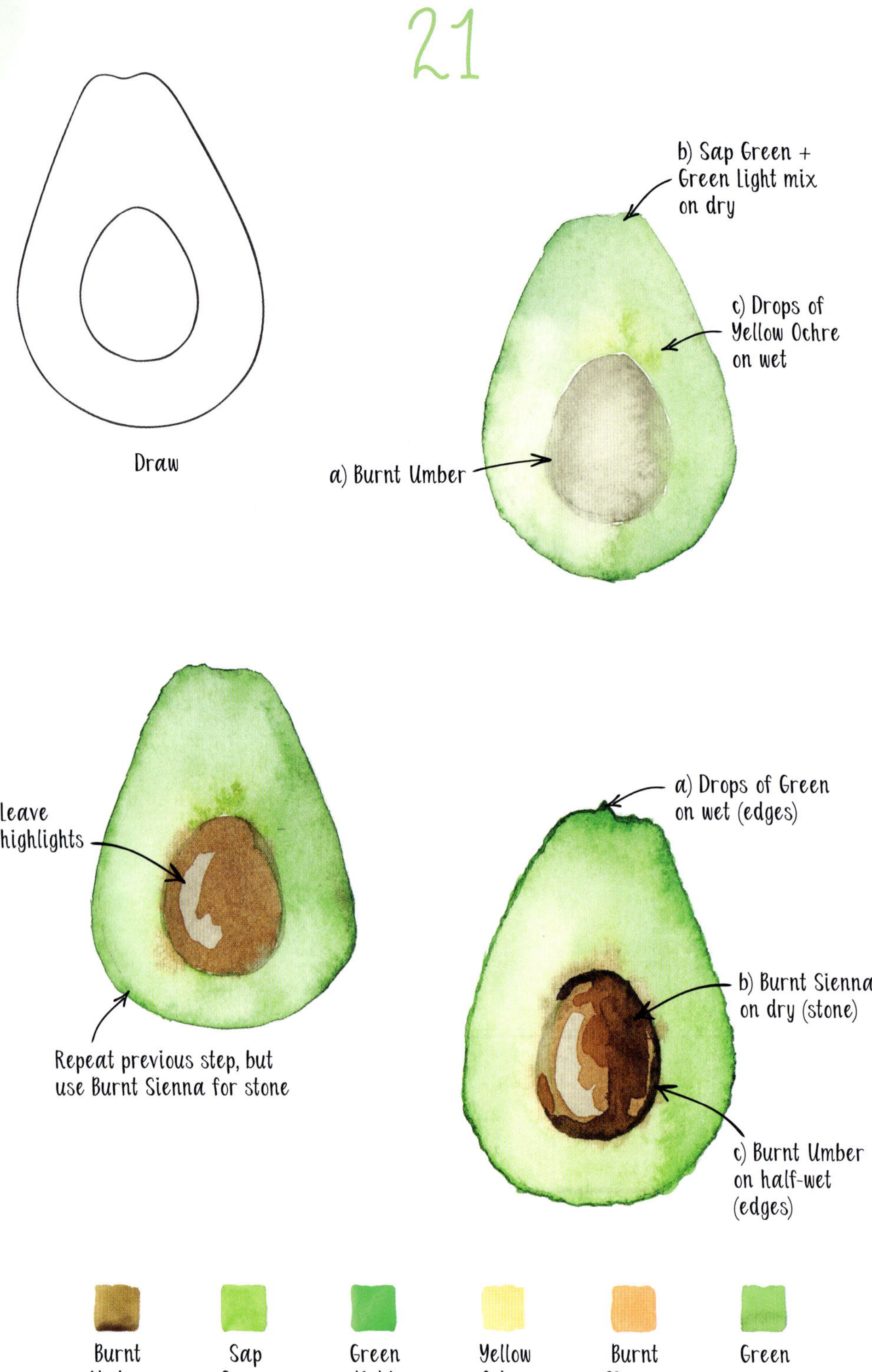

21
Draw
b) Sap Green +
Green Light mix
on dry
c) Drops of
Yellow Ochre
on wet
a) Burnt Umber
leave
highlights
Repeat previous step, but
use Burnt Sienna for stone
a) Drops of Green
on wet (edges)
b) Burnt Sienna
on dry (stone)
c) Burnt Umber
on half-wet
(edges)
Burnt
Umber
Sap
Green
Green
Light
Yellow
Ochre
Burnt
Sienna
Green

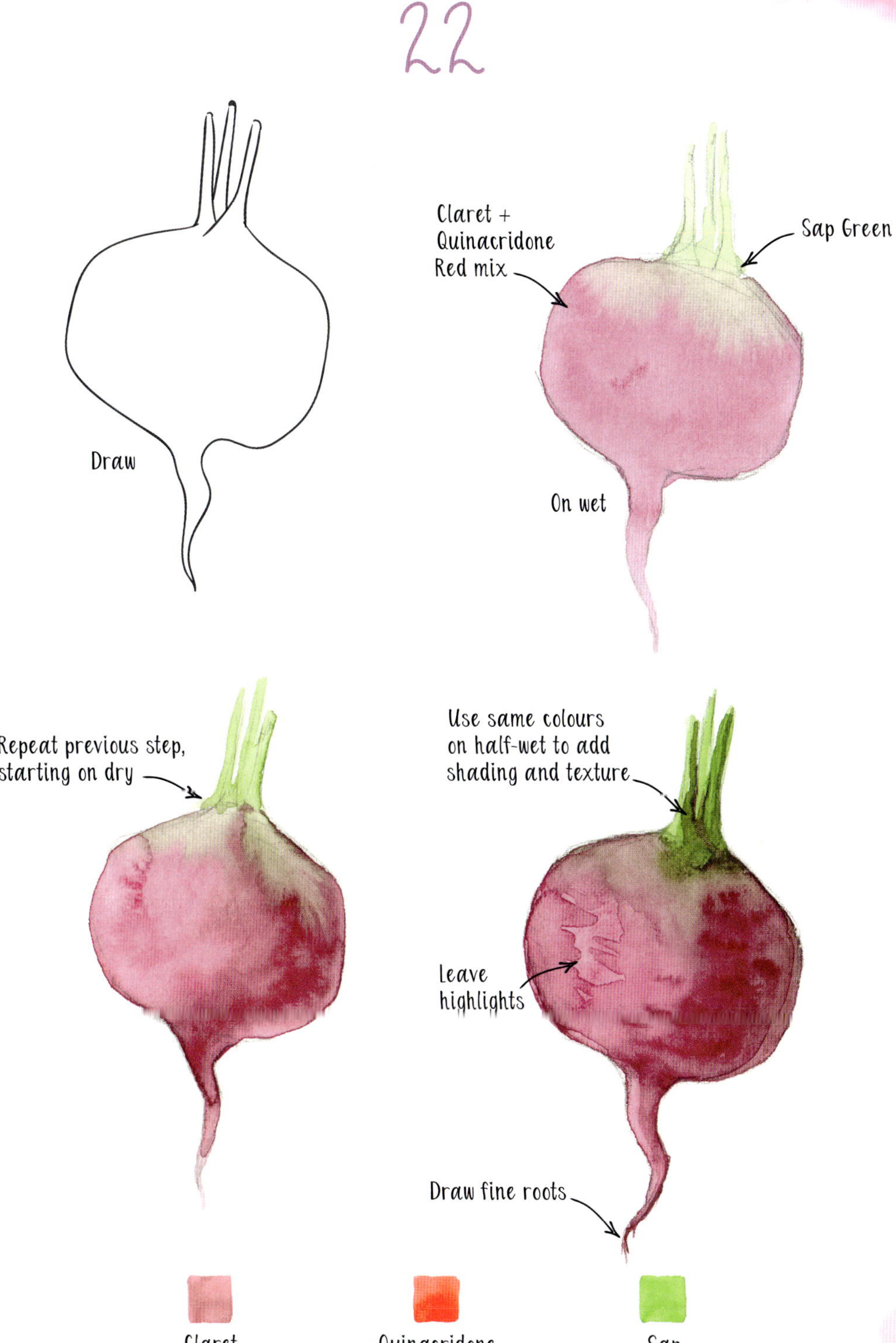

22
Draw
Claret +
Quinacridone
Red mix
Sap Green
On wet
Repeat previous step,
starting on dry
Use same colours
on half-wet to add
shading and texture
Leave
highlights
Draw fine roots
Claret
Quinacridone
Red
Sap
Green

23

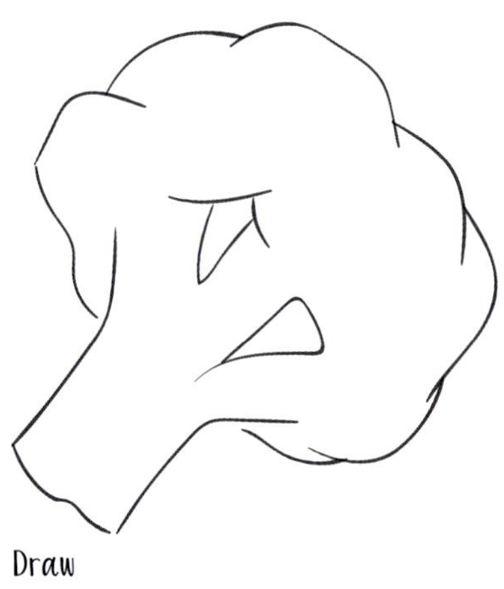

Draw

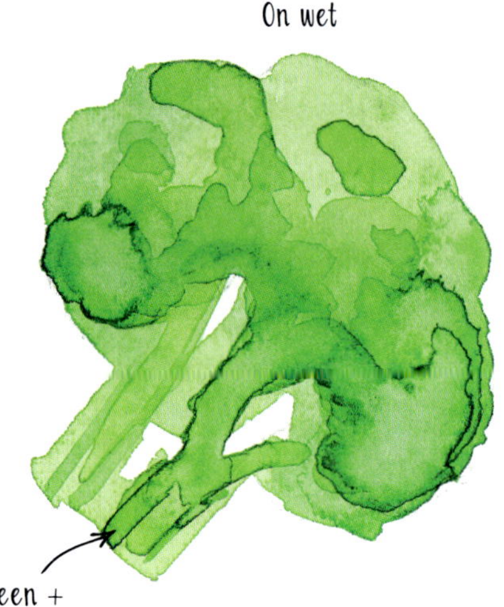

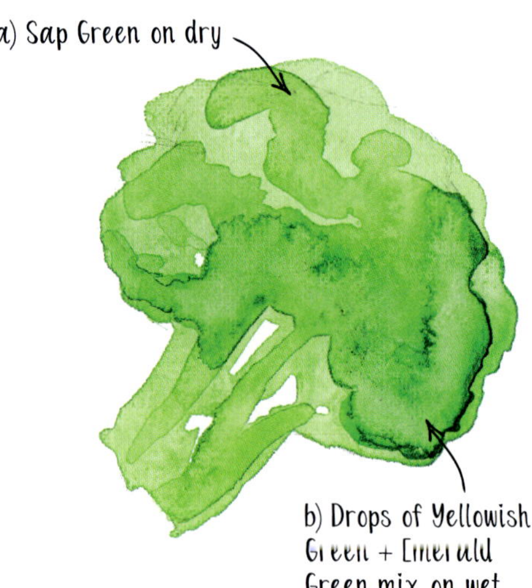

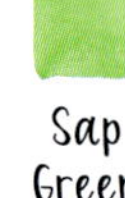

Sap
Green

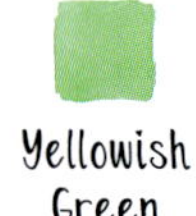

Yellowish
Green

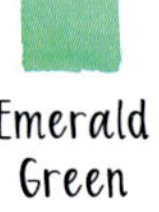

Emerald
Green

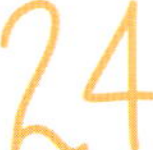

24

Draw

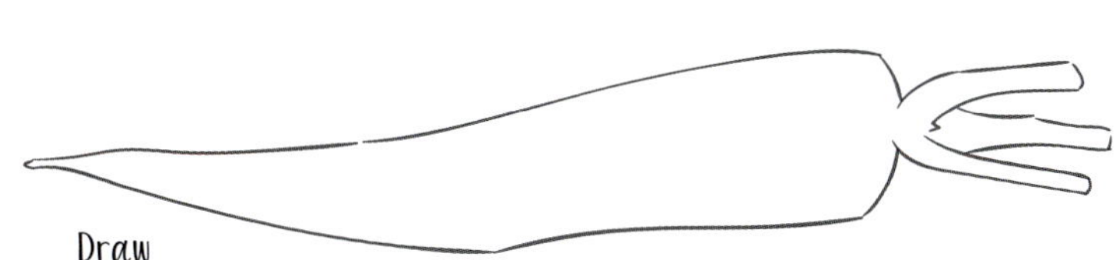

Cadmium Yellow

On wet

Red Ochre

Sap Green

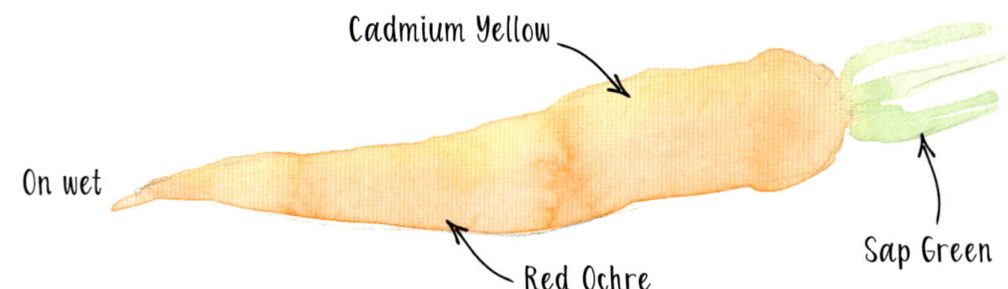

a) Repeat previous step, starting on dry

b) Drops of Cadmium Orange on wet

Leave highlights

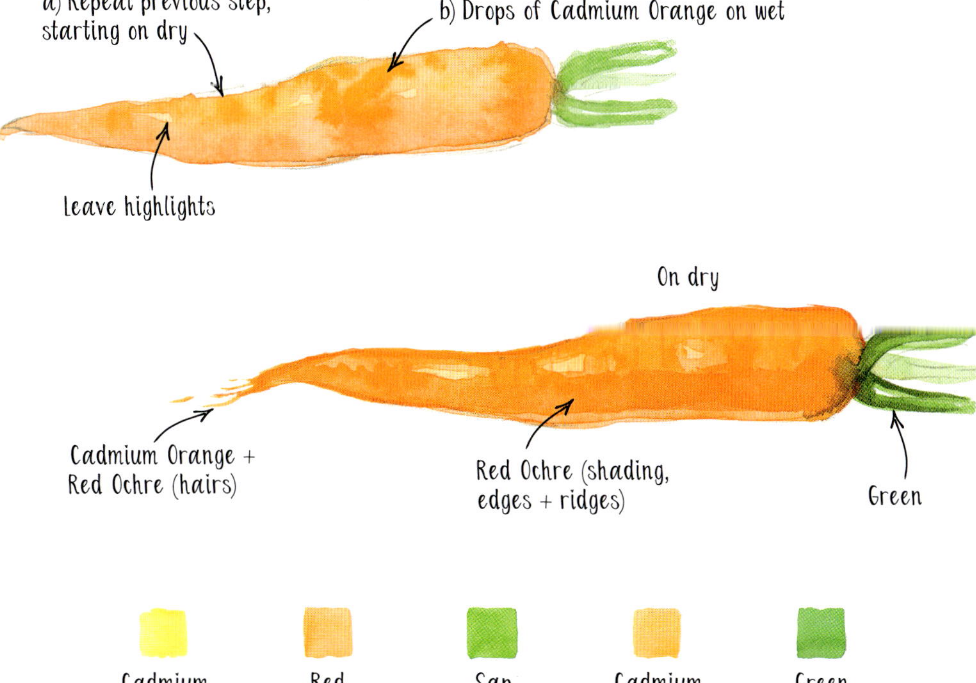

On dry

Cadmium Orange +
Red Ochre (hairs)

Red Ochre (shading,
edges + ridges)

Green

Cadmium
Yellow

Red
Ochre

Sap
Green

Cadmium
Orange

Green

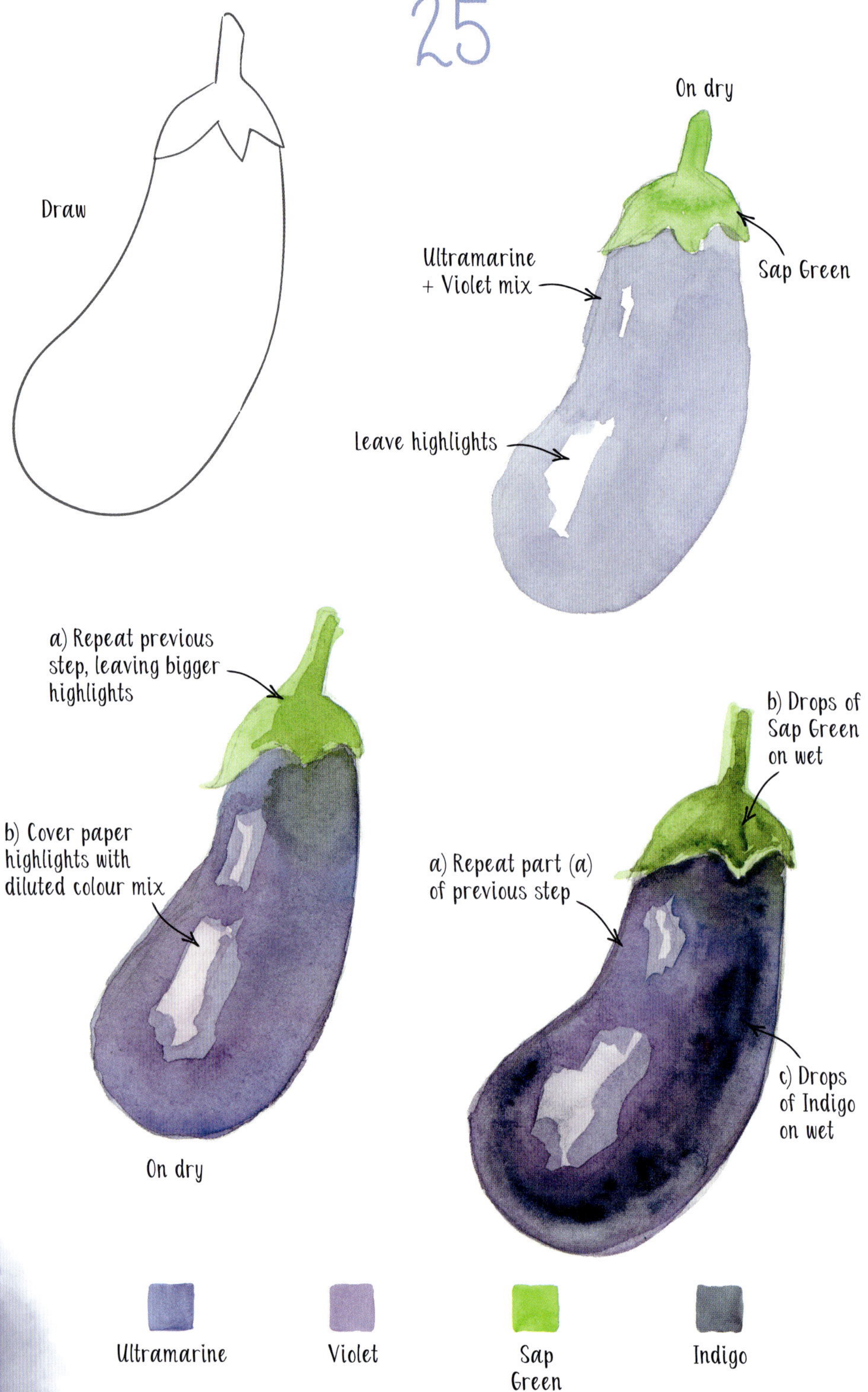
25
Draw
On dry
Ultramarine + Violet mix
Sap Green
Leave highlights
a) Repeat previous step, leaving bigger highlights
b) Cover paper highlights with diluted colour mix
On dry
b) Drops of Sap Green on wet
a) Repeat part (a) of previous step
c) Drops of Indigo on wet
Ultramarine
Violet
Sap Green
Indigo

26

Draw

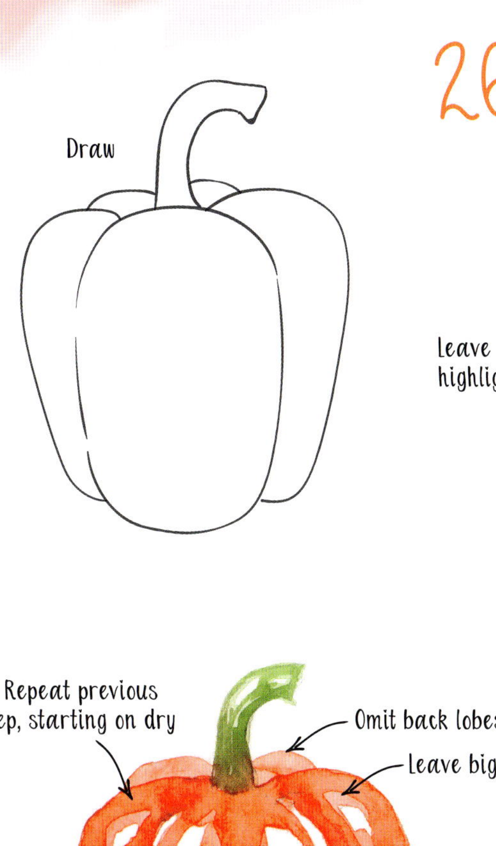

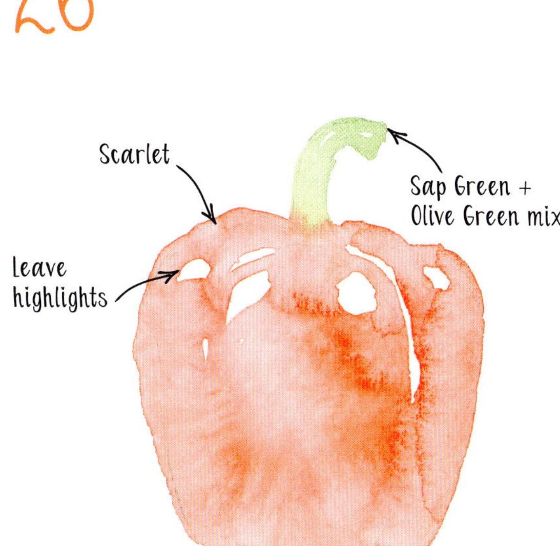

On wet

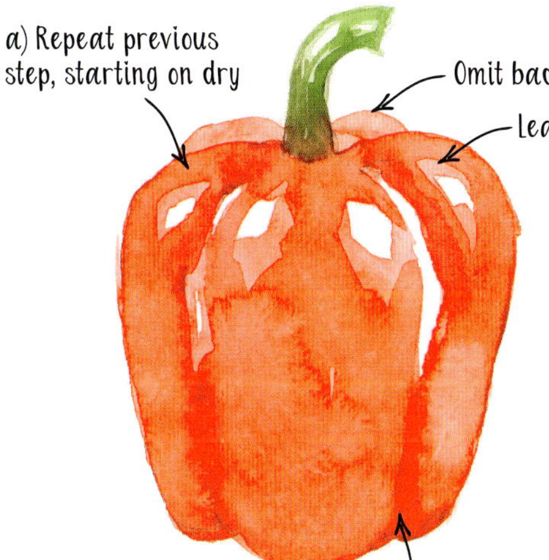

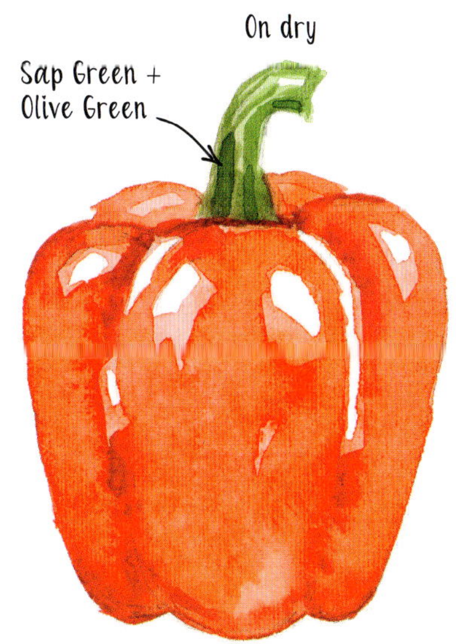

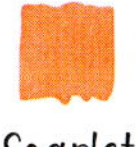

Scarlet

Sap
Green

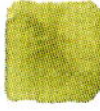

Olive
Green

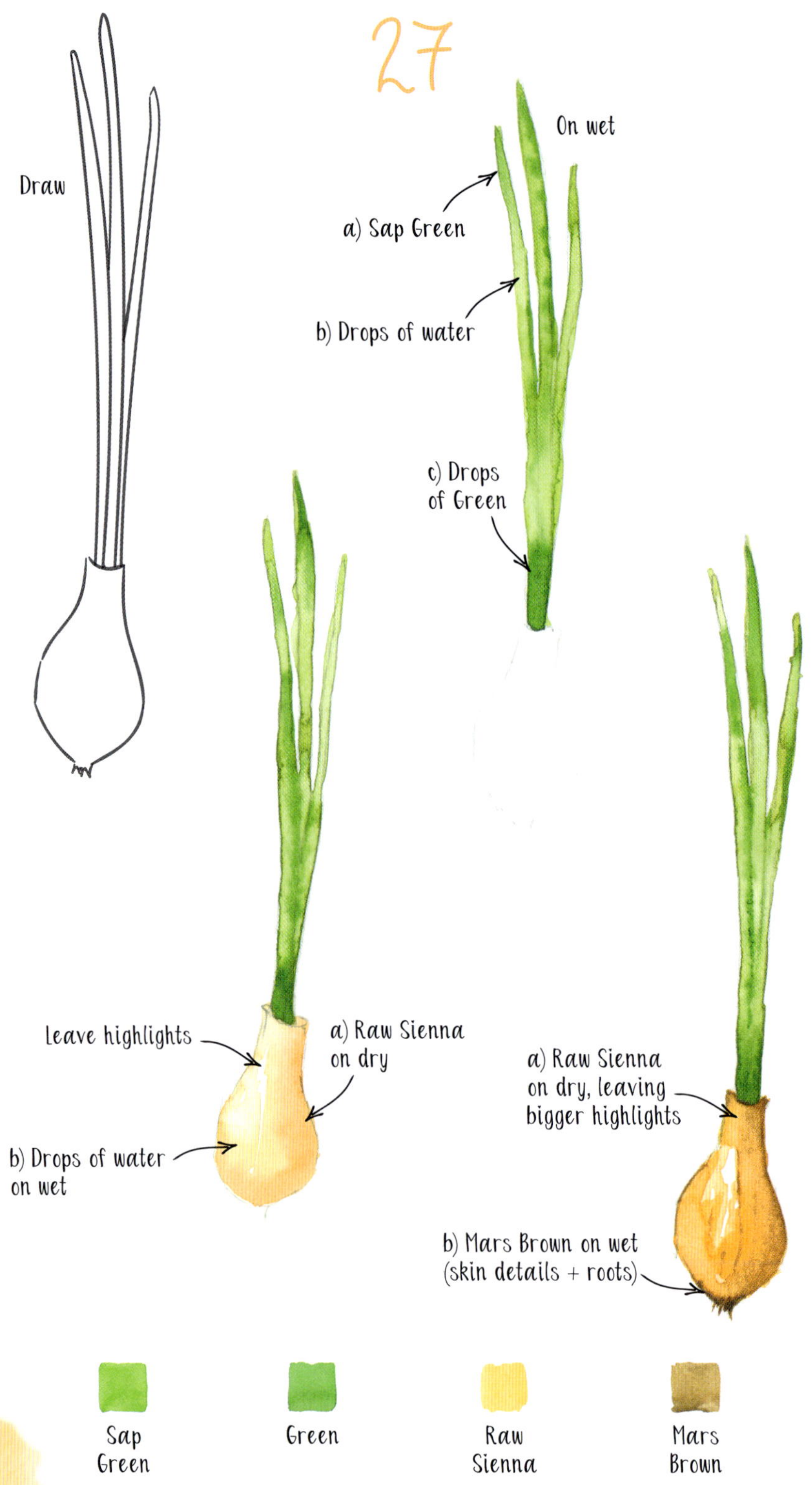
27
Draw
On wet
a) Sap Green
b) Drops of water
c) Drops
of Green
leave highlights
a) Raw Sienna
on dry
a) Raw Sienna
on dry, leaving
bigger highlights
b) Drops of water
on wet
b) Mars Brown on wet
(skin details + roots)
Sap
Green
Green
Raw
Sienna
Mars
Brown

28

Draw

Yellow Ochre
Sap Green
On wet

Two layers of Yellowish
Green (to define bracts)
Apply second layer
to shaded side only
On dry

Sap Green
On half-wet

Sap
Green

Yellow
Ochre

Yellowish
Green

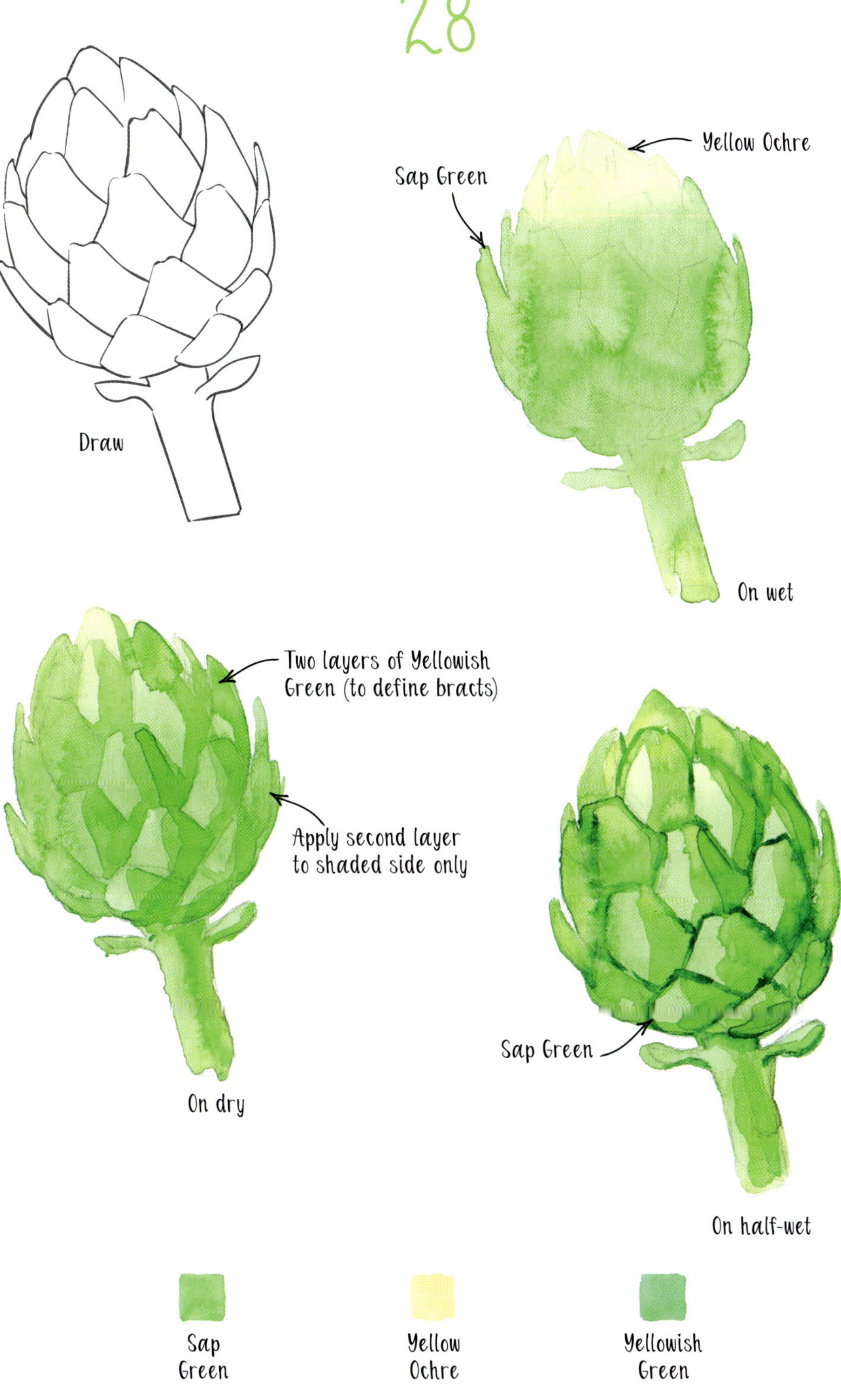

29

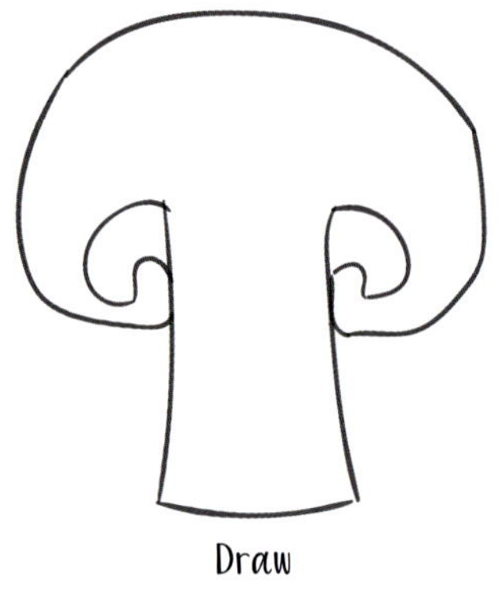

Draw

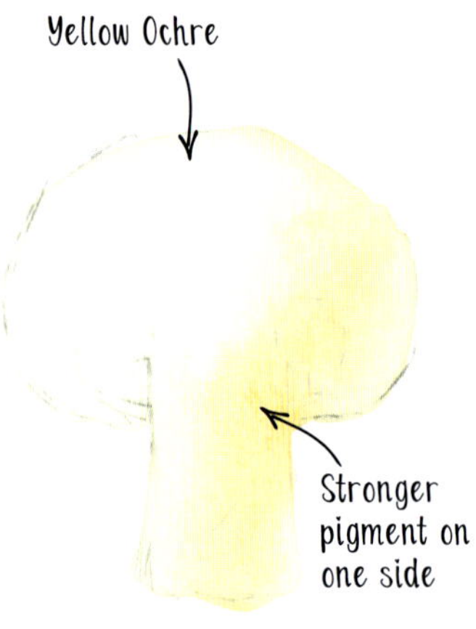

On wet

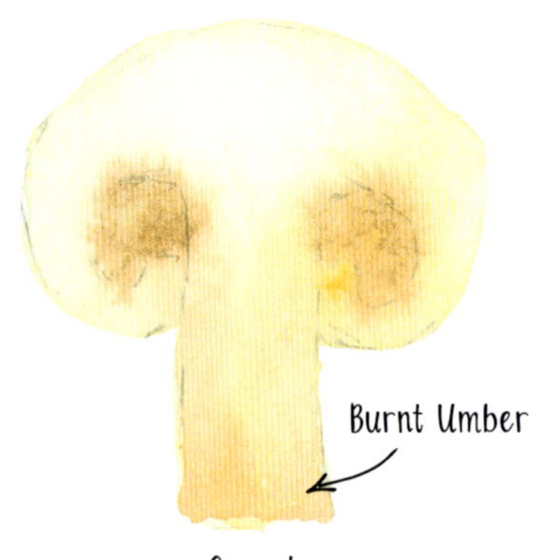

On wet

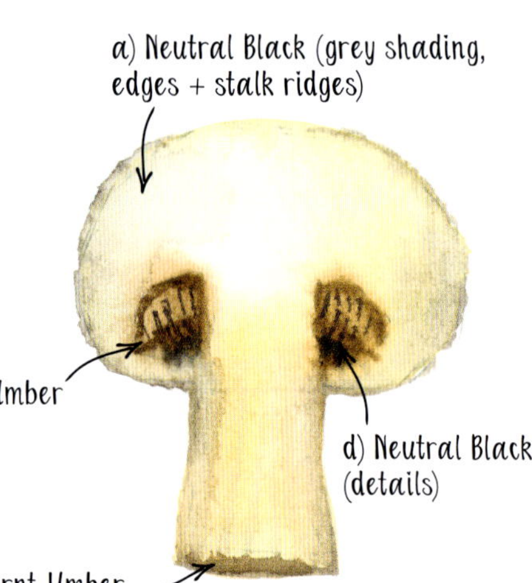

On dry

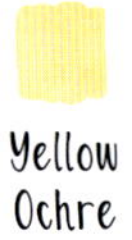

Yellow
Ochre

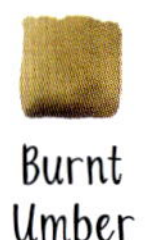

Burnt
Umber

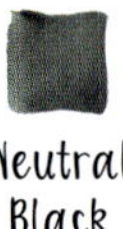

Neutral
Black

30

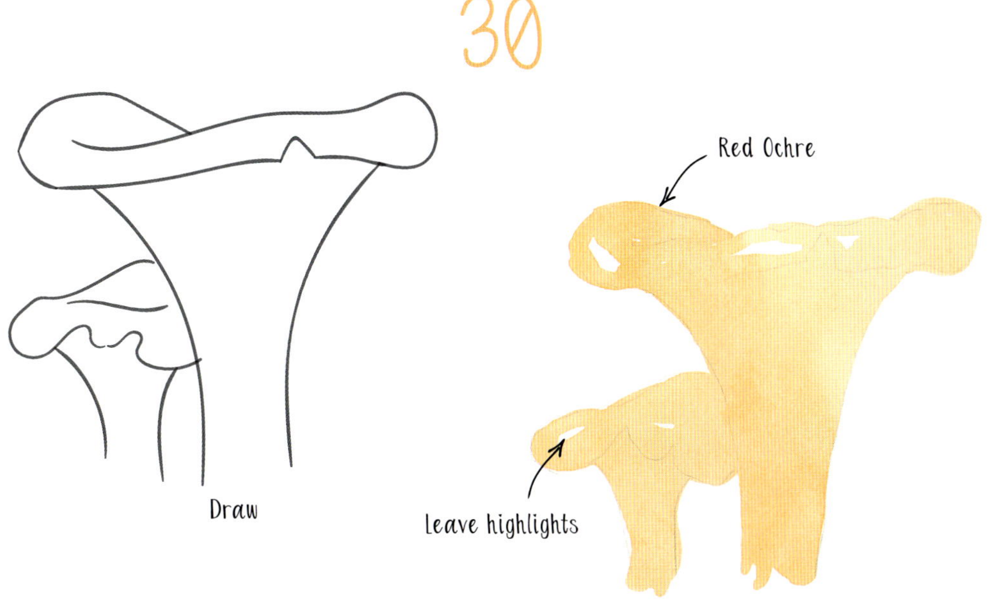

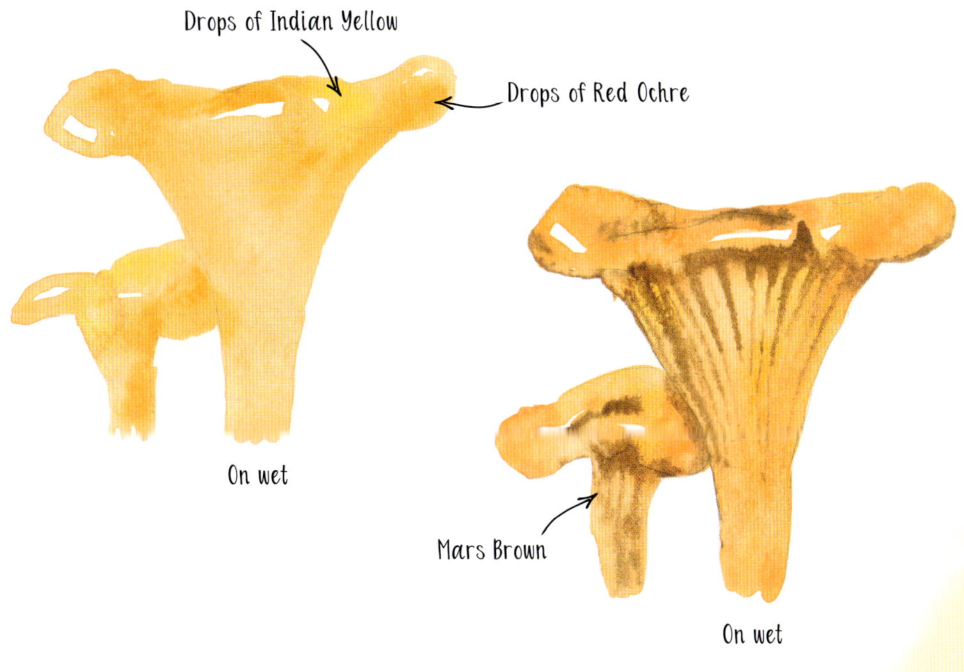

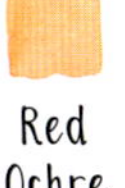

Red
Ochre

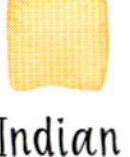

Indian
Yellow

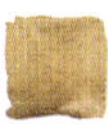

Mars
Brown

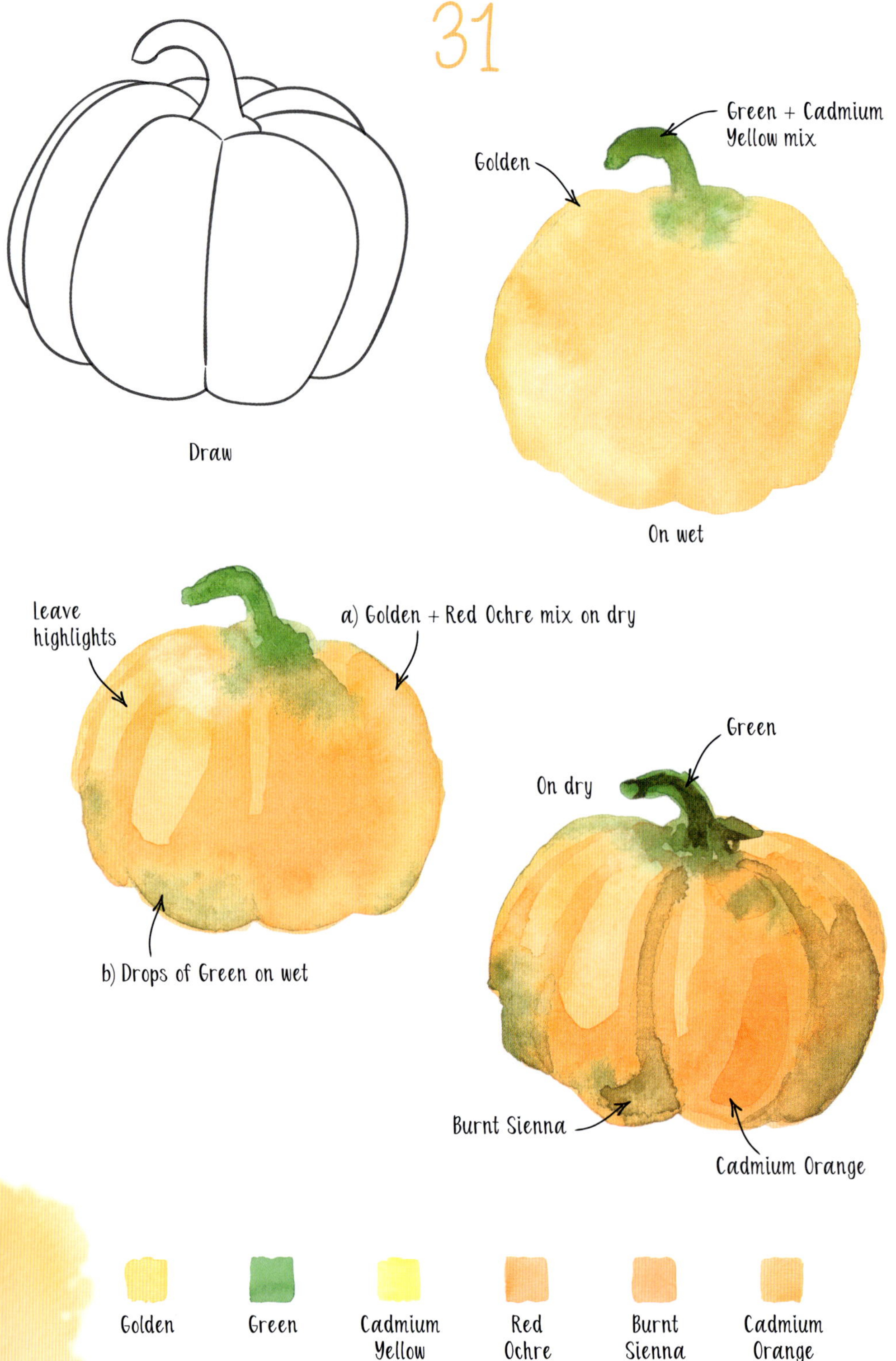
31
Draw
Golden
Green + Cadmium Yellow mix
On wet
leave highlights
a) Golden + Red Ochre mix on dry
b) Drops of Green on wet
On dry
Green
Burnt Sienna
Cadmium Orange
Golden
Green
Cadmium Yellow
Red Ochre
Burnt Sienna
Cadmium Orange

32

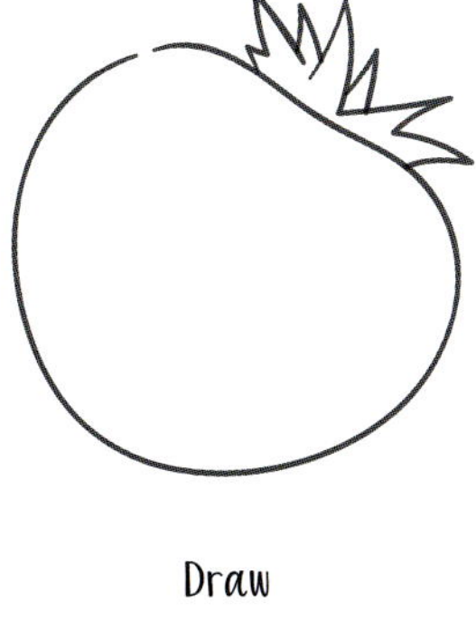

Draw

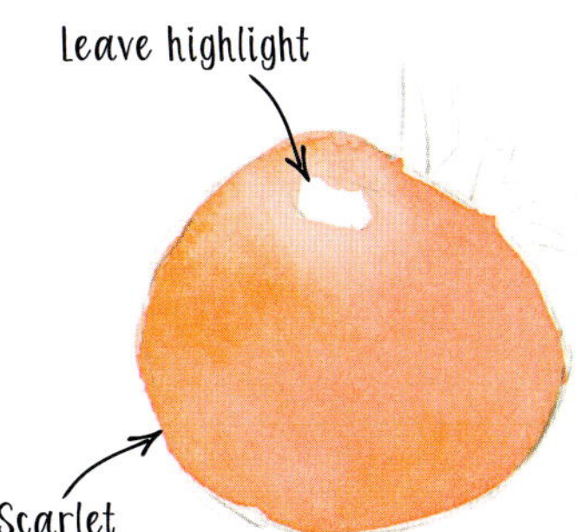

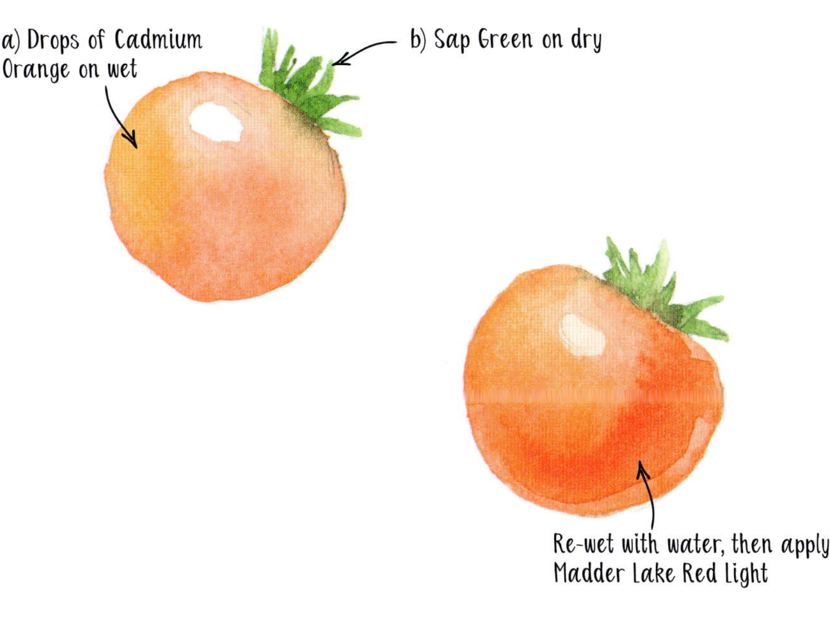

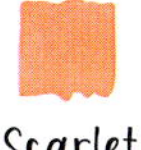

Scarlet

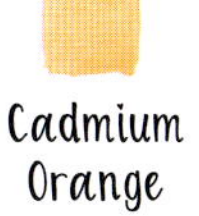

Cadmium
Orange

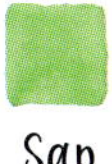

Sap
Green

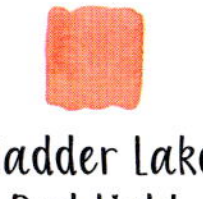

Madder Lake
Red Light

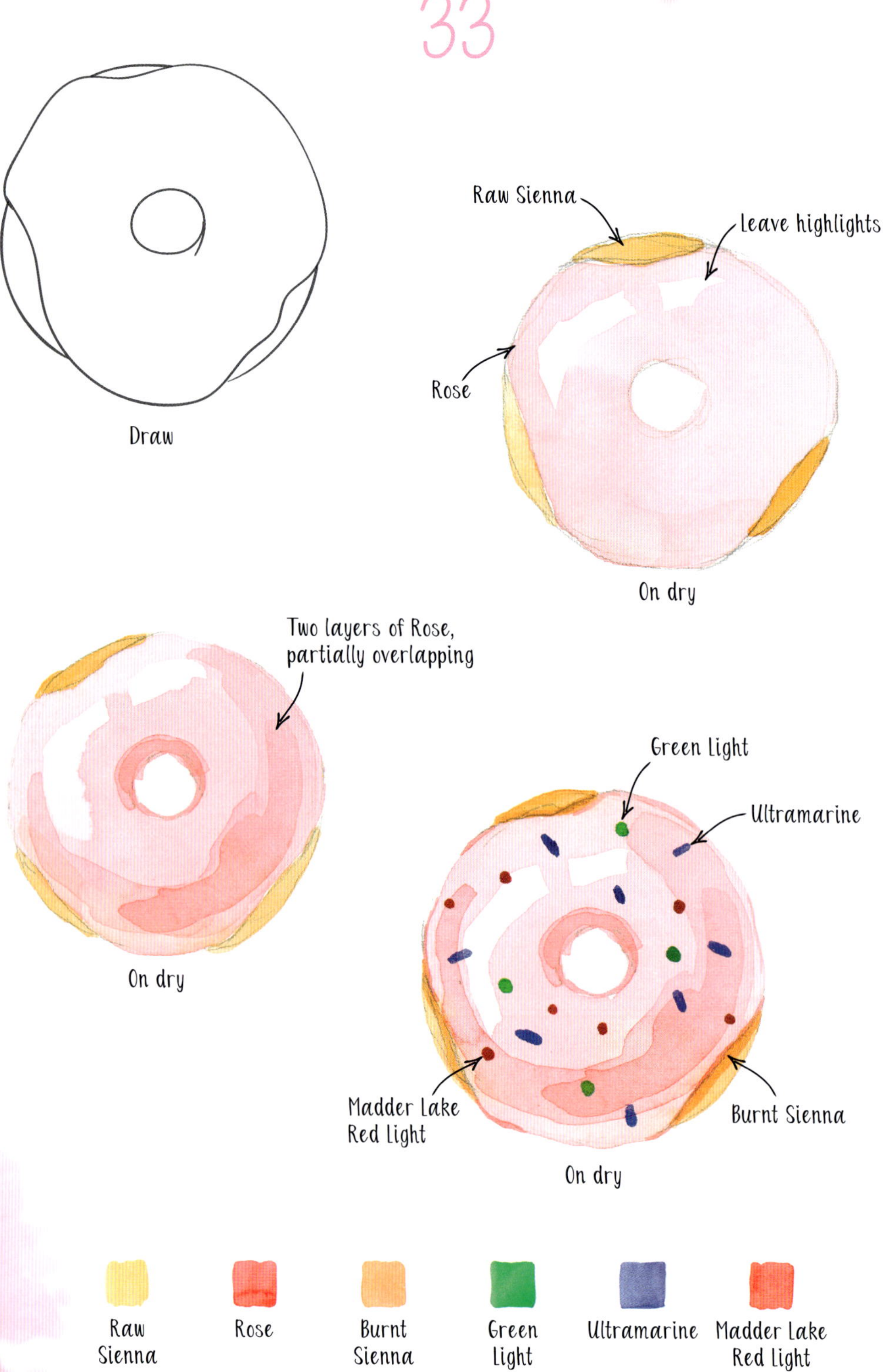
33
Draw
Raw Sienna
leave highlights
Rose
On dry
Two layers of Rose,
partially overlapping
On dry
Green light
Ultramarine
Madder Lake
Red light
Burnt Sienna
On dry
Raw
Sienna
Rose
Burnt
Sienna
Green
Light
Ultramarine
Madder Lake
Red light

34

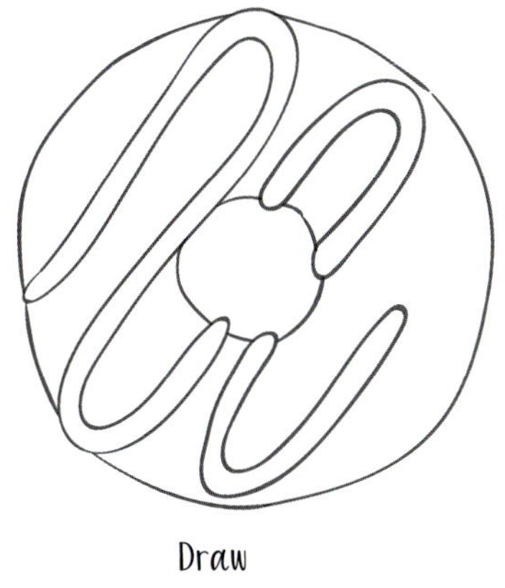

Draw

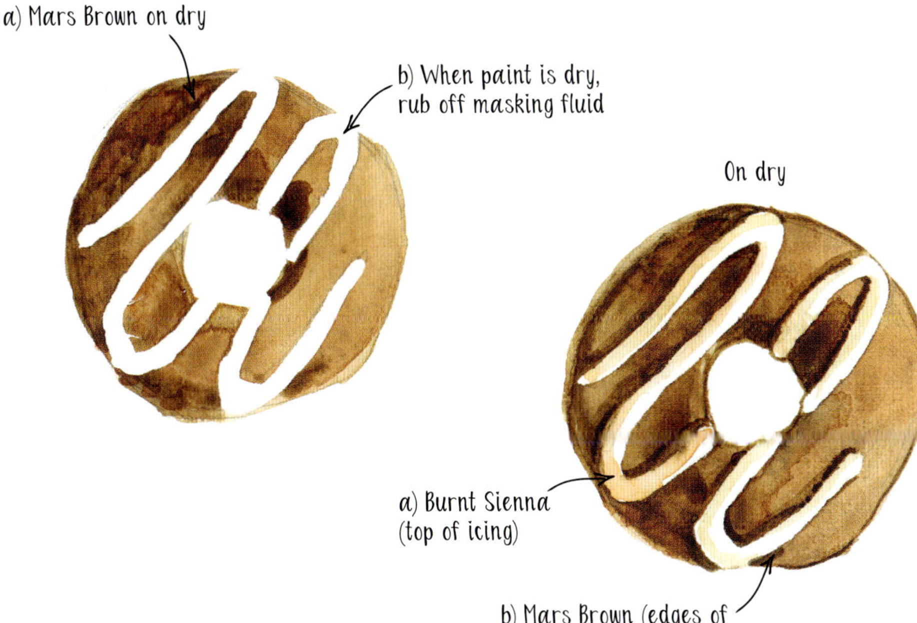

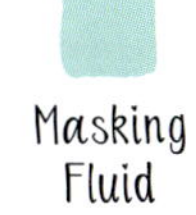

Masking
Fluid

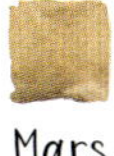

Mars
Brown

Burnt
Sienna

35

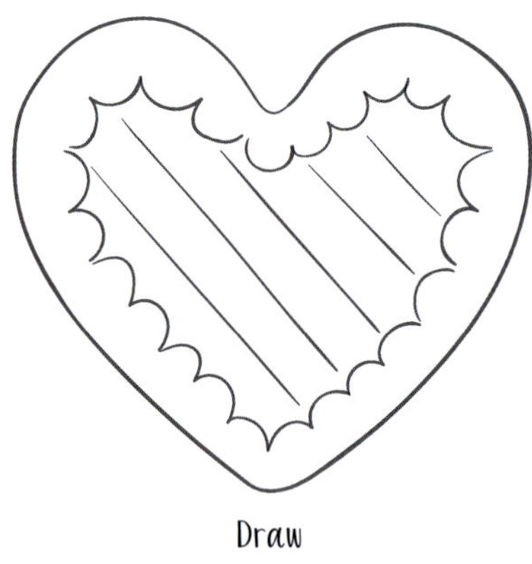

Draw

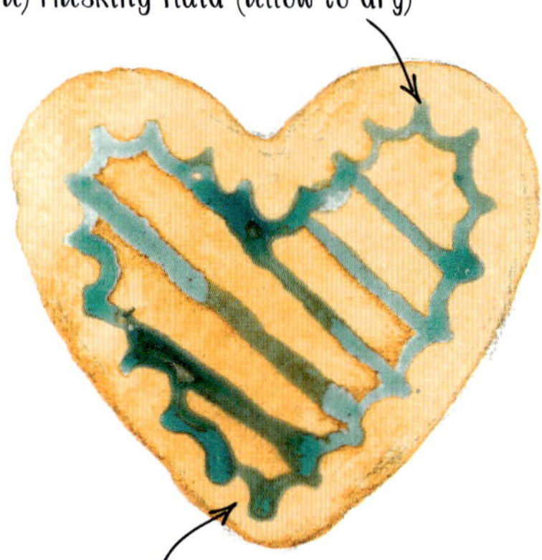

a) Masking fluid (allow to dry)

b) Red Ochre +
Raw Sienna mix

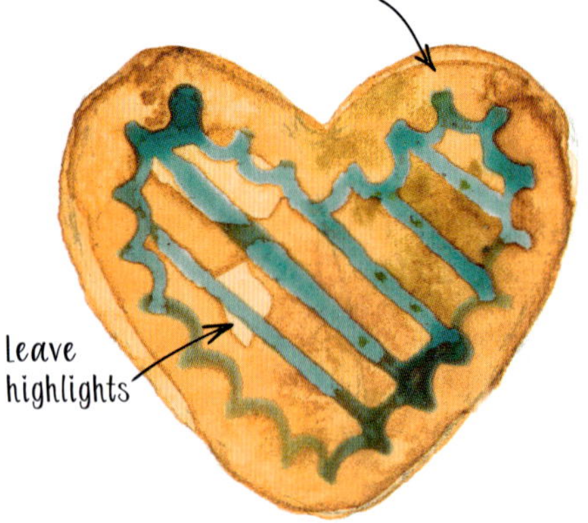

Second layer of Red Ochre + Raw Sienna mix

leave
highlights

On dry

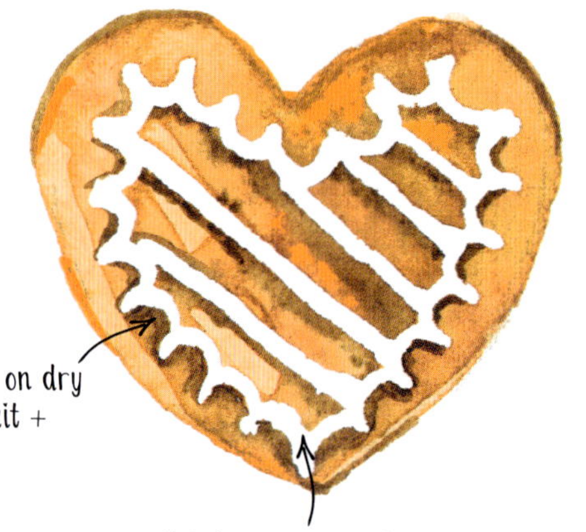

a) Mars Brown on dry
(edges of biscuit +
icing shadows)

b) When paint is dry,
rub off masking fluid

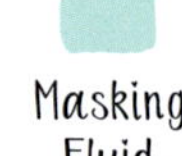

Masking
Fluid

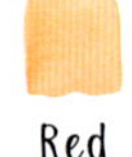

Red
Ochre

Raw
Sienna

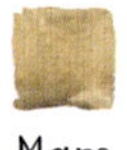

Mars
Brown

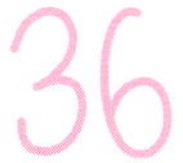

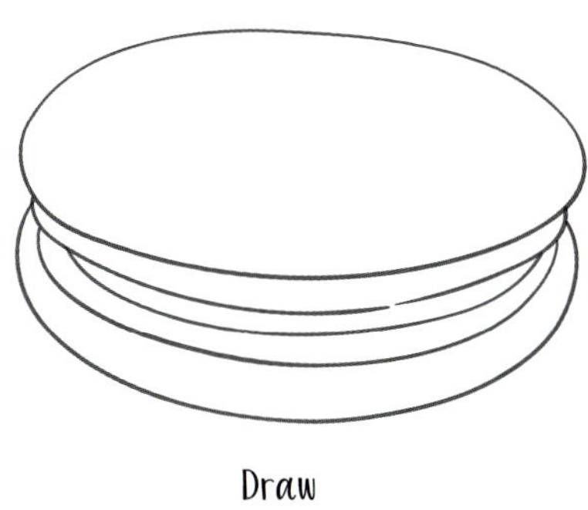

Draw

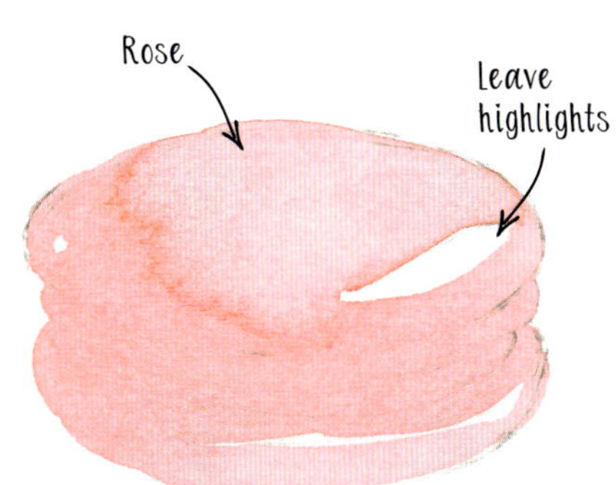

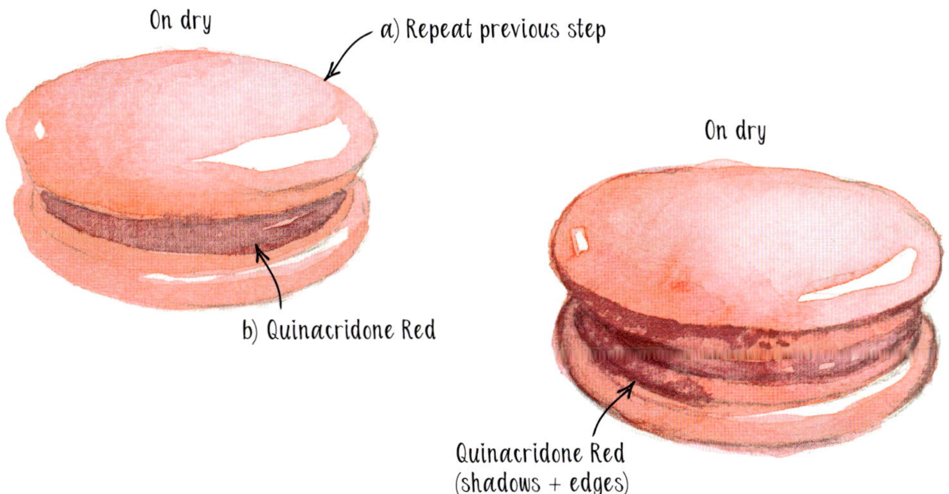

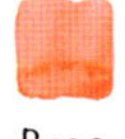

Rose

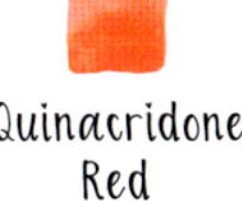

Quinacridone
Red

37

Draw
a) Mars Brown
Leave highlights
On dry
b) Quinacridone Lilac + Rose mix
a) Repeat previous step
b) Drops of Azure on wet
c) Drops Quinacridone Lilac on wet (edges)
a) Mars Brown on dry
b) Drops of Sepia on wet
c) Quinacridone Lilac + Rose mix on dry
Mars Brown
Quinacridone Lilac
Rose
Azure
Sepia

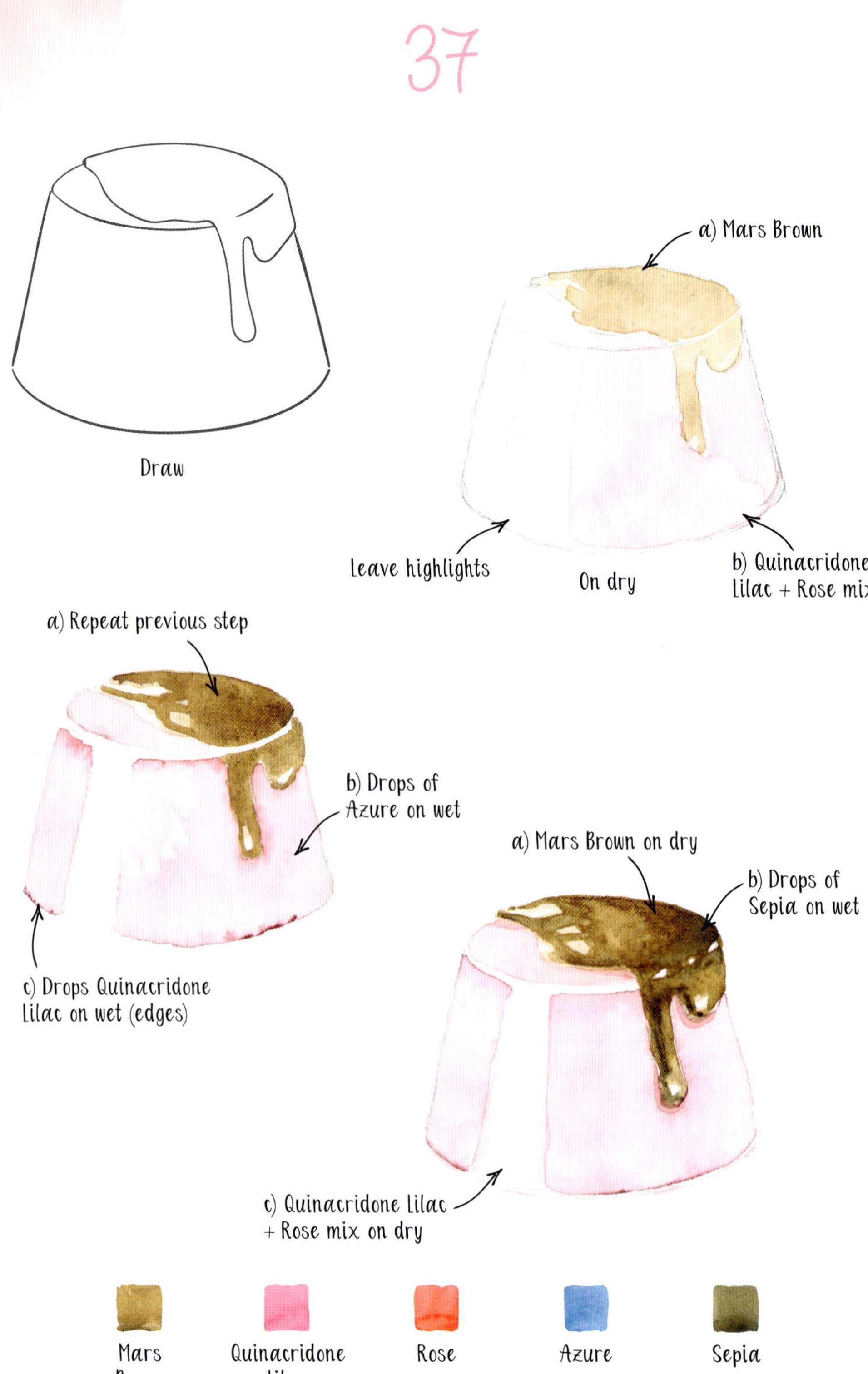

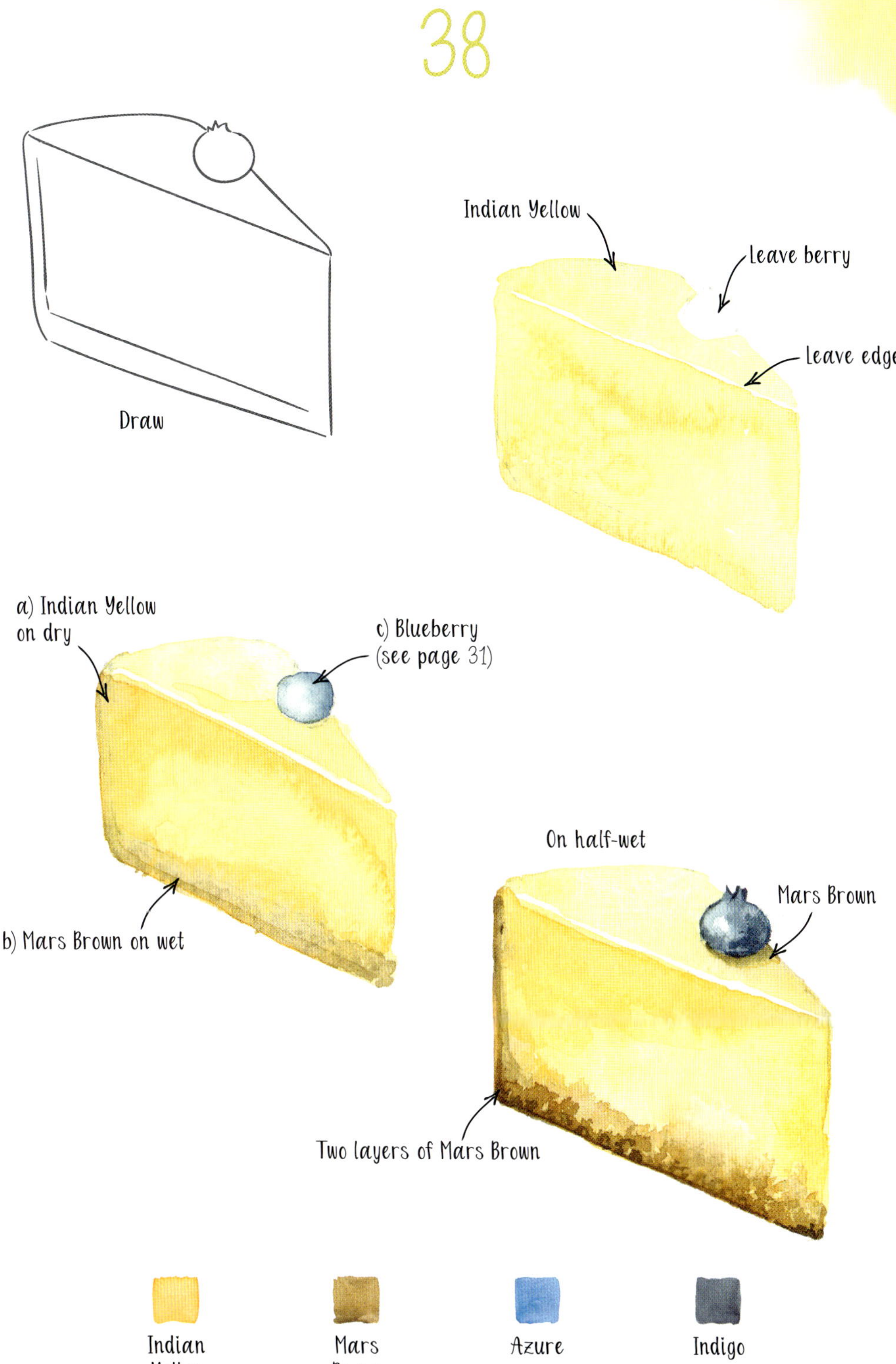
38
Draw
Indian Yellow
leave berry
leave edge
a) Indian Yellow
on dry
c) Blueberry
(see page 31)
b) Mars Brown on wet
On half-wet
Mars Brown
Two layers of Mars Brown
Indian
Yellow
Mars
Brown
Azure
Indigo

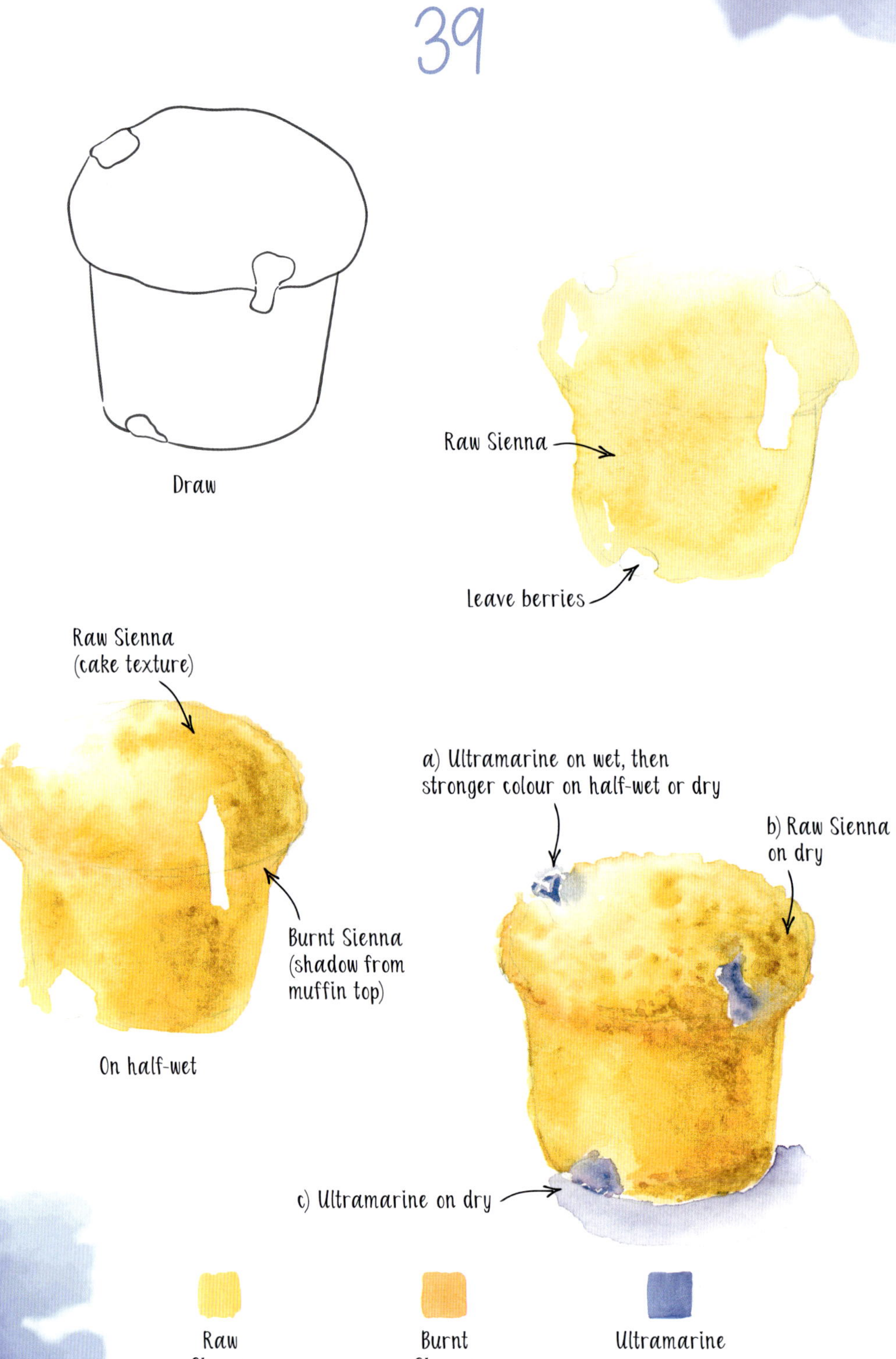
39

Draw

Raw Sienna

leave berries

Raw Sienna
(cake texture)

Burnt Sienna
(shadow from
muffin top)

On half-wet

a) Ultramarine on wet, then
stronger colour on half-wet or dry

b) Raw Sienna
on dry

c) Ultramarine on dry

Raw
Sienna

Burnt
Sienna

Ultramarine

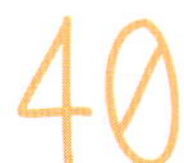

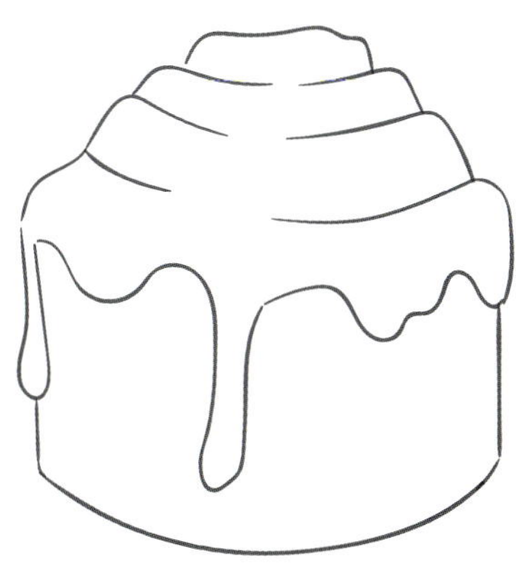

Draw

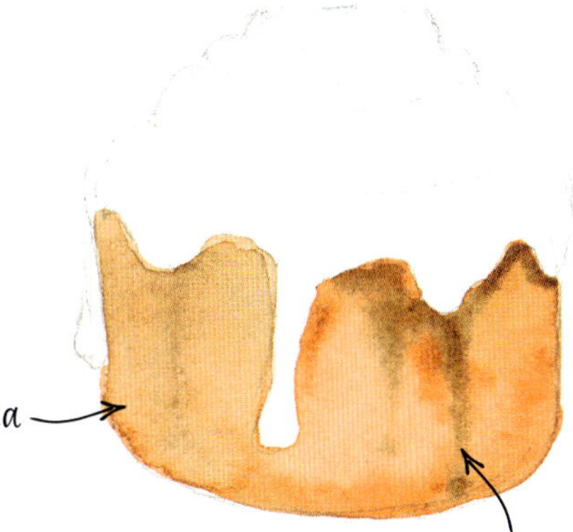

a) Burnt Sienna

b) Drops of Burnt
Umber on wet

a) Yellow Ochre on dry

b) Burnt Umber +
Burnt Sienna on wet

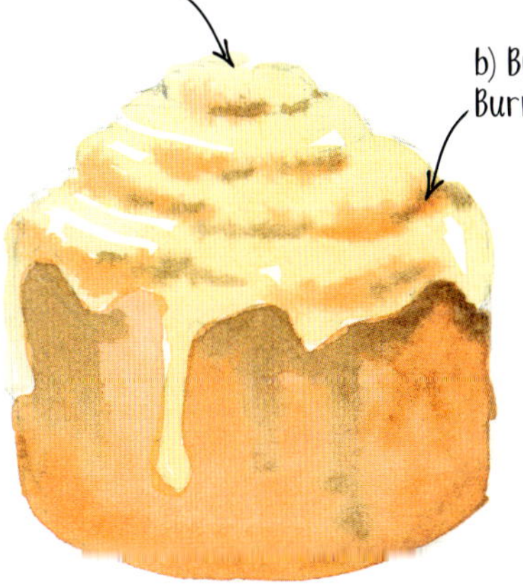

a) Burnt Umber
on half-wet

b) Burnt Umber on dry
(icing shadow + base
of bun)

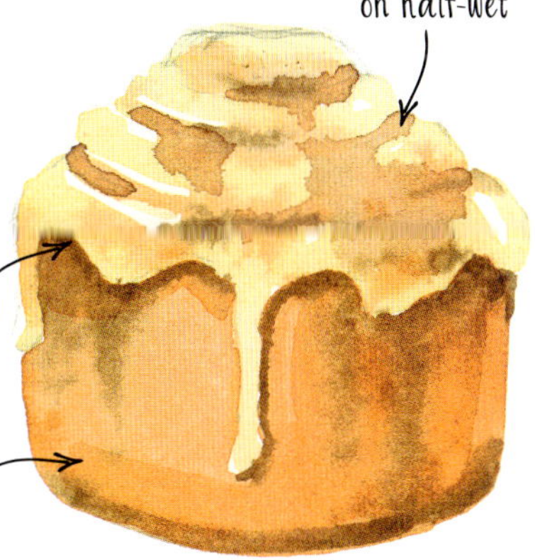

c) Burnt Sienna on dry

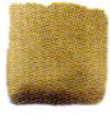

Burnt
Sienna

Burnt
Umber

Yellow
Ochre

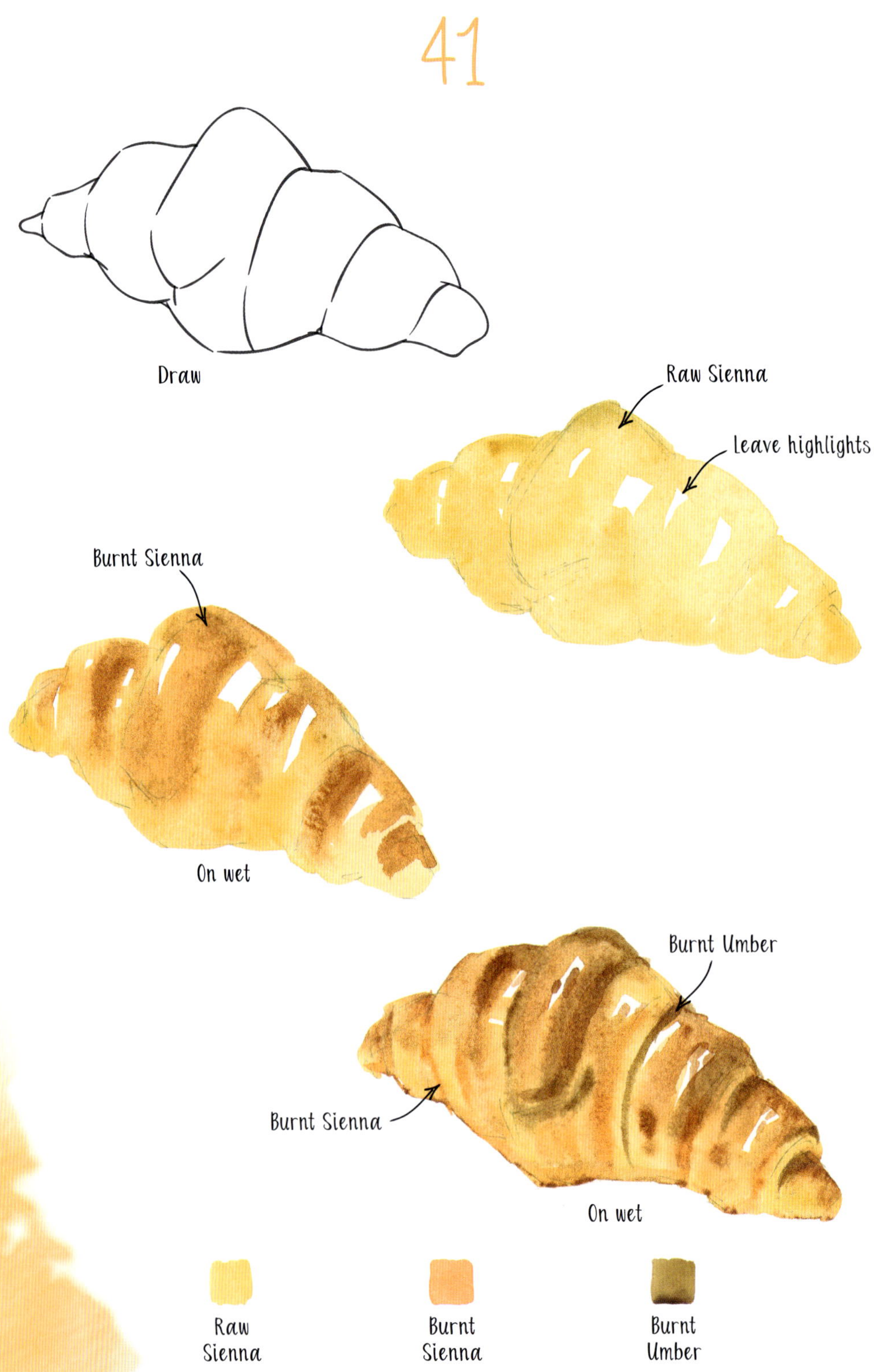
41
Draw
Raw Sienna
leave highlights
Burnt Sienna
On wet
Burnt Umber
Burnt Sienna
On wet
Raw
Sienna
Burnt
Sienna
Burnt
Umber

42

Draw

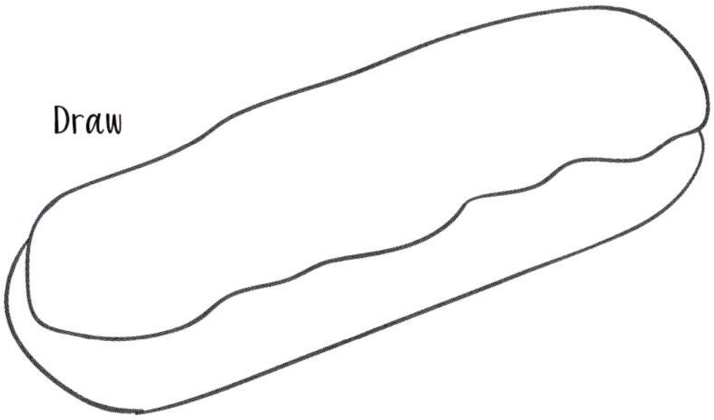

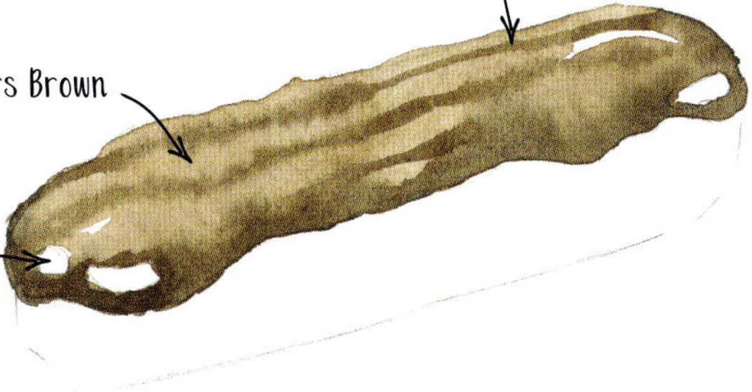

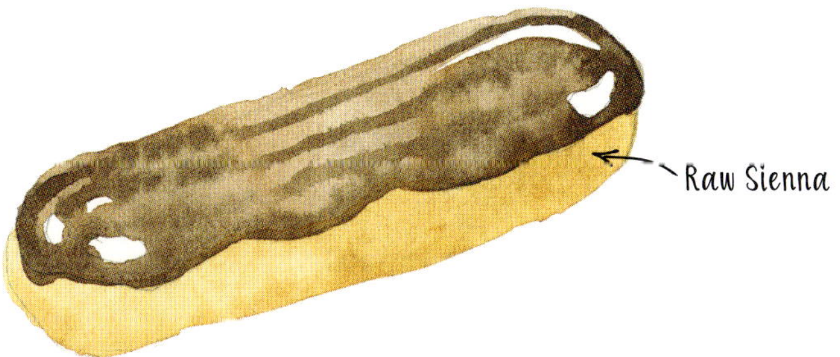

a) Mars Brown

b) Stripes of Mars
Brown on half-wet

leave highlights

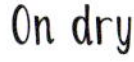

Raw Sienna

On dry

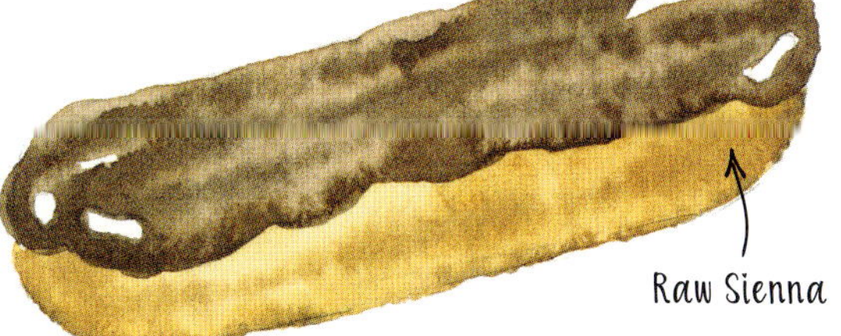

Raw Sienna

On half-wet

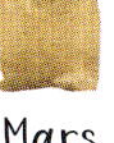

Mars
Brown

Raw
Sienna

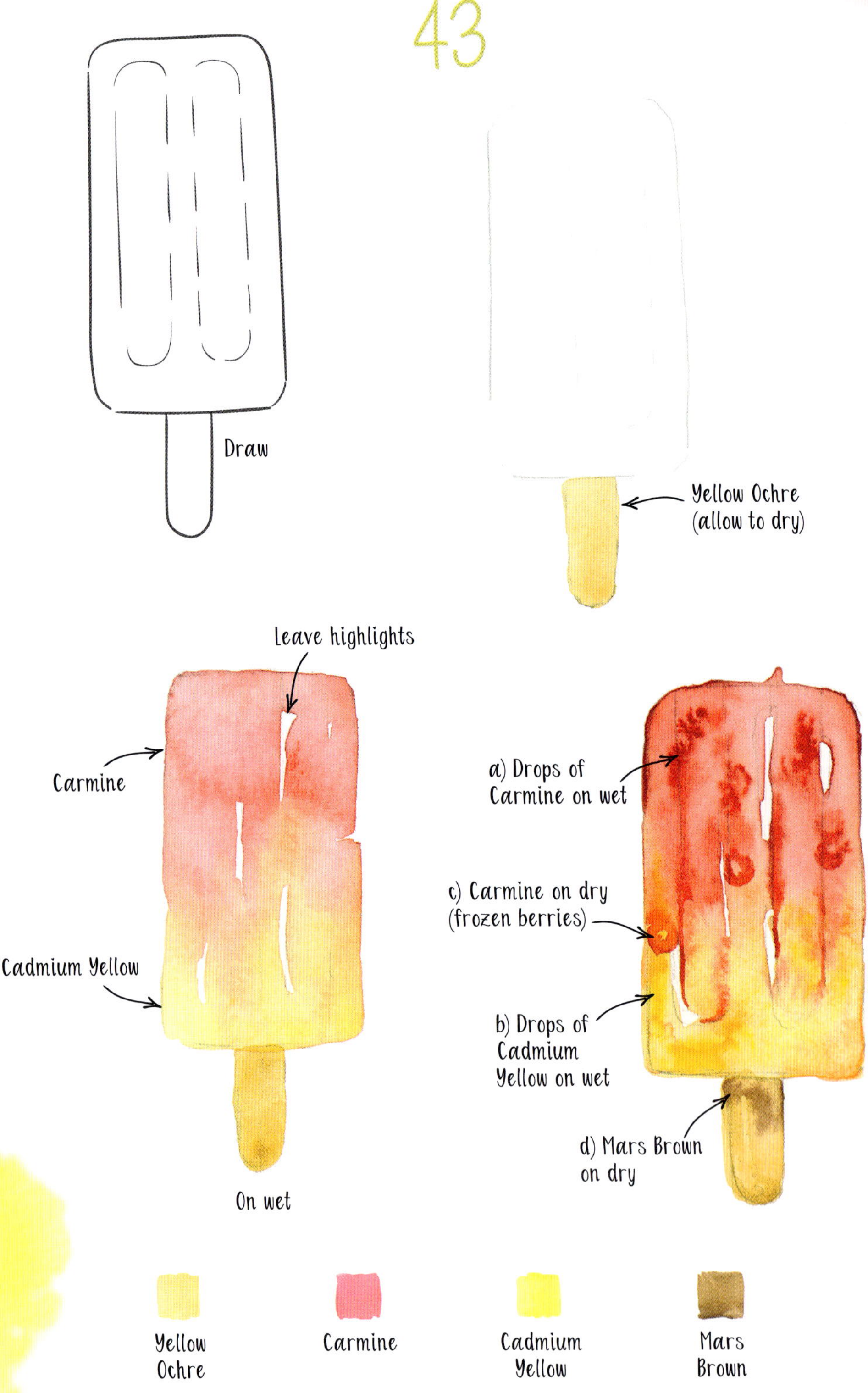

43

Draw

Yellow Ochre
(allow to dry)

Leave highlights

Carmine

Cadmium Yellow

On wet

a) Drops of
Carmine on wet

c) Carmine on dry
(frozen berries)

b) Drops of
Cadmium
Yellow on wet

d) Mars Brown
on dry

Yellow
Ochre

Carmine

Cadmium
Yellow

Mars
Brown

44

Rose
leave
highlights
Draw
a) Drops of
Rose on wet
b) Raw Sienna
on dry
c) Drops of Burnt
Sienna on wet
Mars Brown
Burnt Sienna
On dry
Rose
Raw
Sienna
Burnt
Sienna
Mars
Brown

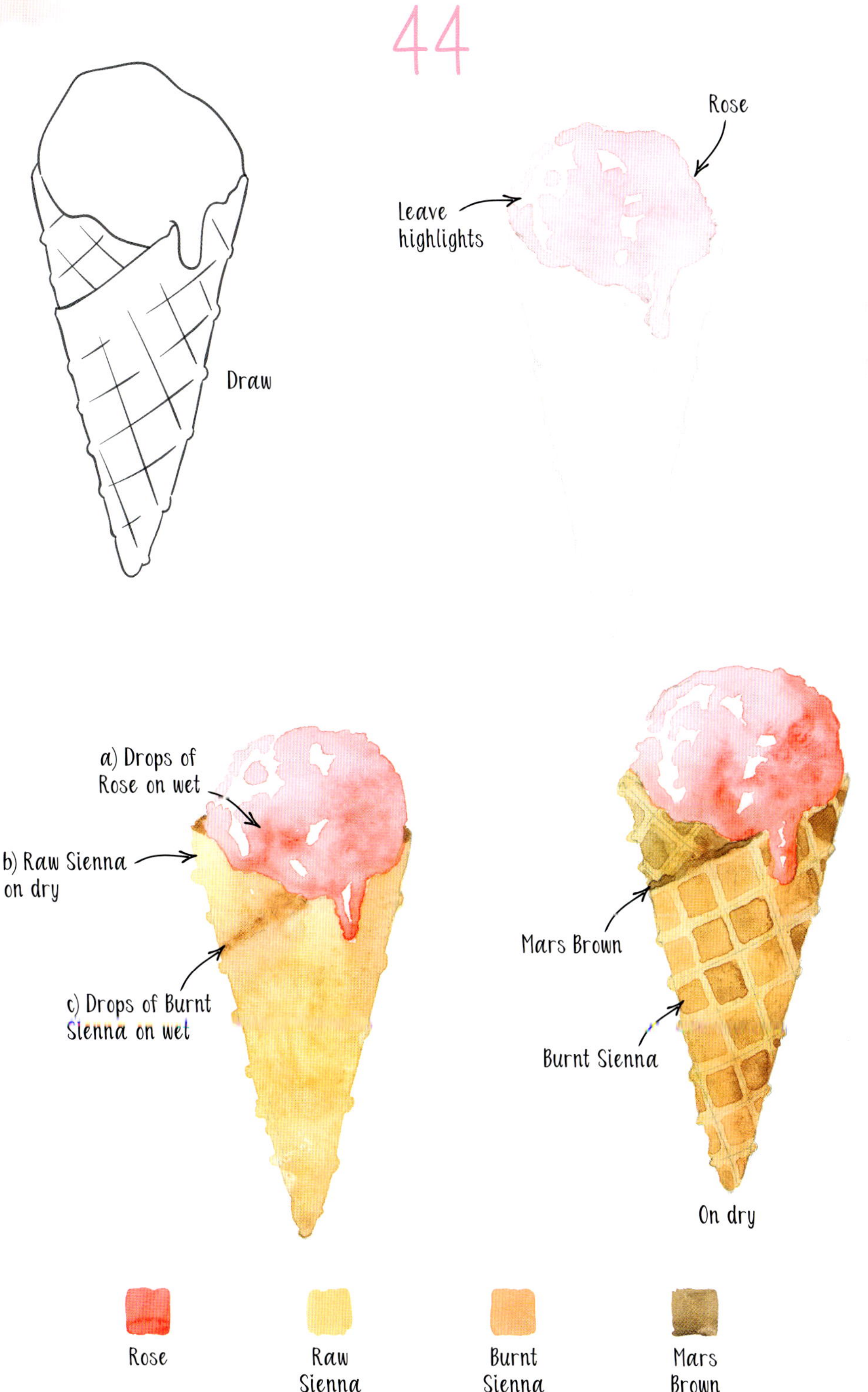

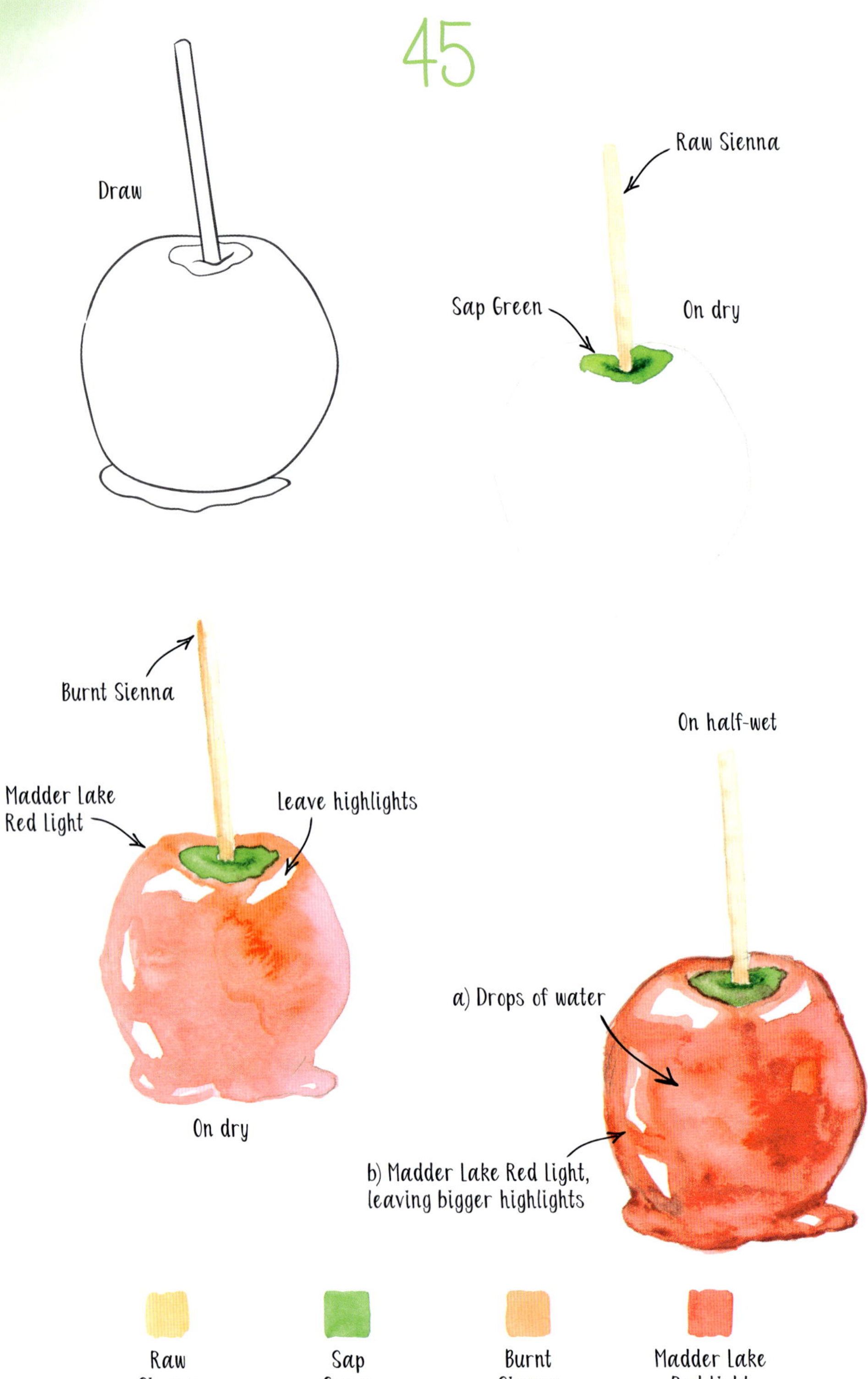
45
Draw
Raw Sienna
Sap Green
On dry
Burnt Sienna
Madder Lake
Red Light
leave highlights
On half-wet
a) Drops of water
On dry
b) Madder Lake Red light,
leaving bigger highlights
Raw
Sienna
Sap
Green
Burnt
Sienna
Madder Lake
Red light

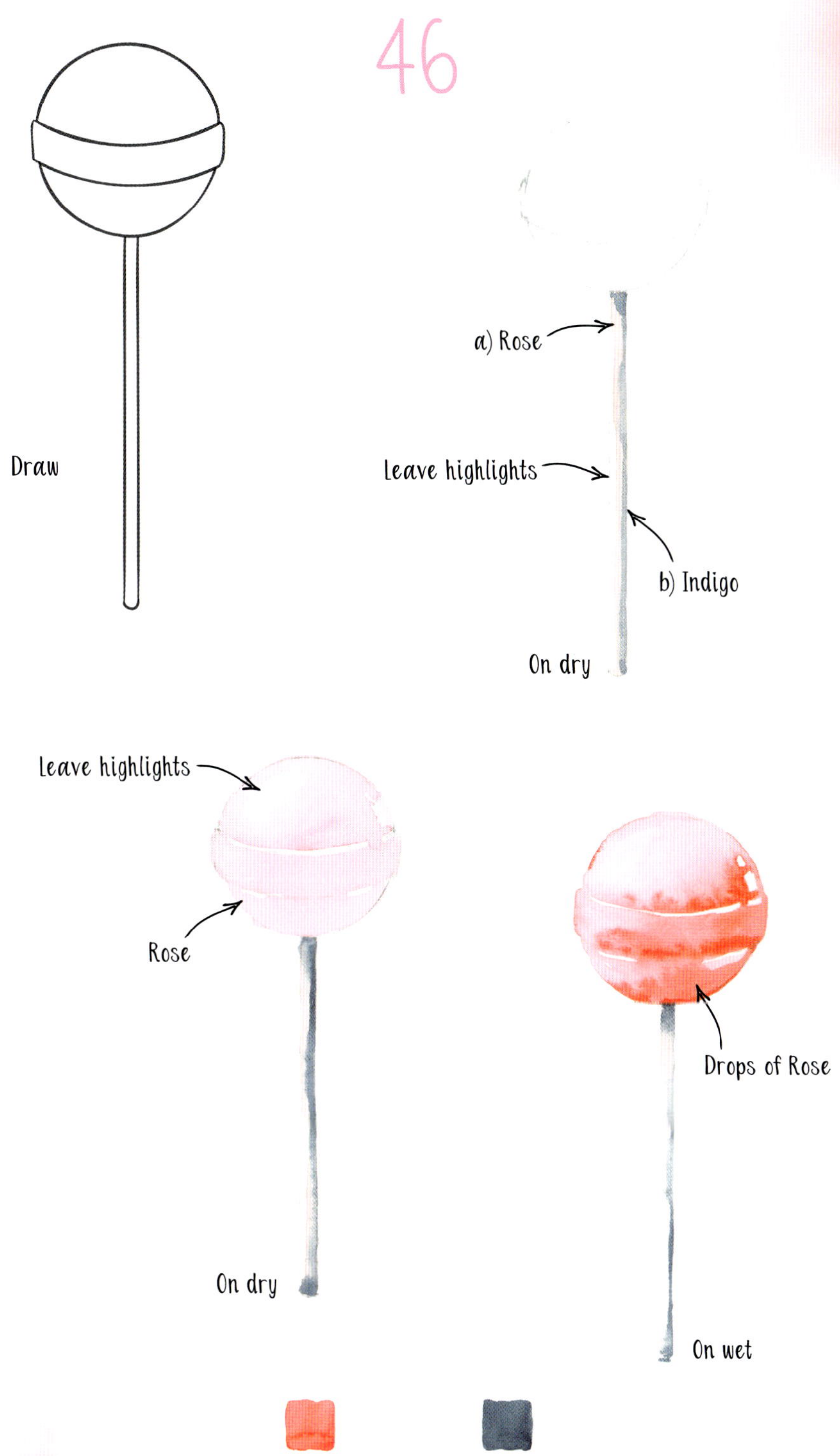
46
Draw
a) Rose
Leave highlights
b) Indigo
On dry
leave highlights
Rose
On dry
Drops of Rose
On wet
Rose
Indigo

47

Draw
English Red
Burnt Sienna
On half-wet
b) English Red on dry
a) Burnt Sienna on wet
c) Burnt Umber on dry
English Red
Burnt Sienna
Burnt Umber

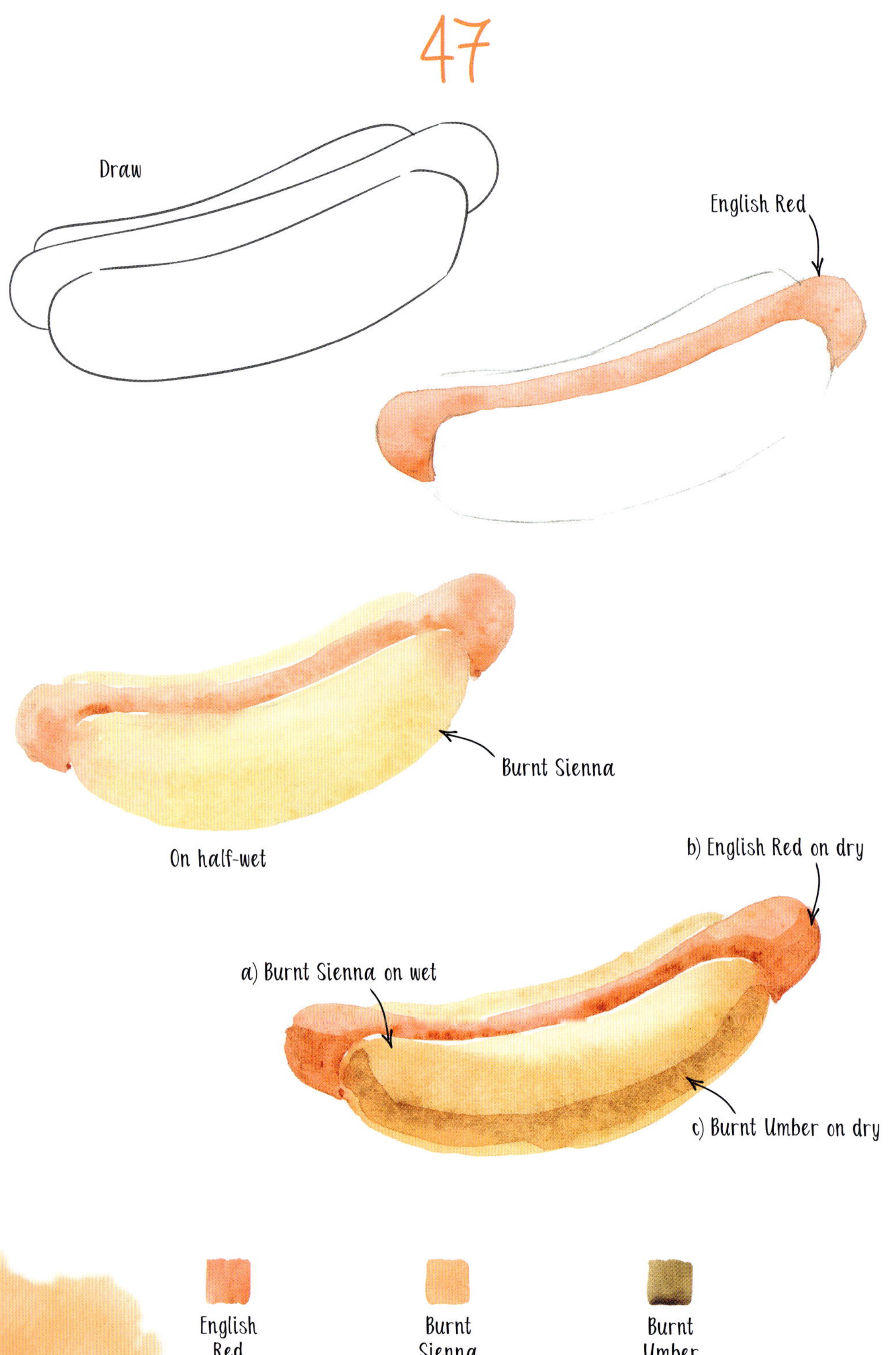

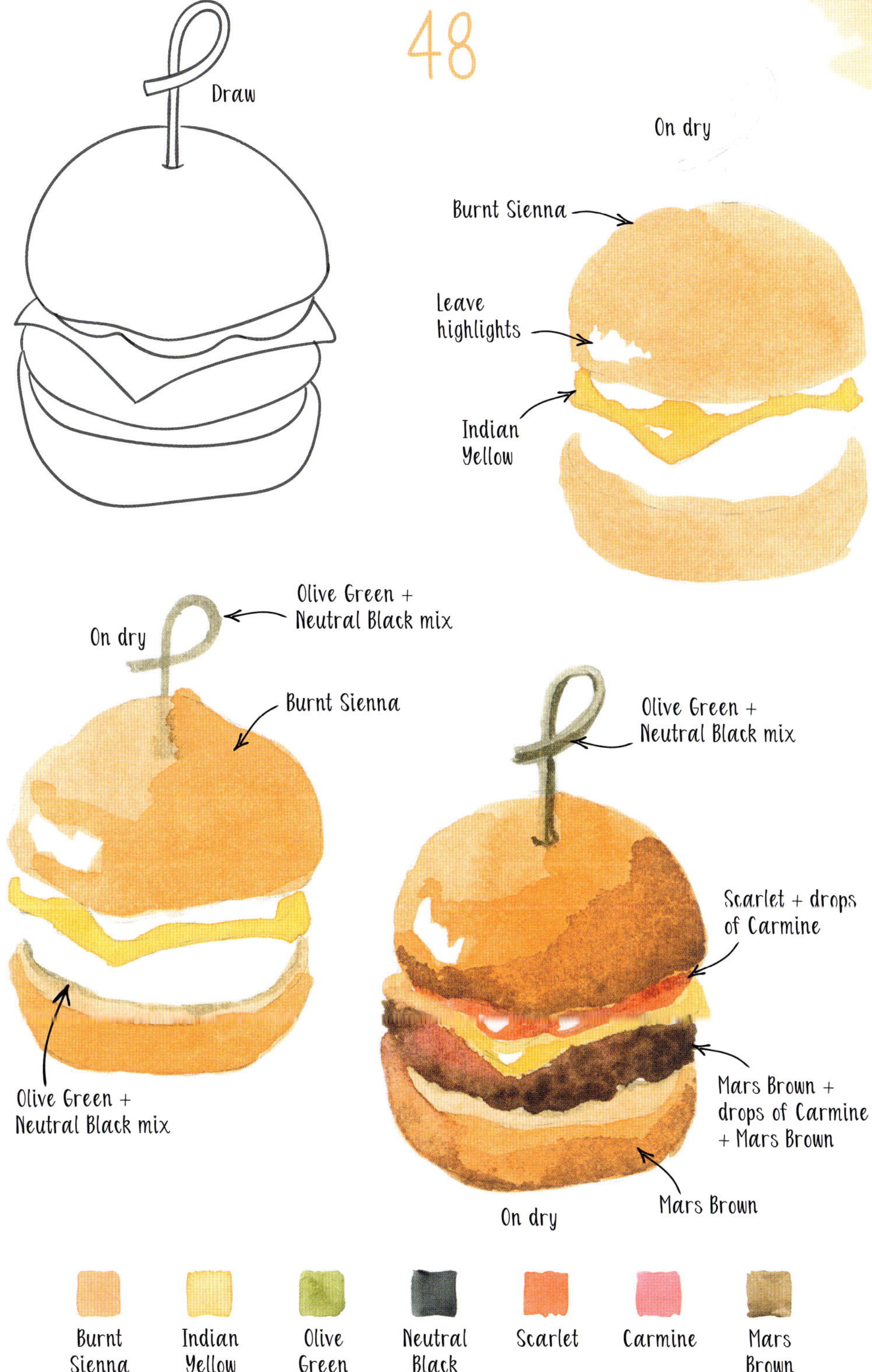
Draw
48
On dry
Burnt Sienna
Leave
highlights
Indian
Yellow
Olive Green +
Neutral Black mix
On dry
Burnt Sienna
Olive Green +
Neutral Black mix
Scarlet + drops
of Carmine
Mars Brown +
drops of Carmine
+ Mars Brown
Olive Green +
Neutral Black mix
Mars Brown
On dry
Burnt
Sienna
Indian
Yellow
Olive
Green
Neutral
Black
Scarlet
Carmine
Mars
Brown

49

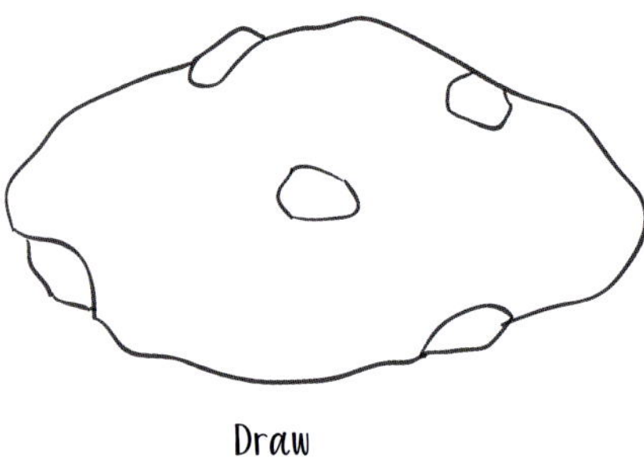

Draw

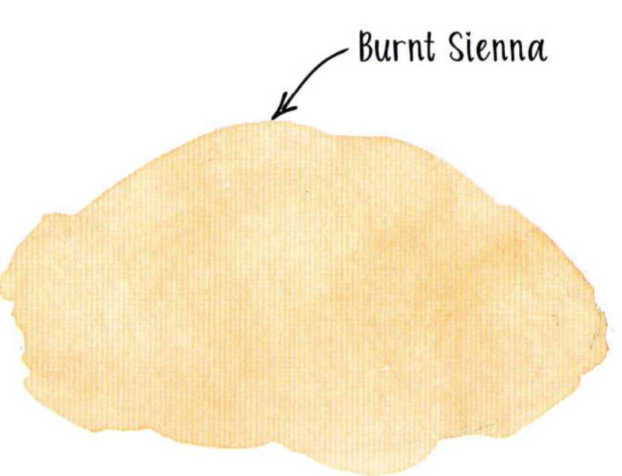

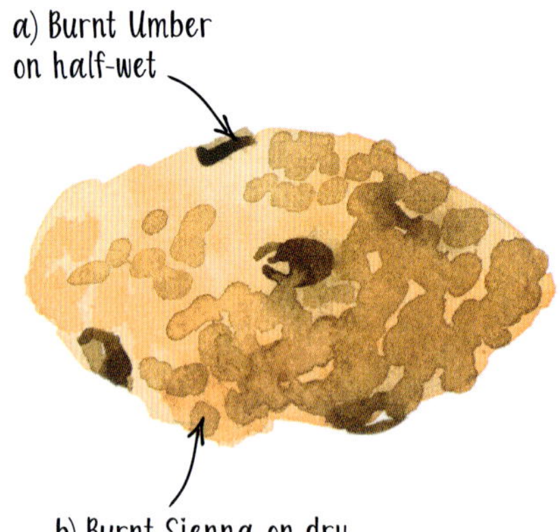

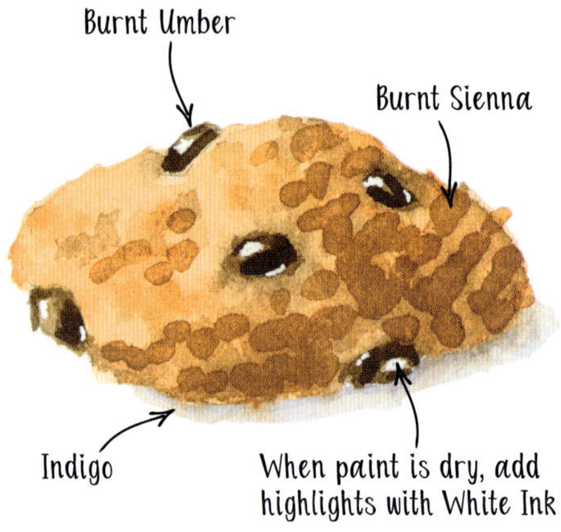

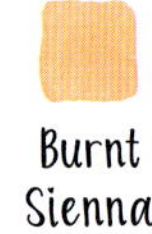

Burnt
Sienna

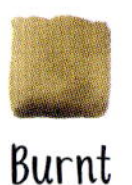

Burnt
Umber

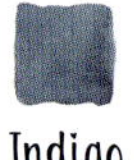

Indigo

White
Ink

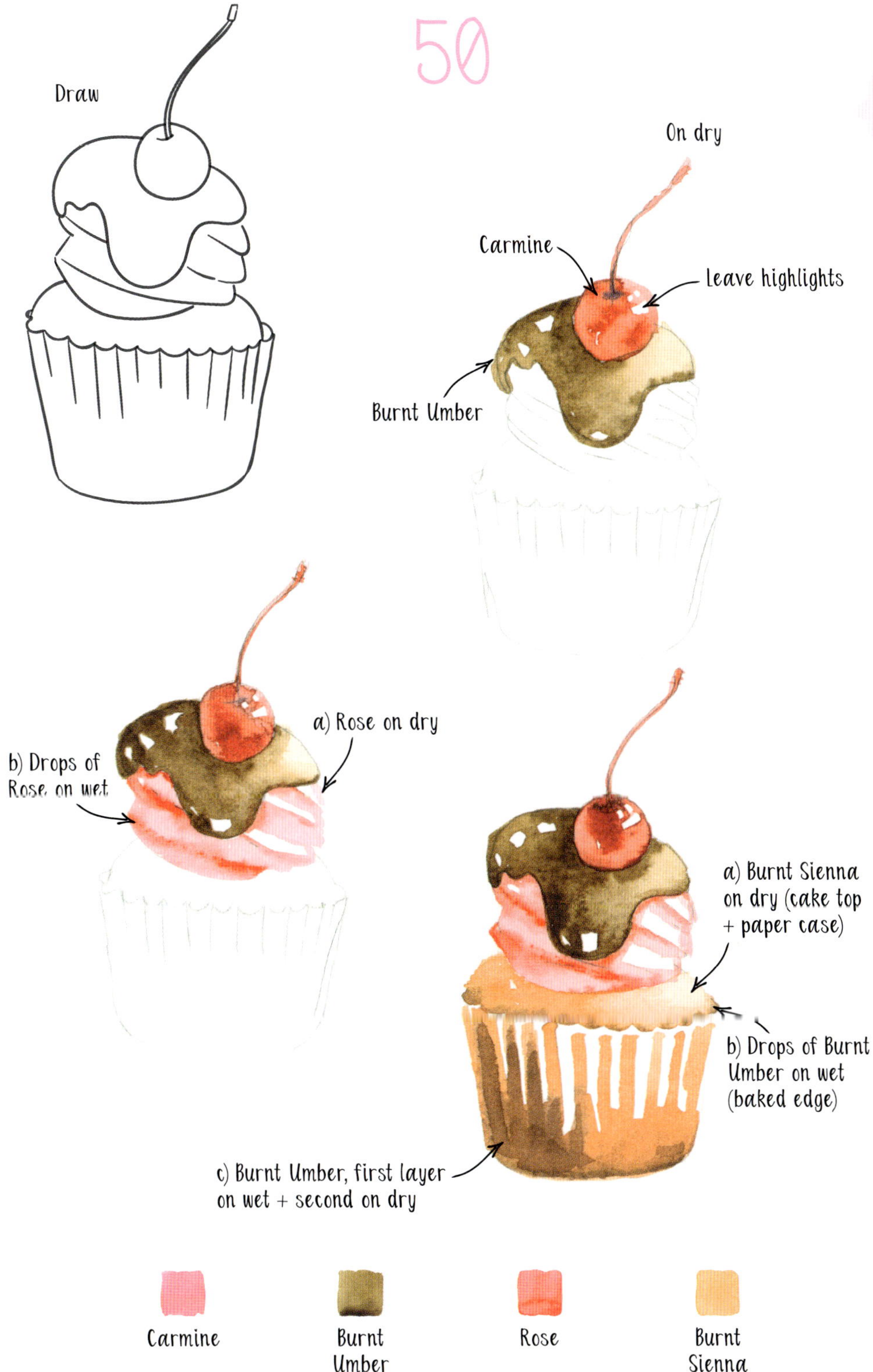

Draw

50

On dry

Carmine

leave highlights

Burnt Umber

a) Rose on dry

b) Drops of
Rose on wet

a) Burnt Sienna
on dry (cake top
+ paper case)

b) Drops of Burnt
Umber on wet
(baked edge)

c) Burnt Umber, first layer
on wet + second on dry

Carmine

Burnt
Umber

Rose

Burnt
Sienna

51

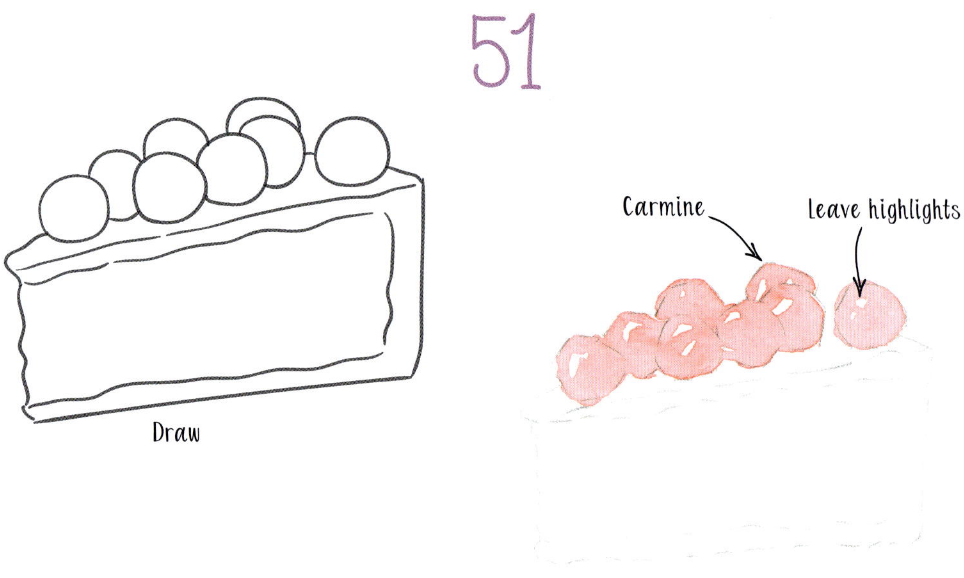

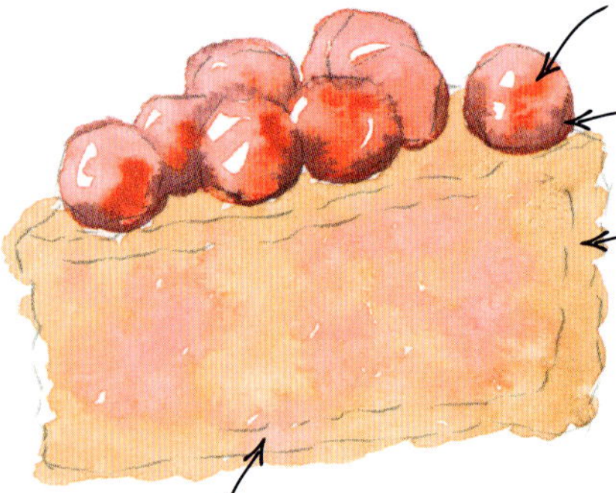

a) Drops of Carmine on wet

b) Drops of Claret on wet

c) Burnt Sienna on dry

d) Drops of Rose on wet

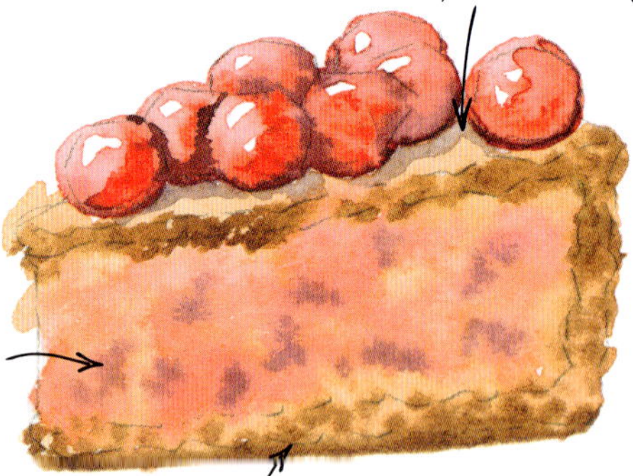

c) Claret on dry

a) Drops of Claret on wet

b) Burnt Sienna on half-wet

Carmine

Claret

Burnt Sienna

Rose

52

Draw
a) Indian Yellow
b) Drops of Burnt Sienna on wet
Leave highlights
Burnt Sienna
Indian Yellow
On dry
Rose
Burnt Umber
On dry
Indian Yellow
Burnt Sienna
Rose
Burnt Umber

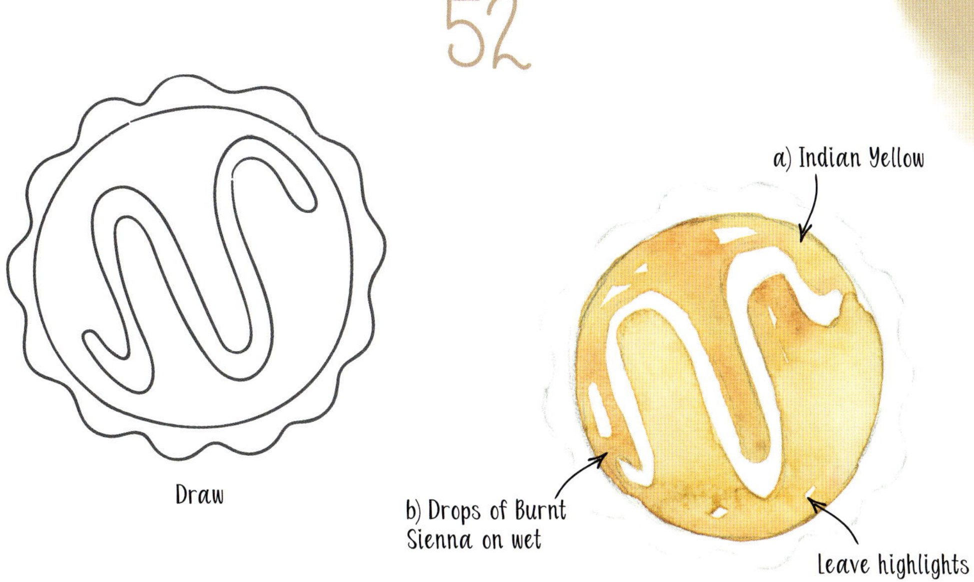

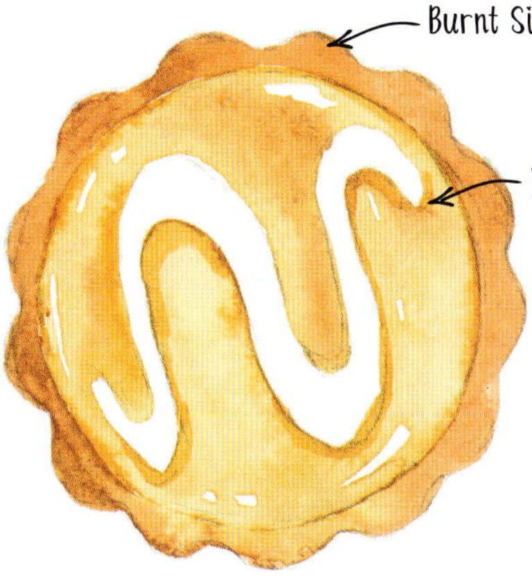

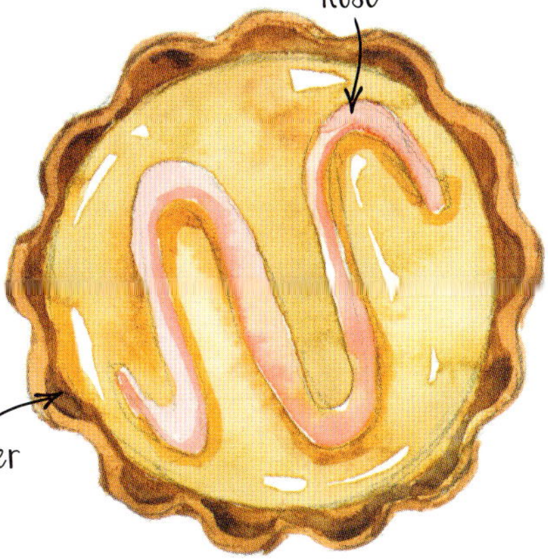

53

Draw
a) Yellow Ochre
b) Burnt Sienna
On dry

On wet
Carmine
Olive Green
Cadmium Yellow
Mars Brown
(icing
shadow +
cake base)
Burnt Sienna + Mars Brown
(cake texture + icing shadow)
On dry

Yellow
Ochre
Burnt
Sienna
Mars
Brown
Carmine
Olive
Green
Cadmium
Yellow

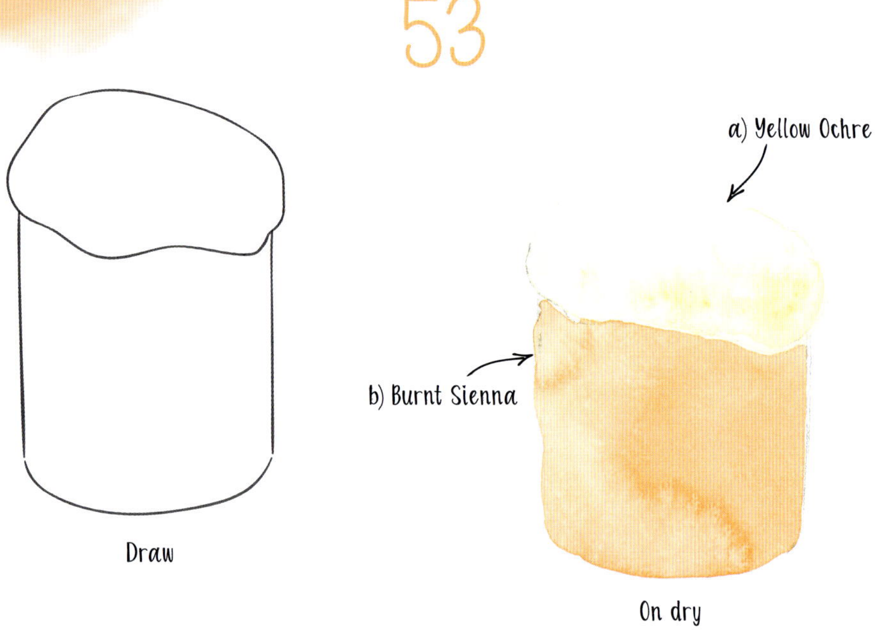

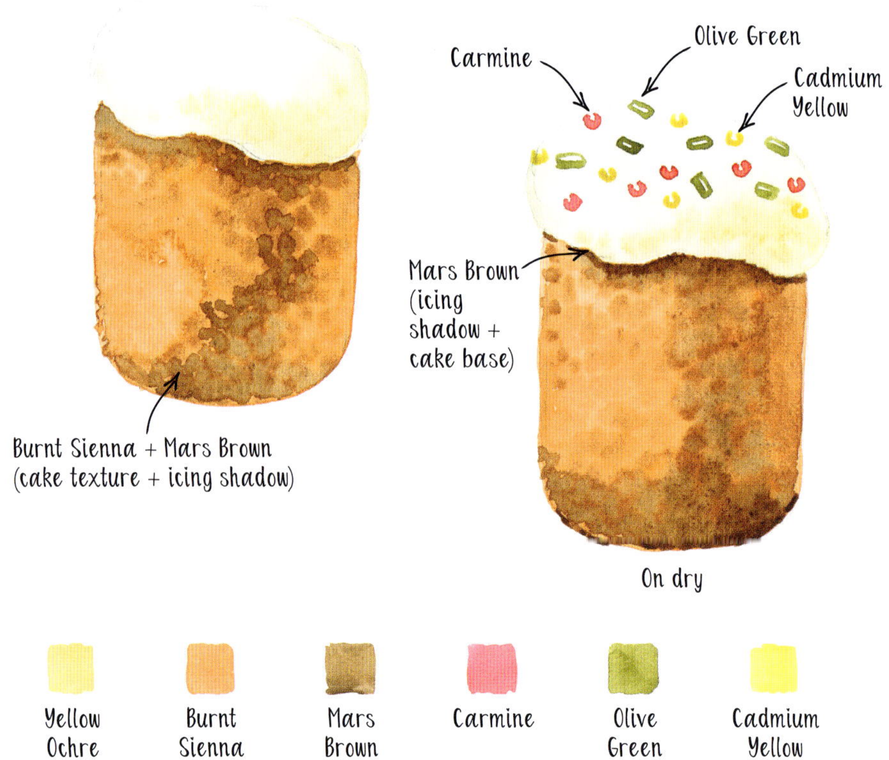

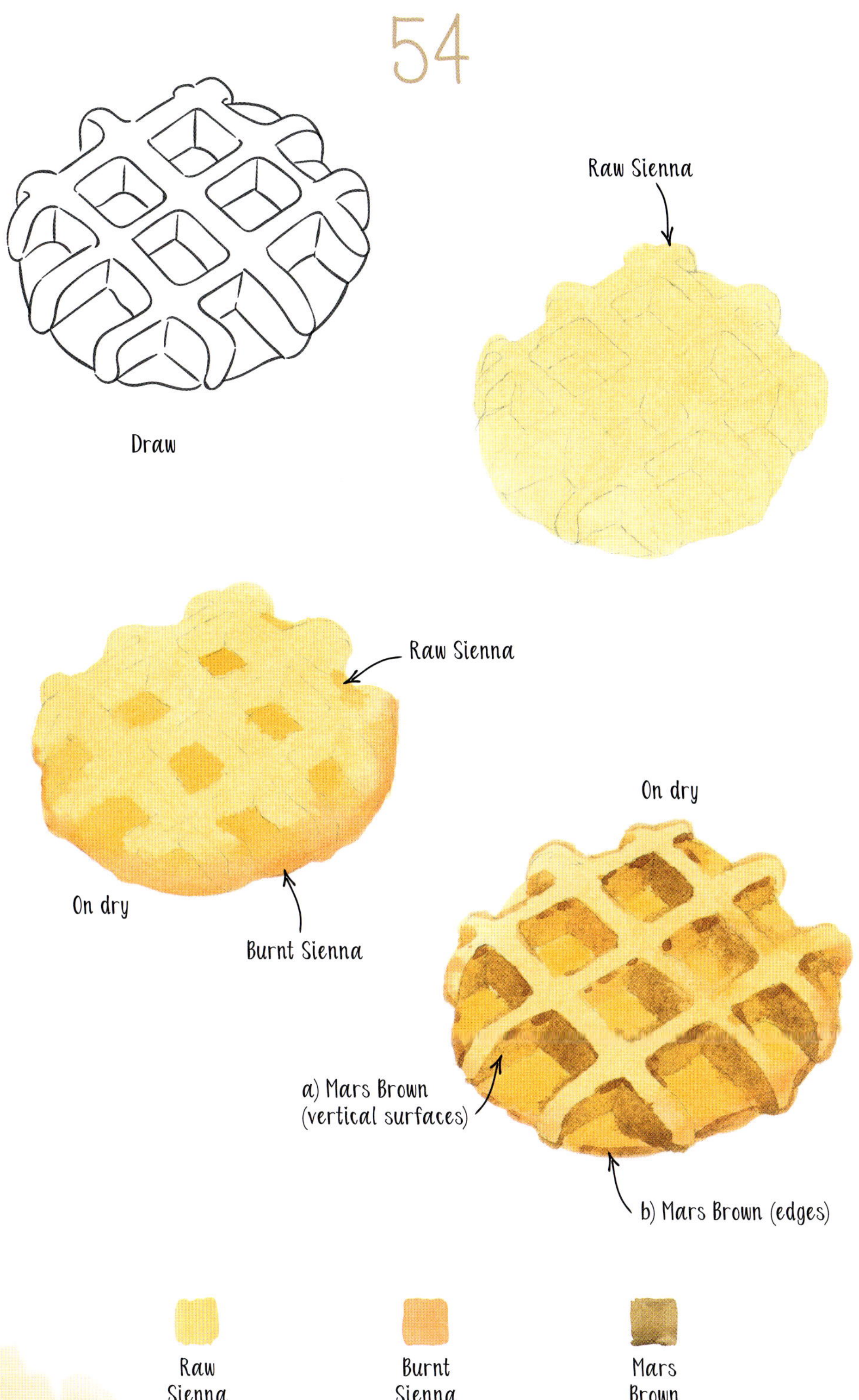

54
Draw
Raw Sienna
Raw Sienna
On dry
On dry
Burnt Sienna
a) Mars Brown
(vertical surfaces)
b) Mars Brown (edges)
Raw
Sienna
Burnt
Sienna
Mars
Brown

55

Draw

Yellow Ochre
Indigo
leave highlights

On dry

a) Cadmium Yellow on dry
c) Scarlet on wet
b) Carmine graduating upwards to Cadmium Yellow on wet
Leave highlights

c) Scarlet on dry (stalk + cherry)
d) Violet on dry
a) Starting on dry, repeat part (b) of previous step but work from top downwards
e) Indigo on dry
b) Drops of Carmine on wet, then draw bottom edge of glass

Indigo
Yellow Ochre
Cadmium Yellow
Carmine
Scarlet
Violet

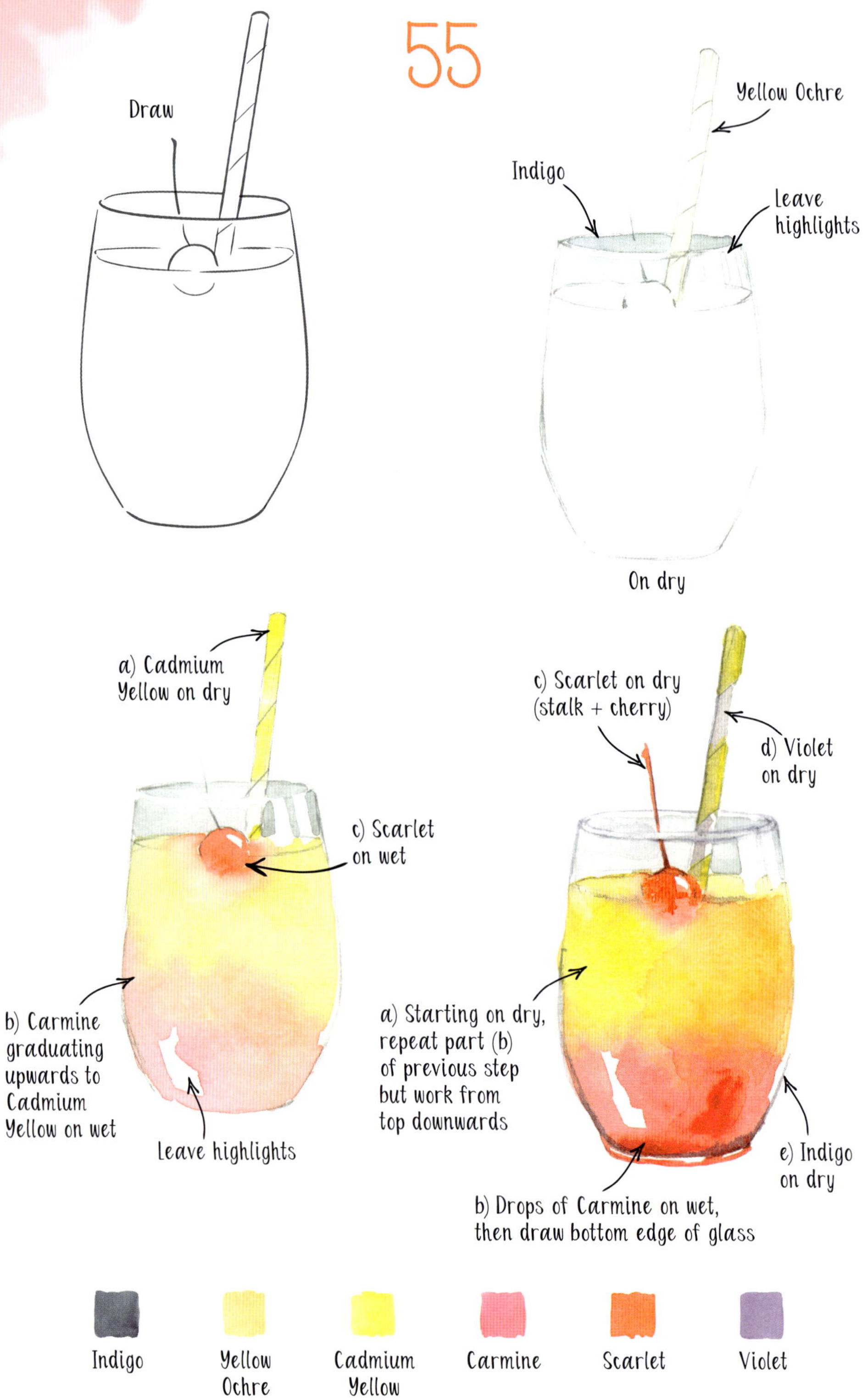

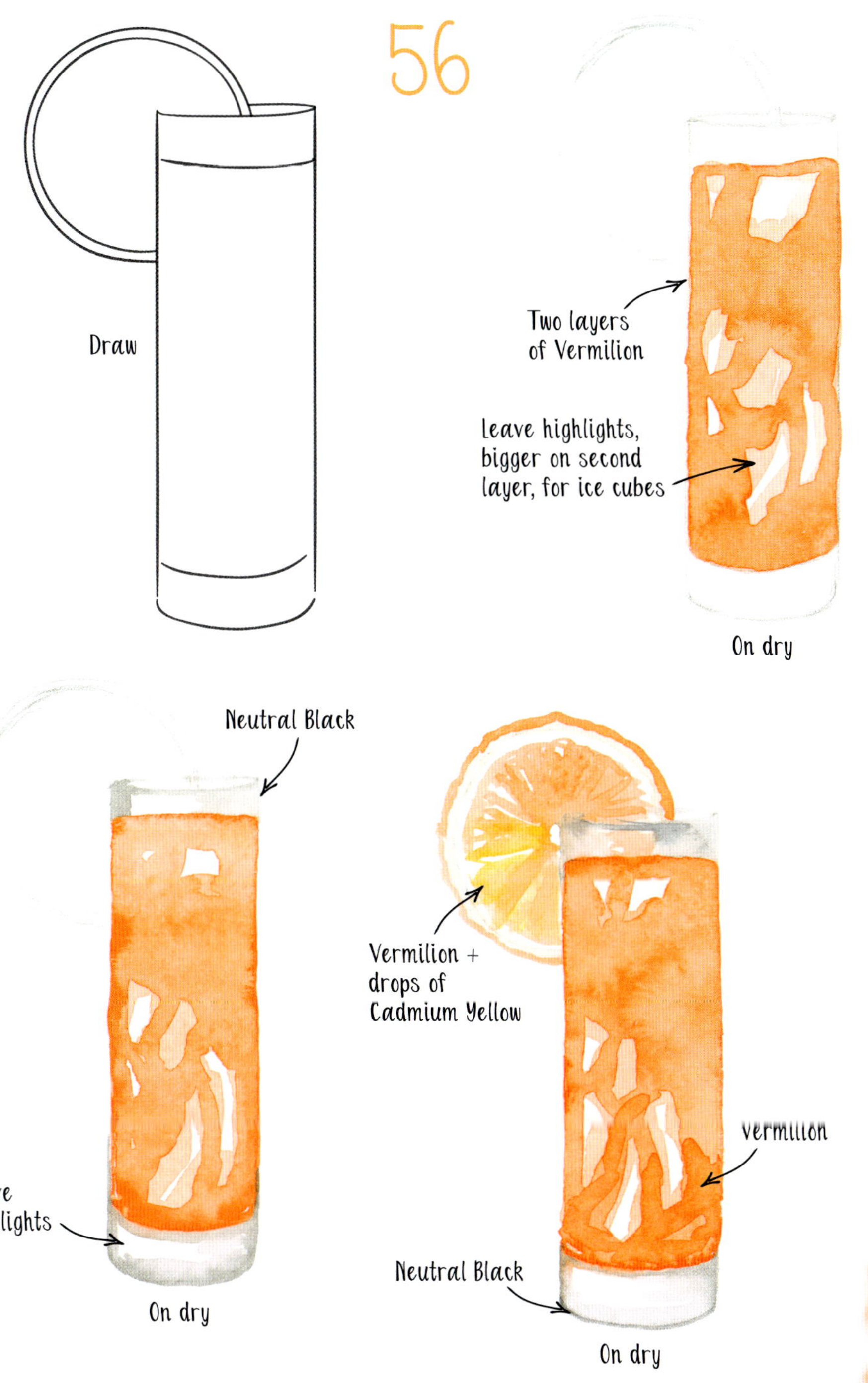
Draw
56
Two layers
of Vermilion
Leave highlights,
bigger on second
layer, for ice cubes
On dry
Neutral Black
Vermilion +
drops of
Cadmium Yellow
Vermilion
Leave
highlights
Neutral Black
On dry
On dry
Vermilion
Neutral
Black
Cadmium
Yellow

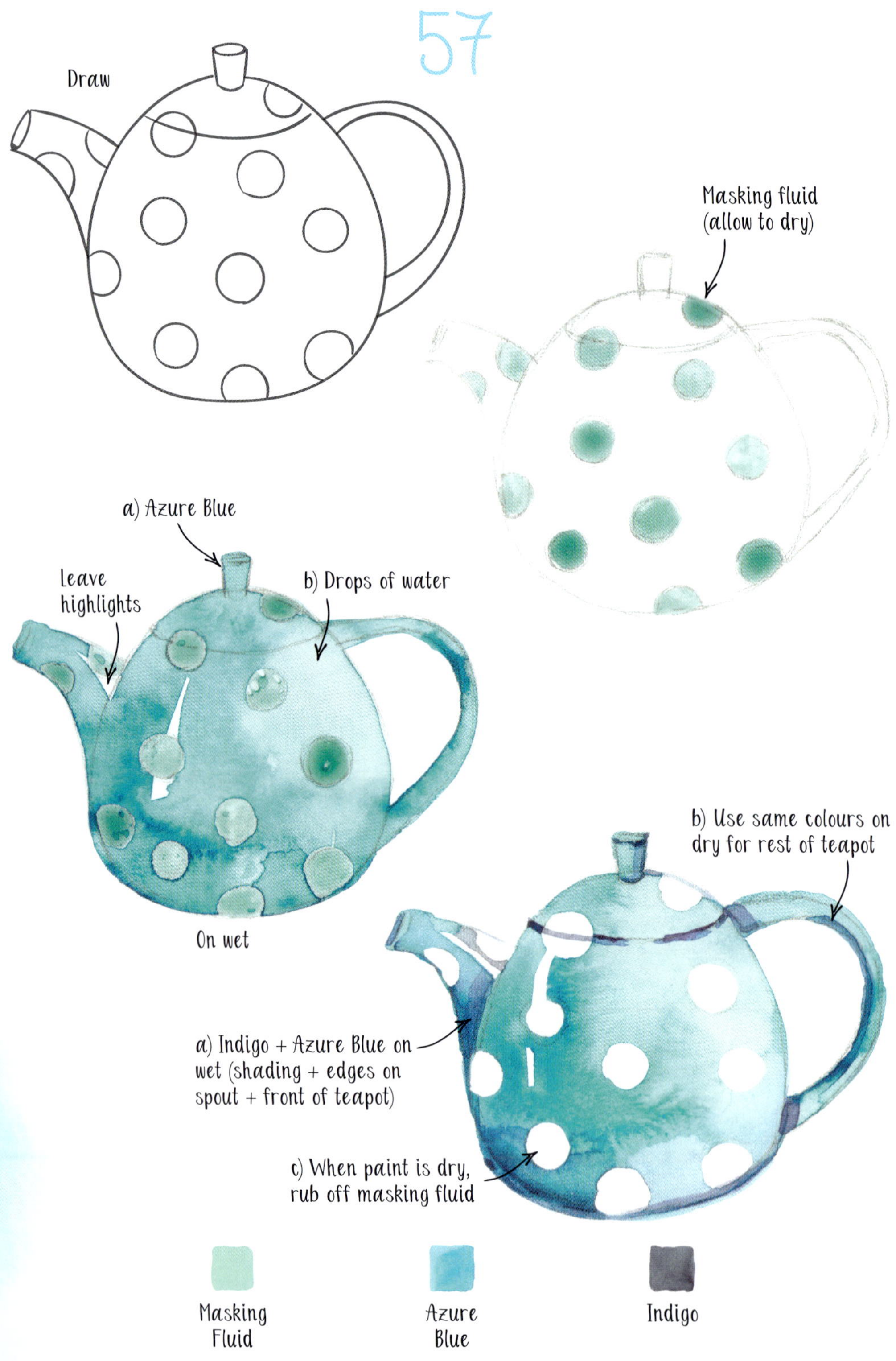
57
Draw
Masking fluid
(allow to dry)
a) Azure Blue
leave
highlights
b) Drops of water
On wet
b) Use same colours on
dry for rest of teapot
a) Indigo + Azure Blue on
wet (shading + edges on
spout + front of teapot)
c) When paint is dry,
rub off masking fluid
Masking
Fluid
Azure
Blue
Indigo

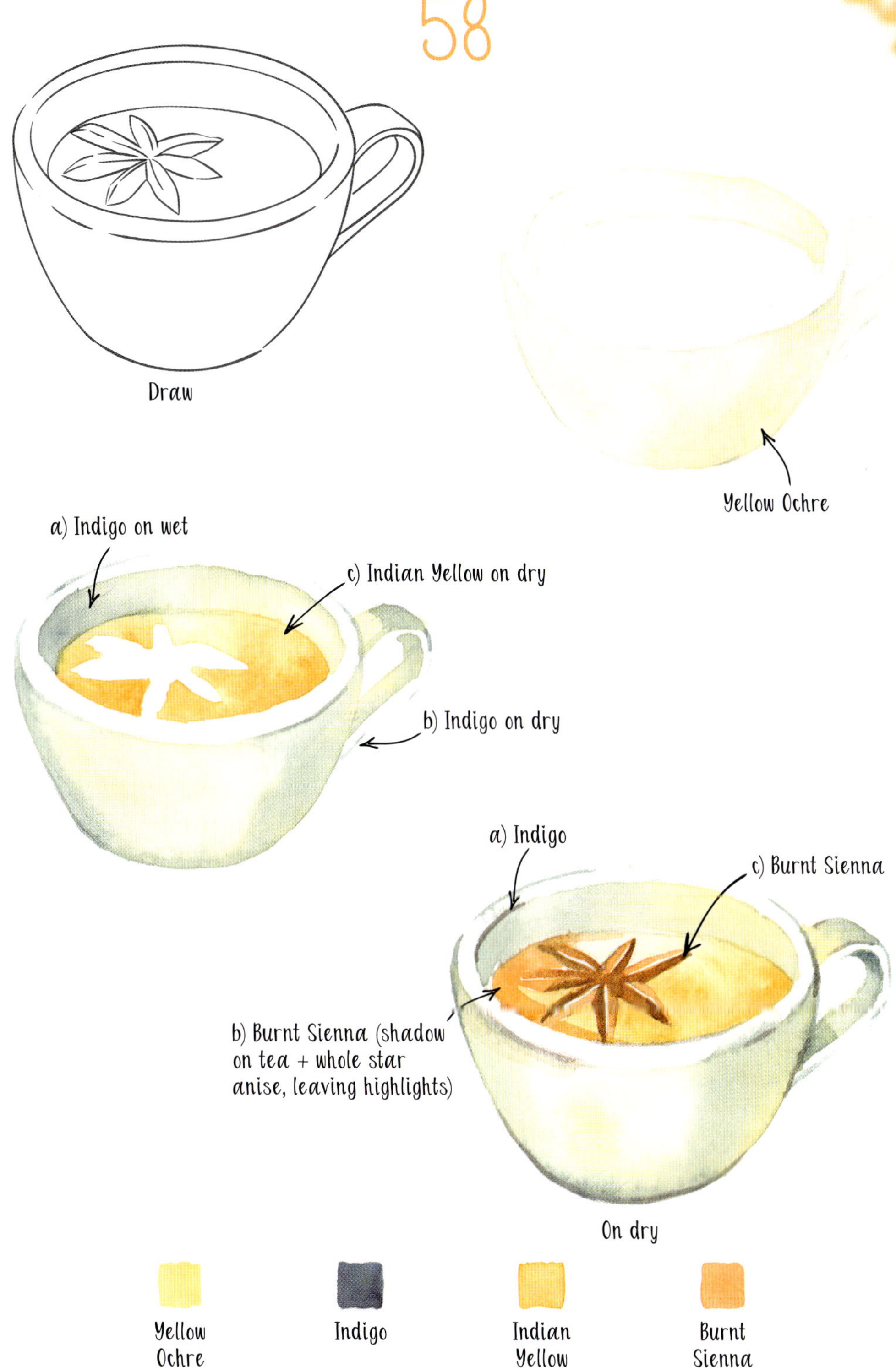
58
Draw
Yellow Ochre
a) Indigo on wet
c) Indian Yellow on dry
b) Indigo on dry
a) Indigo
c) Burnt Sienna
b) Burnt Sienna (shadow
on tea + whole star
anise, leaving highlights)
On dry
Yellow
Ochre
Indigo
Indian
Yellow
Burnt
Sienna

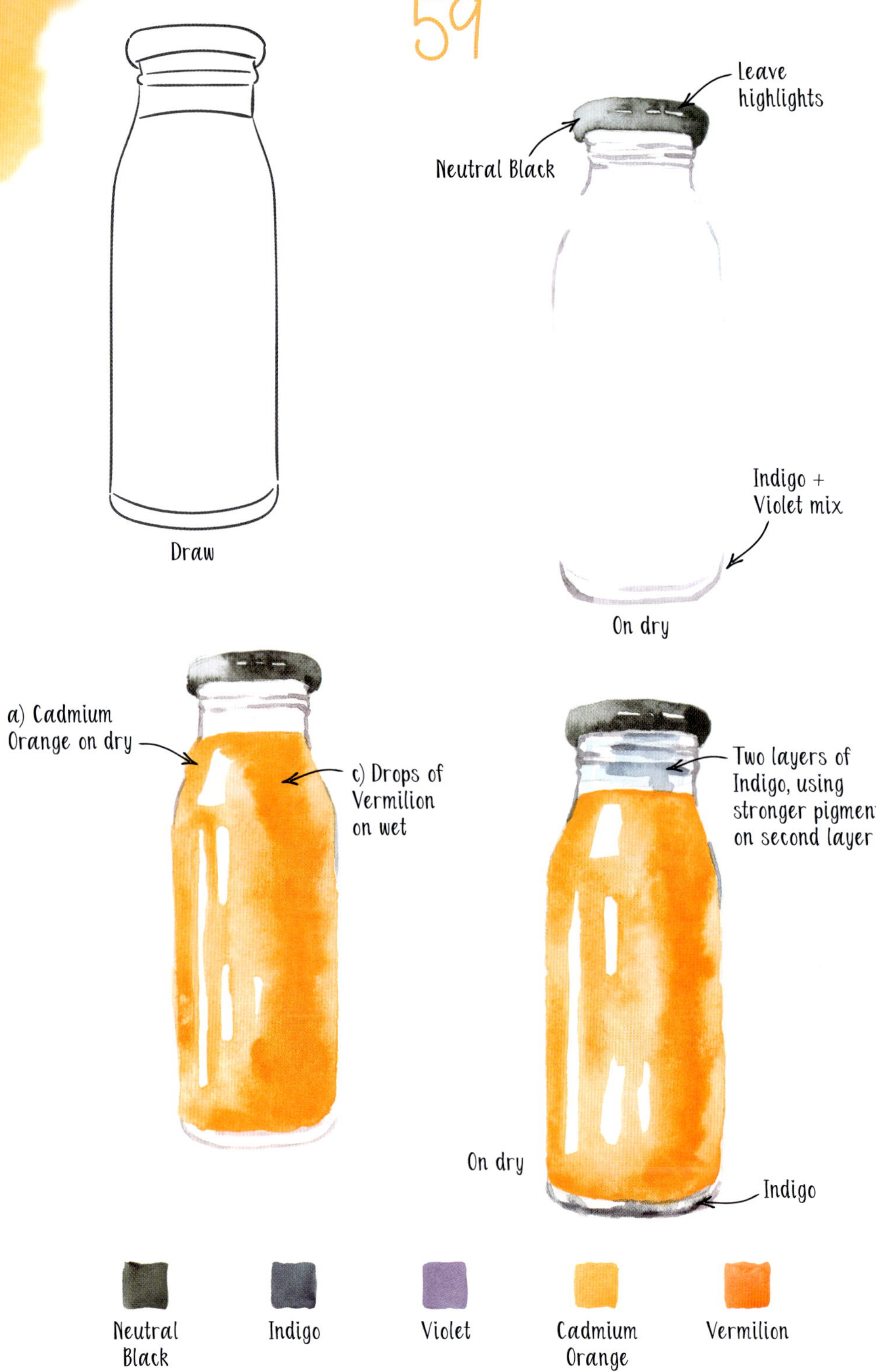
59
leave highlights
Neutral Black
Indigo + Violet mix
On dry
a) Cadmium Orange on dry
c) Drops of Vermilion on wet
Two layers of Indigo, using stronger pigment on second layer
On dry
Indigo
Draw
Neutral Black
Indigo
Violet
Cadmium Orange
Vermilion

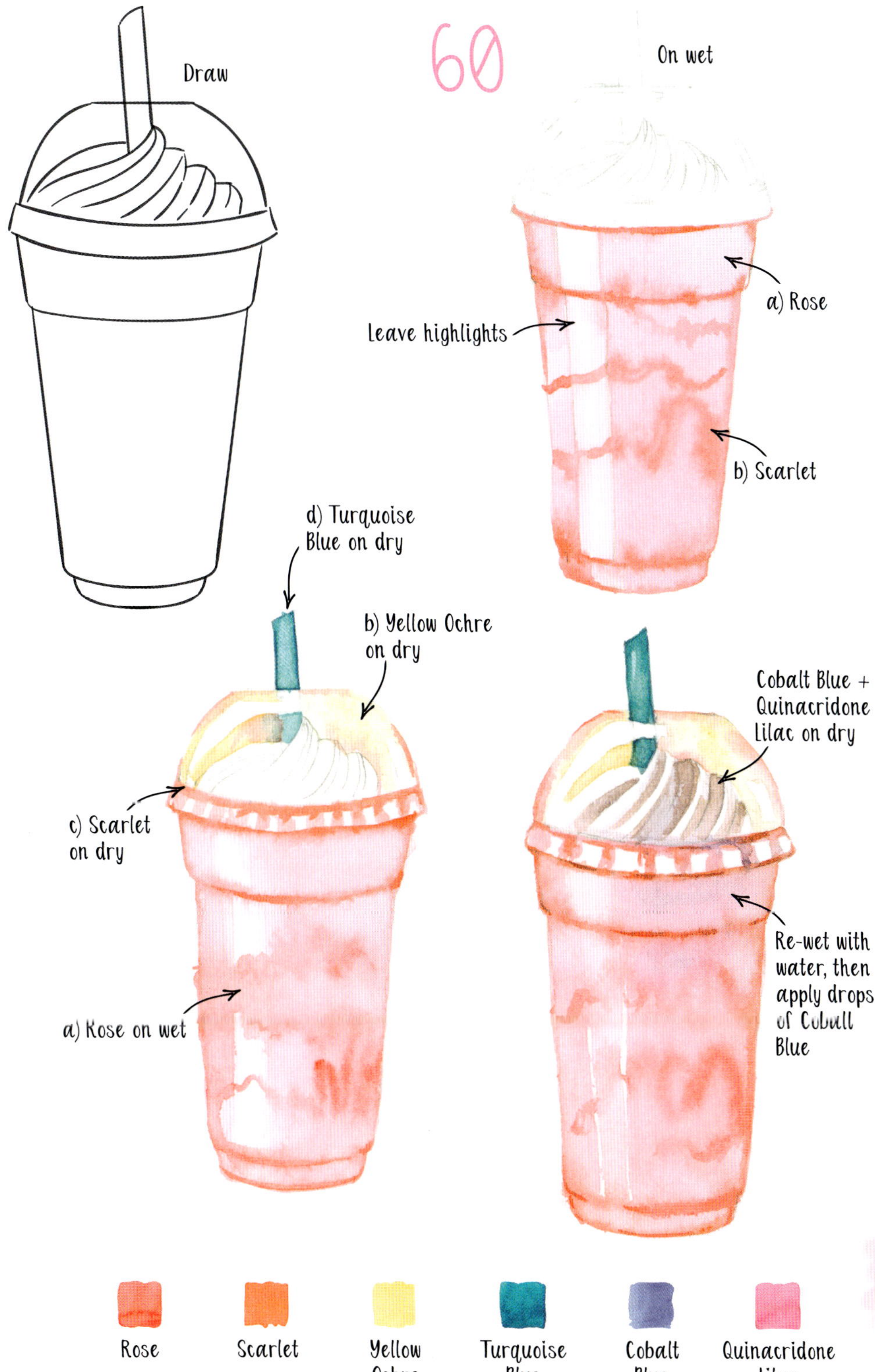

Draw
60
On wet
leave highlights
a) Rose
b) Scarlet
d) Turquoise Blue on dry
b) Yellow Ochre on dry
Cobalt Blue + Quinacridone Lilac on dry
c) Scarlet on dry
Re-wet with water, then apply drops of Cobalt Blue
a) Rose on wet
Rose
Scarlet
Yellow Ochre
Turquoise Blue
Cobalt Blue
Quinacridone Lilac

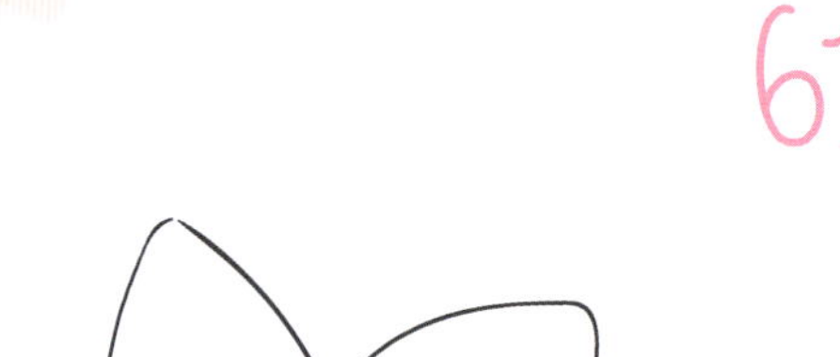

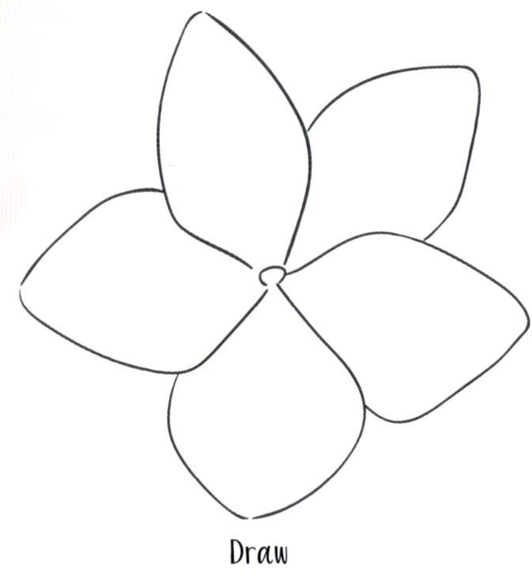

Draw

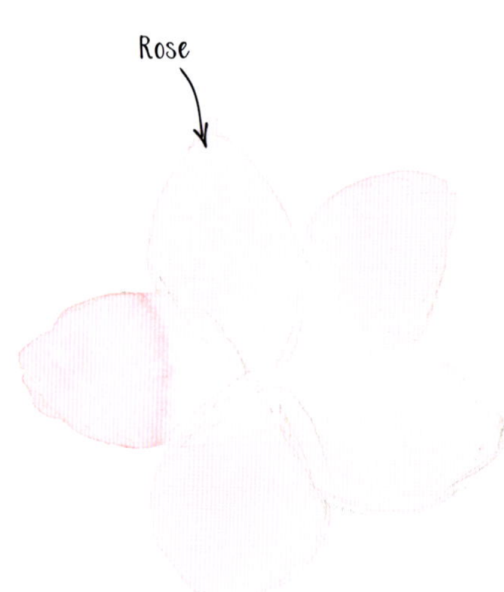

Rose

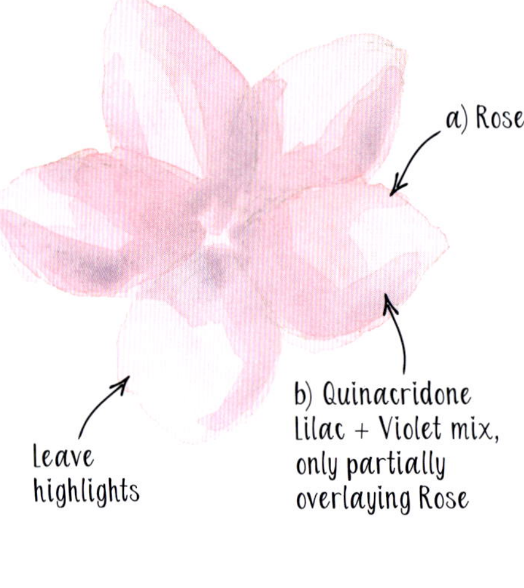

On dry

a) Rose

b) Quinacridone Lilac + Violet mix, only partially overlaying Rose

leave highlights

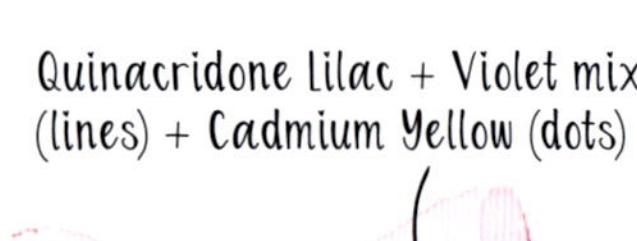

Quinacridone Lilac + Violet mix (lines) + Cadmium Yellow (dots)

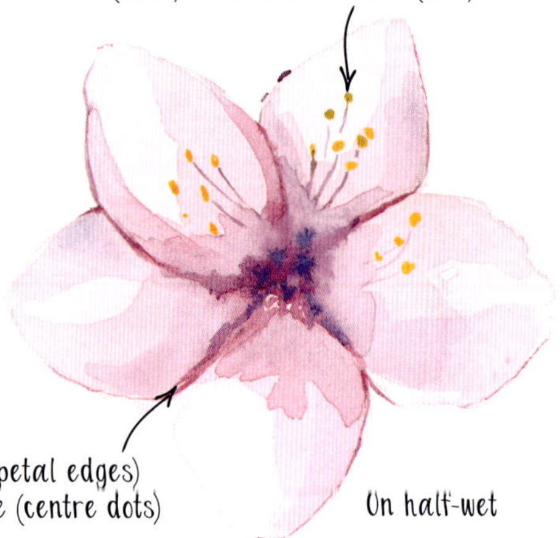

Violet (petal edges) + Azure (centre dots)

On half-wet

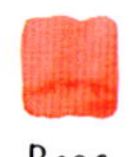

Rose

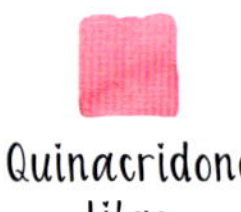

Quinacridone Lilac

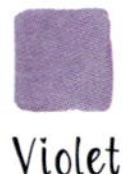

Violet

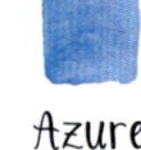

Azure

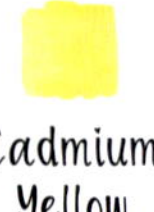

Cadmium Yellow

62

Draw
On wet
Sap Green
Quinacridone
Lilac
Violet
Repeat previous step,
starting on dry
Violet
Sap Green
On half-wet
Sap
Green
Quinacridone
Lilac
Violet

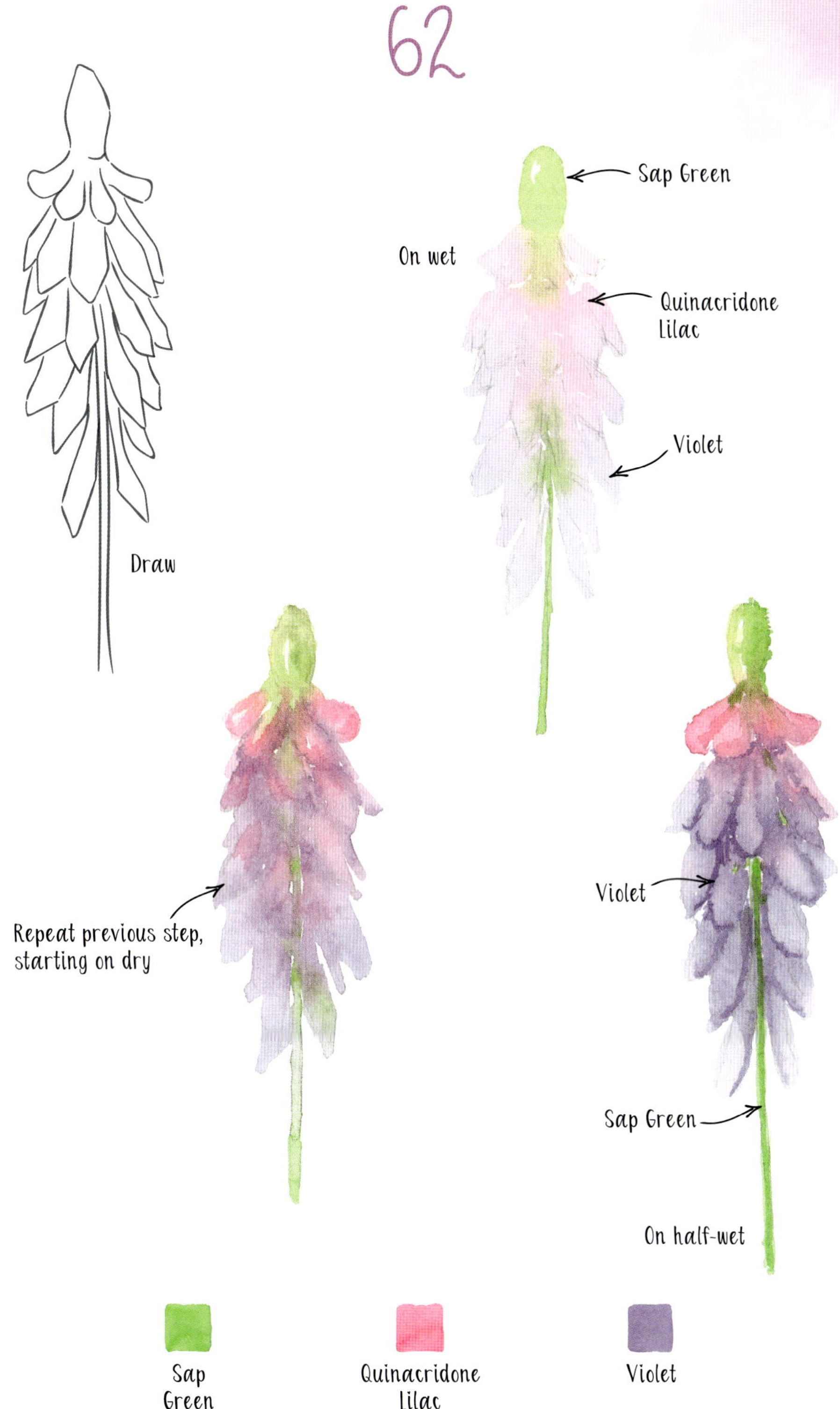

63

Draw

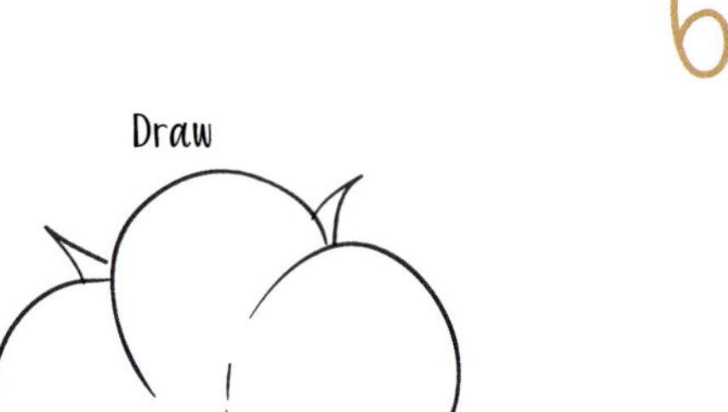

a) Cover with water,
then work on half-wet

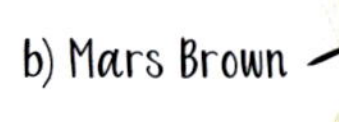

b) Mars Brown

c) Neutral Black
(outer edges)

a) Yellow Ochre on wet
(outer edges)

b) Mars Brown
on wet (centre)

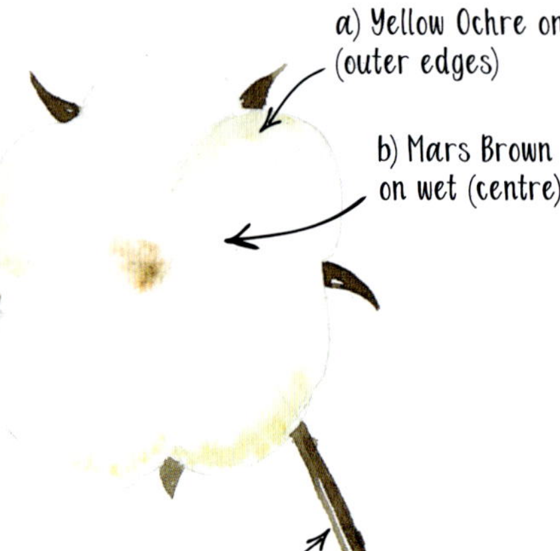

c) Sepia on dry

a) Re-wet with water, then apply
Neutral Black on half-wet (around
edges + to define segments)

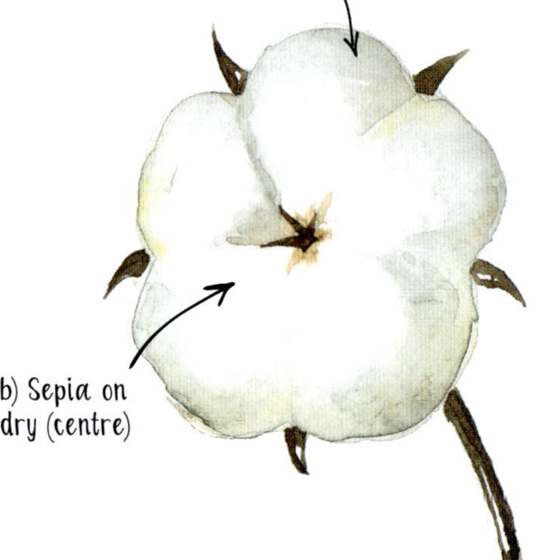

b) Sepia on
dry (centre)

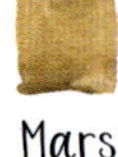

Mars
Brown

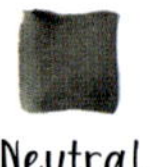

Neutral
Black

Yellow
Ochre

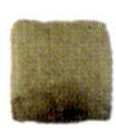

Sepia

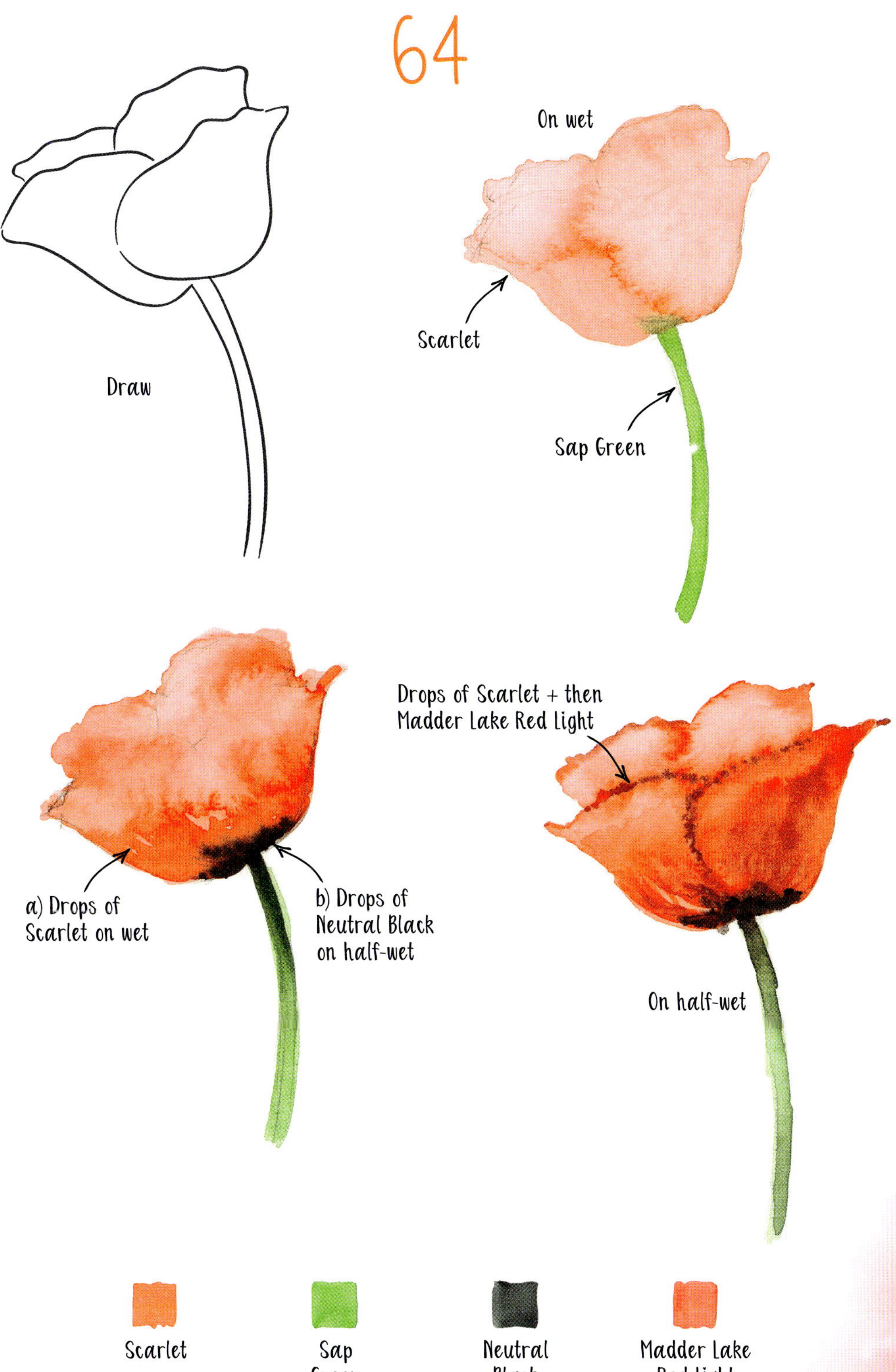

64
Draw
On wet
Scarlet
Sap Green
Drops of Scarlet + then
Madder Lake Red Light
a) Drops of
Scarlet on wet
b) Drops of
Neutral Black
on half-wet
On half-wet
Scarlet
Sap
Green
Neutral
Black
Madder Lake
Red Light

65

Draw
Sap Green
Cadmium Yellow
On dry
Indian Yellow
Green
a) Repeat previous step, painting shorter petals on this layer
b) Green on wet
On half-wet
Sap Green
Cadmium Yellow
Green
Indian Yellow

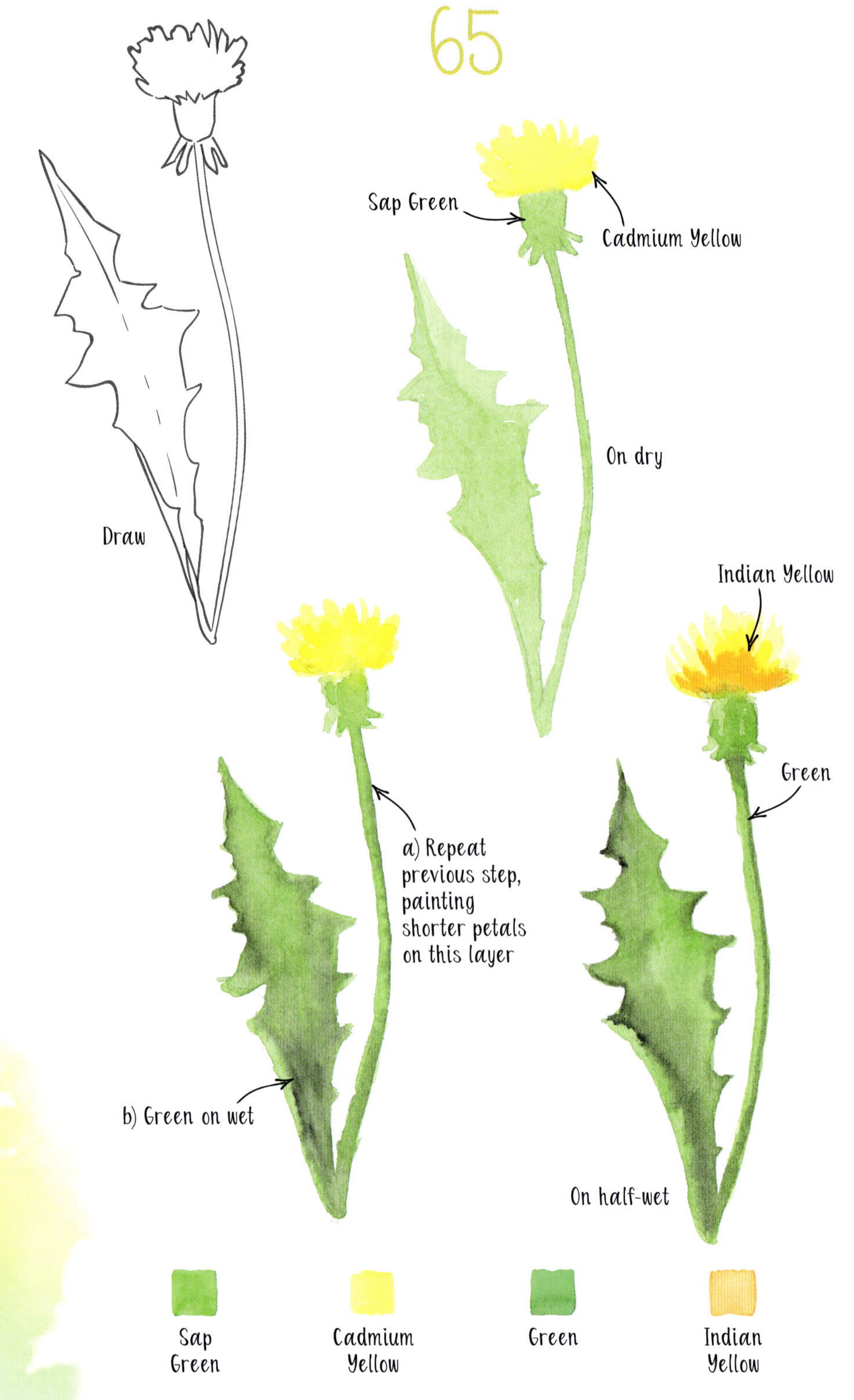

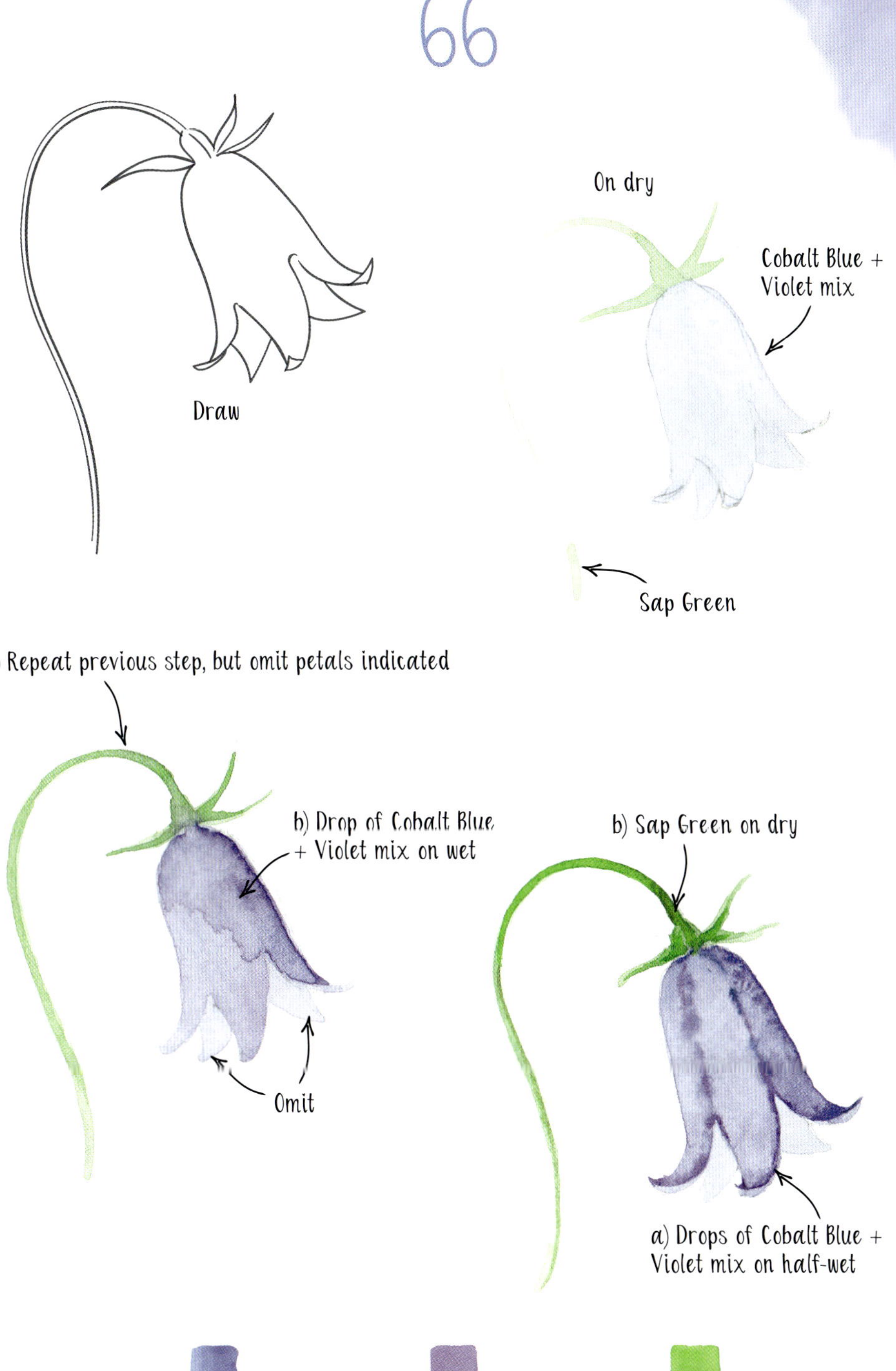
66
Draw
On dry
Cobalt Blue + Violet mix
Sap Green
a) Repeat previous step, but omit petals indicated
b) Drop of Cobalt Blue + Violet mix on wet
Omit
b) Sap Green on dry
a) Drops of Cobalt Blue + Violet mix on half-wet
Cobalt Blue
Violet
Sap Green

67

Draw
Rose
On wet
Green
Drops of Rose
Drops of Rose
On wet
Drops of Umber
Drops of Green light
Umber (leaf veins)
On wet
Rose
Green
Umber
Green Light

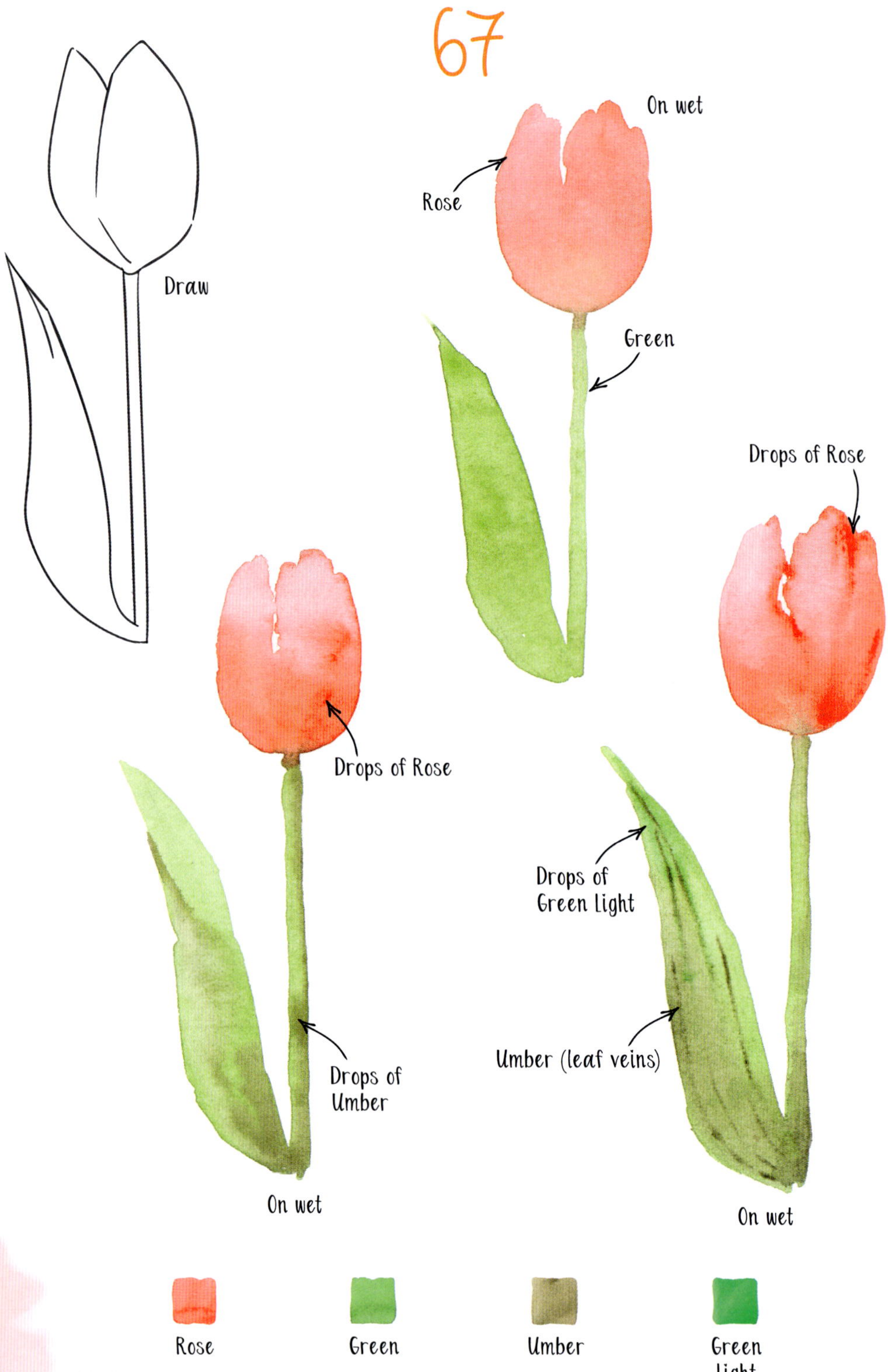

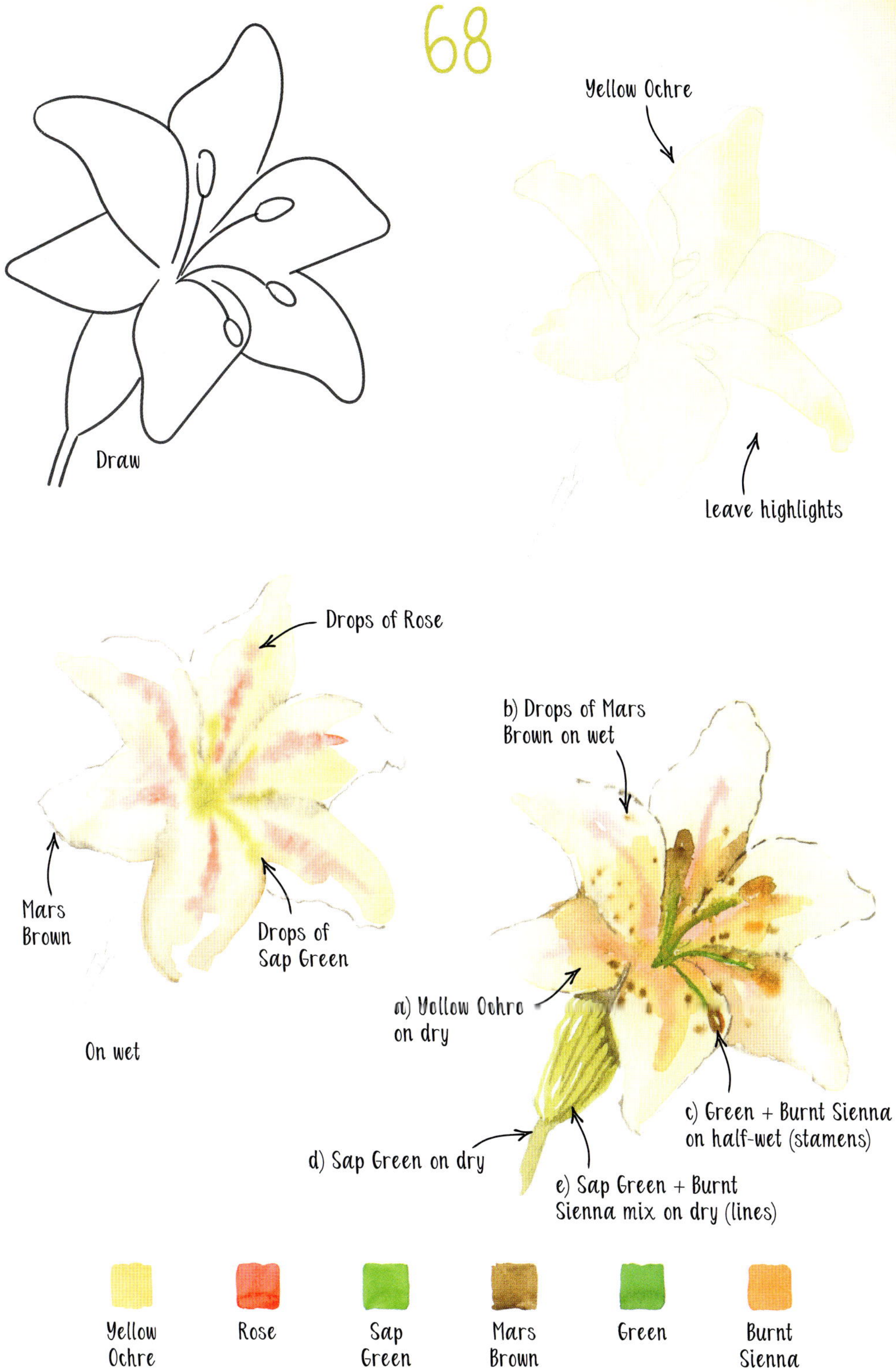

68
Draw
Yellow Ochre
leave highlights
Drops of Rose
Mars
Brown
Drops of
Sap Green
On wet
b) Drops of Mars
Brown on wet
a) Yellow Ochre
on dry
c) Green + Burnt Sienna
on half-wet (stamens)
d) Sap Green on dry
e) Sap Green + Burnt
Sienna mix on dry (lines)
Yellow
Ochre
Rose
Sap
Green
Mars
Brown
Green
Burnt
Sienna

69

Draw

Cadmium Yellow
leave
highlights

a) Drops of
Indian Yellow
+ Sap Green
on wet

b) Neutral Black on dry

a) Drops of Neutral Black on wet

b) Sap Green on dry

Cadmium
Yellow

Indian
Yellow

Sap
Green

Neutral
Black

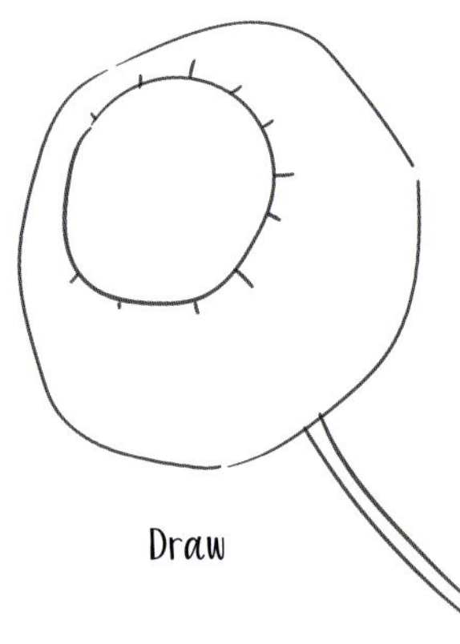

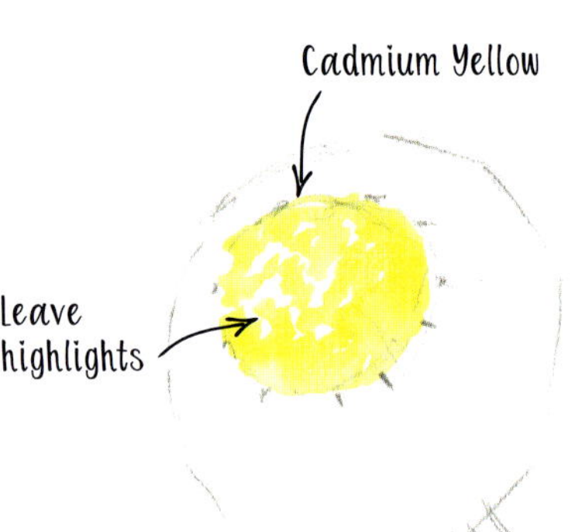

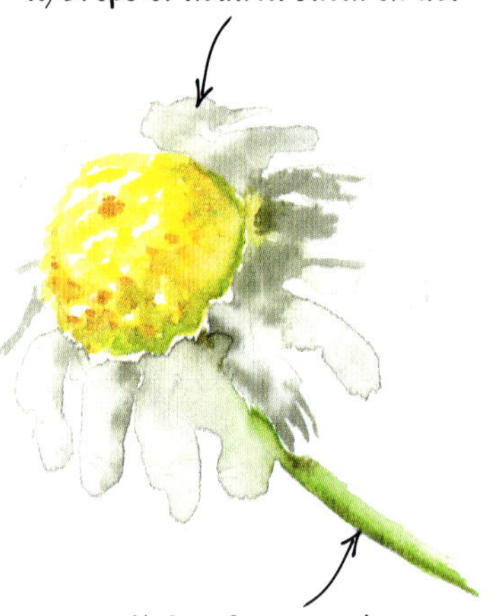

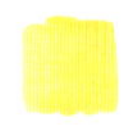

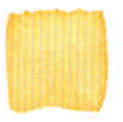

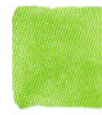

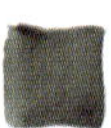

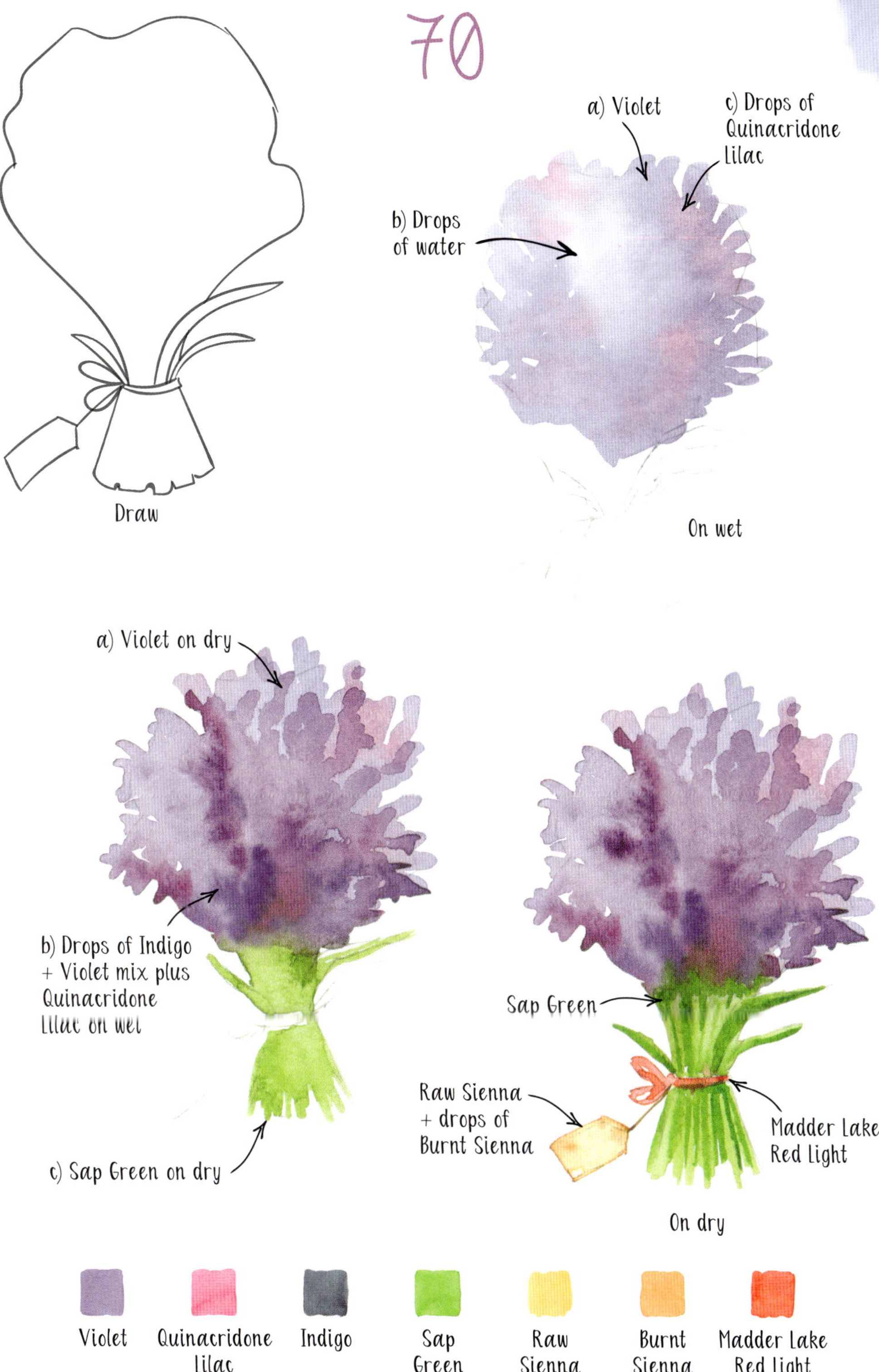
70
a) Violet
c) Drops of Quinacridone Lilac
b) Drops of water
On wet
a) Violet on dry
b) Drops of Indigo + Violet mix plus Quinacridone Lilac on wet
c) Sap Green on dry
Draw
Sap Green
Raw Sienna + drops of Burnt Sienna
Madder Lake Red light
On dry
Violet
Quinacridone Lilac
Indigo
Sap Green
Raw Sienna
Burnt Sienna
Madder Lake Red light

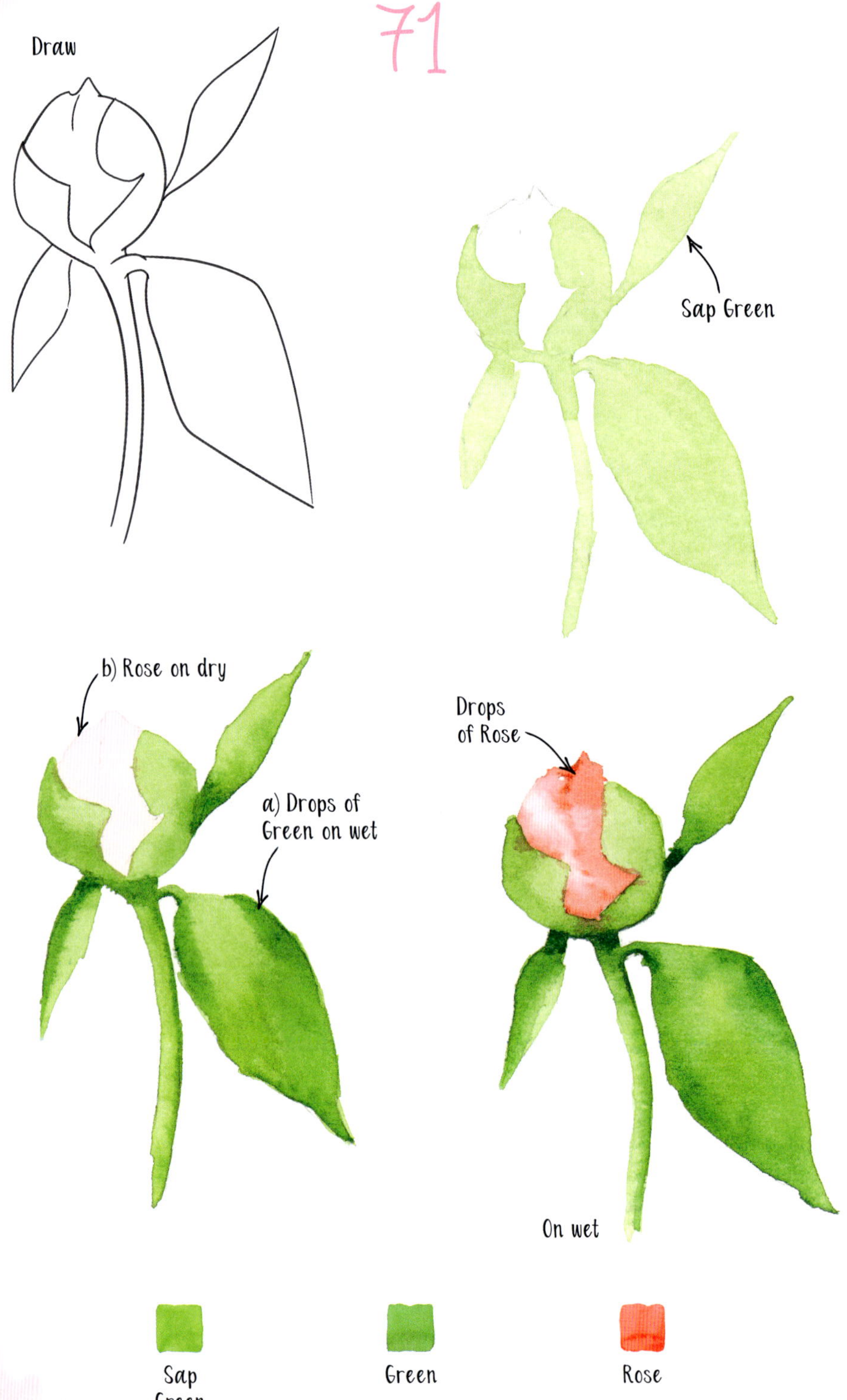
Draw
71
Sap Green
b) Rose on dry
a) Drops of
Green on wet
Drops
of Rose
On wet
Sap
Green
Green
Rose

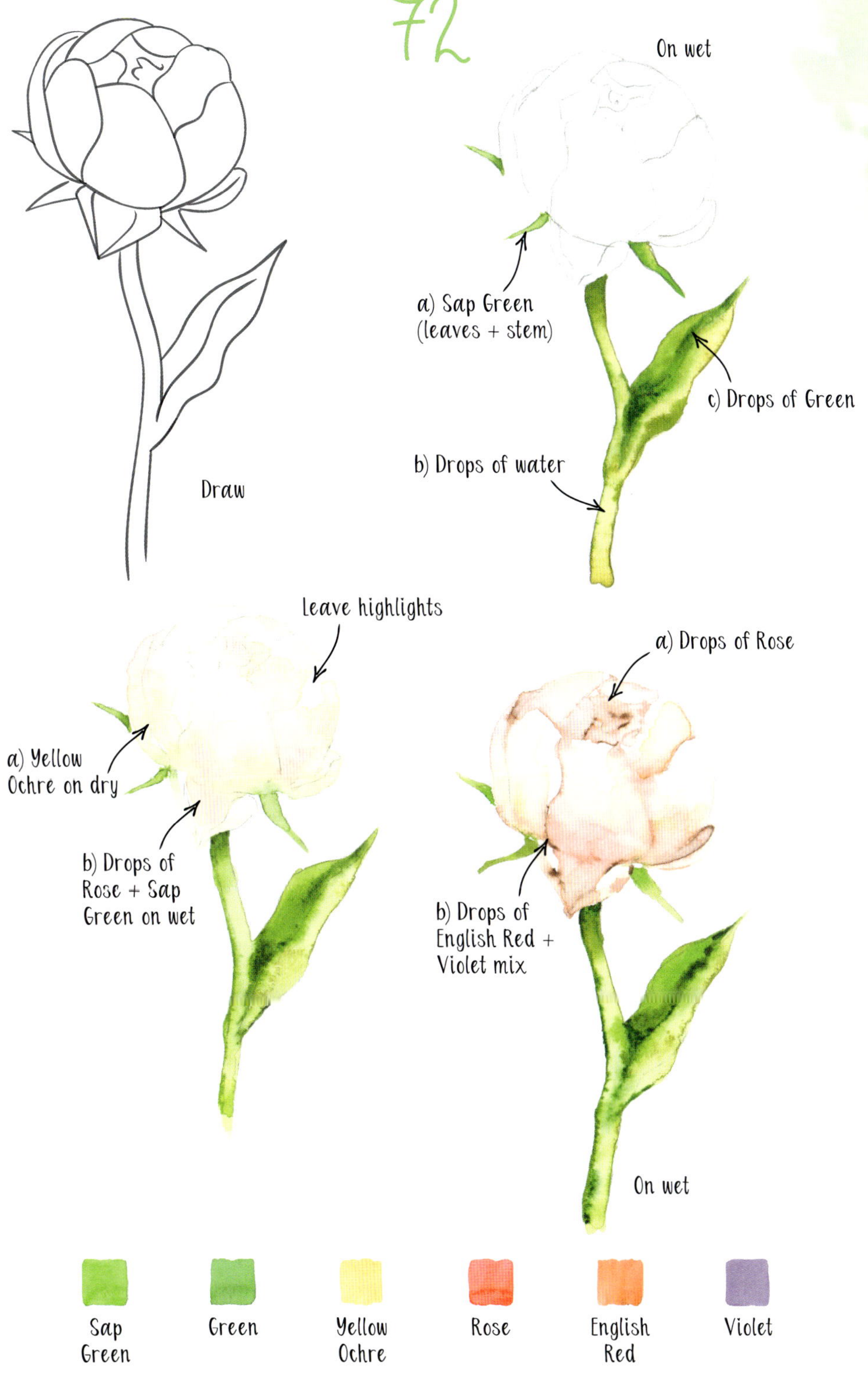
72

Draw

On wet

a) Sap Green
(leaves + stem)

c) Drops of Green

b) Drops of water

leave highlights

a) Yellow
Ochre on dry

b) Drops of
Rose + Sap
Green on wet

a) Drops of Rose

b) Drops of
English Red +
Violet mix

On wet

Sap
Green

Green

Yellow
Ochre

Rose

English
Red

Violet

73

Draw
a) Mars Brown
b) Drops of Sepia
leave highlights
On wet
Cadmium Yellow
Drops of Mars Brown + Sepia (flower centre)
On half-wet
Red Ochre
On half-wet
Mars Brown
Sepia
Cadmium Yellow
Red Ochre

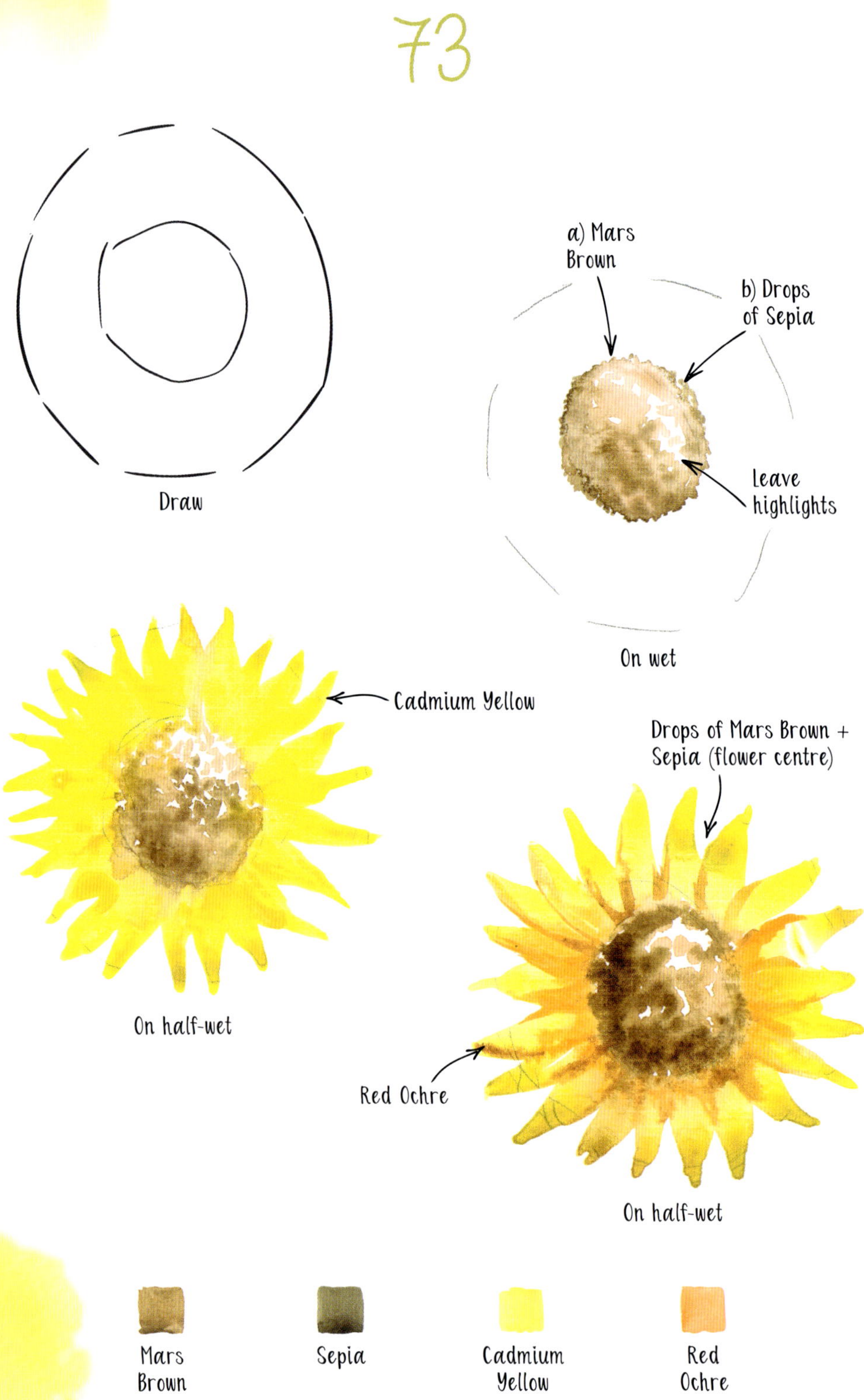

74

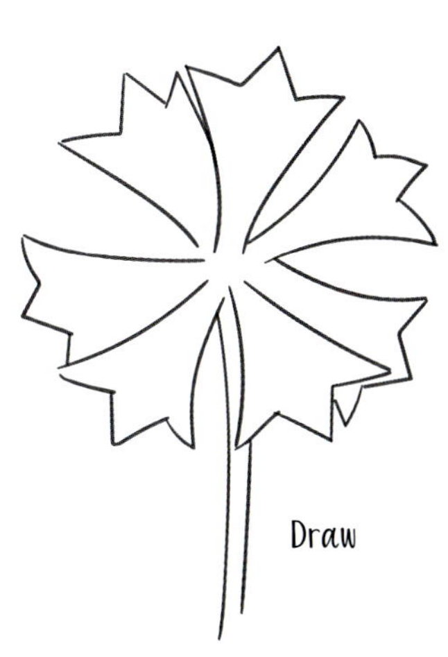

Draw

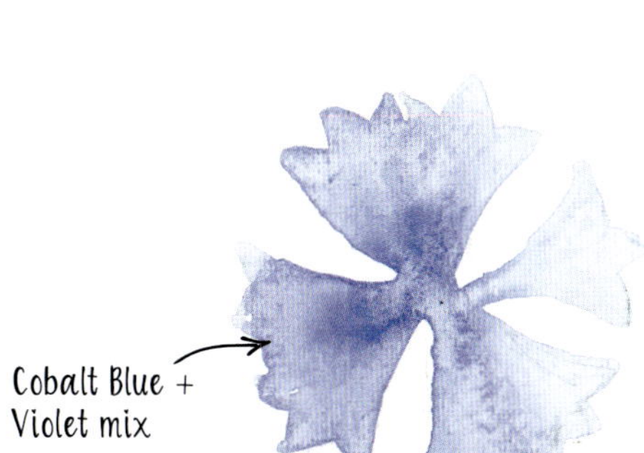

Cobalt Blue +
Violet mix

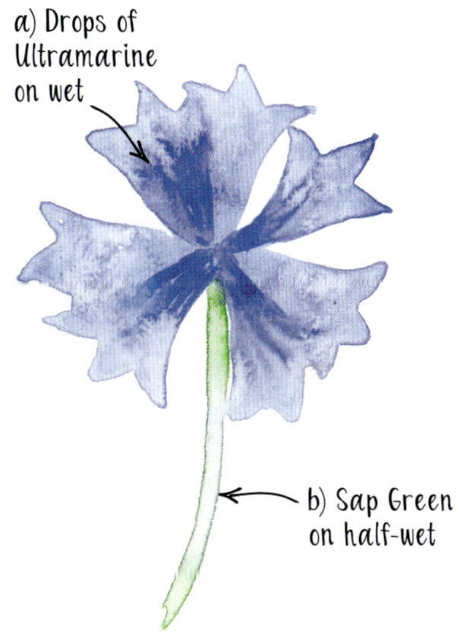

a) Drops of
Ultramarine
on wet

b) Sap Green
on half-wet

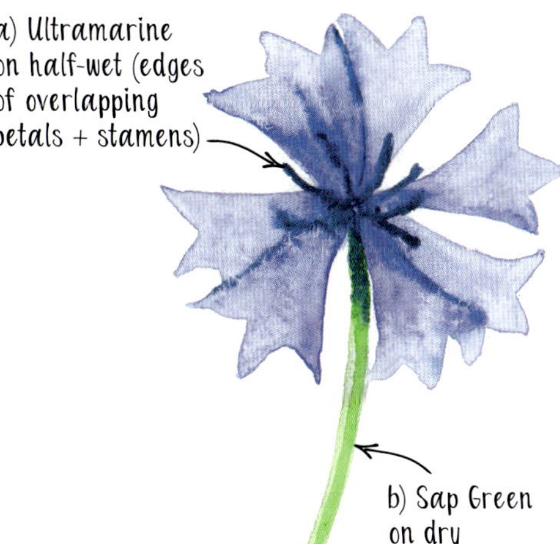

a) Ultramarine
on half-wet (edges
of overlapping
petals + stamens)

b) Sap Green
on dry

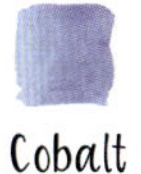

Cobalt
Blue

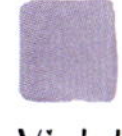

Violet

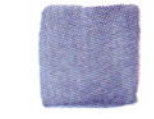

Ultramarine

Sap
Green

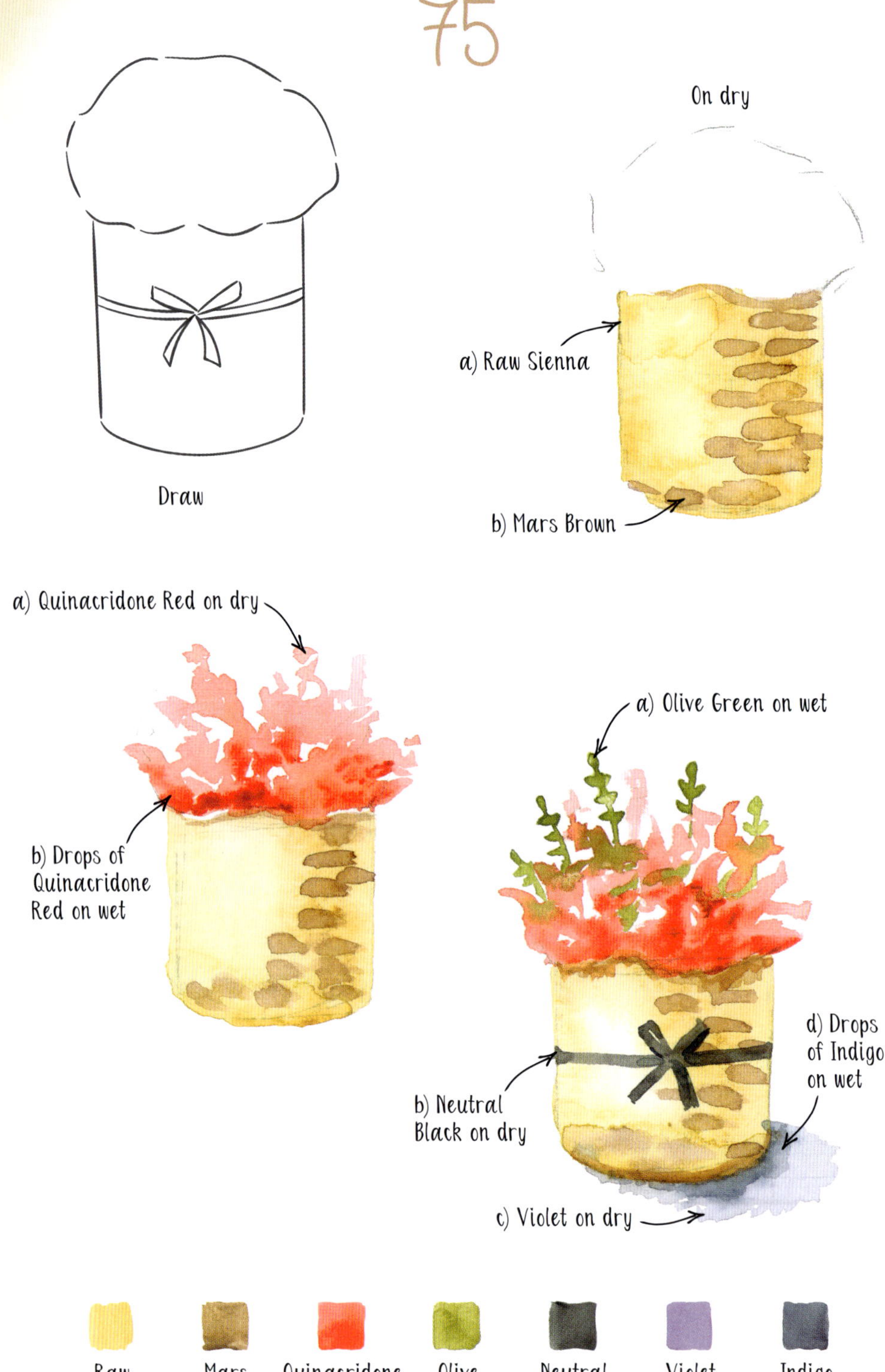
75
Draw
On dry
a) Raw Sienna
b) Mars Brown
a) Quinacridone Red on dry
b) Drops of Quinacridone Red on wet
a) Olive Green on wet
d) Drops of Indigo on wet
b) Neutral Black on dry
c) Violet on dry
Raw Sienna
Mars Brown
Quinacridone Red
Olive Green
Neutral Black
Violet
Indigo

76

Draw

Rose, stronger at
centre of flowers

leave
highlights

a) Sap Green

b) Cadmium
Yellow

On dry

c) Mars Brown
on dry

b) Green
on dry

a) Indian Yellow
on half-wet

d) Raw Sienna on dry

Rose

Sap
Green

Cadmium
Yellow

Indian
Yellow

Green

Mars
Brown

Raw
Sienna

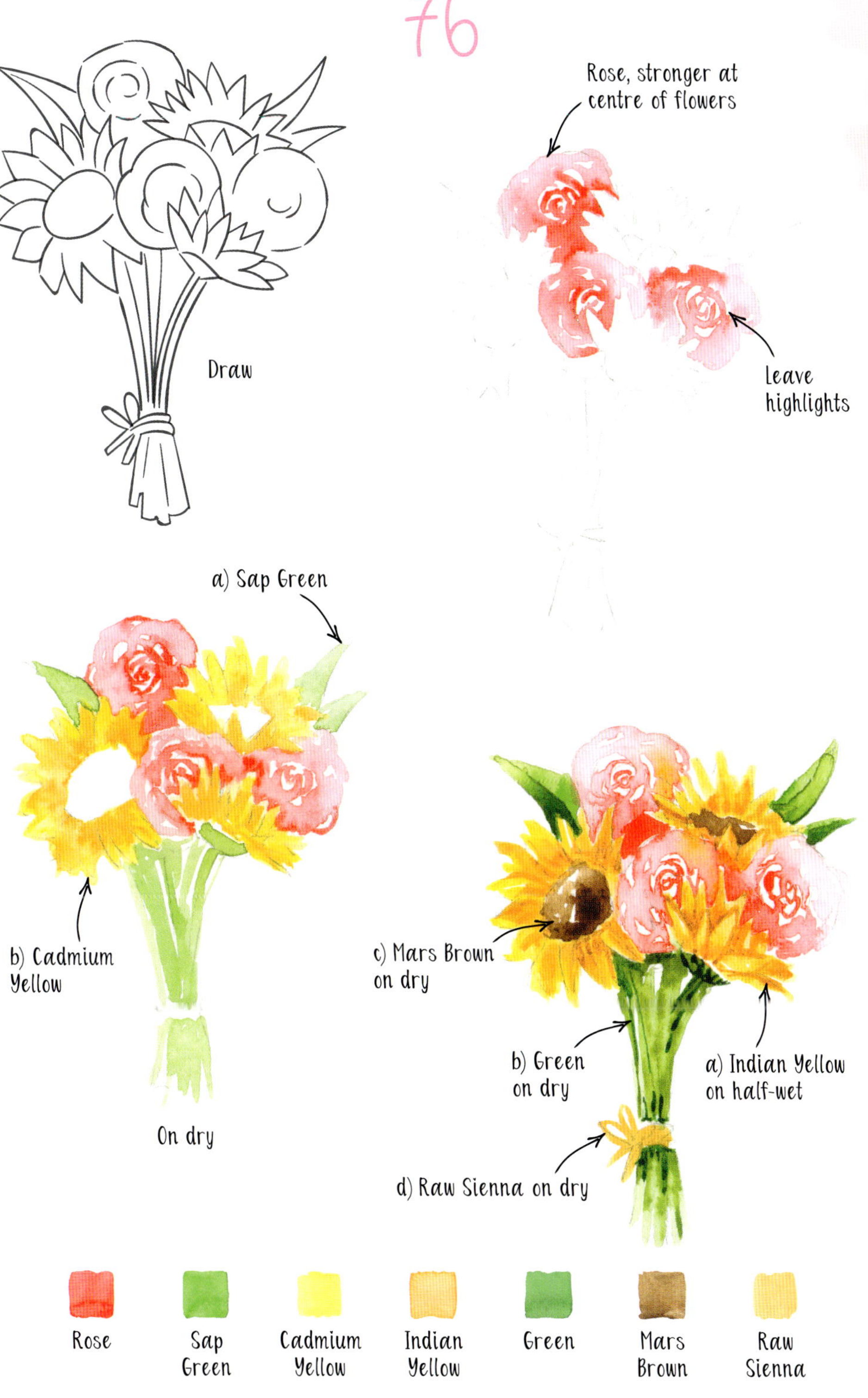

77

Draw
Raw Sienna
Sap Green
On wet
Repeat previous step, starting on dry
Green
Burnt Umber
On wet
Raw
Sienna
Sap
Green
Green
Burnt
Umber

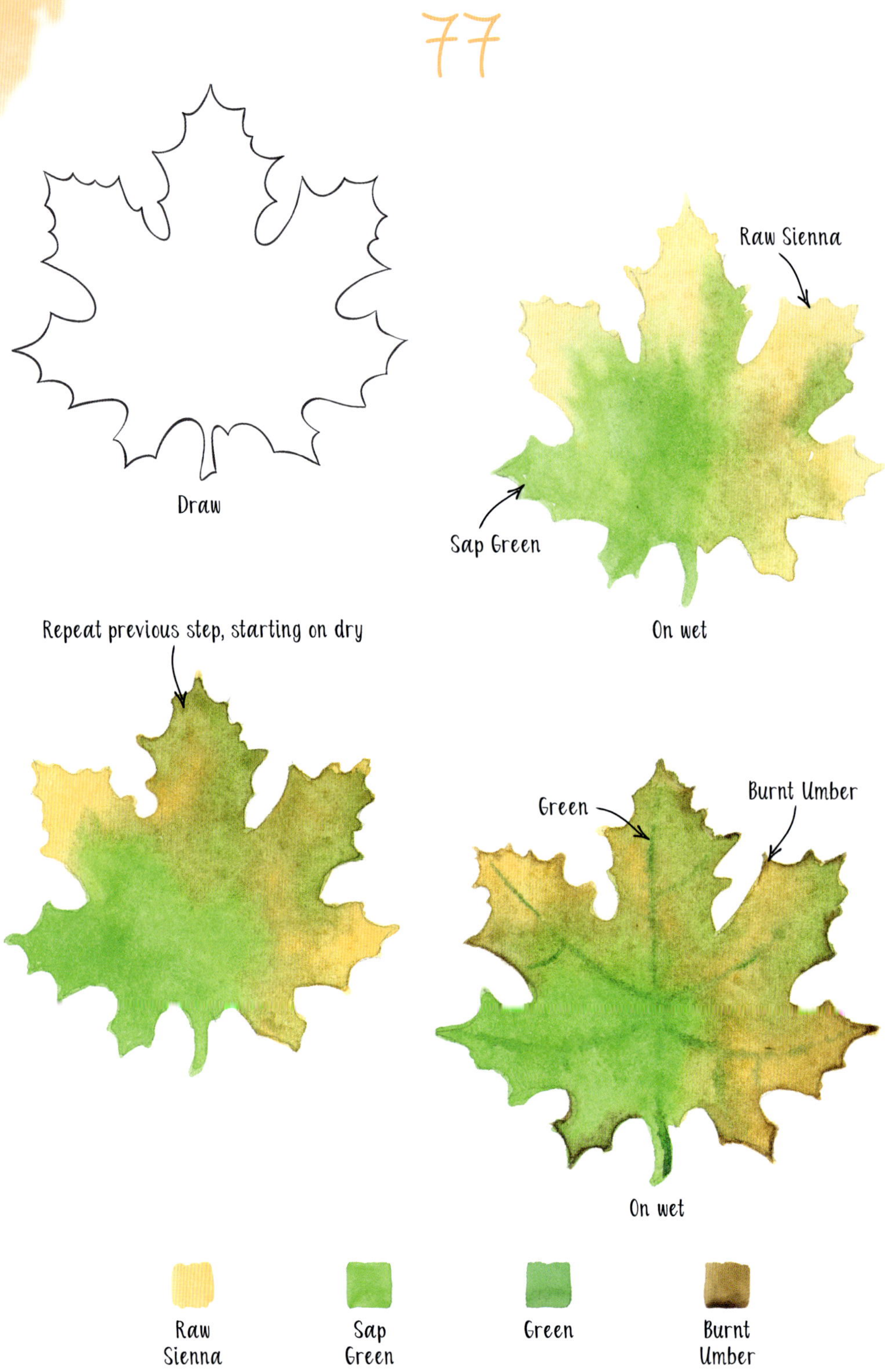

78

Draw
Sap Green
On half-wet
Green
On dry
Green
Green
Sap
Green
Green

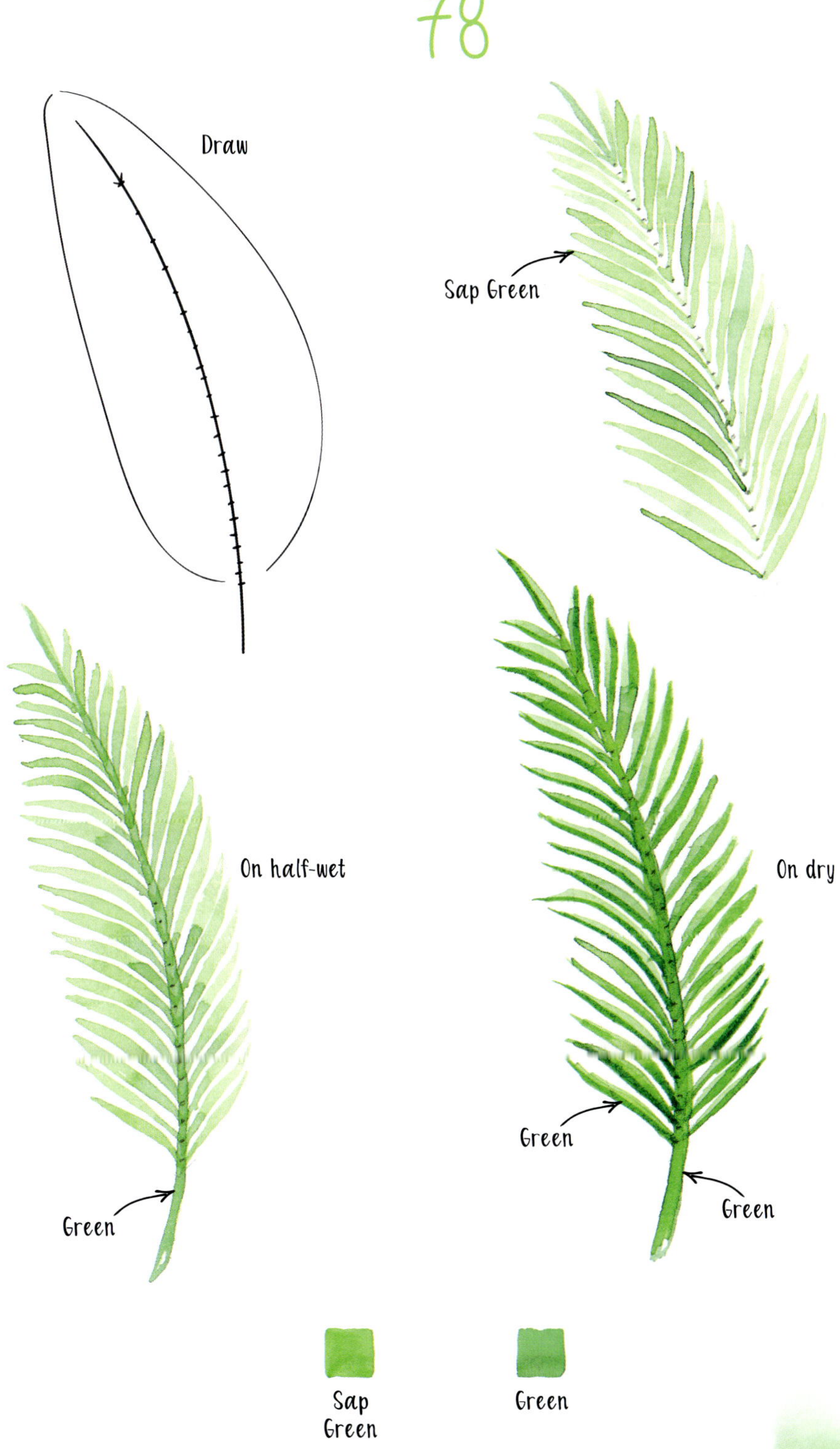

79

Draw

Sap Green

a) Drops of Cadmium
Yellow on half-wet
(top two leaves)

Leave highlights on
bottom two leaves

b) Green on dry

Repeat previous step,
starting on dry + applying
Green while Cadmium
Yellow is still wet

Sap
Green

Cadmium
Yellow

Green

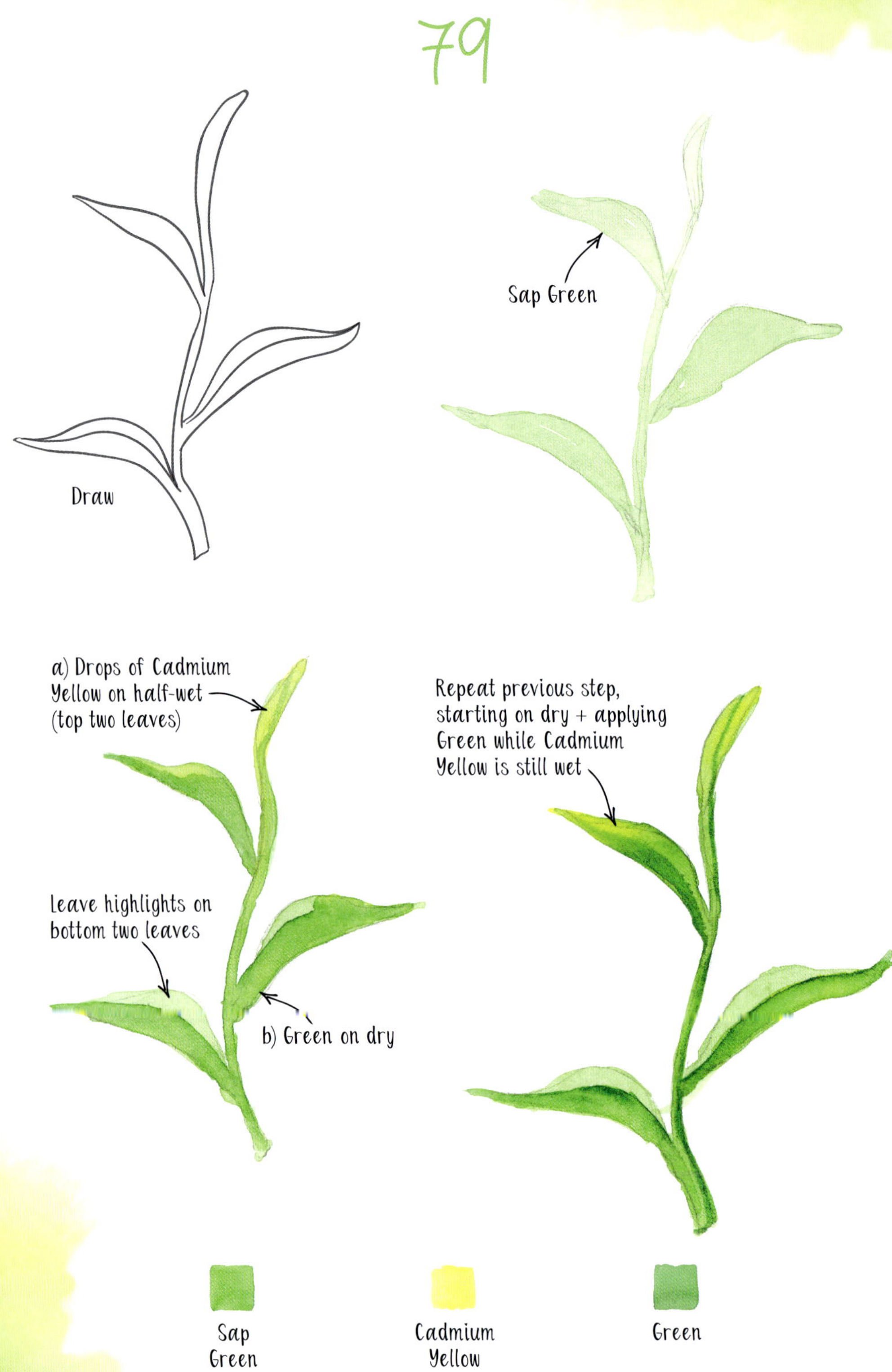

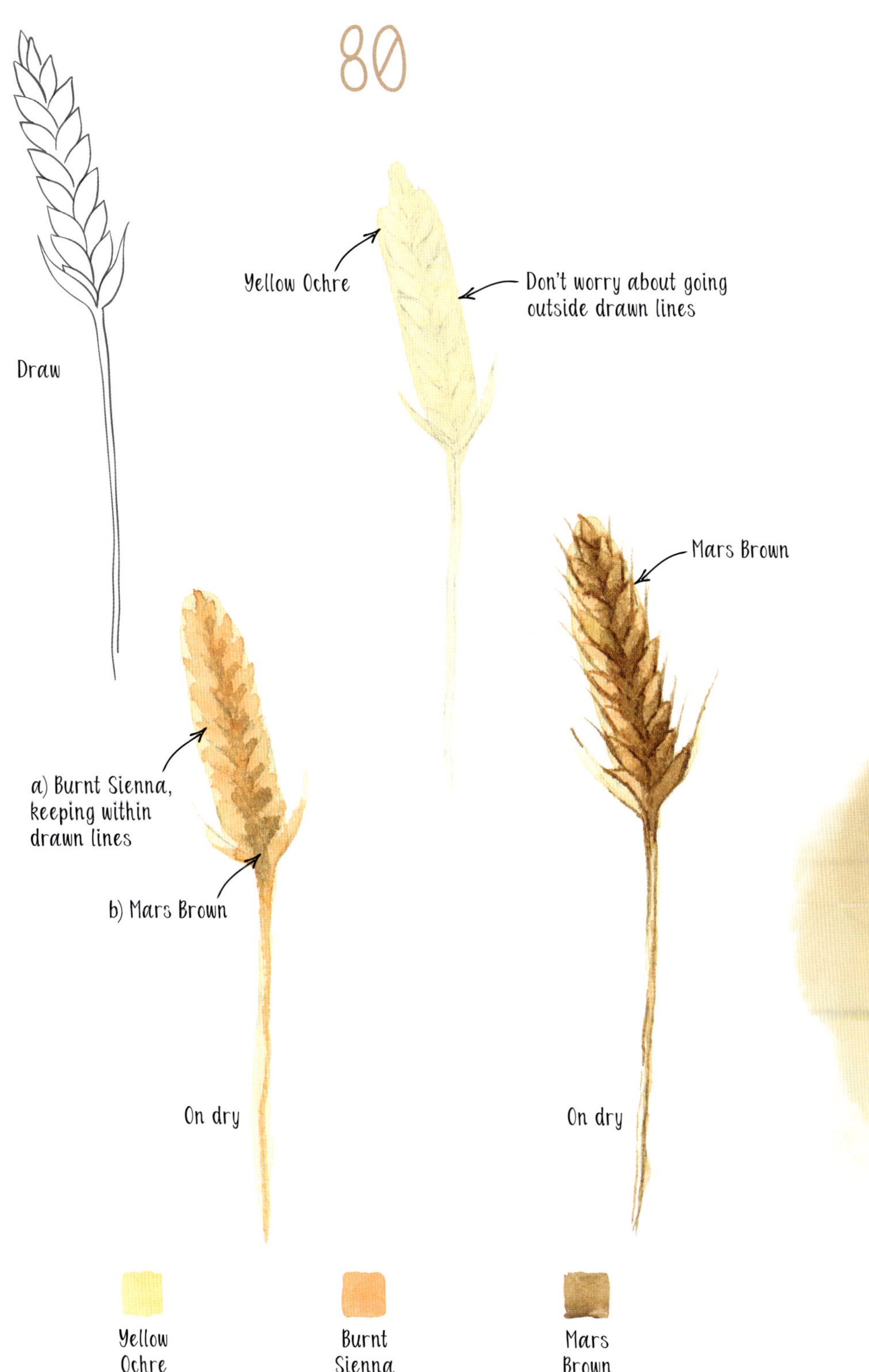
80
Draw
Yellow Ochre
Don't worry about going outside drawn lines
Mars Brown
a) Burnt Sienna, keeping within drawn lines
b) Mars Brown
On dry
On dry
Yellow Ochre
Burnt Sienna
Mars Brown

81

Draw
leave highlight
a) Raw Sienna
b) Burnt Sienna
c) Drop of water
On wet

a) Repeat previous step, starting on dry
leave more highlights
b) Drops of Sepia on half-wet
b) Sepia on half-wet (crisscross texture) + dry (stalk)
a) Drops of Sepia on half-wet
Raw Sienna
Burnt Sienna
Sepia

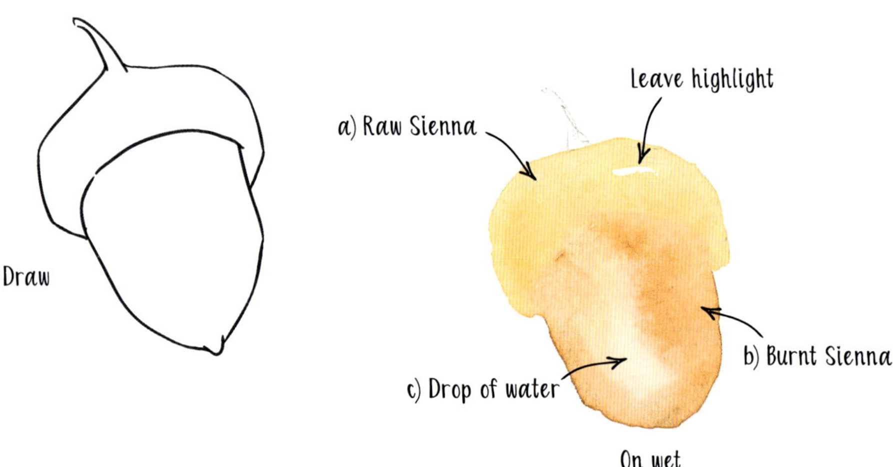

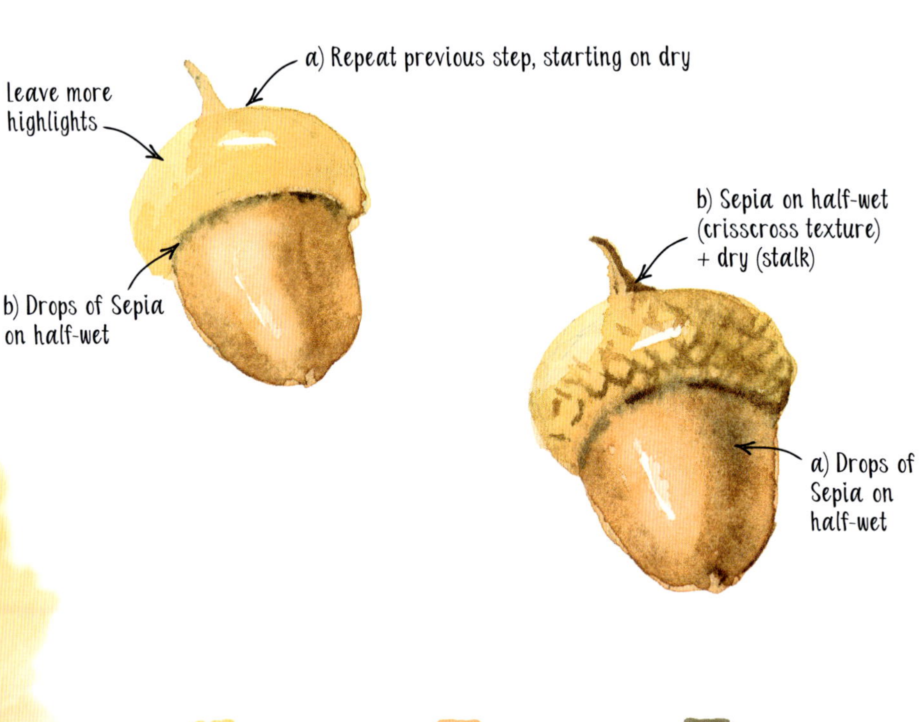

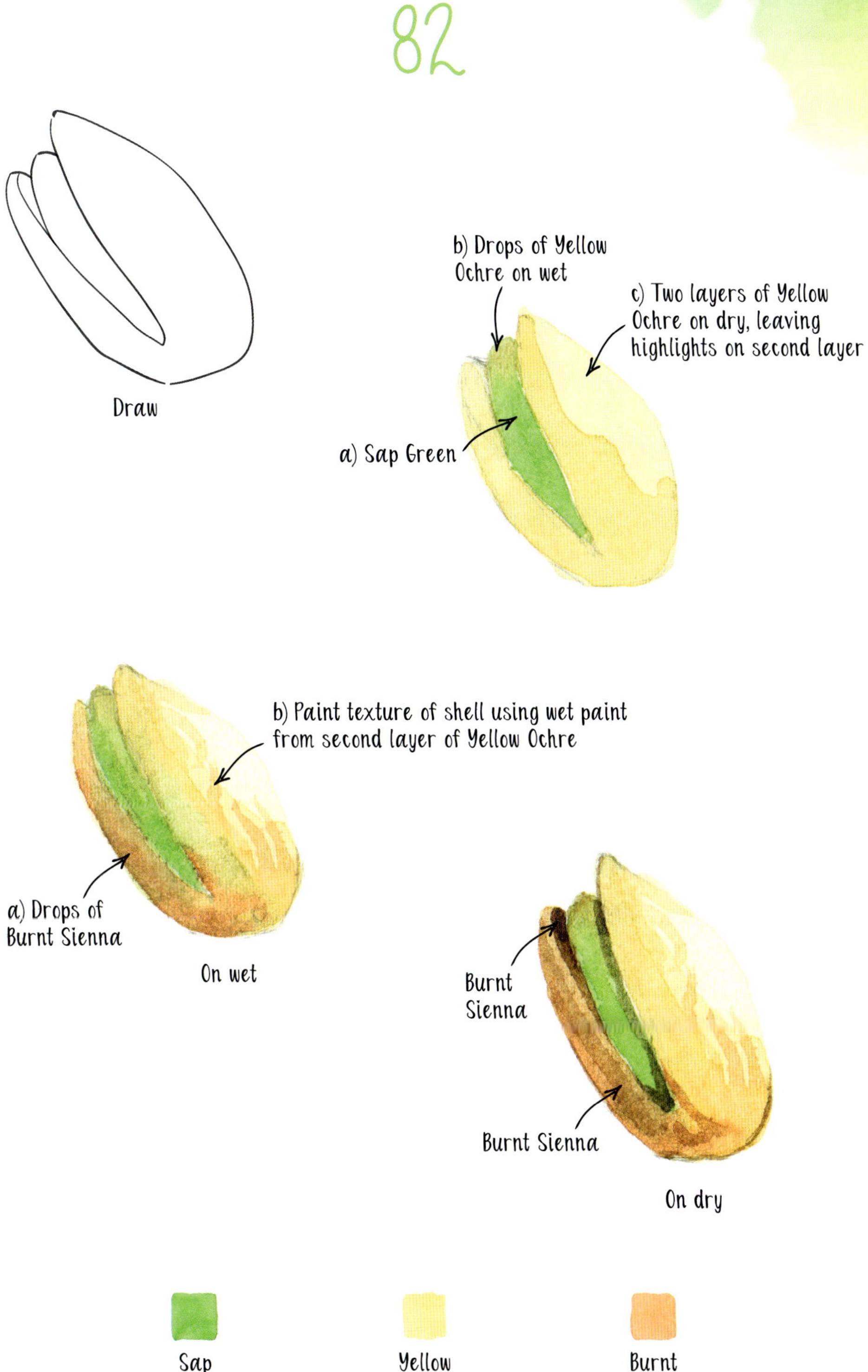
82

Draw

b) Drops of Yellow Ochre on wet

c) Two layers of Yellow Ochre on dry, leaving highlights on second layer

a) Sap Green

b) Paint texture of shell using wet paint from second layer of Yellow Ochre

a) Drops of Burnt Sienna

On wet

Burnt Sienna

Burnt Sienna

On dry

Sap Green

Yellow Ochre

Burnt Sienna

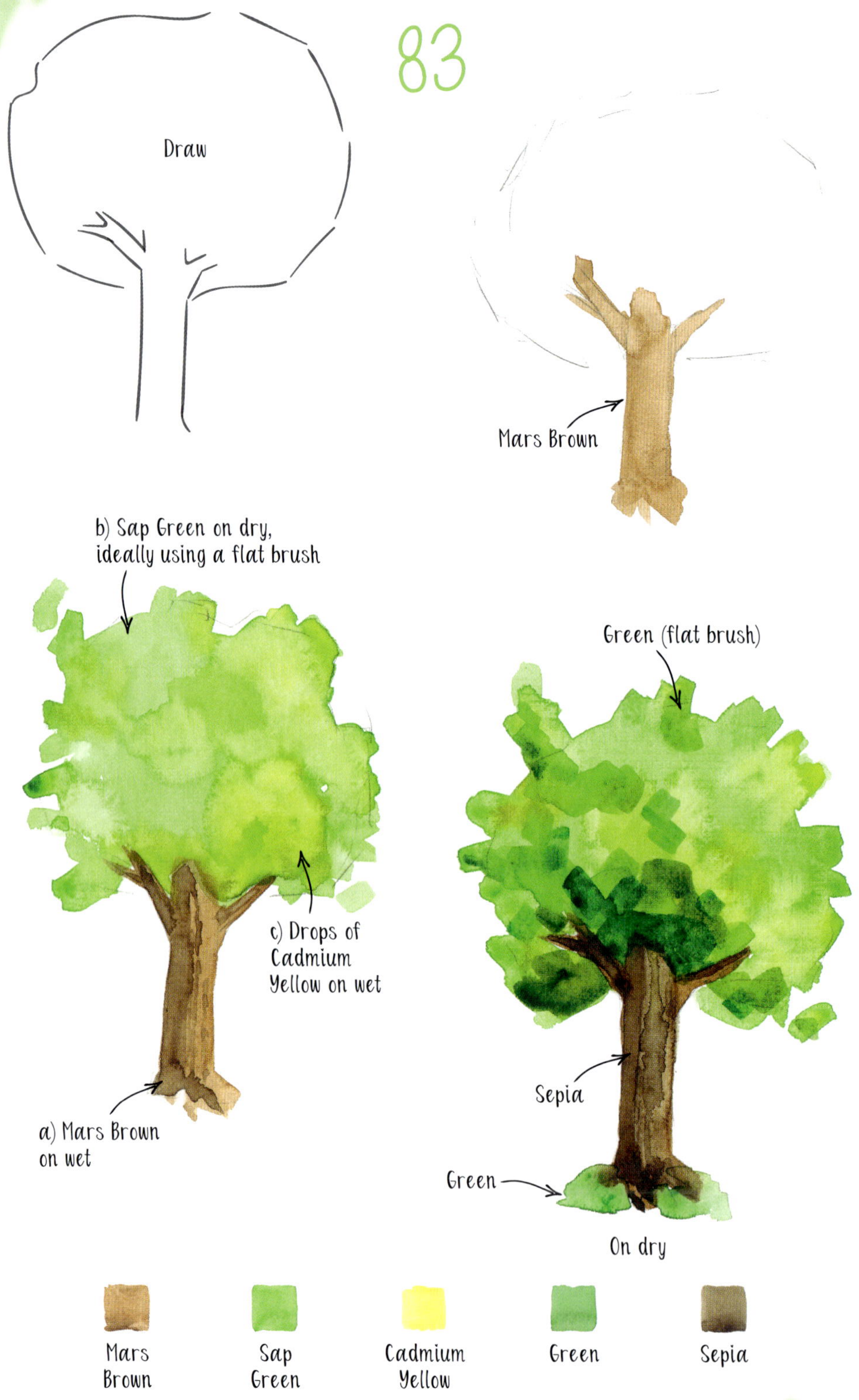
Draw
83
Mars Brown
b) Sap Green on dry,
ideally using a flat brush
Green (flat brush)
c) Drops of
Cadmium
Yellow on wet
Sepia
a) Mars Brown
on wet
Green
On dry
Mars
Brown
Sap
Green
Cadmium
Yellow
Green
Sepia

84

Draw
a) Mars Brown
b) Sap Green on dry
c) Drops of Green on wet
leave highlights
On dry
Olive Green
Leave highlights
Mars Brown
Two layers of Olive Green, leaving bigger highlights on each layer
On dry
Mars Brown
Sap Green
Green
Olive Green

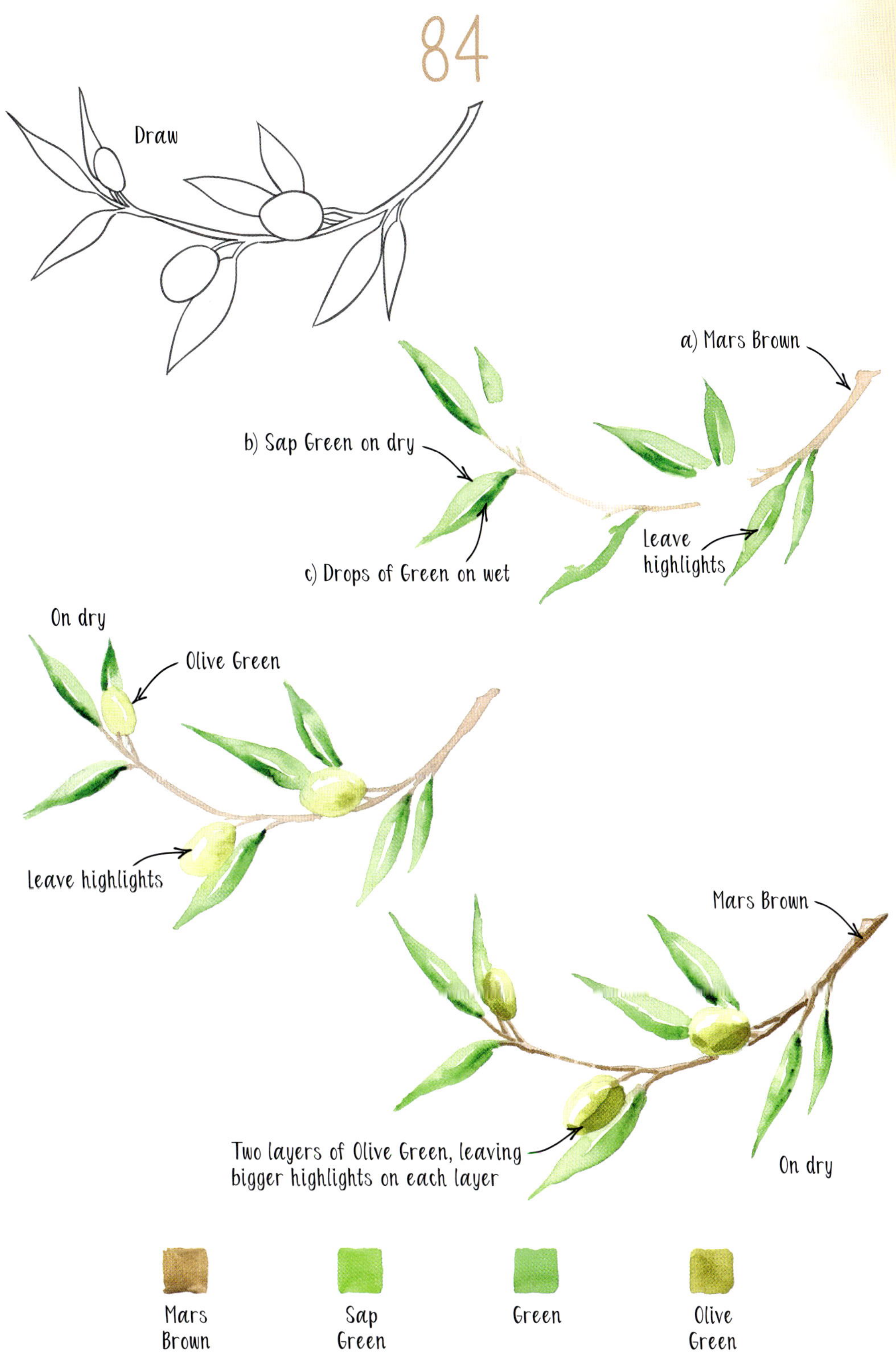

85

Draw

Two layers
of Mars Brown,
leaving highlights
on second layer

On dry

a) Sap Green
on dry

b) Drops of
Emerald
Green
on wet

c) Quinacridone
Lilac on dry

leave
highlights

On dry

Quinacridone
Lilac

Emerald
Green

Mars
Brown

Mars
Brown

Sap
Green

Emerald
Green

Quinacridone
Lilac

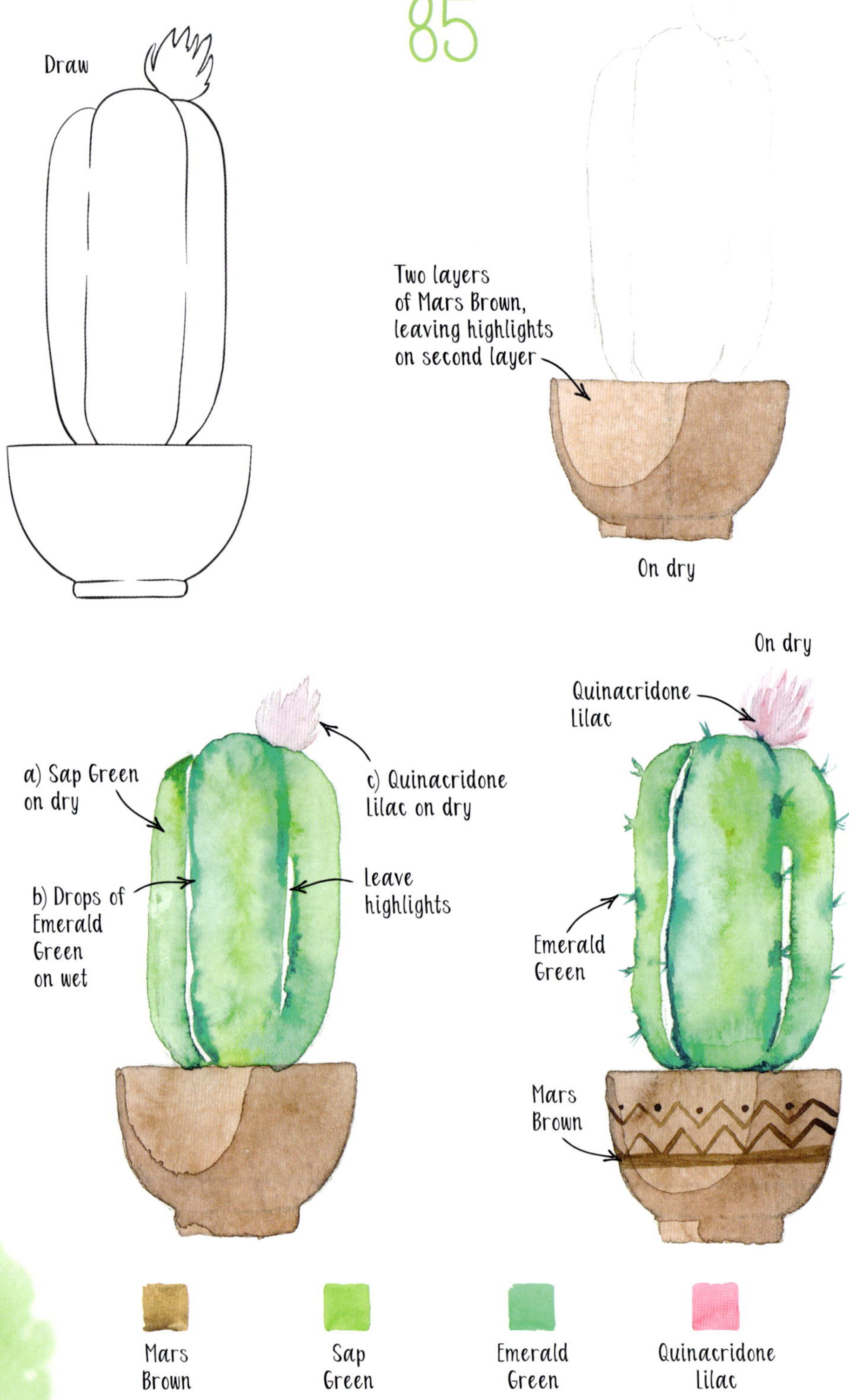

86

Draw
a) Masking fluid
(allow to dry)
c) Quinacridone Lilac
b) Sap Green
On wet

Starting on dry, apply second layer
of same colours to foreground leaves
a) Starting on dry, apply third layer
to form shading on foreground leaves
c) When paint
is dry, rub off
masking fluid
b) Burnt Sienna on dry, then
drops of Burnt Umber on wet
Masking
Fluid
Sap
Green
Quinacridone
Lilac
Burnt
Sienna
Burnt
Umber

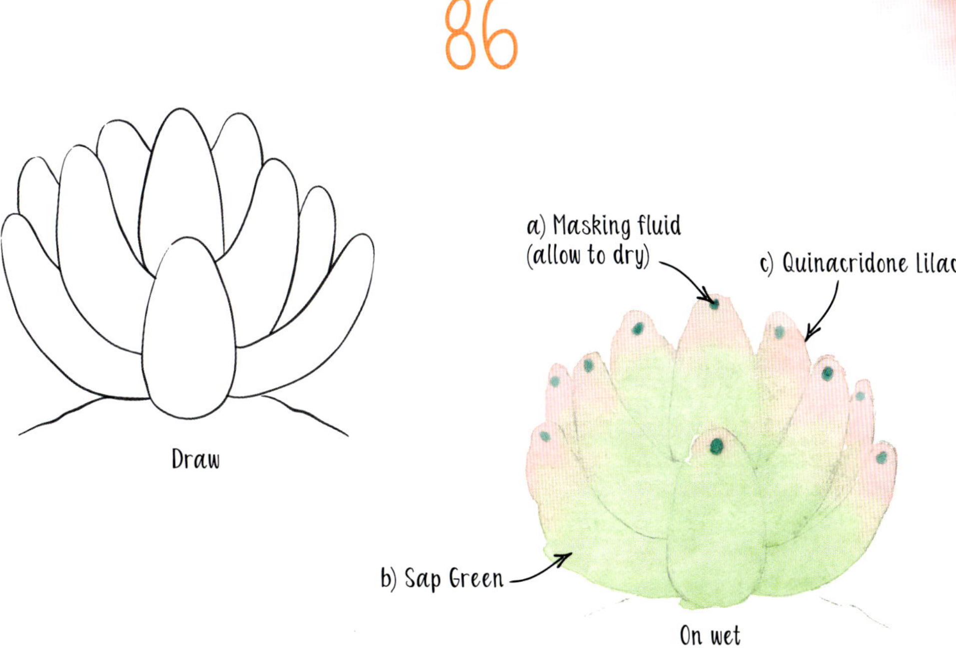

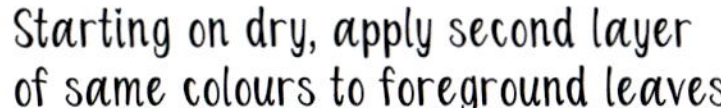

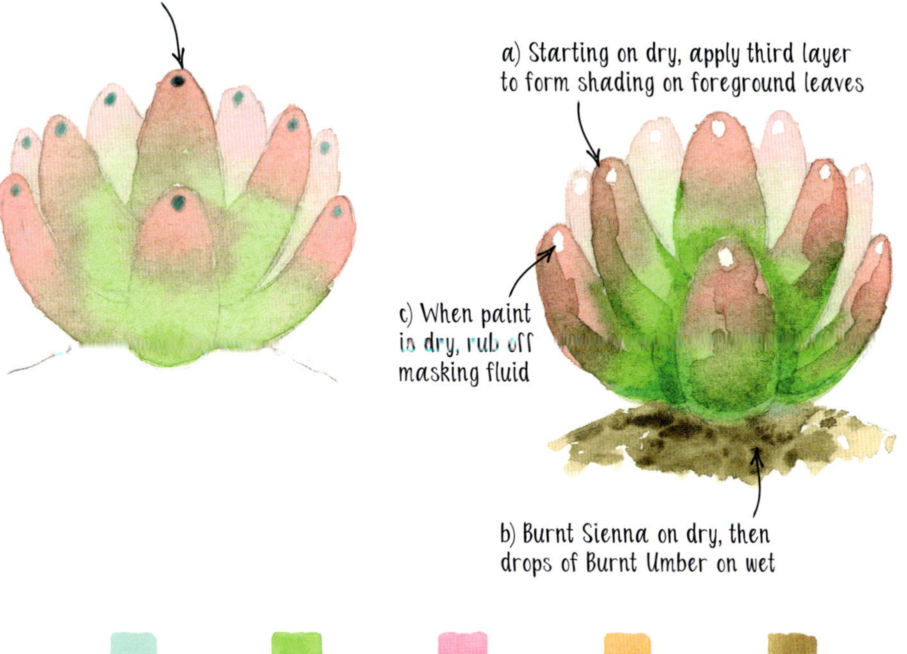

87

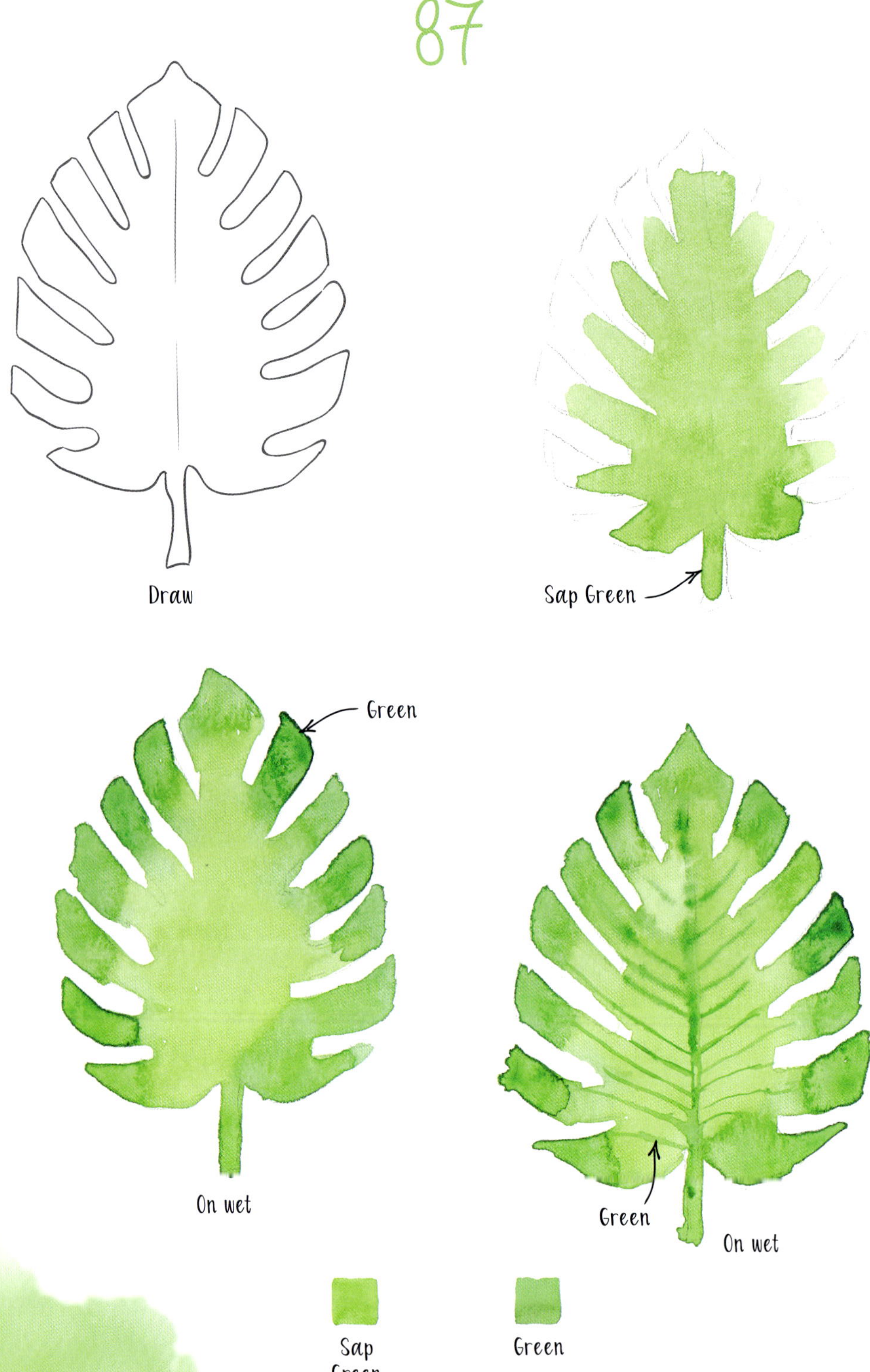

88

Draw

a) Masking fluid
(allow to dry)

b) Scarlet

On wet

Second layer
of Scarlet

Burnt Sienna

c) When paint is dry,
rub off masking fluid

a) Scarlet on dry,
leaving highlight

d) Indigo

b) Indigo + Burnt Sienna mix on
half-wet, then on dry for details

Masking
Fluid

Scarlet

Burnt
Sienna

Indigo

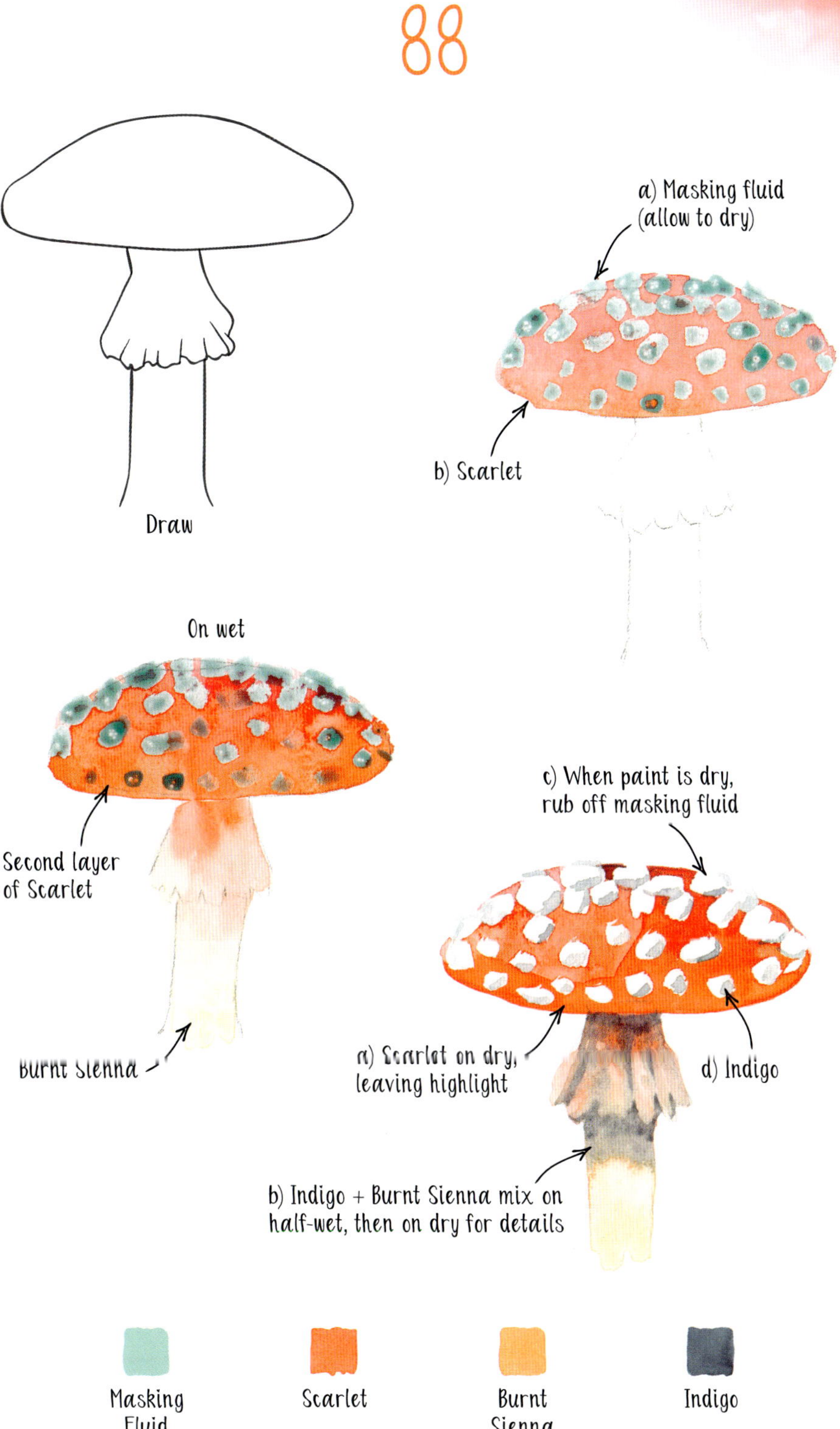

89

Draw

On wet

Azure

Violet

b) Drops of
Indigo on wet

Drops of
Azure +
Violet

a) Salt
on wet

On wet

c) When paint is dry, rub off salt

Azure

Violet

Sea
Salt

Indigo

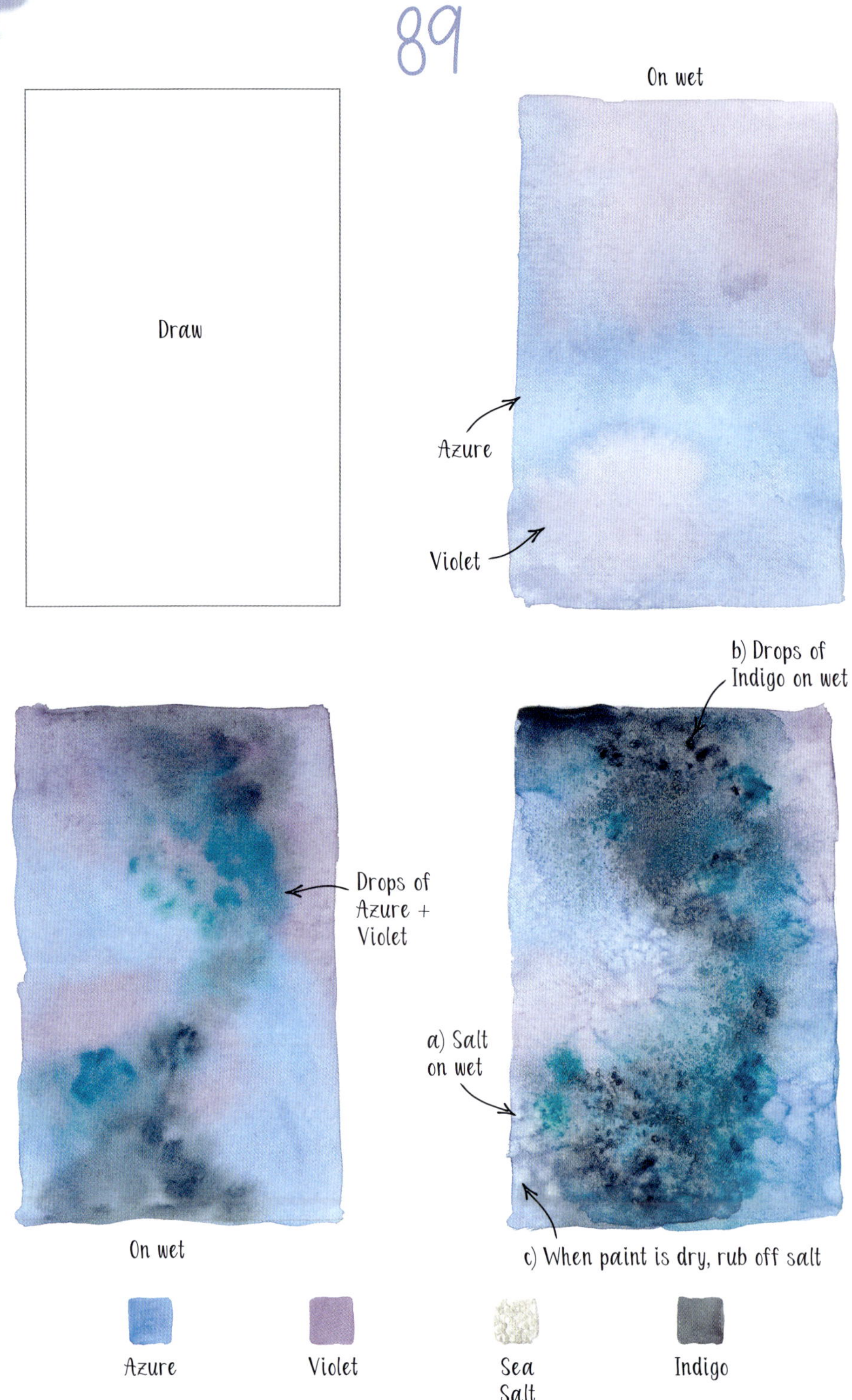

90

Draw

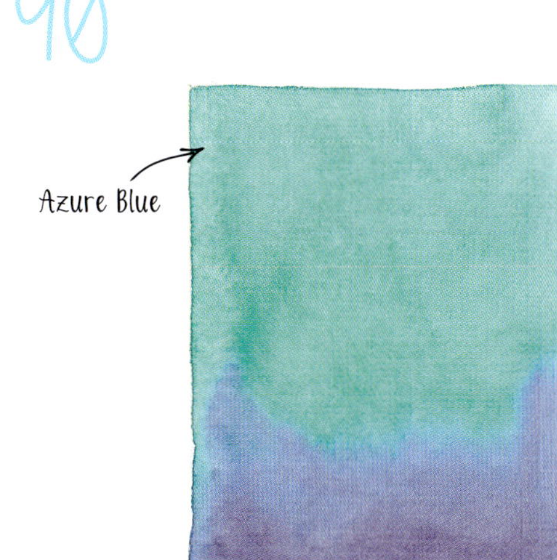

On wet

On wet

On half-wet

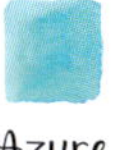

Azure
Blue

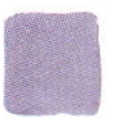

Violet

Indigo

91

Draw
a) Azure Blue
On wet
Leave highlights
b) Drops of Azure Blue

Drops of Neutral Black
On wet

Neutral Black (antennae, body + wing edges)
Azure Blue
On half-wet

Azure
Blue

Neutral
Black

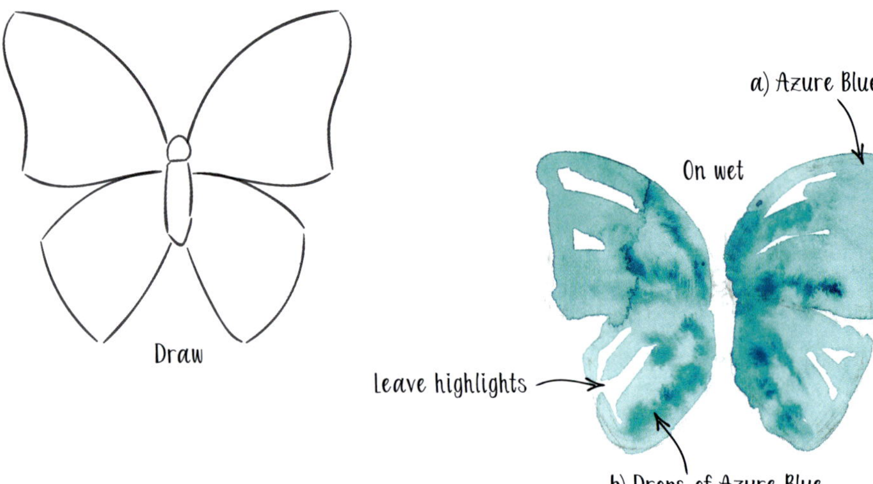

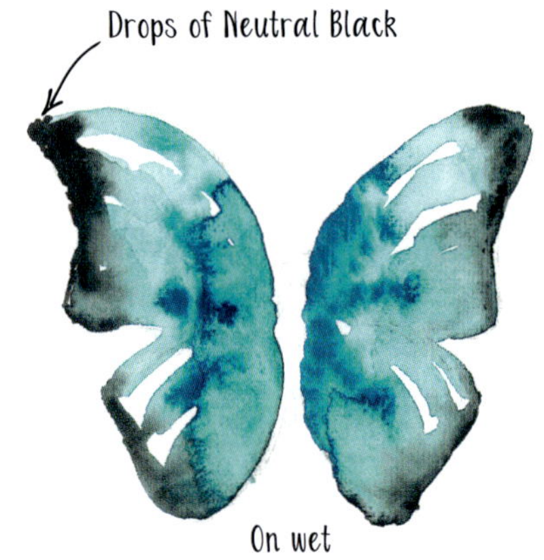

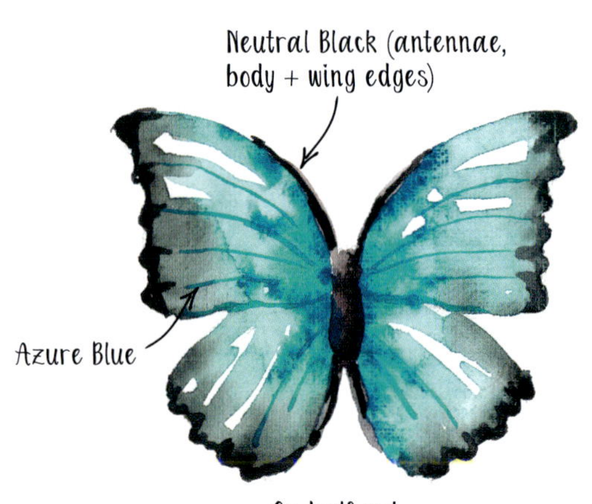

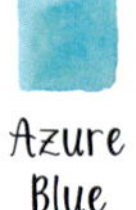

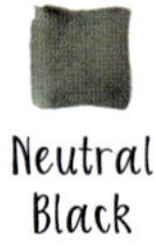

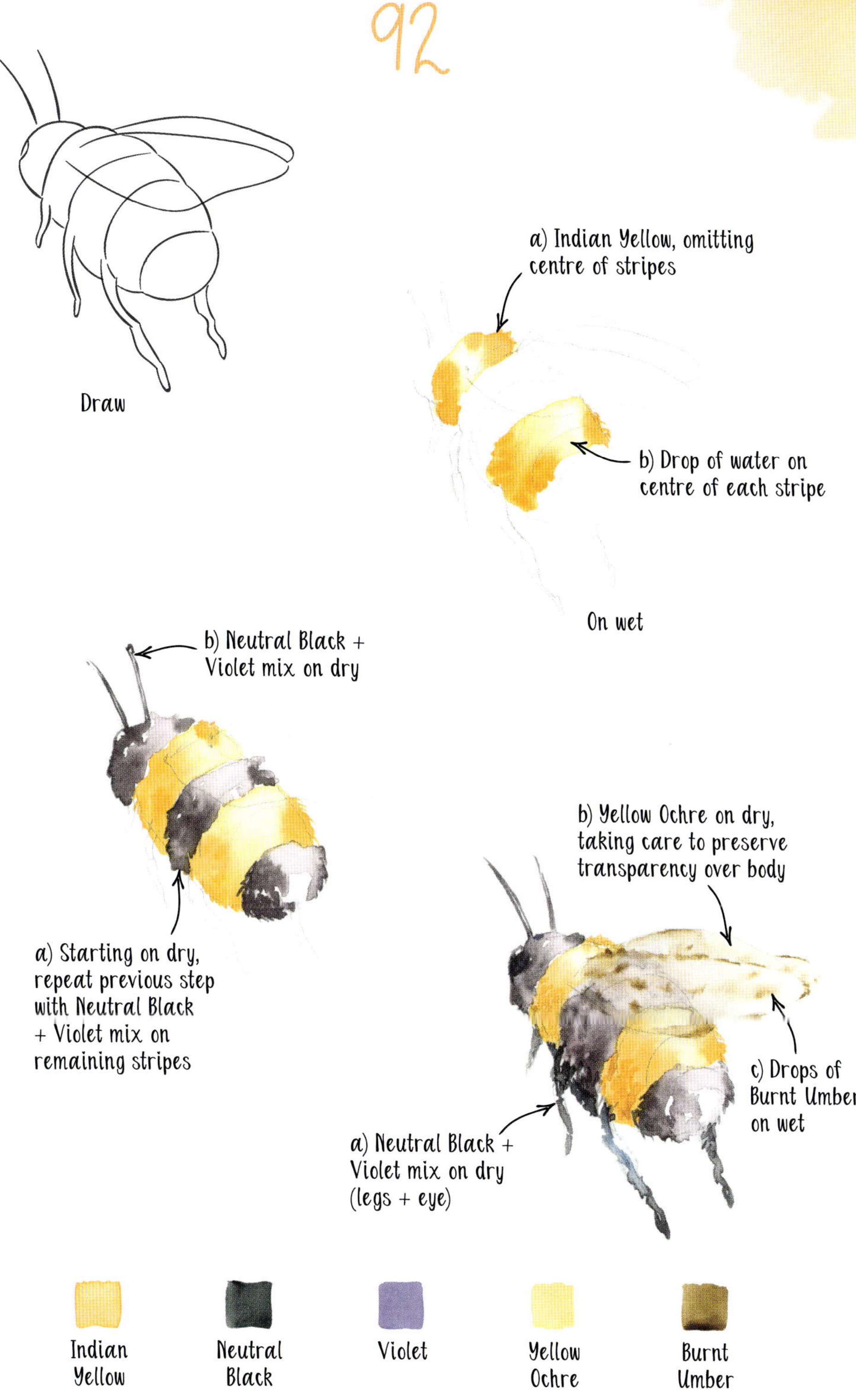

92

Draw

a) Indian Yellow, omitting centre of stripes

b) Drop of water on centre of each stripe

On wet

b) Neutral Black + Violet mix on dry

a) Starting on dry, repeat previous step with Neutral Black + Violet mix on remaining stripes

b) Yellow Ochre on dry, taking care to preserve transparency over body

c) Drops of Burnt Umber on wet

a) Neutral Black + Violet mix on dry (legs + eye)

Indian Yellow

Neutral Black

Violet

Yellow Ochre

Burnt Umber

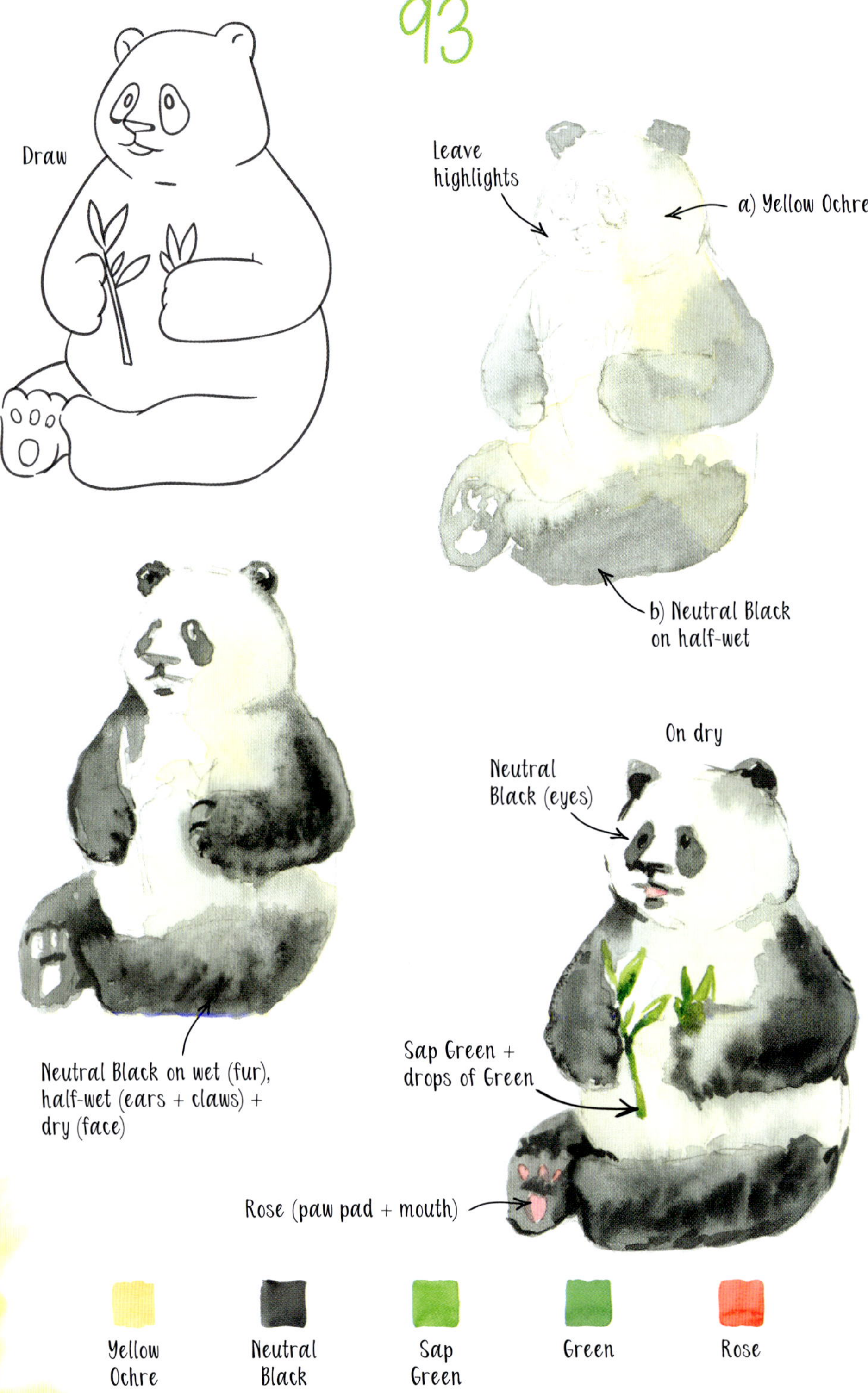

93
Draw
leave highlights
a) Yellow Ochre
b) Neutral Black on half-wet
Neutral Black on wet (fur), half-wet (ears + claws) + dry (face)
On dry
Neutral Black (eyes)
Sap Green + drops of Green
Rose (paw pad + mouth)
Yellow Ochre
Neutral Black
Sap Green
Green
Rose

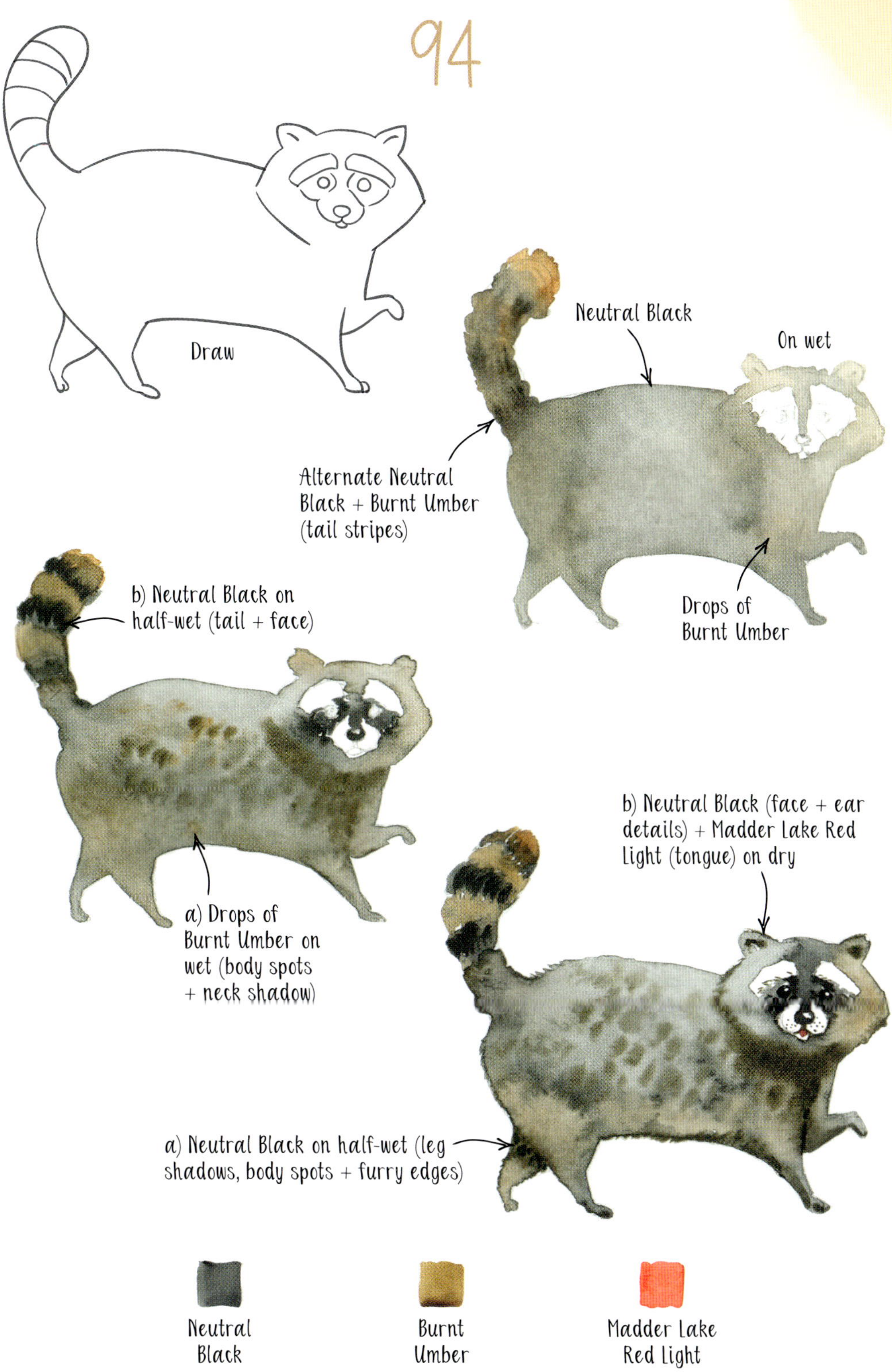

94
Draw
Neutral Black
On wet
Alternate Neutral Black + Burnt Umber (tail stripes)
Drops of Burnt Umber
b) Neutral Black on half-wet (tail + face)
a) Drops of Burnt Umber on wet (body spots + neck shadow)
b) Neutral Black (face + ear details) + Madder Lake Red Light (tongue) on dry
a) Neutral Black on half-wet (leg shadows, body spots + furry edges)
Neutral Black
Burnt Umber
Madder Lake Red light

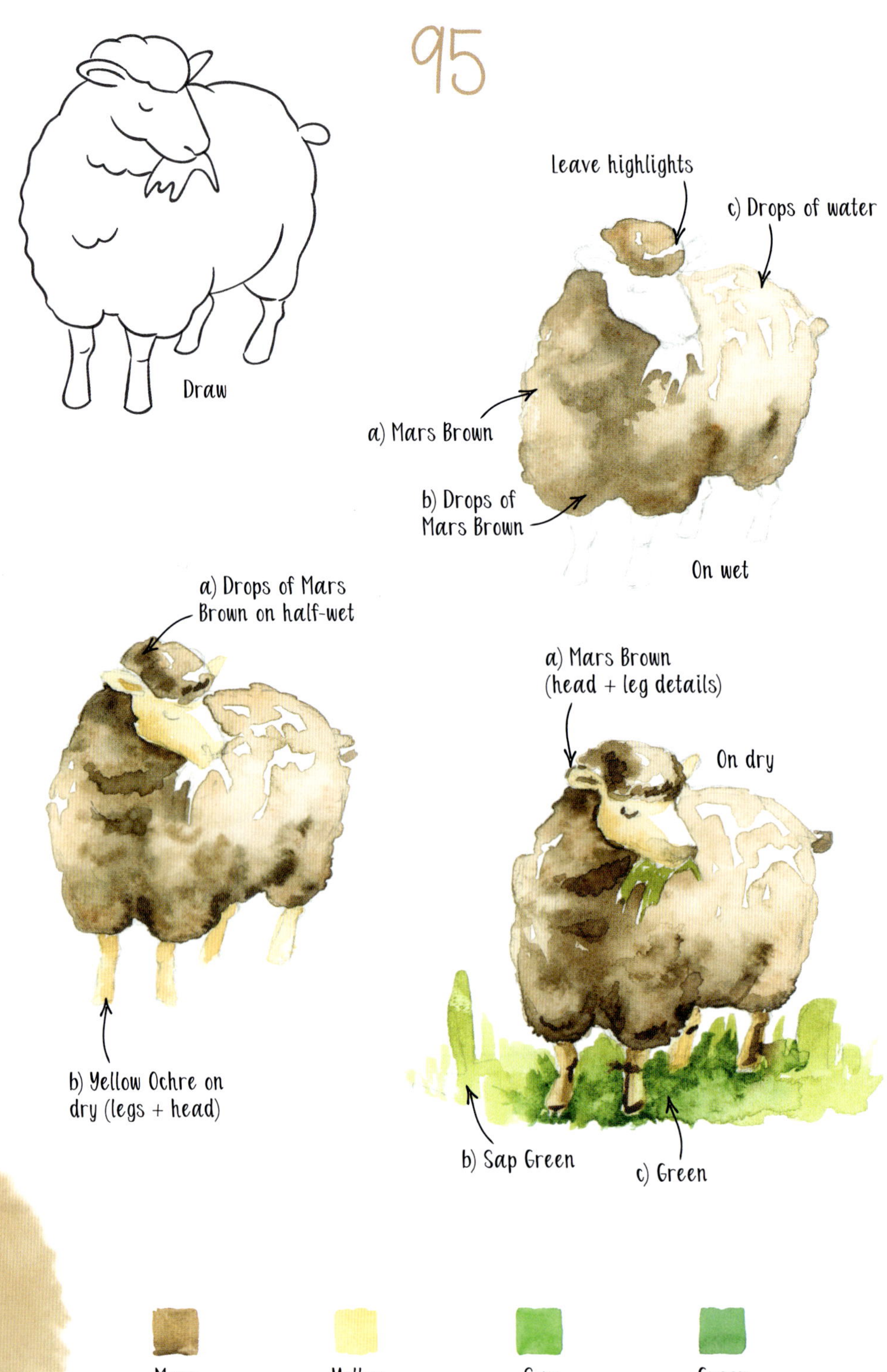
95

Draw

leave highlights

c) Drops of water

a) Mars Brown

b) Drops of
Mars Brown

On wet

a) Drops of Mars
Brown on half-wet

b) Yellow Ochre on
dry (legs + head)

a) Mars Brown
(head + leg details)

On dry

b) Sap Green

c) Green

Mars
Brown

Yellow
Ochre

Sap
Green

Green

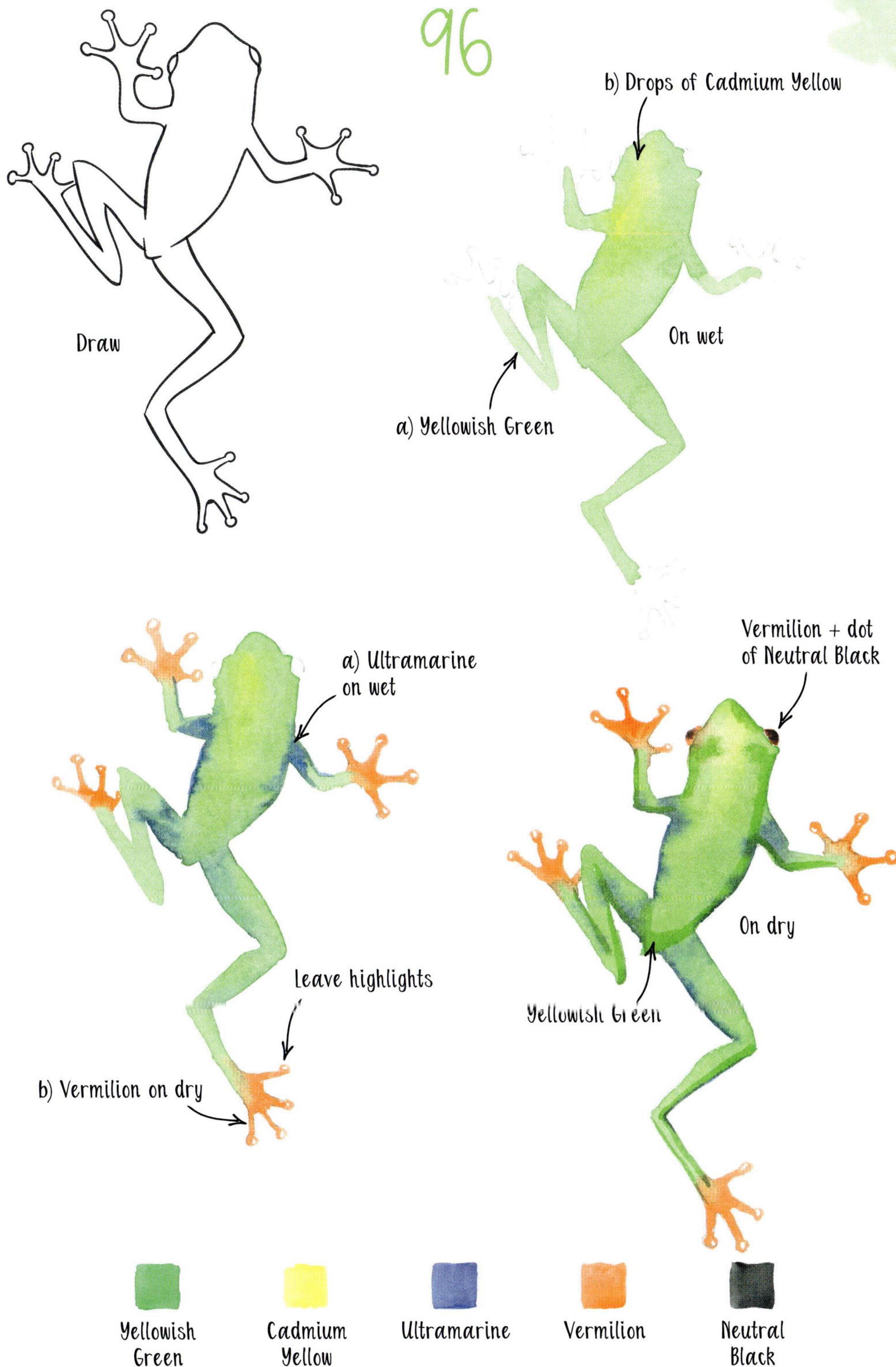
96
Draw
b) Drops of Cadmium Yellow
On wet
a) Yellowish Green
a) Ultramarine on wet
Vermilion + dot of Neutral Black
Leave highlights
On dry
b) Vermilion on dry
Yellowish Green
Yellowish Green
Cadmium Yellow
Ultramarine
Vermilion
Neutral Black

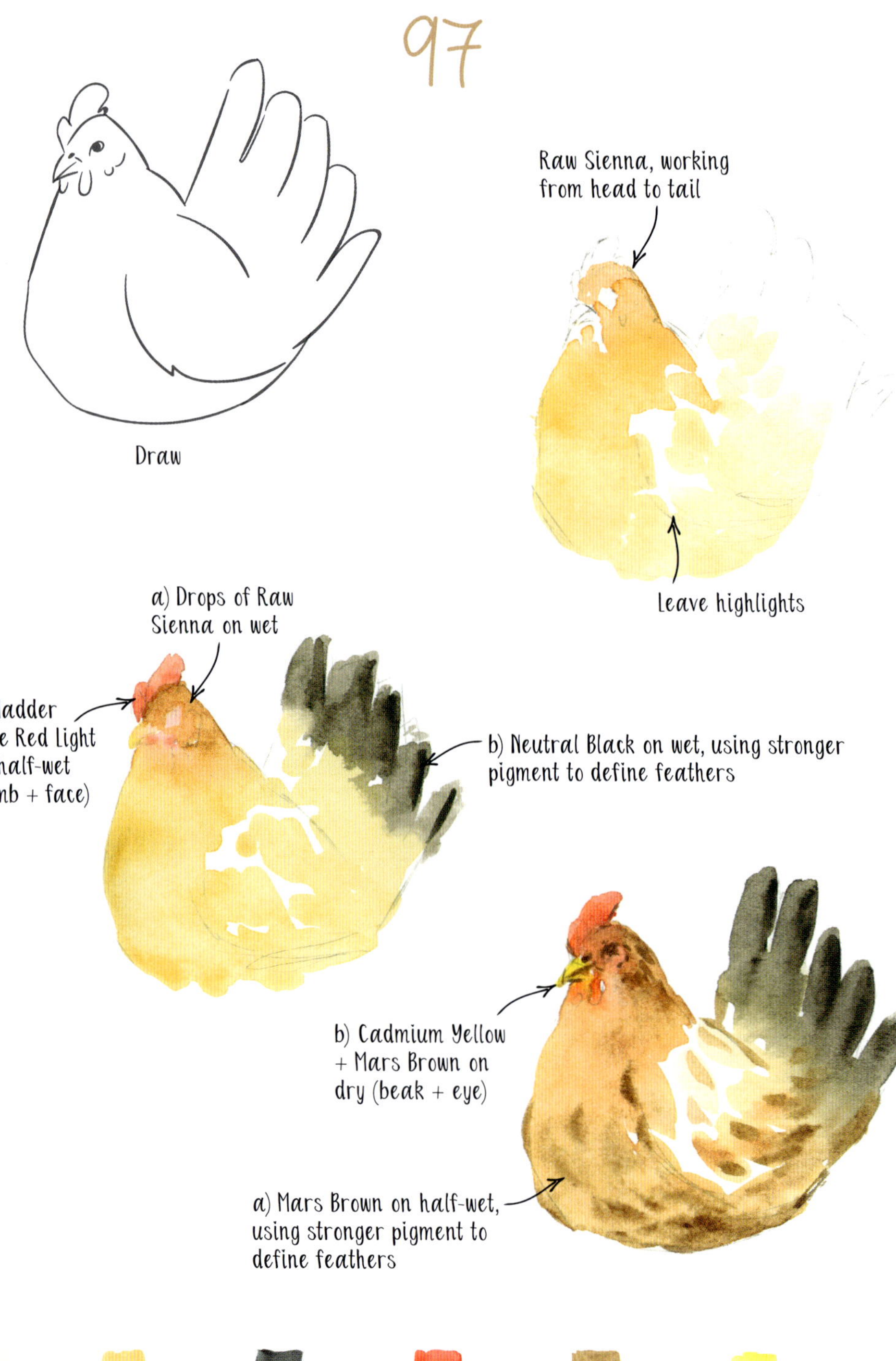
97

Draw

Raw Sienna, working
from head to tail

leave highlights

a) Drops of Raw
Sienna on wet

c) Madder
Lake Red Light
on half-wet
(comb + face)

b) Neutral Black on wet, using stronger
pigment to define feathers

b) Cadmium Yellow
+ Mars Brown on
dry (beak + eye)

a) Mars Brown on half-wet,
using stronger pigment to
define feathers

Raw
Sienna

Neutral
Black

Madder Lake
Red Light

Mars
Brown

Cadmium
Yellow

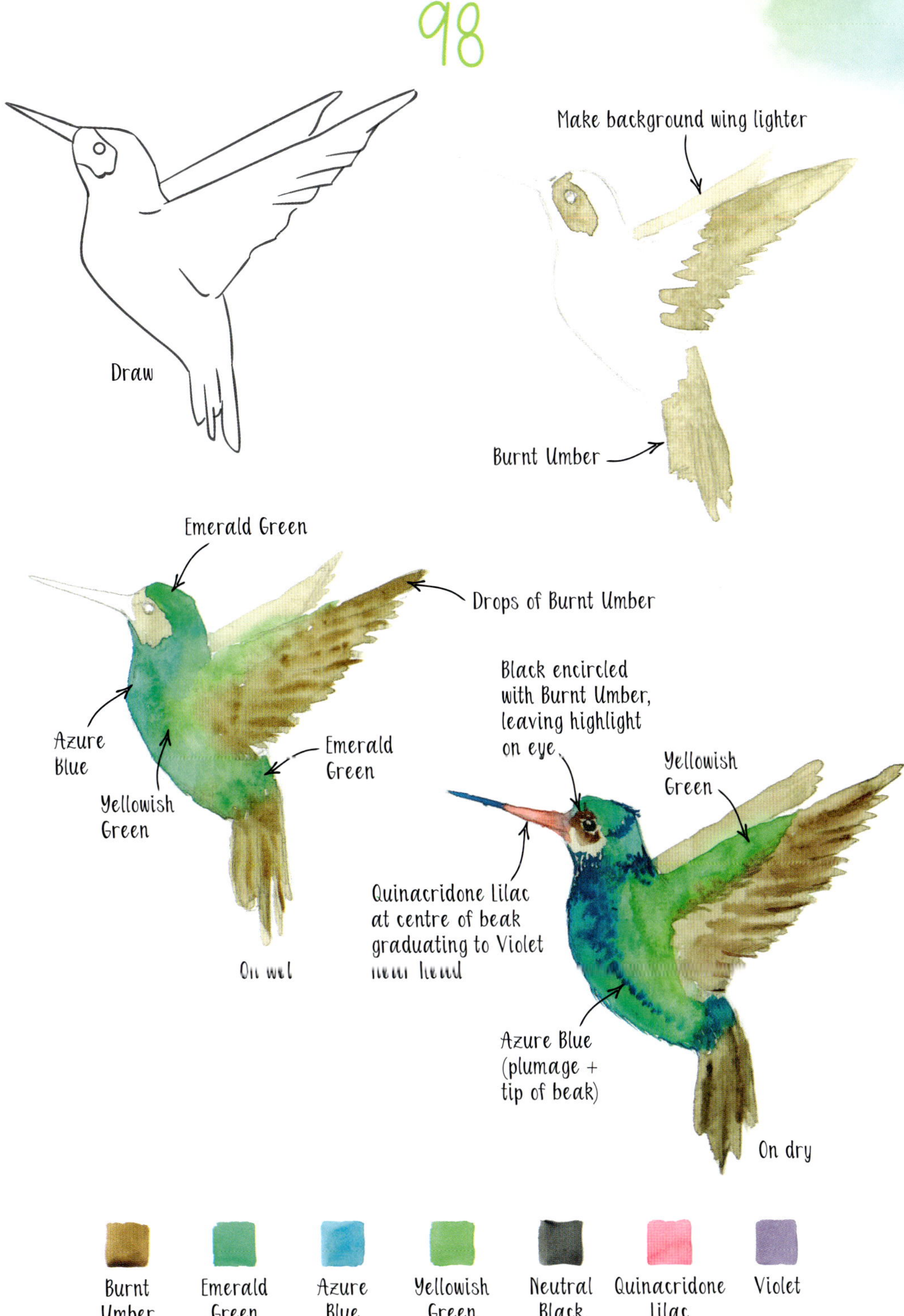
98

Draw

Make background wing lighter

Burnt Umber

Emerald Green

Drops of Burnt Umber

Azure Blue

Yellowish Green

Emerald Green

On wet

Black encircled with Burnt Umber, leaving highlight on eye

Yellowish Green

Quinacridone Lilac at centre of beak graduating to Violet near head

Azure Blue (plumage + tip of beak)

On dry

Burnt Umber

Emerald Green

Azure Blue

Yellowish Green

Neutral Black

Quinacridone Lilac

Violet

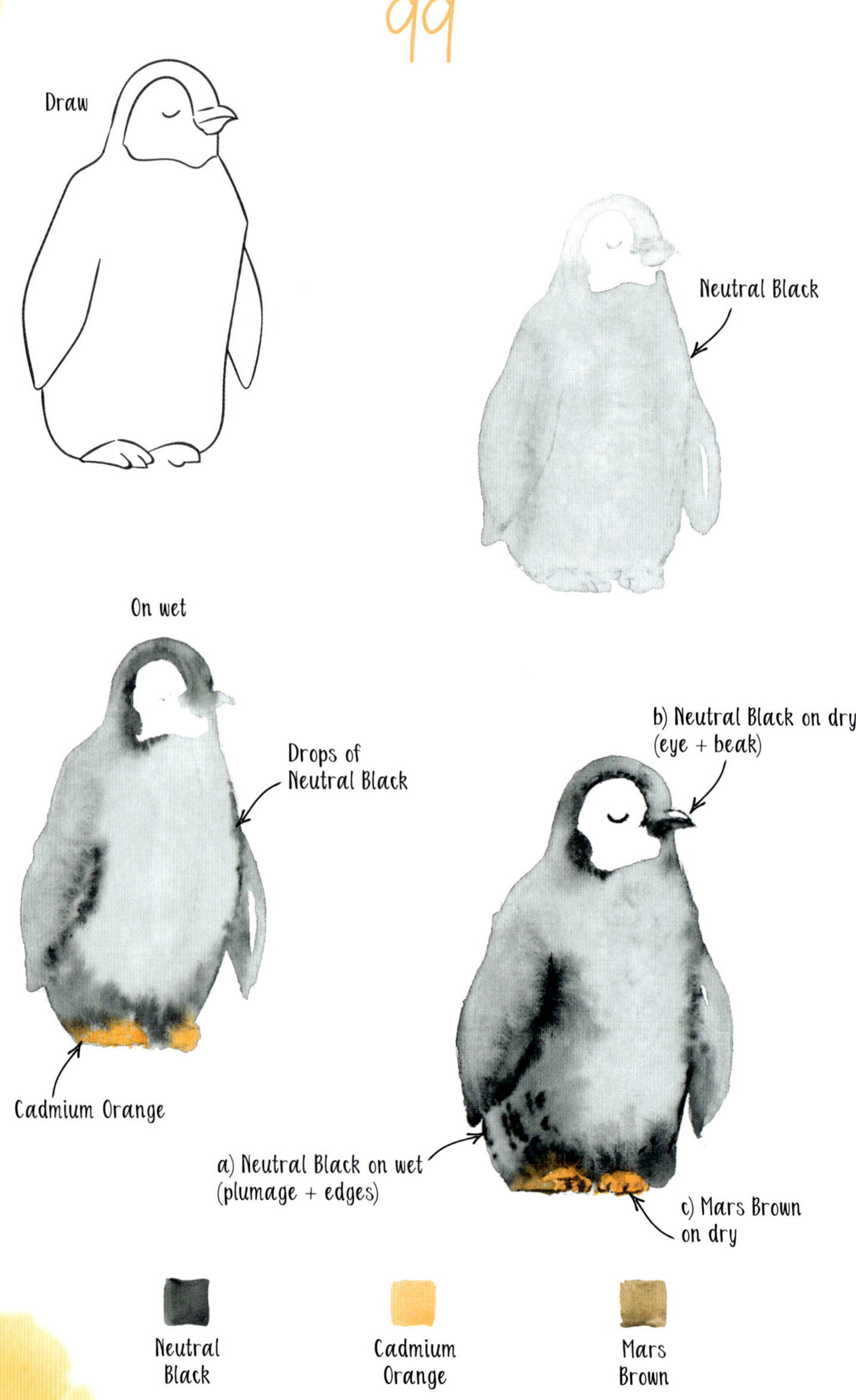
99
Draw
Neutral Black
On wet
Drops of
Neutral Black
Cadmium Orange
b) Neutral Black on dry
(eye + beak)
a) Neutral Black on wet
(plumage + edges)
c) Mars Brown
on dry
Neutral
Black
Cadmium
Orange
Mars
Brown

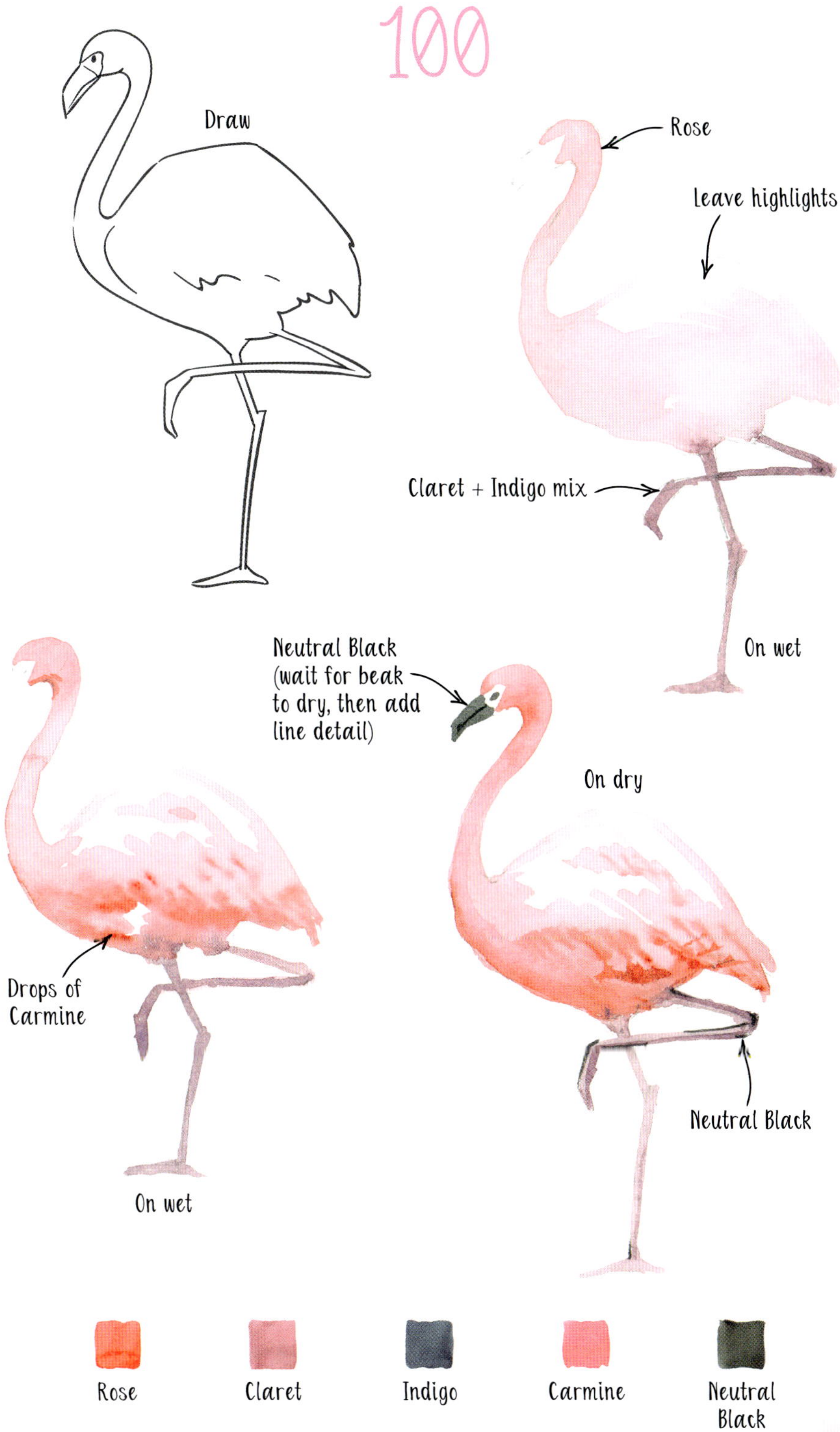
100
Draw
Rose
leave highlights
Claret + Indigo mix
On wet
Neutral Black
(wait for beak
to dry, then add
line detail)
On dry
Drops of
Carmine
On wet
Neutral Black
Rose
Claret
Indigo
Carmine
Neutral
Black

101

Draw
On wet
Azure Blue
Indigo
Burnt Sienna
a) Repeat previous step, starting on dry
On dry
Ultramarine
b) Drops of Ultramarine on wet
c) Ultramarine on dry
Ultramarine
Azure Blue
Indigo
Burnt Sienna

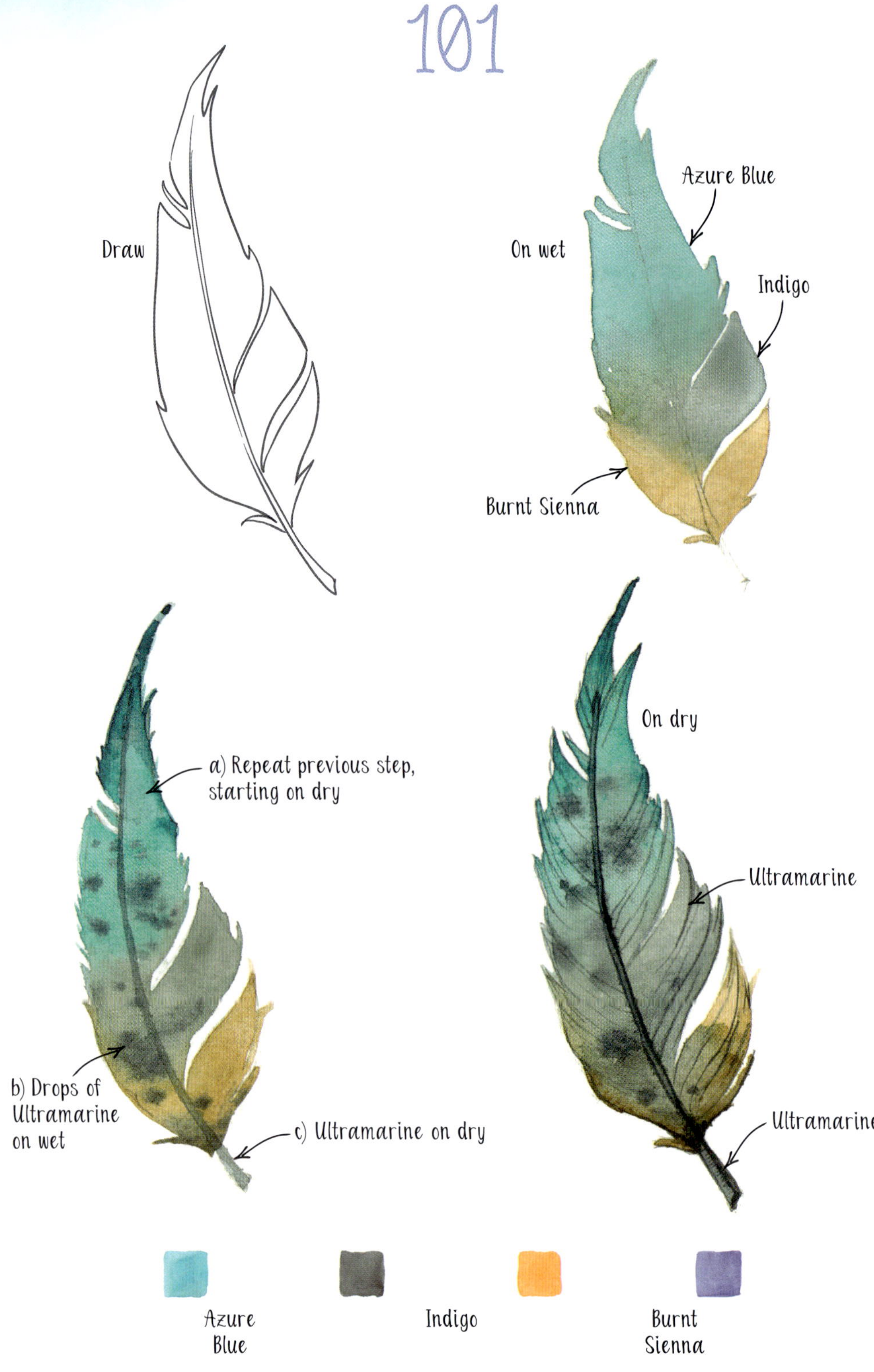

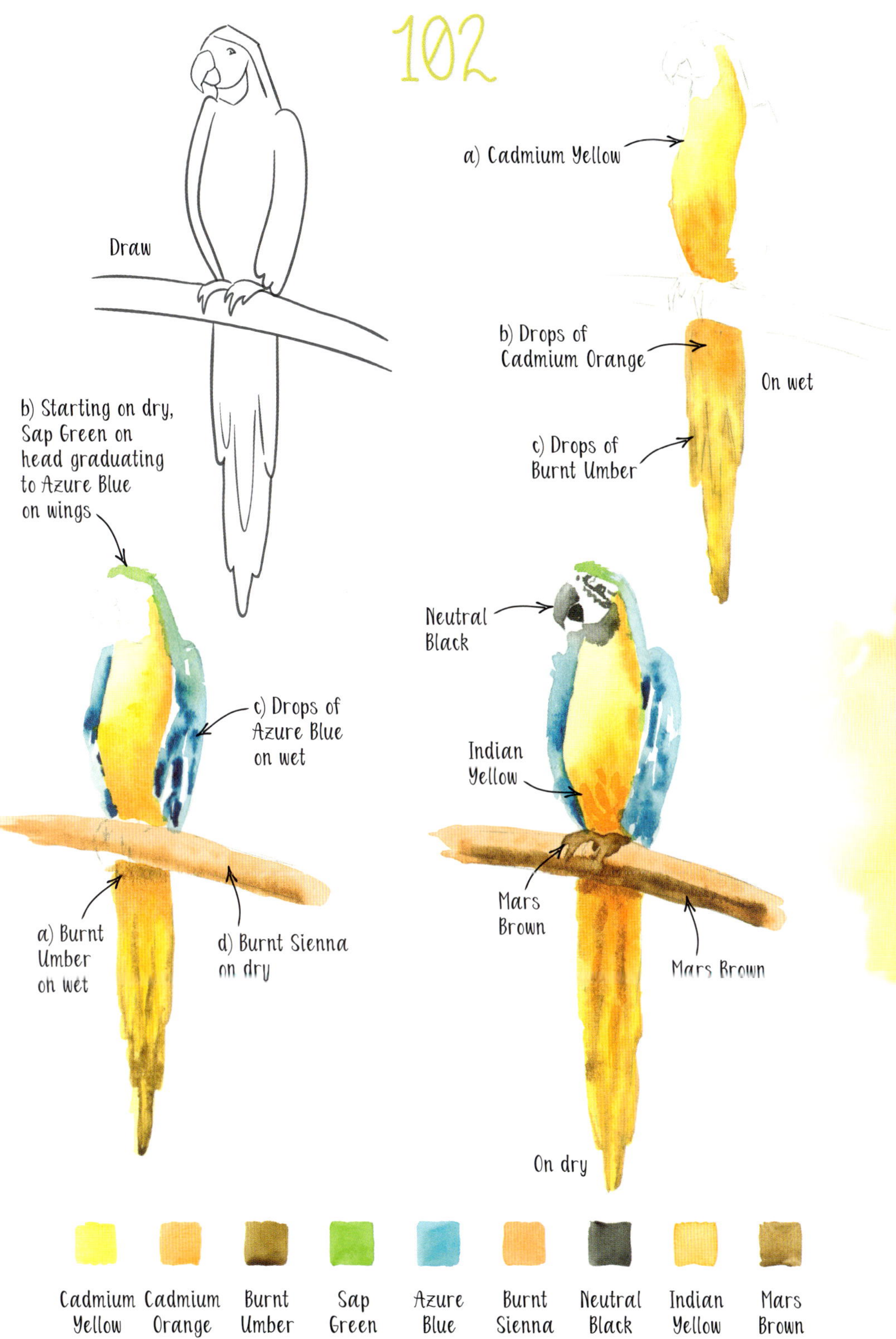
102
Draw
a) Cadmium Yellow
b) Starting on dry, Sap Green on head graduating to Azure Blue on wings
b) Drops of Cadmium Orange
On wet
c) Drops of Burnt Umber
c) Drops of Azure Blue on wet
Neutral Black
Indian Yellow
a) Burnt Umber on wet
d) Burnt Sienna on dry
Mars Brown
Mars Brown
On dry
Cadmium Yellow
Cadmium Orange
Burnt Umber
Sap Green
Azure Blue
Burnt Sienna
Neutral Black
Indian Yellow
Mars Brown

103

Draw

leave highlights

Neutral Black,
strongest near belly

a) Vermilion (bill + feet)

b) Second layer
of Neutral Black

On dry

b) Neutral Black on dry

a) Drops of
Burnt Umber
on wet

Neutral
Black

Vermilion

Burnt
Umber

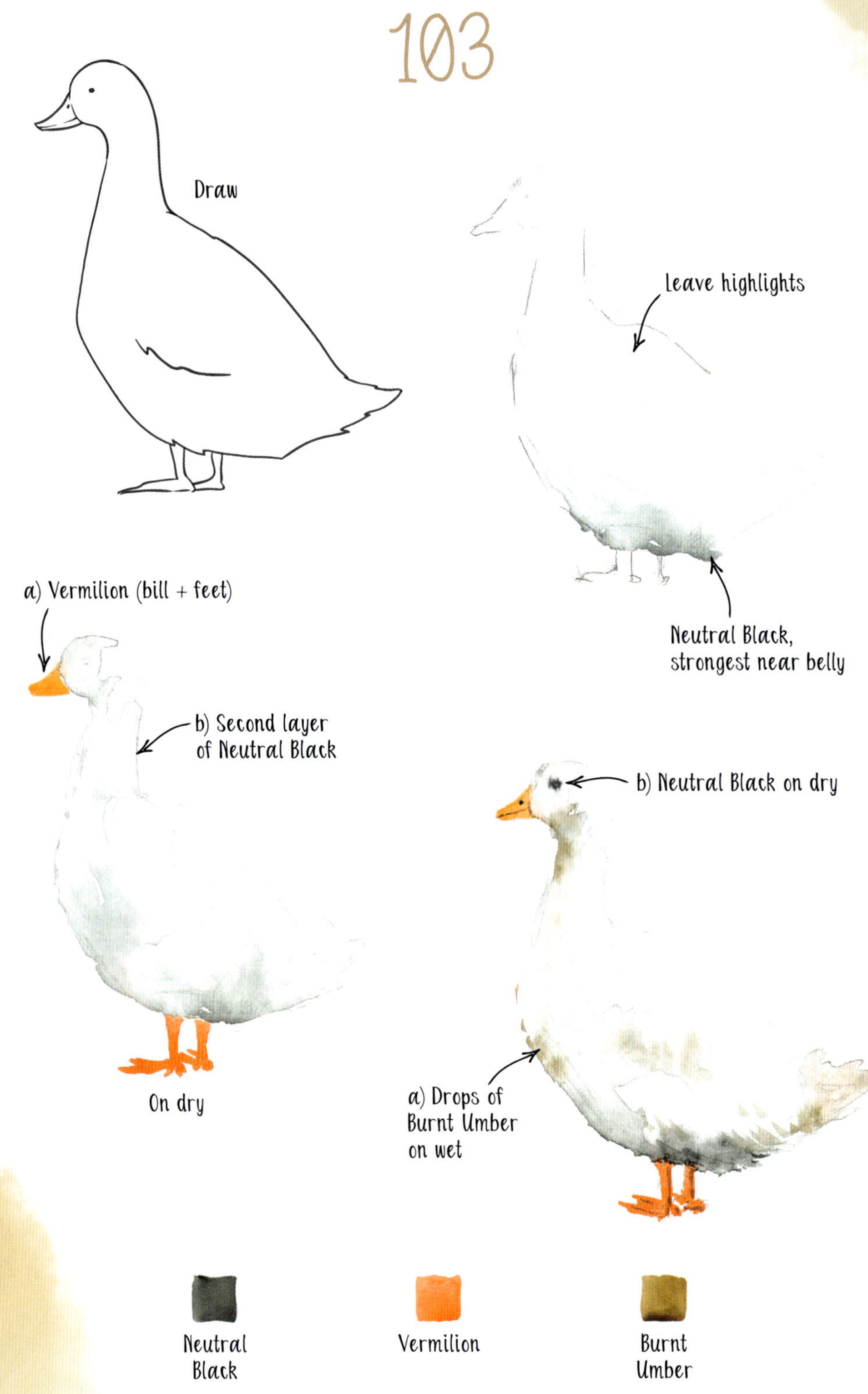

104

Draw
a) Sepia in various dilutions, starting with lightest
b) Drops of Cadmium Orange on wet
c) Cadmium Orange on dry
b) Emerald Green on dry
c) Drops of Green on wet
a) Sepia on dry
a) Drops of Sap Green on wet
b) Cadmium Yellow on dry
c) Drops of Sepia on wet
d) Sepia on dry (eyes)
e) Burnt Umber on dry
Sepia
Cadmium Orange
Emerald Green
Green
Sap Green
Cadmium Yellow
Burnt Umber

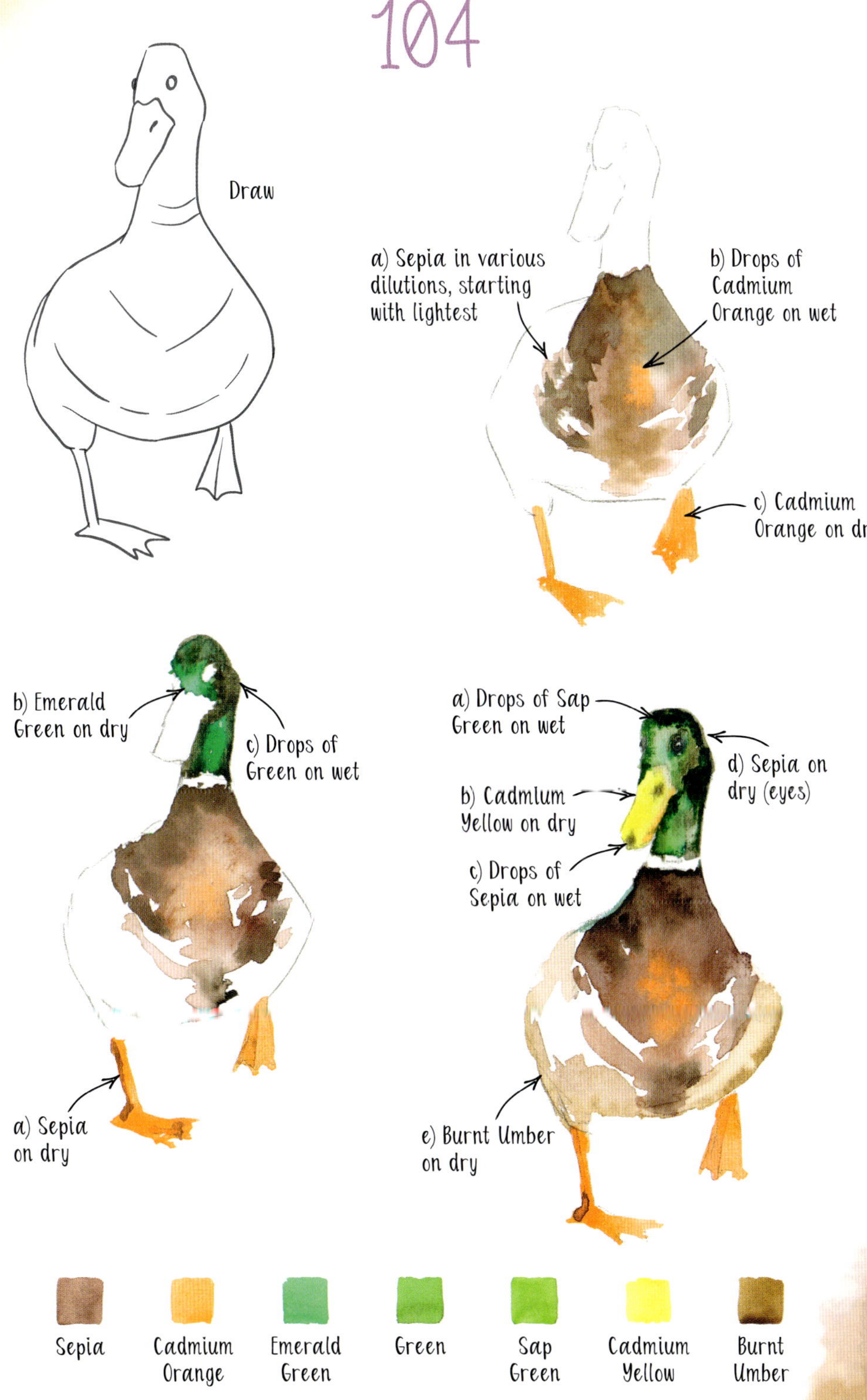

105

Draw

a) Neutral Black
(breast + crown)

On wet

b) Drops of
Burnt Umber

a) Burnt Umber
(head, wings + tail)

c) Cadmium Yellow

b) Drops of
Burnt Umber

leave
highlights

On wet

a) Neutral Black on wet (face + feathers)
+ then on dry (eye + around beak)

b) Cadmium
Orange on dry

d) Olive Green on dry

c) Burnt Umber on
dry (branch + feet)

Neutral
Black

Burnt
Umber

Cadmium
Yellow

Cadmium
Orange

Olive
Green

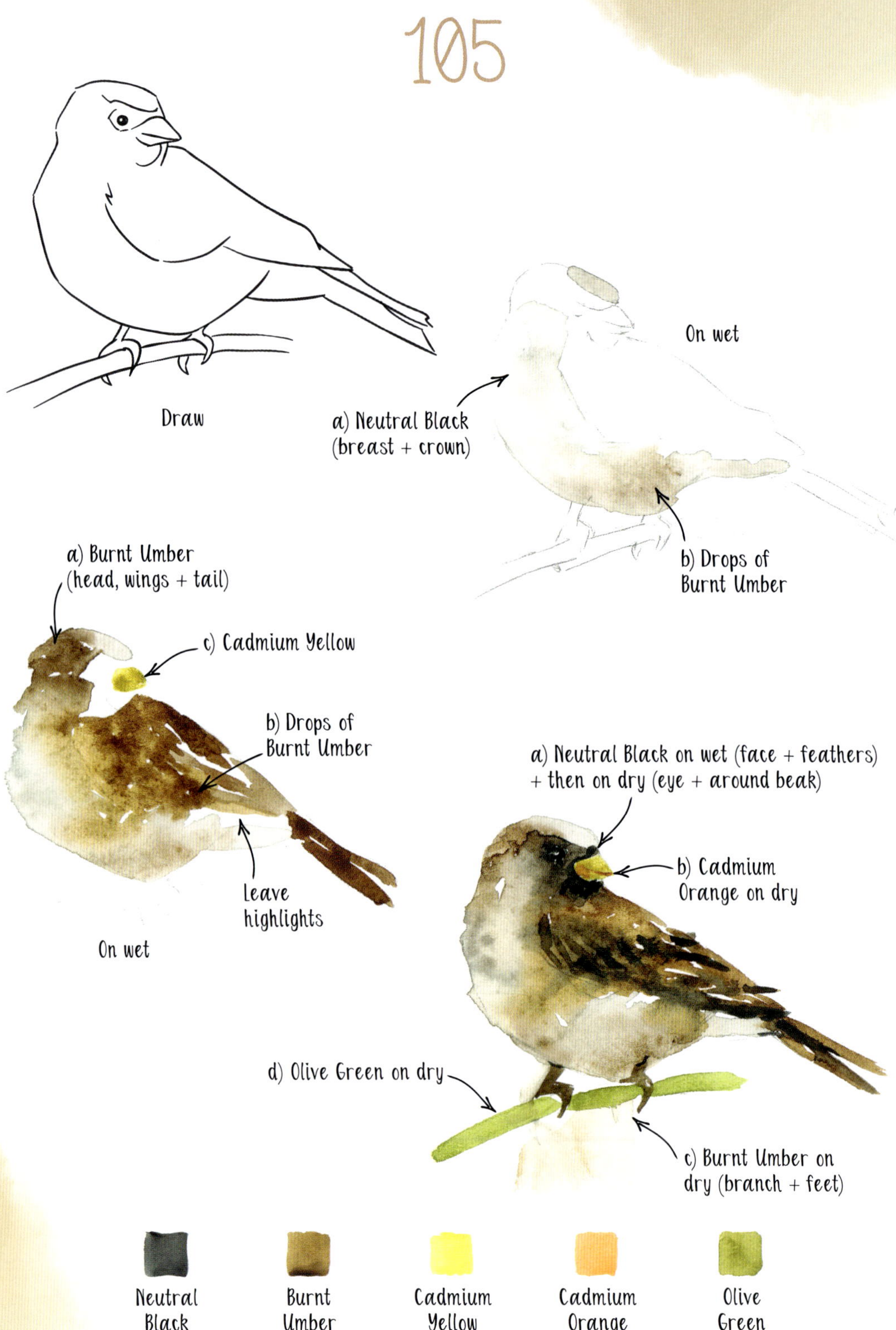

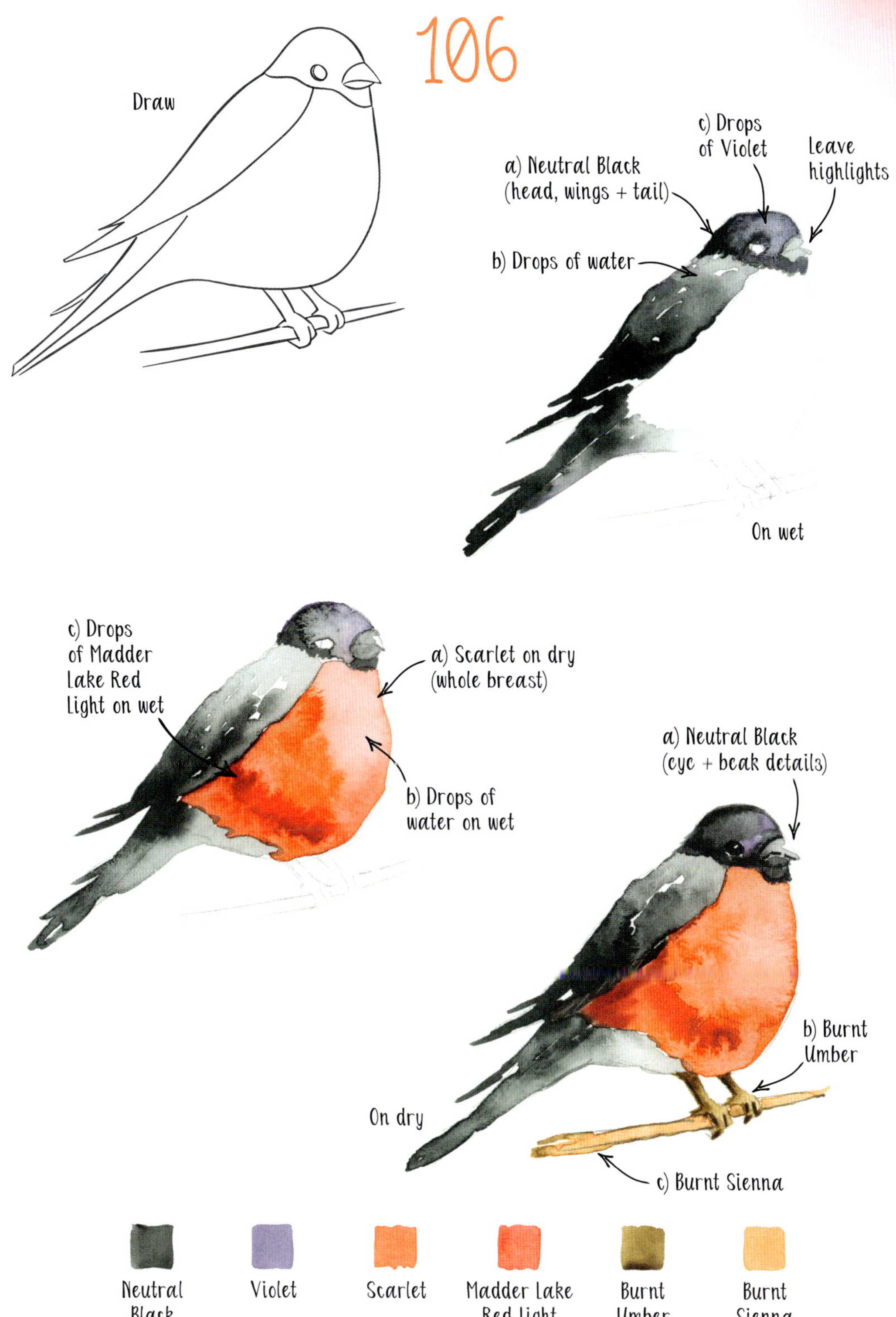

106
Draw
a) Neutral Black
(head, wings + tail)
c) Drops
of Violet
leave
highlights
b) Drops of water
On wet
c) Drops
of Madder
Lake Red
Light on wet
a) Scarlet on dry
(whole breast)
b) Drops of
water on wet
a) Neutral Black
(eye + beak details)
b) Burnt
Umber
On dry
c) Burnt Sienna
Neutral
Black
Violet
Scarlet
Madder Lake
Red Light
Burnt
Umber
Burnt
Sienna

107

Draw
a) Azure Blue
b) Drops of Azure
On wet
Drops of Violet
On wet
Drops of Azure
Drops of Indigo
On wet
Azure Blue
Azure
Violet
Indigo

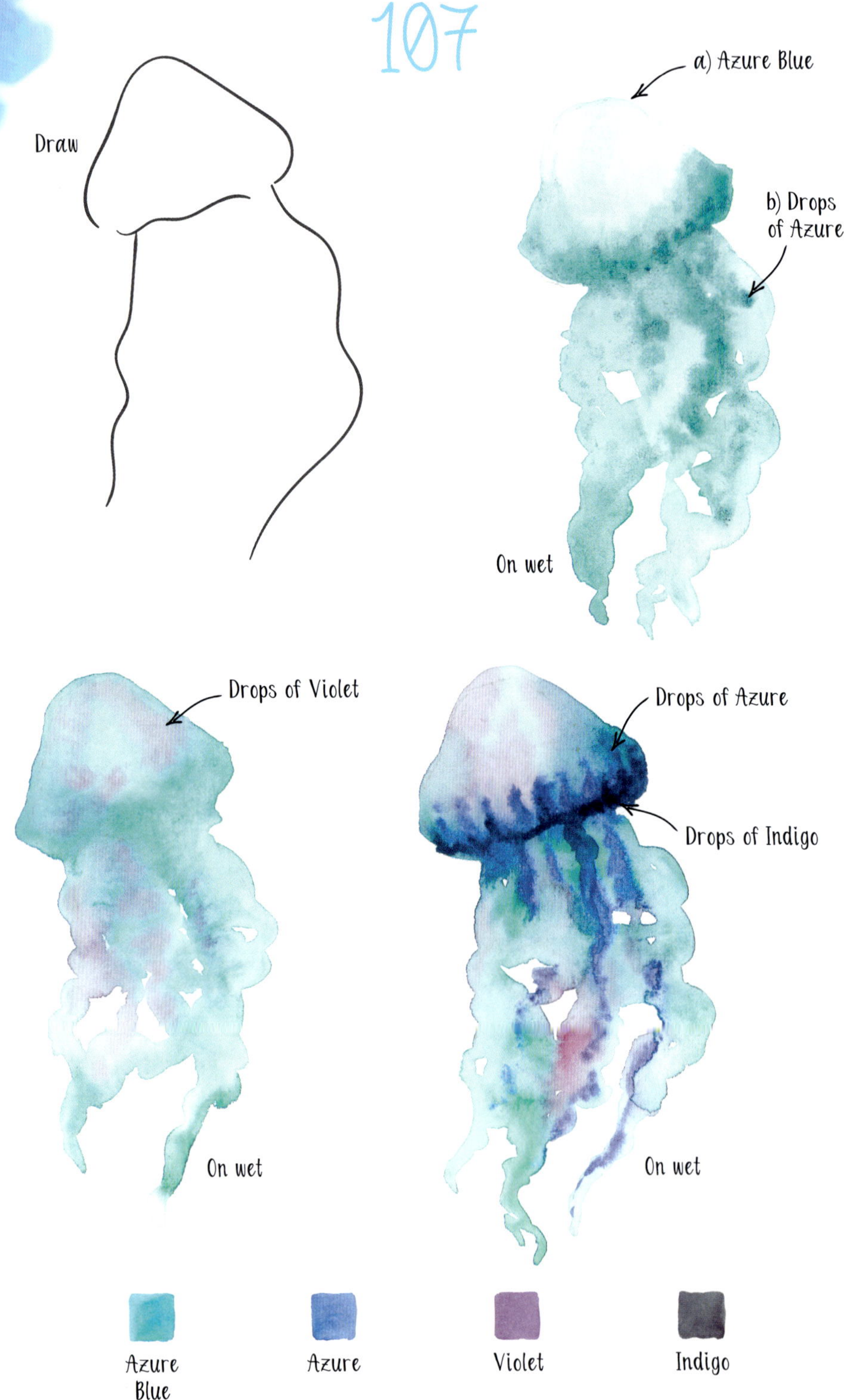

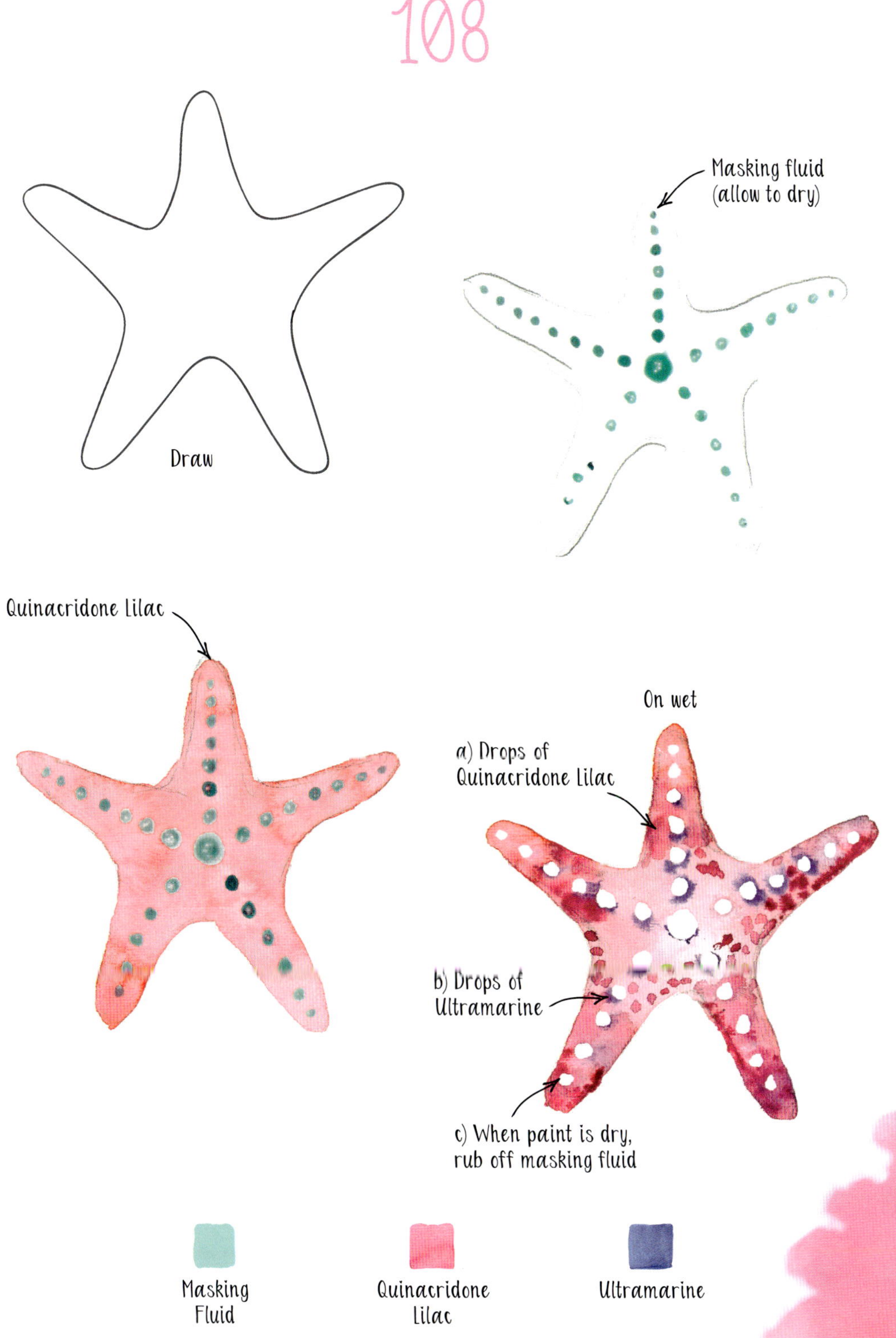

108
Draw
Masking fluid
(allow to dry)
Quinacridone Lilac
On wet
a) Drops of
Quinacridone Lilac
b) Drops of
Ultramarine
c) When paint is dry,
rub off masking fluid
Masking
Fluid
Quinacridone
Lilac
Ultramarine

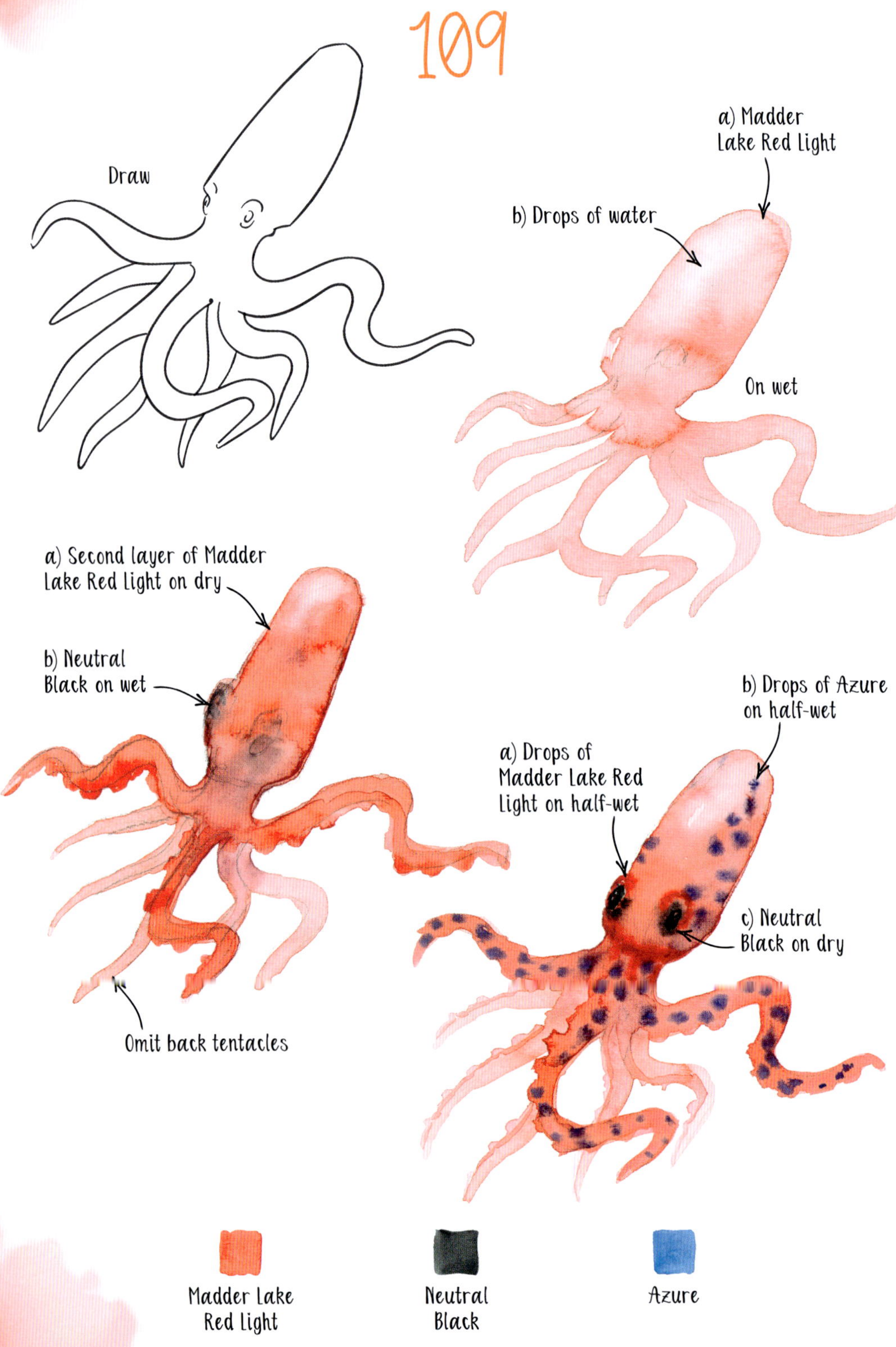

109
Draw
a) Madder Lake Red Light
b) Drops of water
On wet
a) Second layer of Madder Lake Red light on dry
b) Neutral Black on wet
Omit back tentacles
b) Drops of Azure on half-wet
a) Drops of Madder Lake Red light on half-wet
c) Neutral Black on dry
Madder lake Red light
Neutral Black
Azure

110

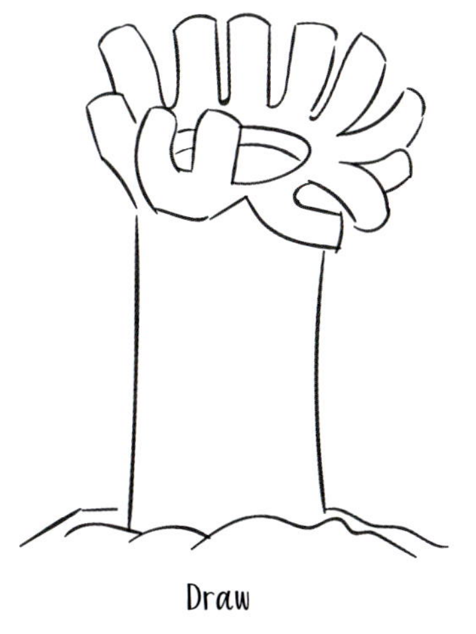

Draw

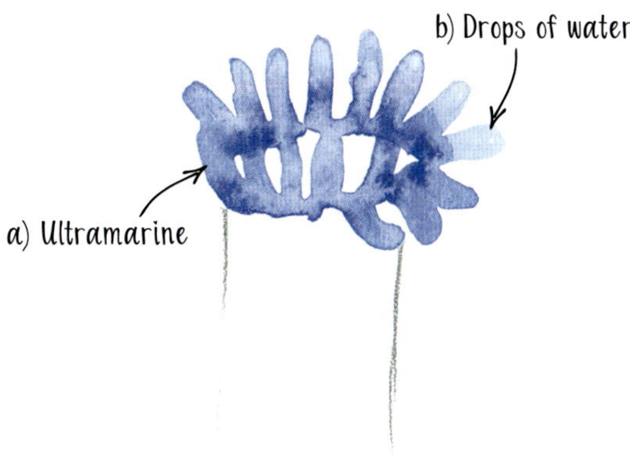

On wet

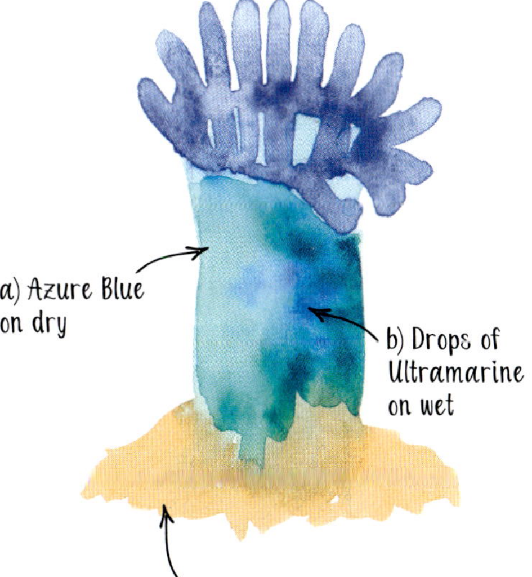

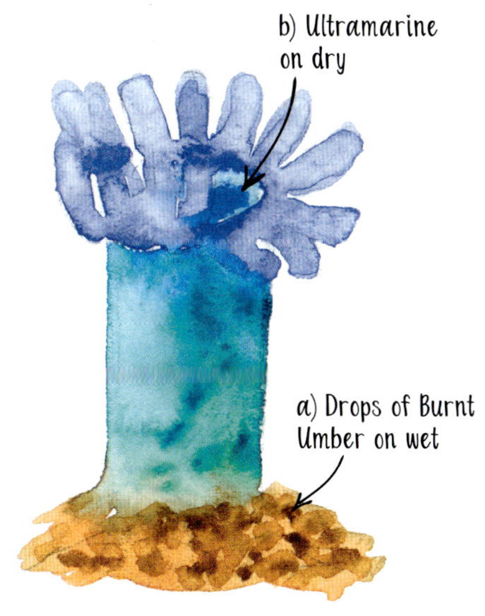

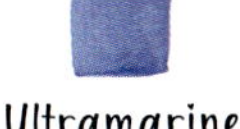

Ultramarine

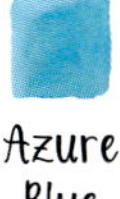

Azure
Blue

Burnt
Sienna

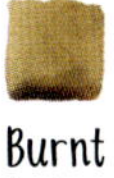

Burnt
Umber

111

Draw
Masking fluid
(allow to dry)
Indigo
a) Drops of Indigo on wet
(shading on tail, fin,
mouth + lower edges)
b) Indigo on dry (eye)
c) When paint is dry,
rub off masking fluid
Masking
Fluid
Indigo

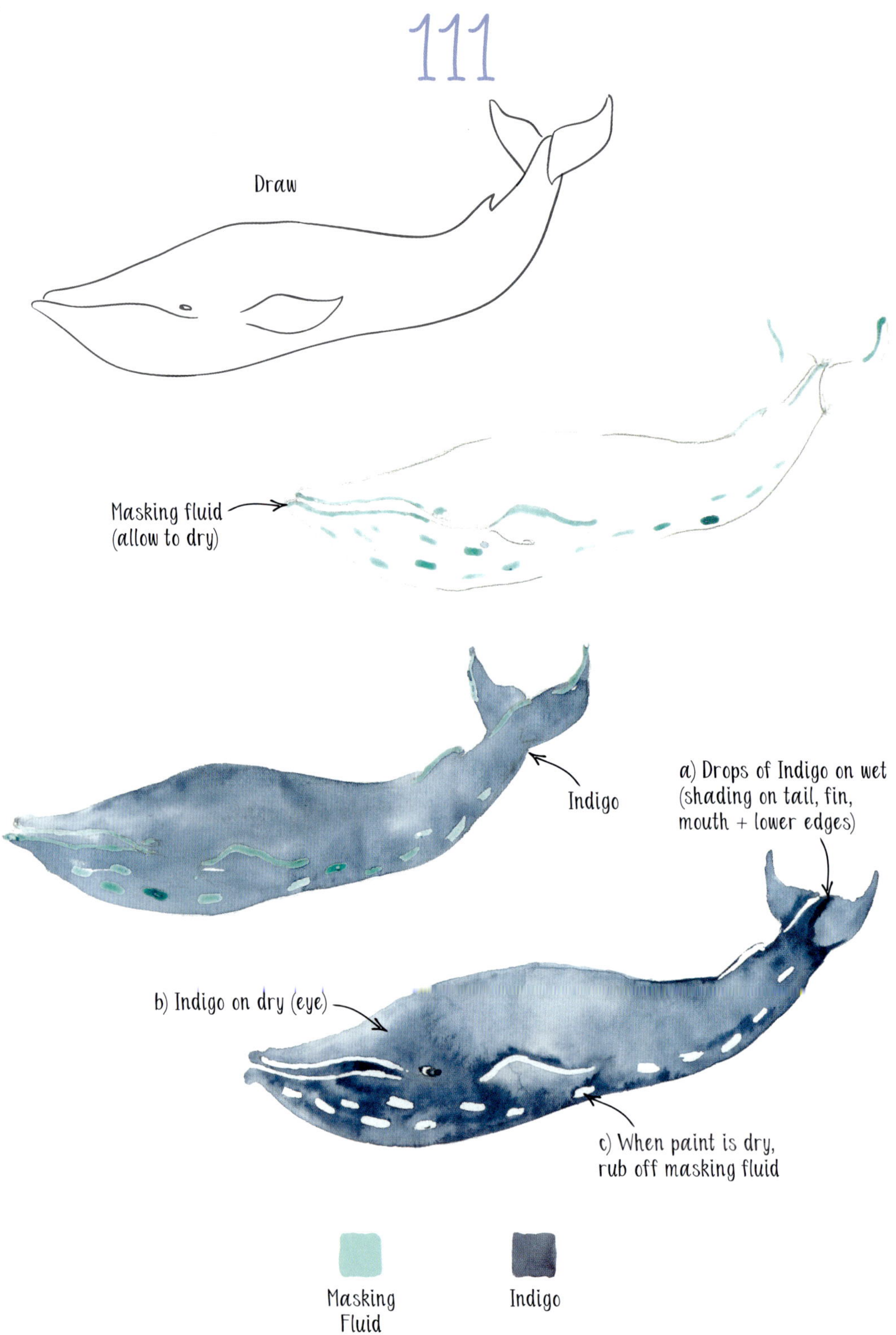

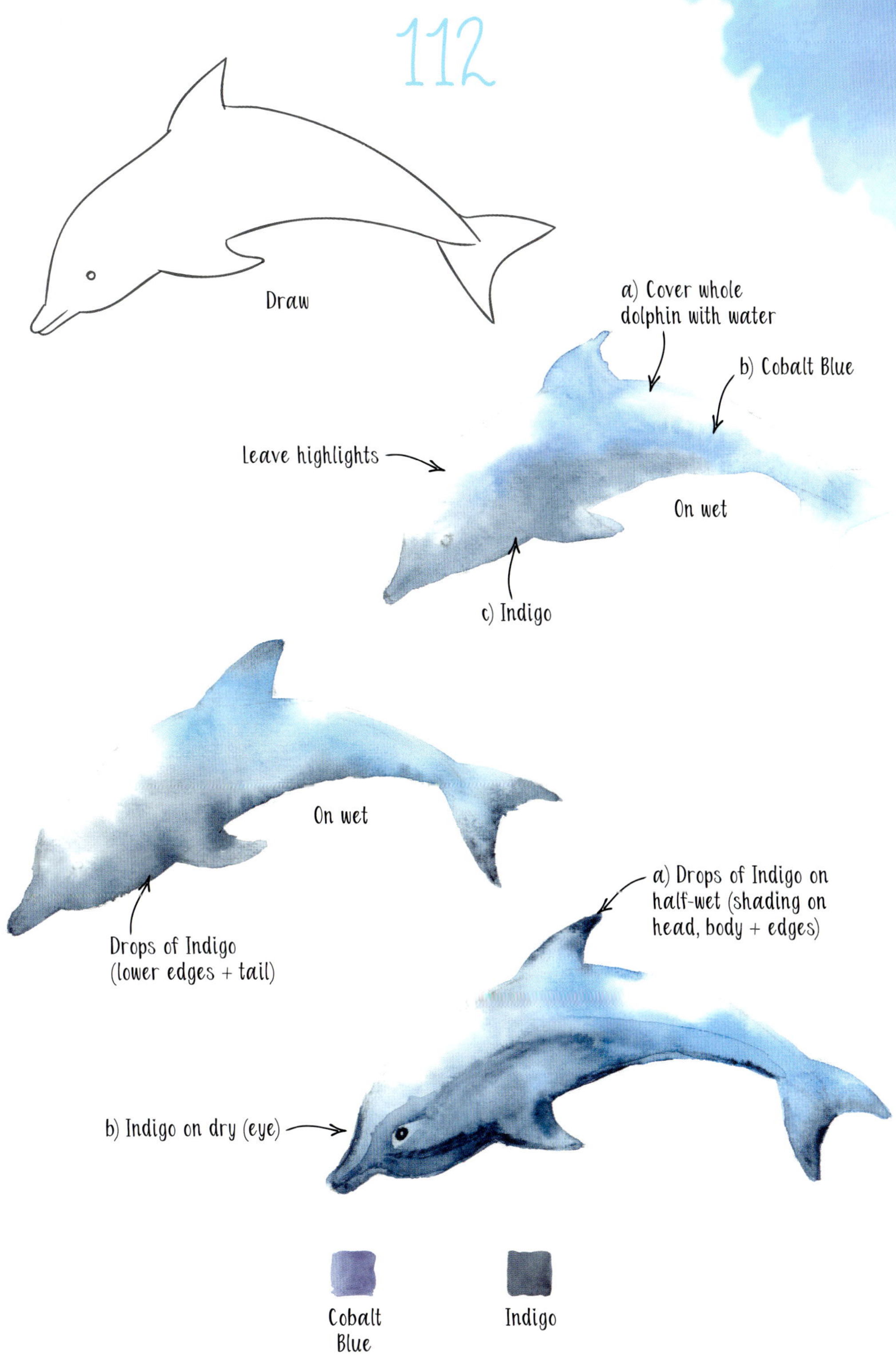

112
Draw
a) Cover whole dolphin with water
b) Cobalt Blue
leave highlights
On wet
c) Indigo
On wet
Drops of Indigo (lower edges + tail)
a) Drops of Indigo on half-wet (shading on head, body + edges)
b) Indigo on dry (eye)
Cobalt Blue
Indigo

113

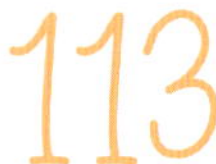

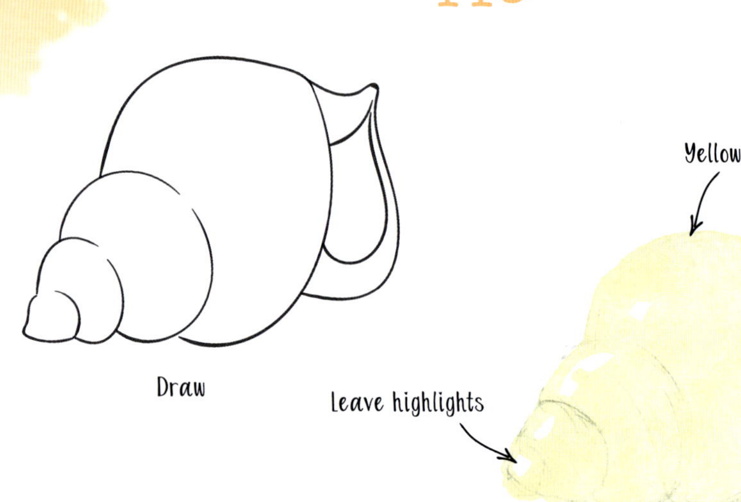

Draw

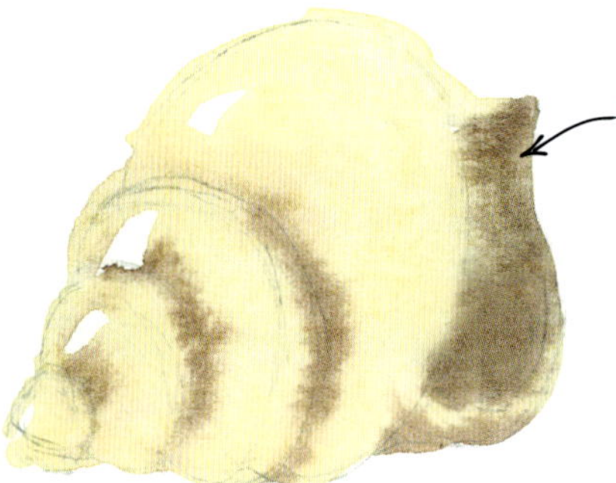

On wet

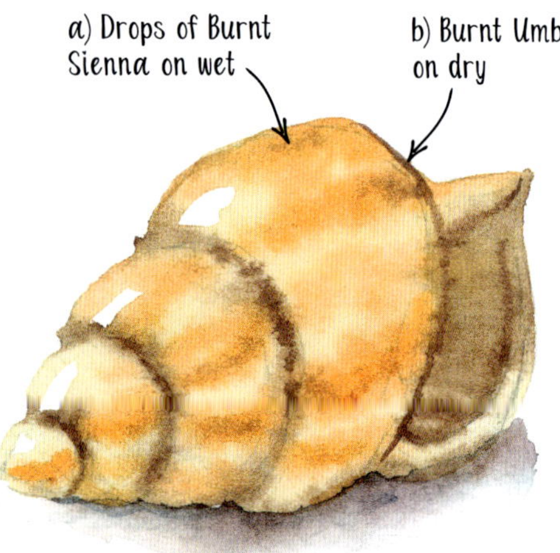

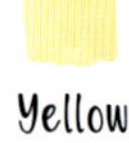

Yellow
Ochre

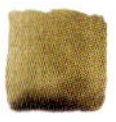

Burnt
Umber

Burnt
Sienna

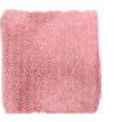

Claret

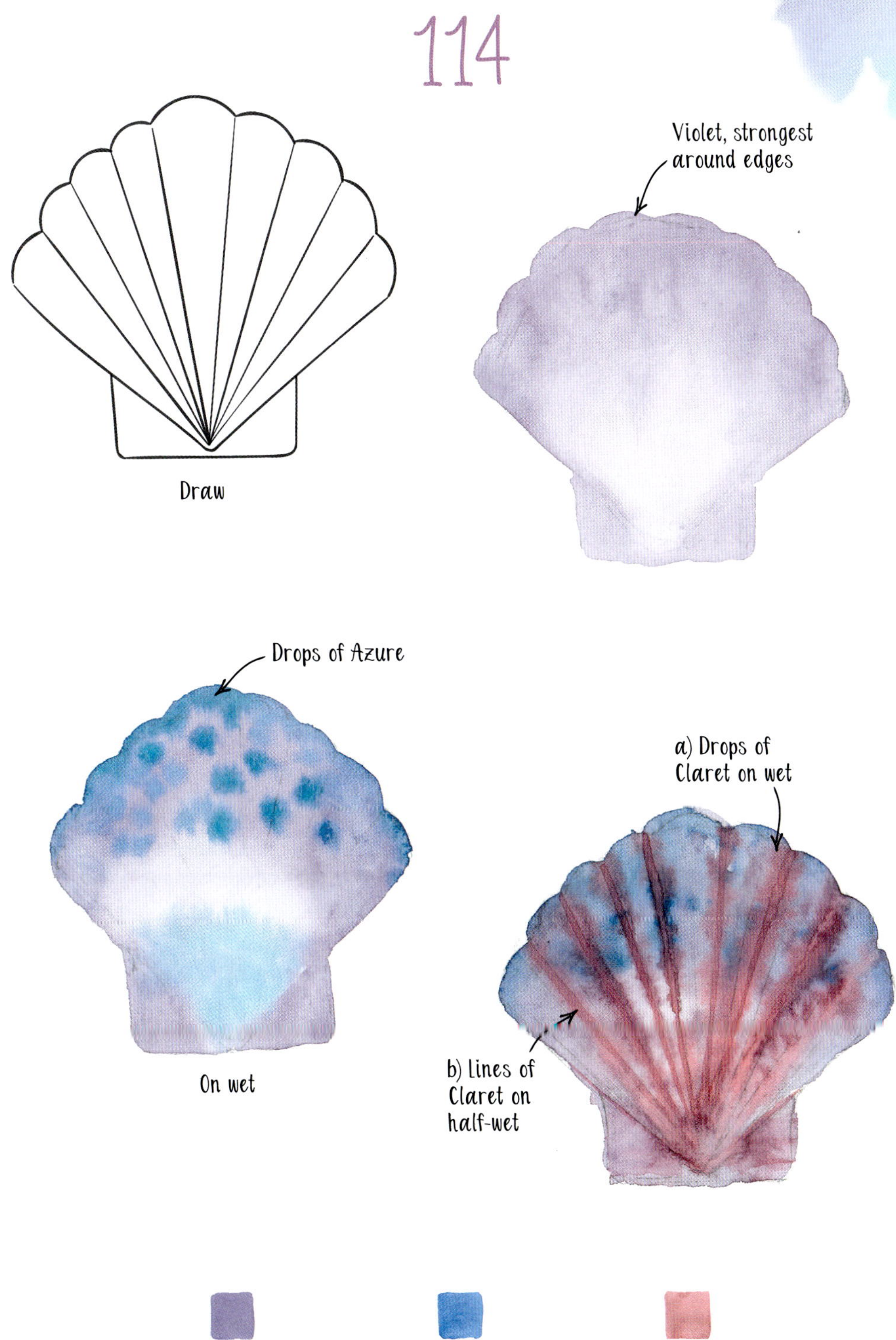
114

Draw

Violet, strongest
around edges

Drops of Azure

On wet

a) Drops of
Claret on wet

b) lines of
Claret on
half-wet

Violet

Azure

Claret

115

Draw
a) Yellow Ochre
b) Drops of Burnt Umber
Leave highlights
On wet
a) Raw Sienna on dry, leaving more highlights
b) Drops of Burnt Umber on wet
Burnt Sienna
Neutral Black (eye)
On dry
Yellow Ochre
Raw Sienna
Burnt Umber
Neutral Black
Burnt Sienna

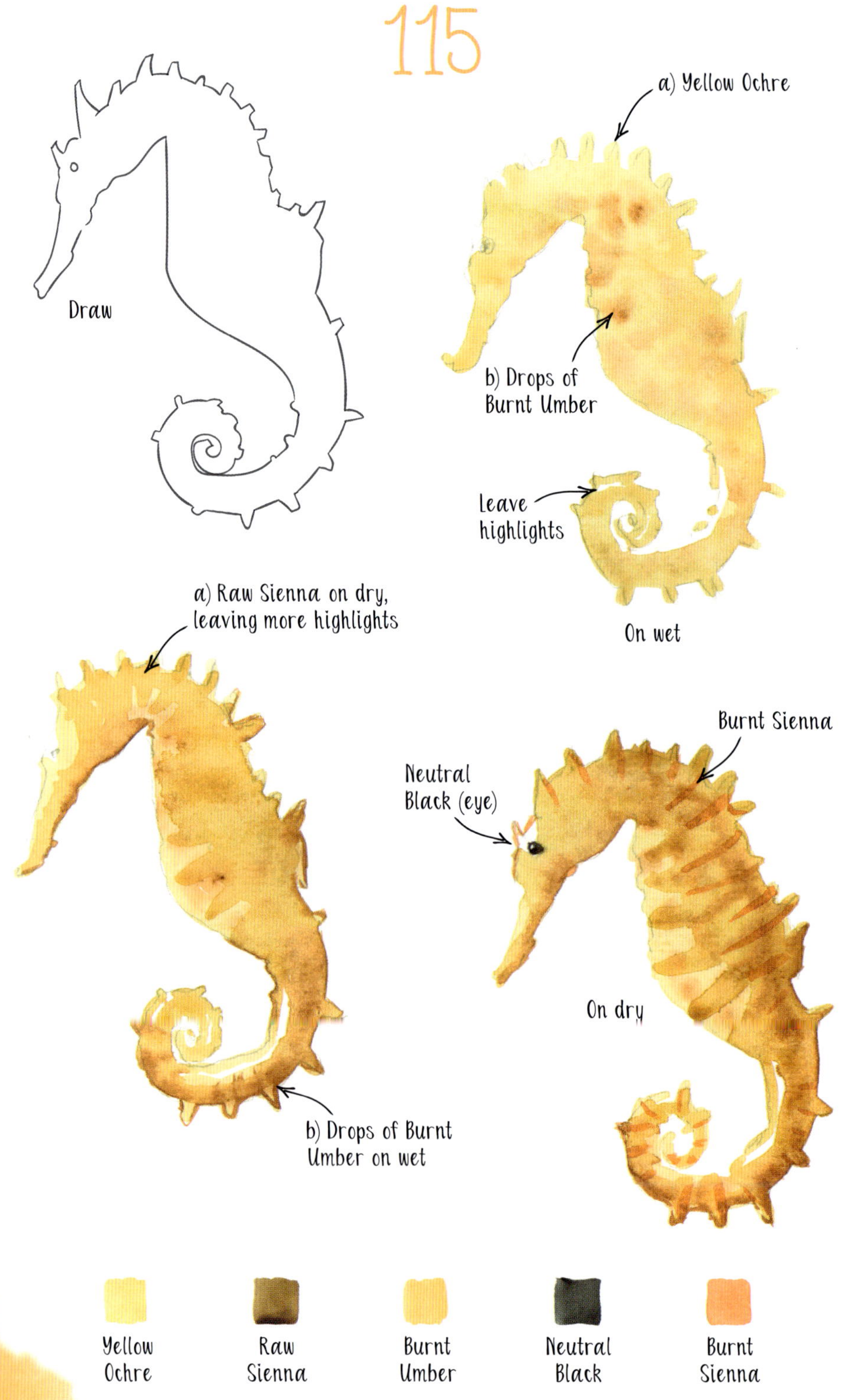

116

Draw

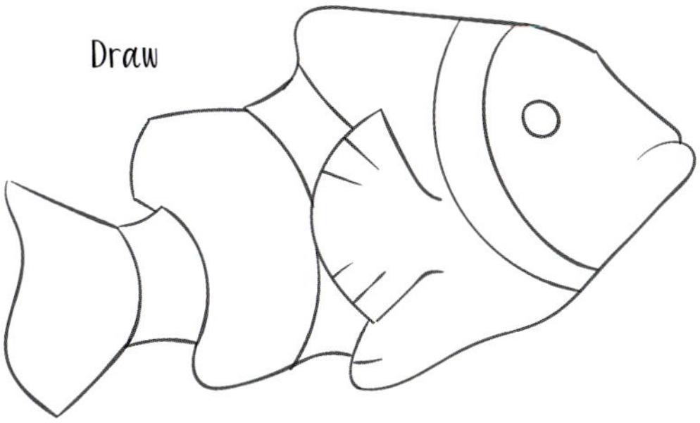

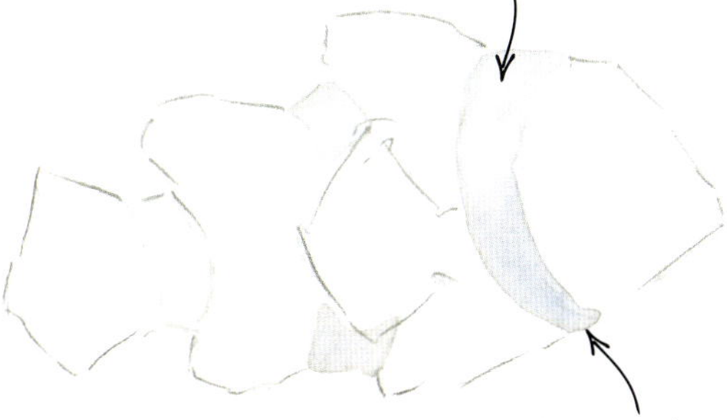

b) Drops of water

On wet

a) Neutral Black

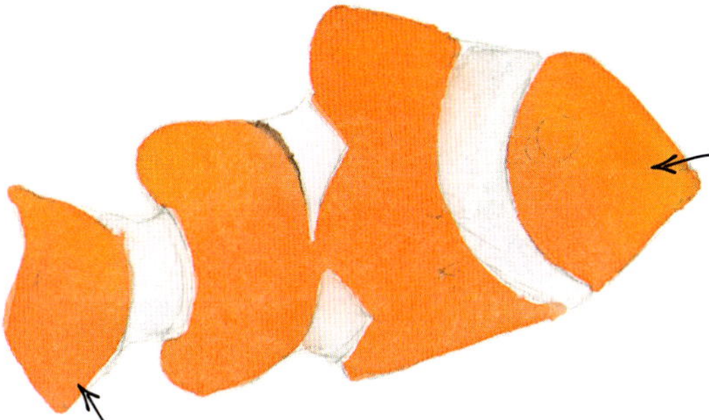

b) Drops of Cadmium Yellow on wet

a) Vermilion on dry

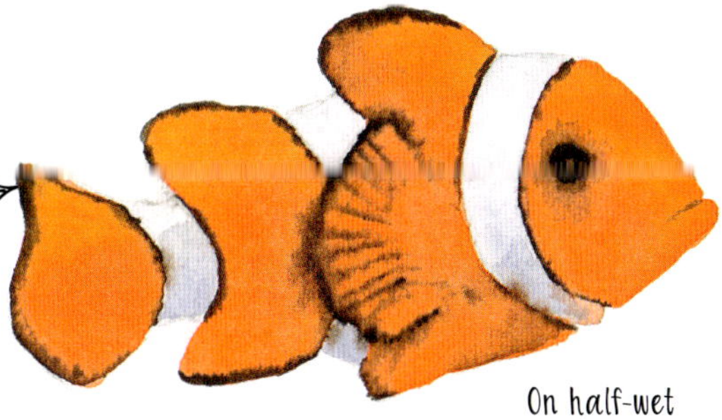

Neutral Black

On half-wet

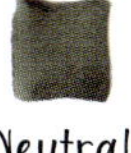

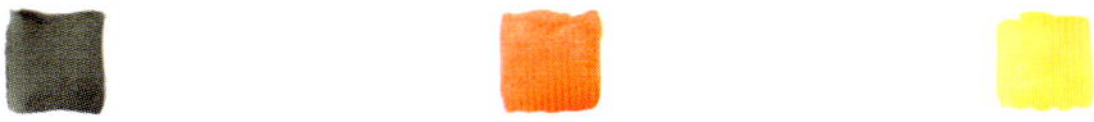

Neutral
Black

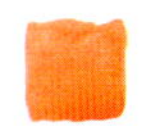

Vermilion

Cadmium
Yellow

117

Draw

On wet

Titian Red +
Yellow Ochre mix

Yellow Ochre

leave highlights

On dry

Second layer of Titian
Red + Yellow Ochre mix

b) Use same colour
mix for antennae

c) Violet on dry

a) Drops of Titian Red +
Yellow Ochre mix on wet

Titian
Red

Yellow
Ochre

Violet

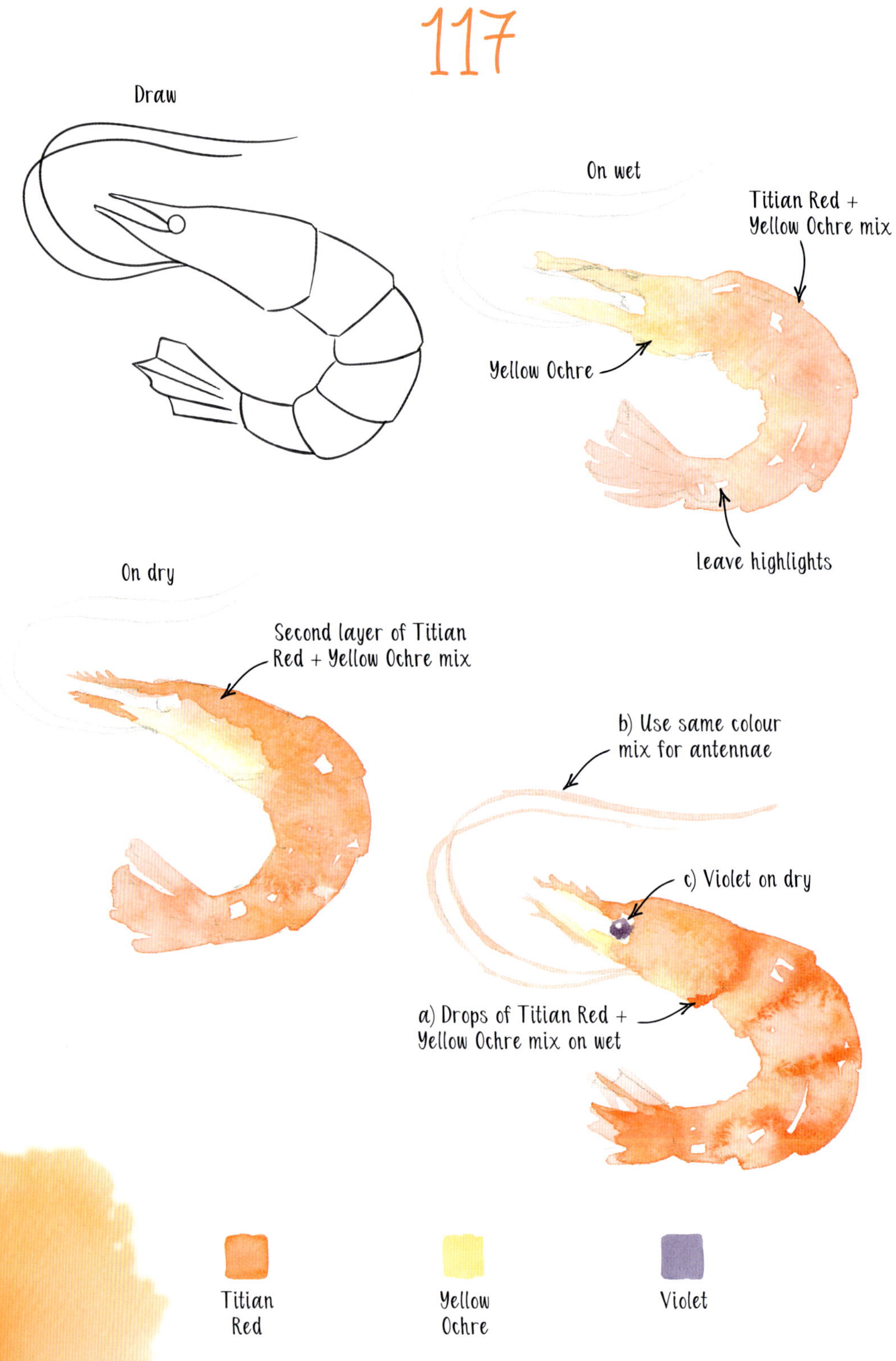

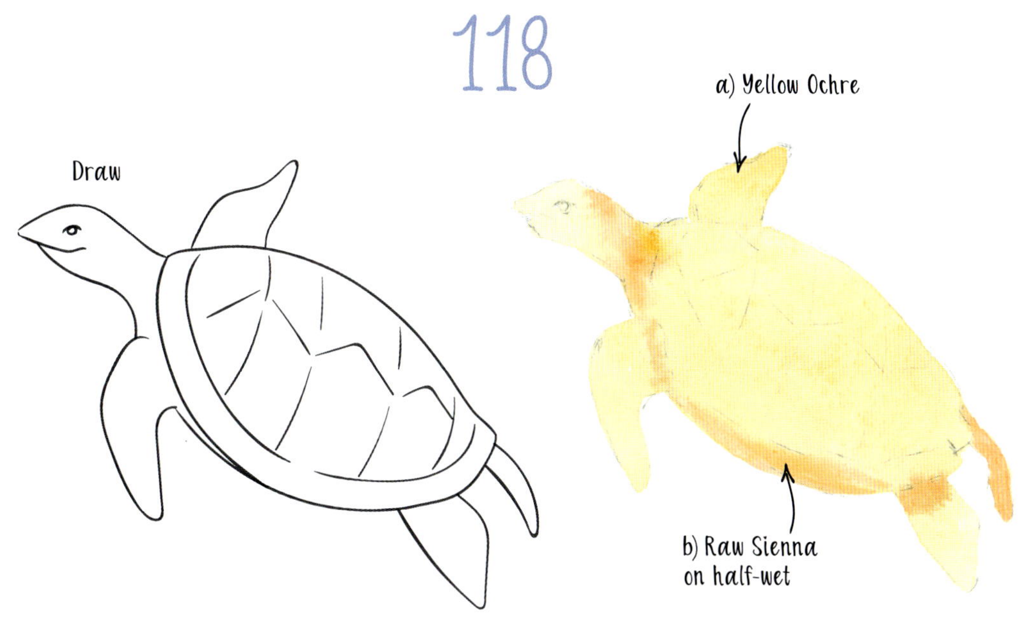
118
Draw
a) Yellow Ochre
b) Raw Sienna
on half-wet

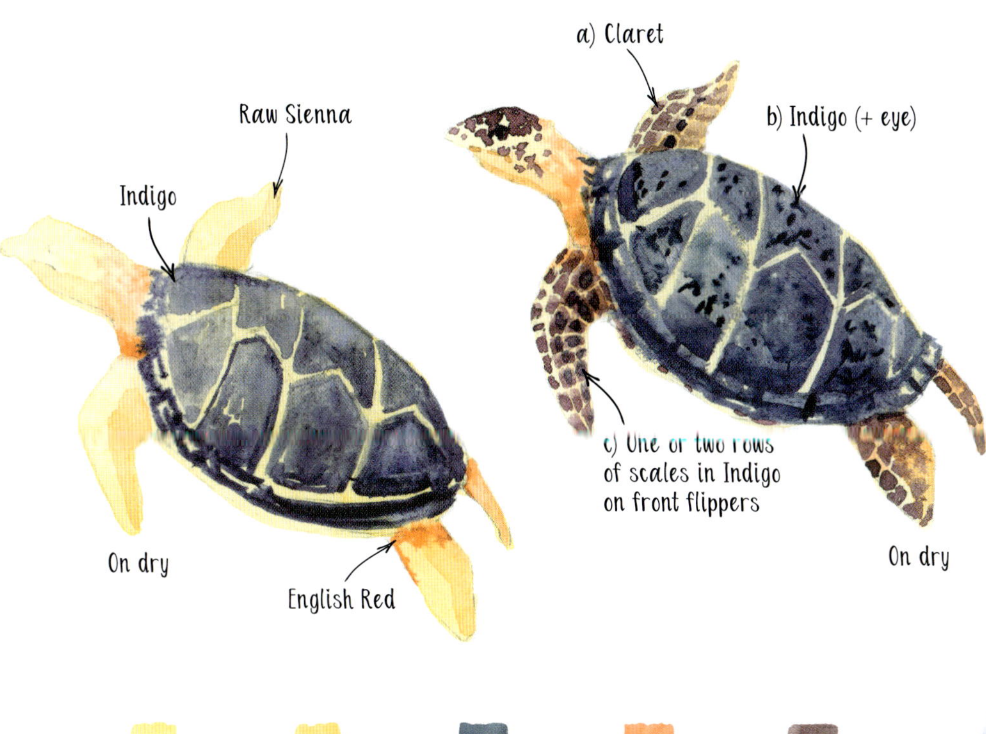
Raw Sienna
Indigo
a) Claret
b) Indigo (+ eye)
c) One or two rows
of scales in Indigo
on front flippers
On dry
English Red
On dry

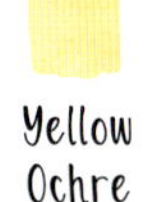
Yellow
Ochre

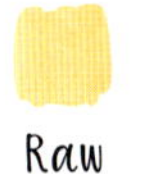
Raw
Sienna

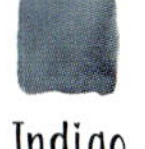
Indigo

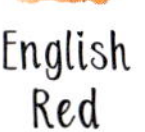
English
Red

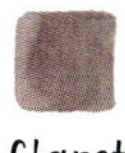
Claret

119

Draw
Raw Sienna
Burnt Sienna
Neutral Black
On dry
Two layers of Scarlet on dry, leaving highlights
leave bigger + extra highlights on second layer
Raw Sienna
Burnt Sienna
Neutral Black
Scarlet

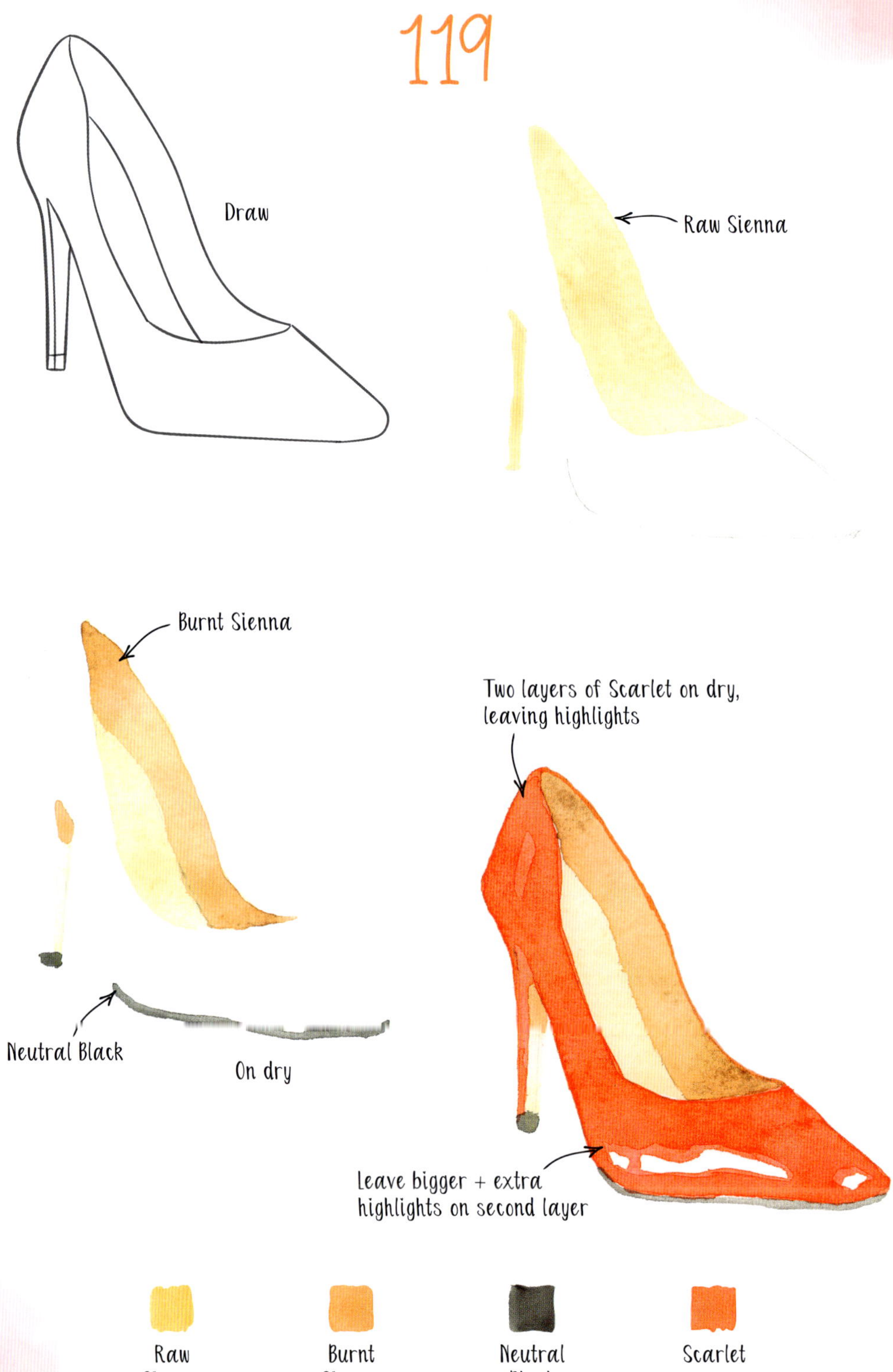

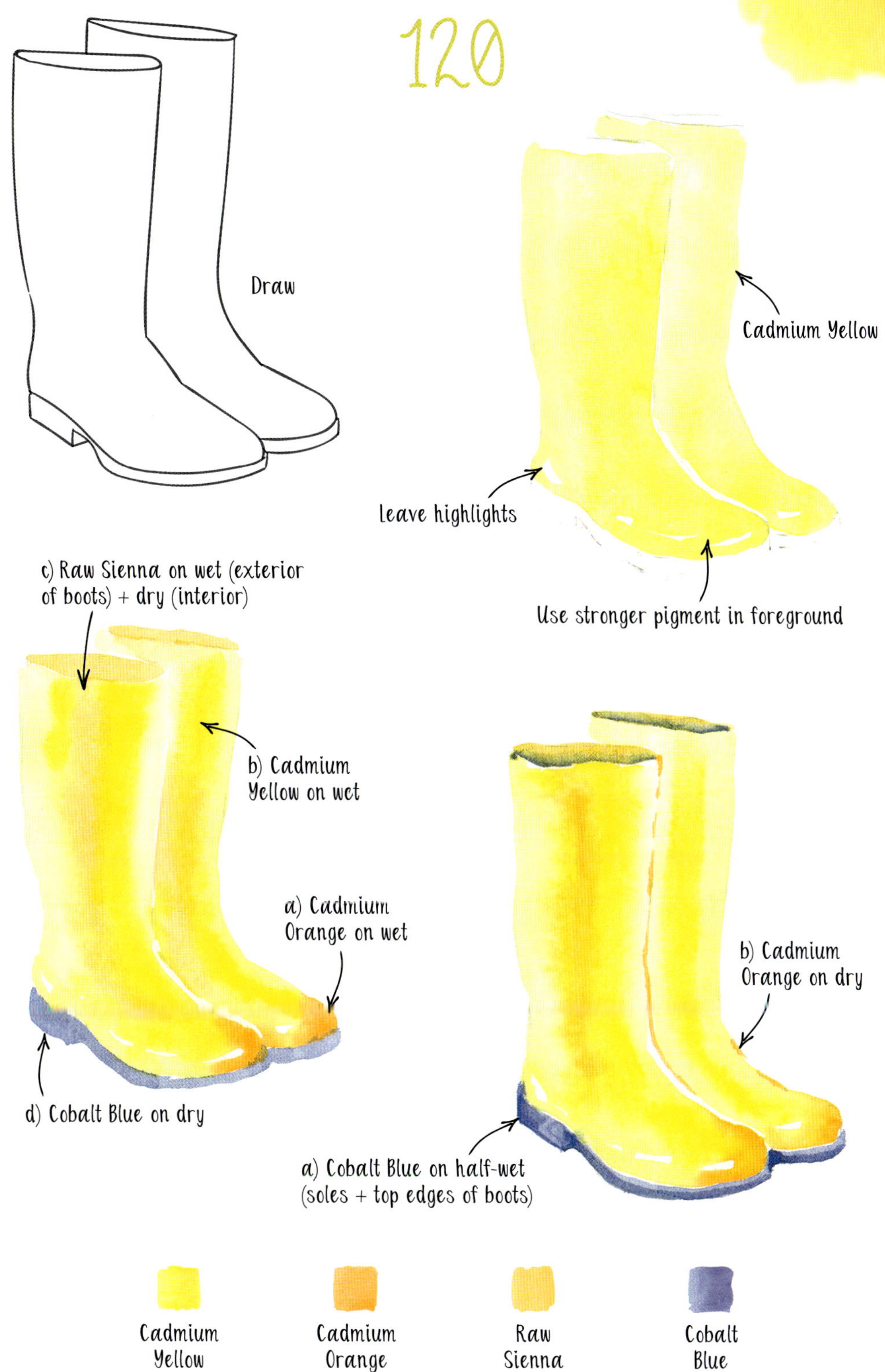
120
Draw
Cadmium Yellow
leave highlights
Use stronger pigment in foreground
c) Raw Sienna on wet (exterior of boots) + dry (interior)
b) Cadmium Yellow on wet
a) Cadmium Orange on wet
d) Cobalt Blue on dry
b) Cadmium Orange on dry
a) Cobalt Blue on half-wet (soles + top edges of boots)
Cadmium Yellow
Cadmium Orange
Raw Sienna
Cobalt Blue

121

Draw
On dry
Azure Blue, strongest near canopy
Neutral Black
Scarlet
On dry
Madder Lake Red Light (outer edges + front panel)
On half-wet
Azure Blue
Neutral Black
Scarlet
Madder Lake Red Light

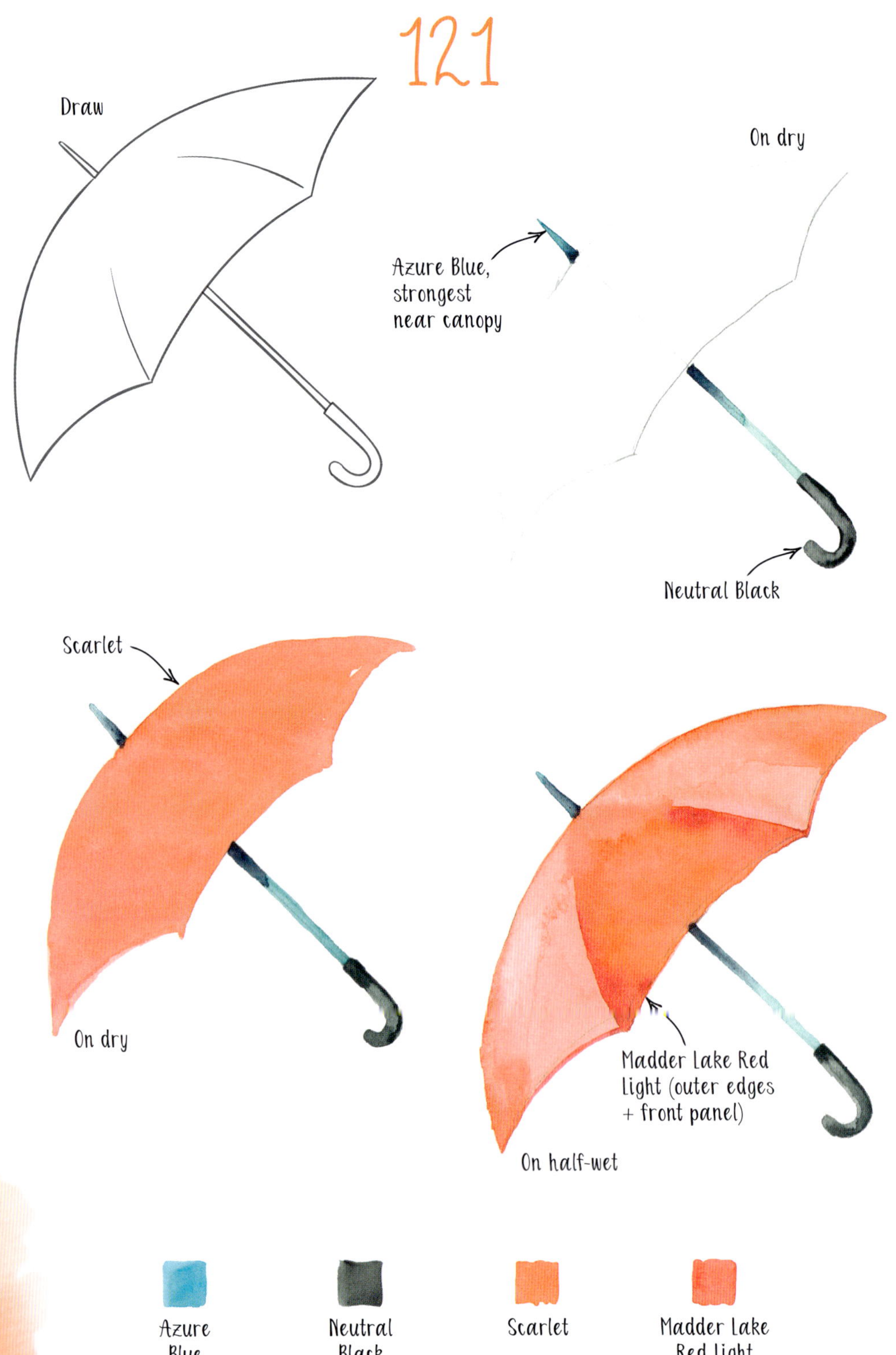

122

Draw
Rose
Use stronger pigment
in foreground

Drops of Burnt Umber on wet
Continue adding drops as the underlayer
dries to create tortoiseshell pattern

a) Burnt Sienna on dry
Leave highlights
b) Drops of water on wet

Rose

Burnt
Umber

Burnt
Sienna

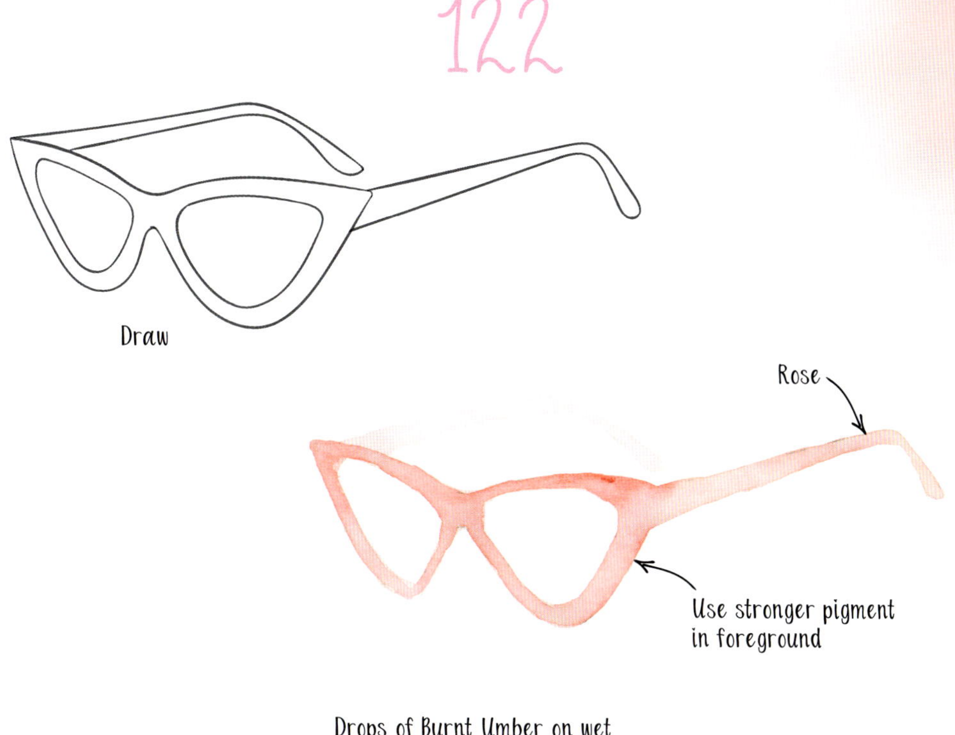

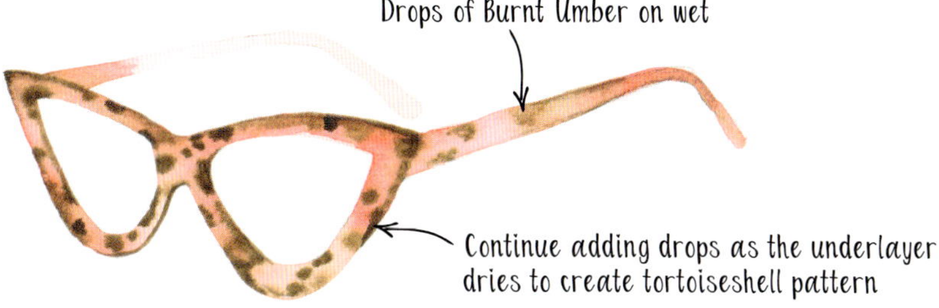

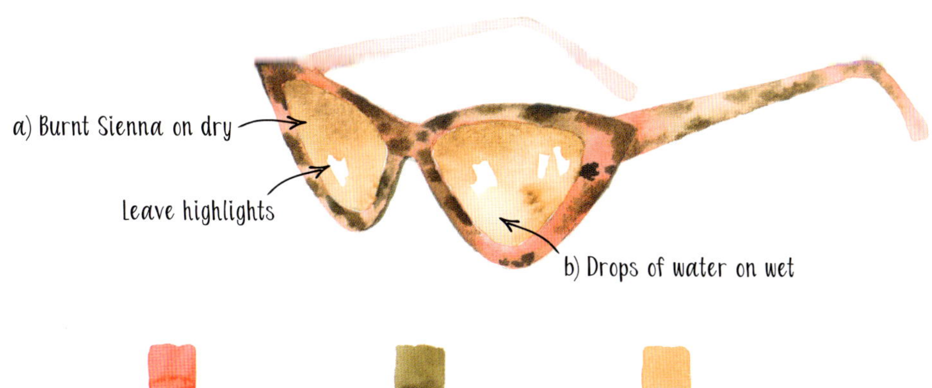

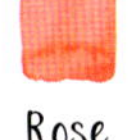

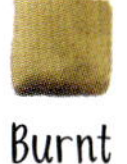

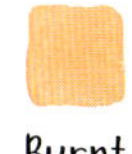

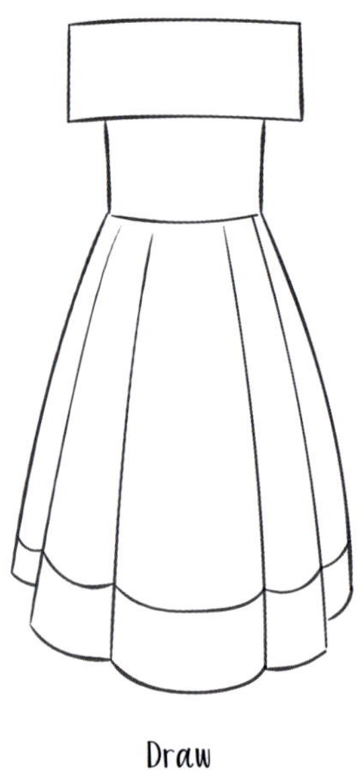

Draw

123

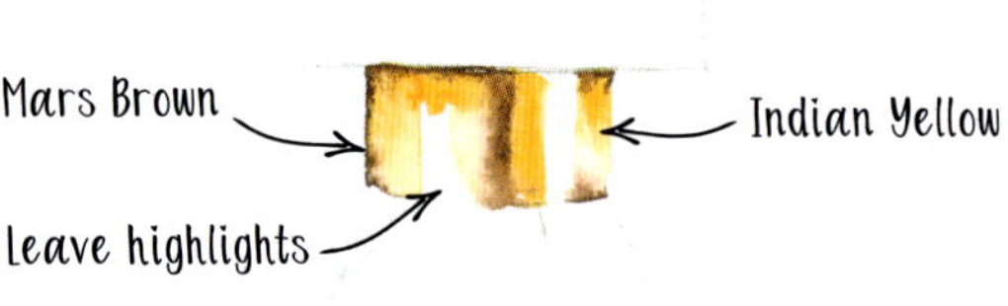

On wet

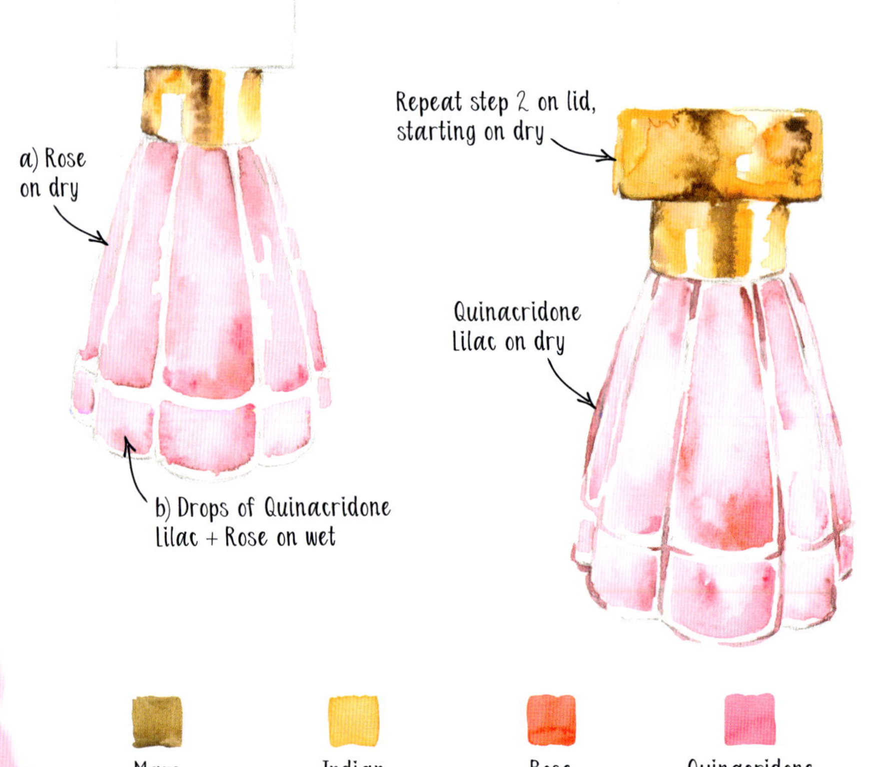

124

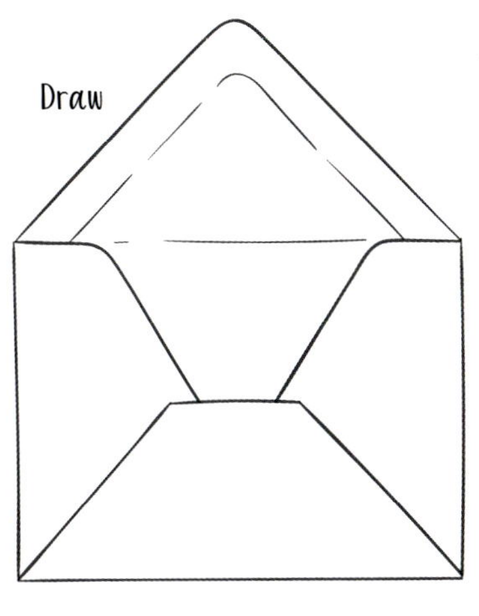

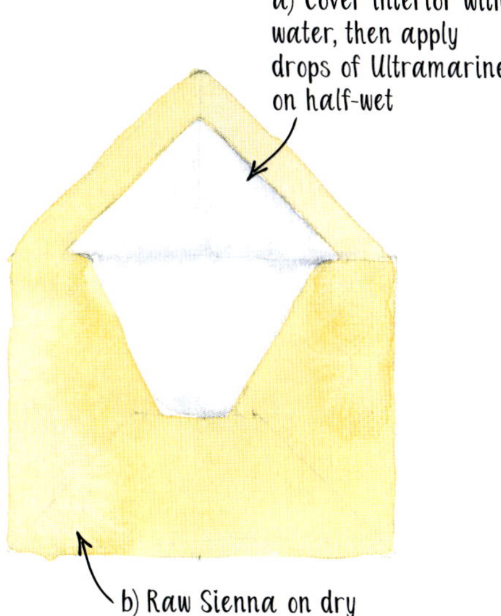

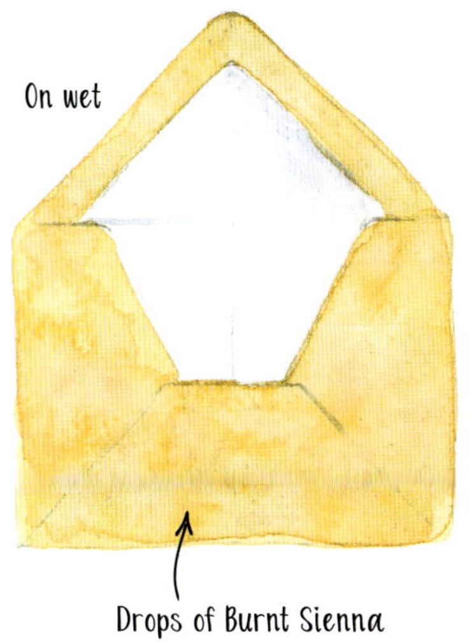

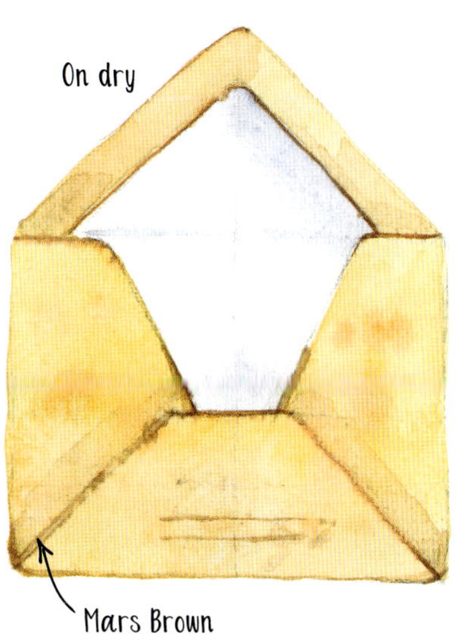

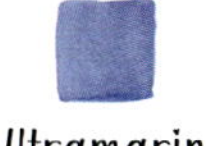

Ultramarine

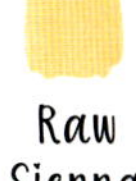

Raw Sienna

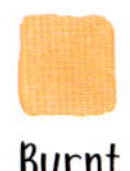

Burnt Sienna

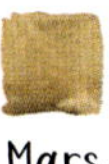

Mars Brown

125

Draw
c) Claret
b) Cadmium Yellow + Golden mix
a) Yellow Ochre
d) Neutral Black
On dry
leave highlights
a) Neutral Black on wet
b) Claret on dry
c) Cadmium Yellow + Golden mix on dry
d) Neutral Black on dry
Claret
Burnt Sienna
On dry
Neutral Black
Yellow Ochre
Cadmium Yellow
Golden
Claret
Neutral Black
Burnt Sienna

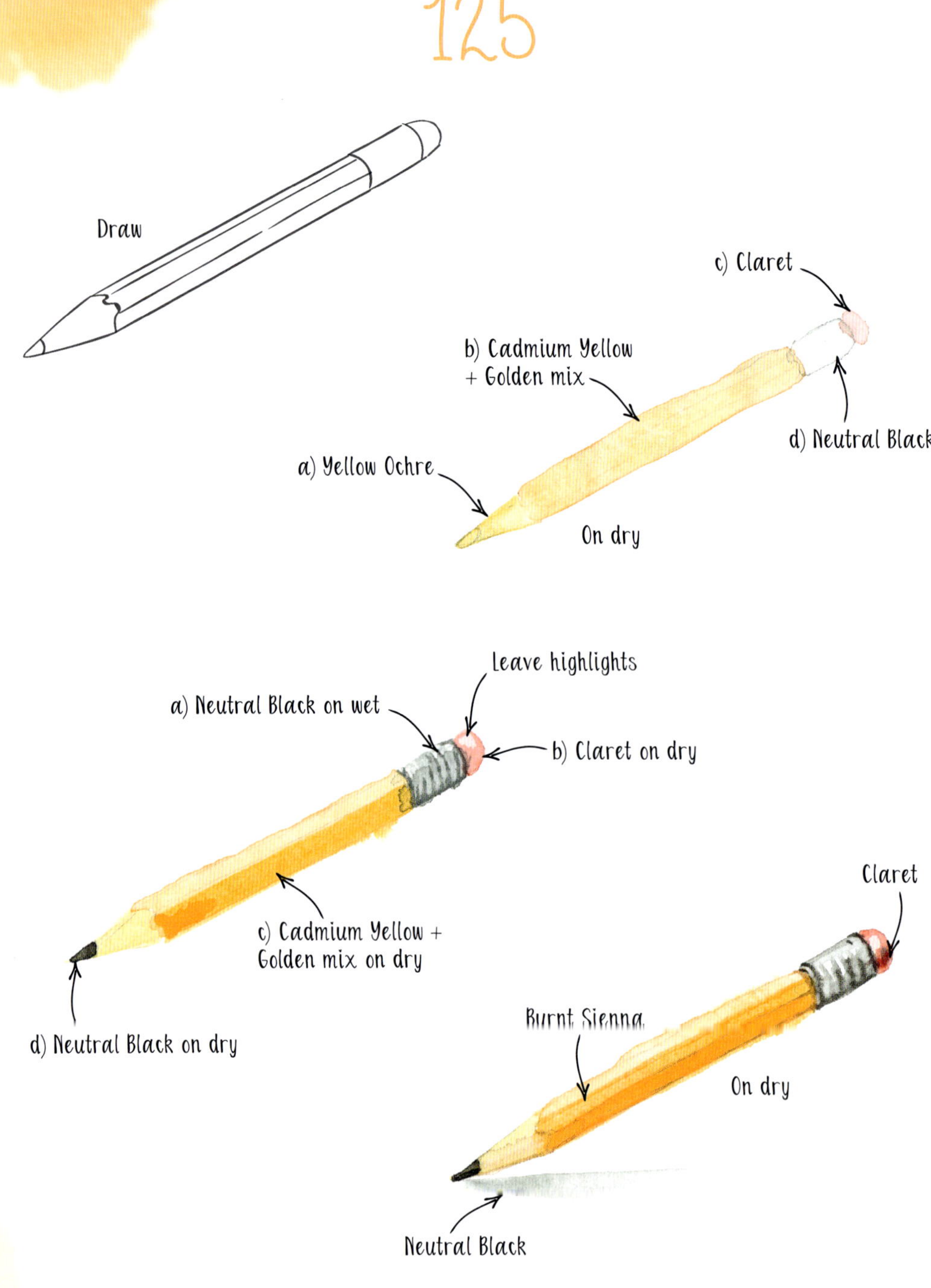

126

Draw

Burnt Sienna

c) Neutral Black on dry, then details on half-wet

leave highlights

a) Mars Brown on dry (whole handle)

b) Drops of Sepia on wet

Mars Brown

leave highlights

On dry

Burnt Sienna

Mars Brown

Sepia

Neutral Black

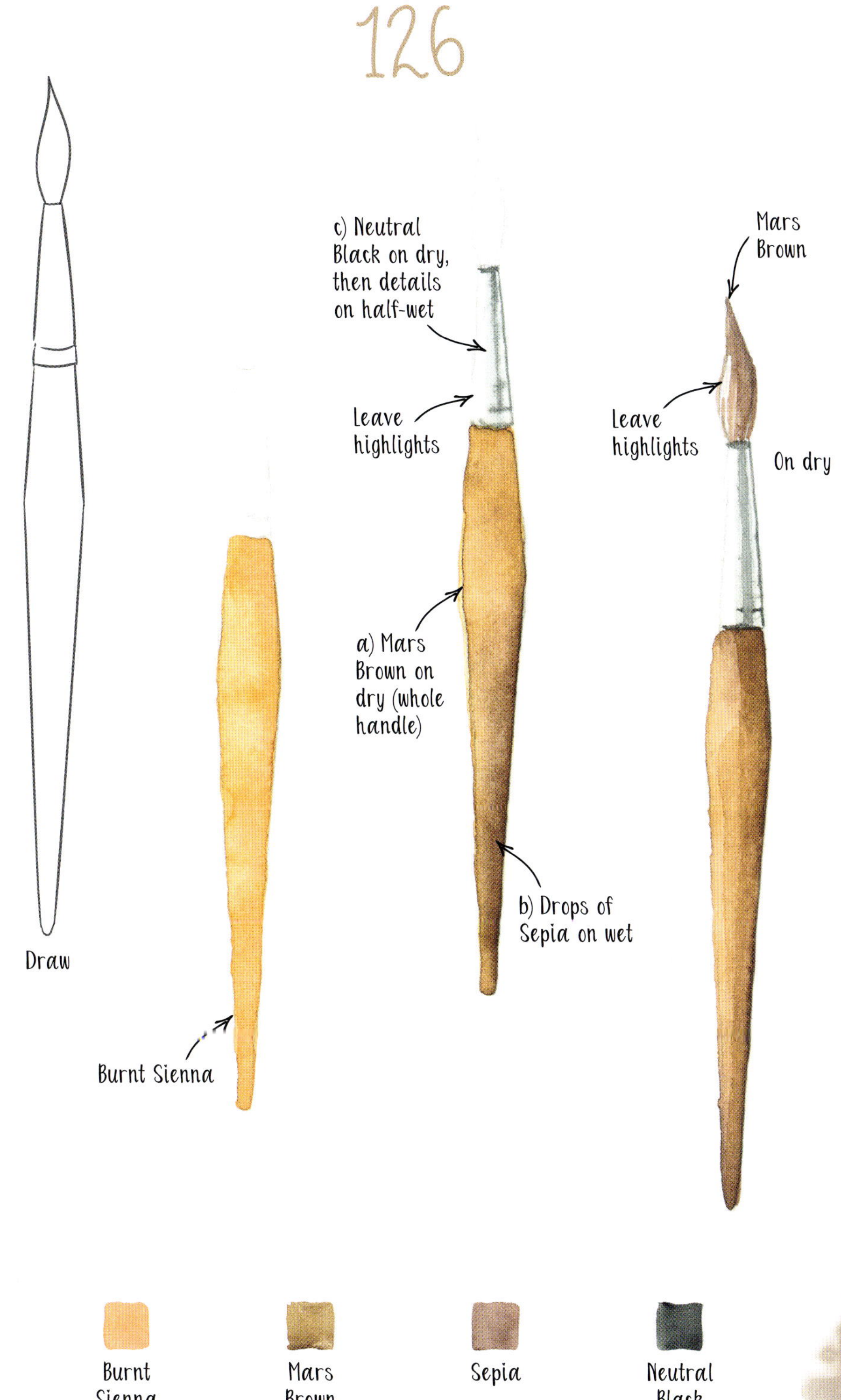

127

Draw

Scarlet
leave highlights
Yellow Ochre
Neutral Black
On dry

Two layers of Sap Green, Azure Blue + Madder Lake Red Light for stripes, leaving highlights on second layer
Scarlet
On dry

Madder Lake Red Light + Neutral Black mix (edges)
Drop of water to mix colours for shadow
On dry

Yellow Ochre
Scarlet
Neutral Black
Sap Green
Azure Blue
Madder Lake Red light

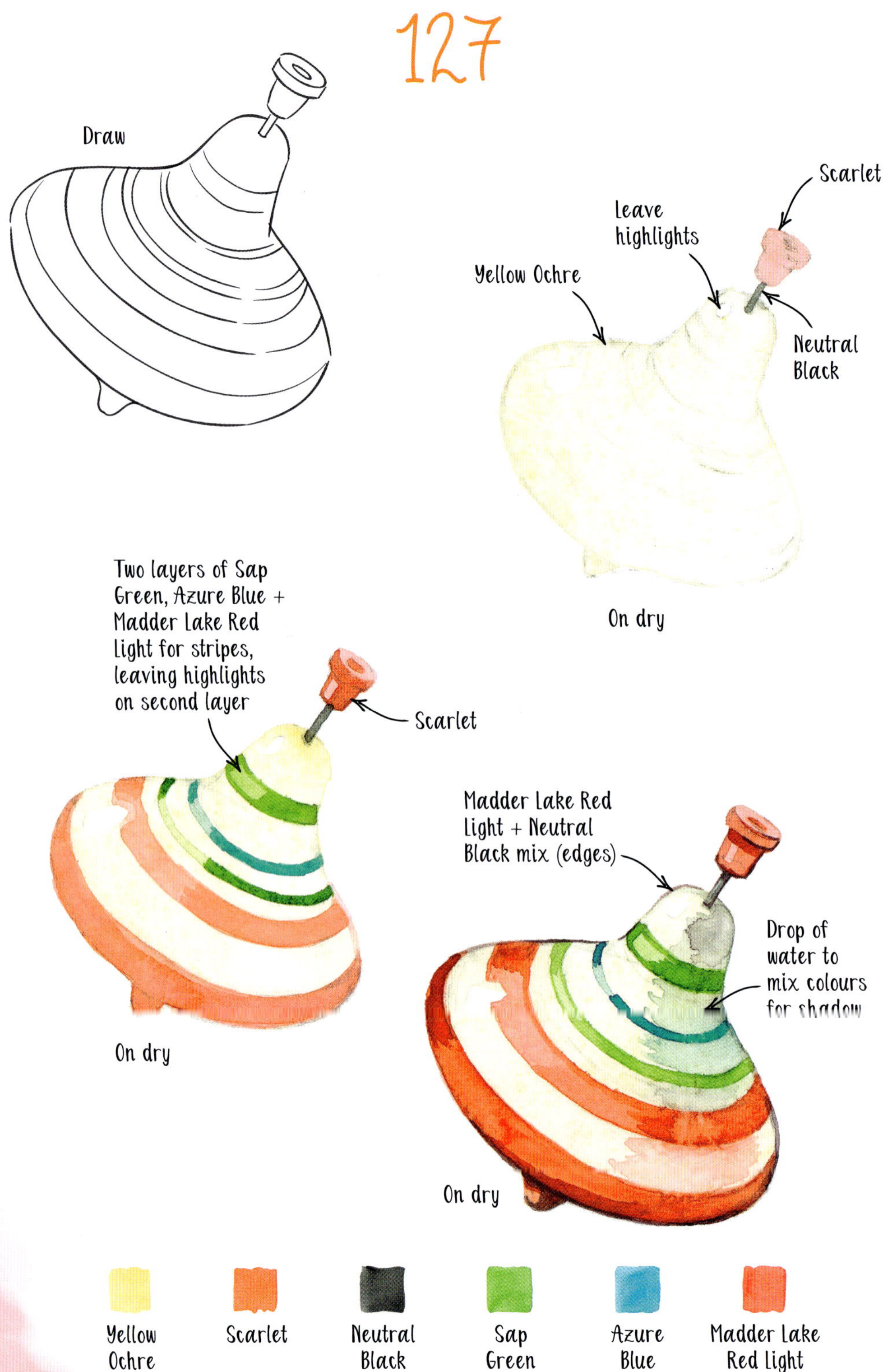

128

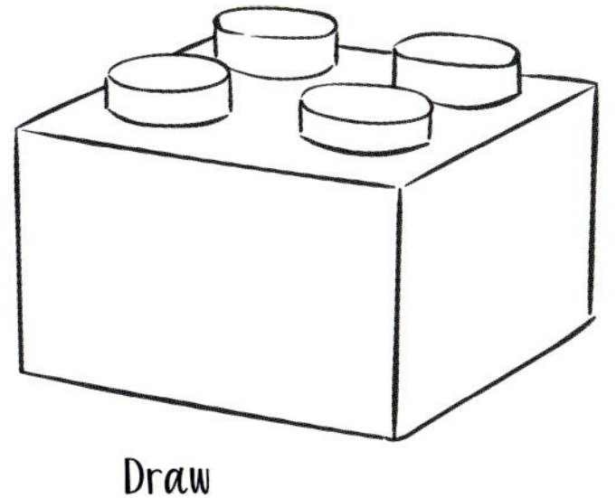

Draw

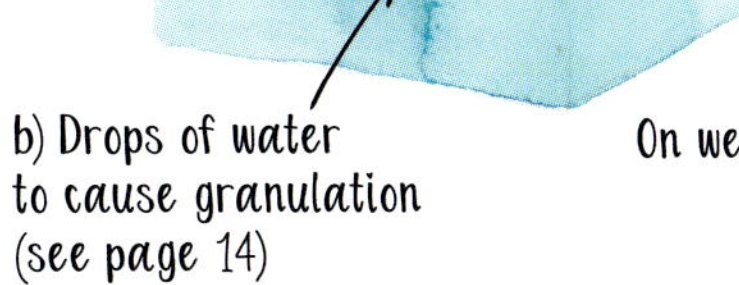

a) Azure Blue

leave highlights

b) Drops of water
to cause granulation
(see page 14)

On wet

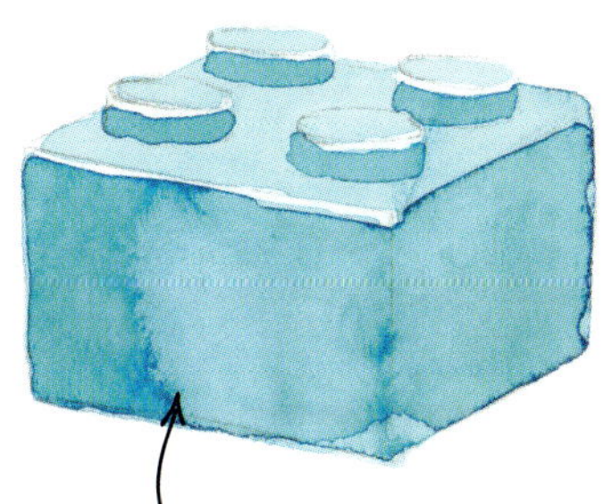

Repeat previous step on vertical
surfaces, starting on dry

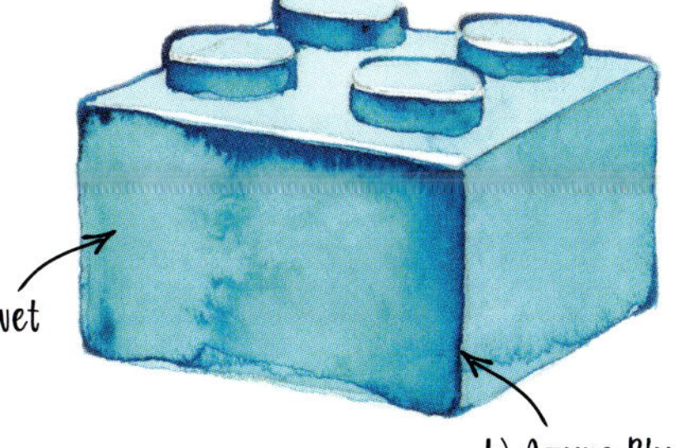

a) Allow to dry, then re-wet
vertical surfaces

b) Azure Blue
on wet (edges)

Azure
Blue

129

Draw
a) Masking fluid (allow to dry)
b) Yellow Ochre
c) Drops of Yellow Ochre on wet

a) Ultramarine on dry
b) Drops of water on wet
c) Madder Lake Red light on dry
Madder Lake Red Light (cheeks + lips), Burnt Umber (eyelashes + hair) + Neutral Black (eyebrows)
When paint is dry, rub off masking fluid
Madder Lake Red light
Violet
On dry

Masking Fluid
Yellow Ochre
Ultramarine
Madder Lake Red Light
Burnt Umber
Neutral Black
Violet

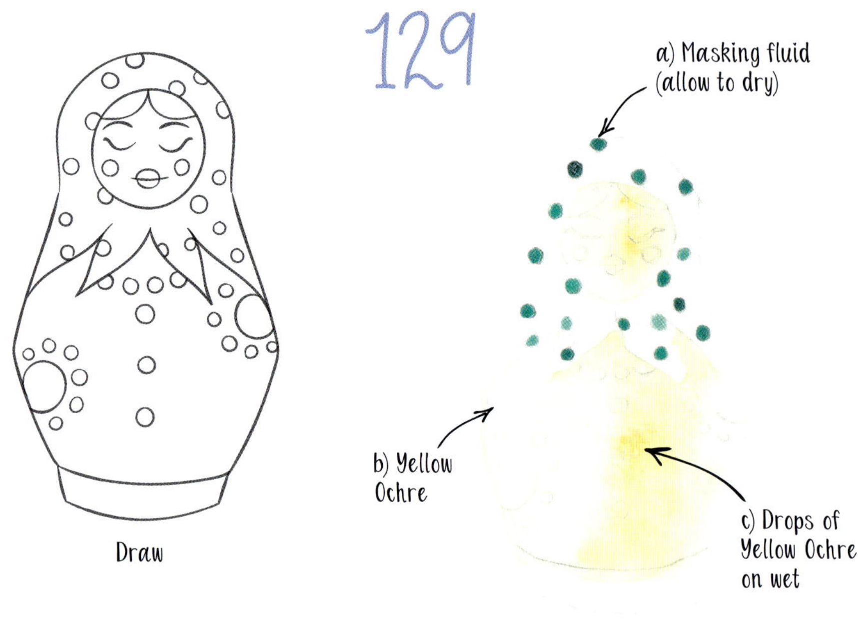

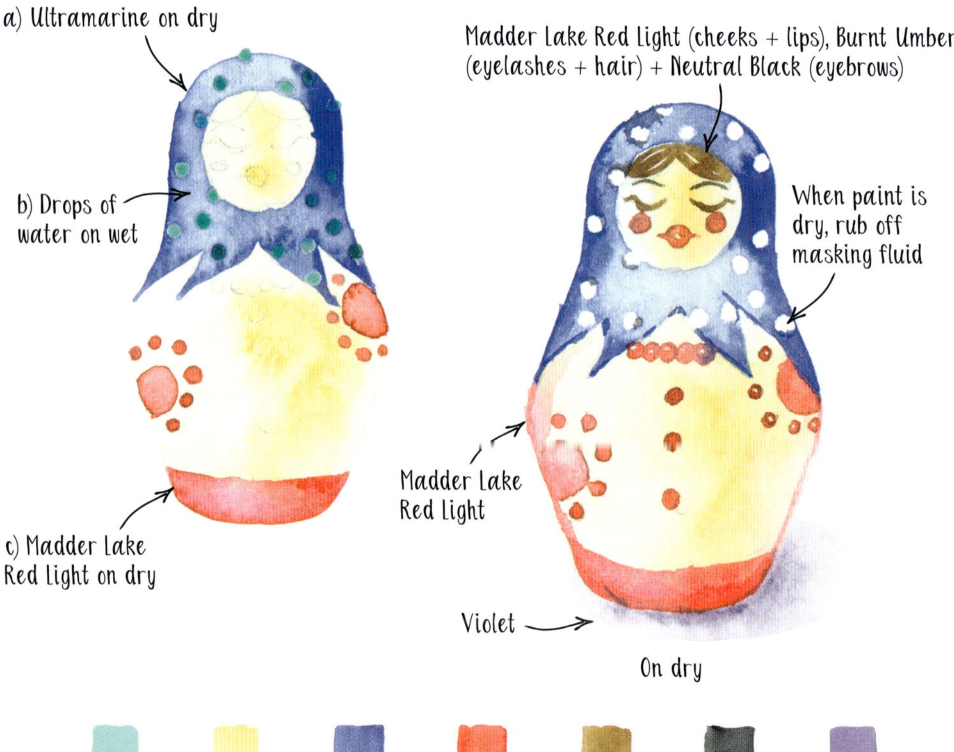

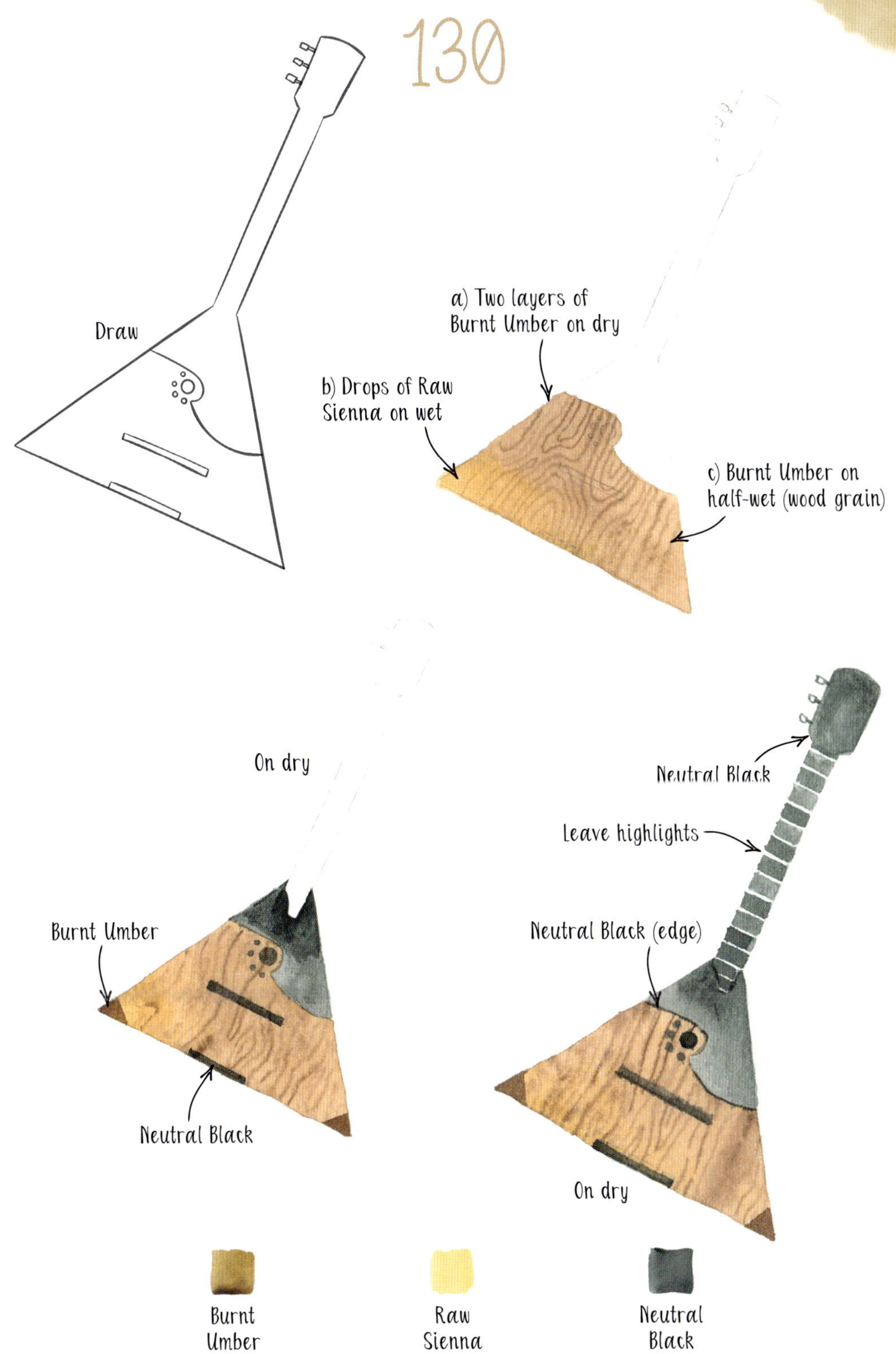
130
Draw
a) Two layers of
Burnt Umber on dry
b) Drops of Raw
Sienna on wet
c) Burnt Umber on
half-wet (wood grain)
On dry
Burnt Umber
Neutral Black
Neutral Black
leave highlights
Neutral Black (edge)
On dry
Burnt
Umber
Raw
Sienna
Neutral
Black

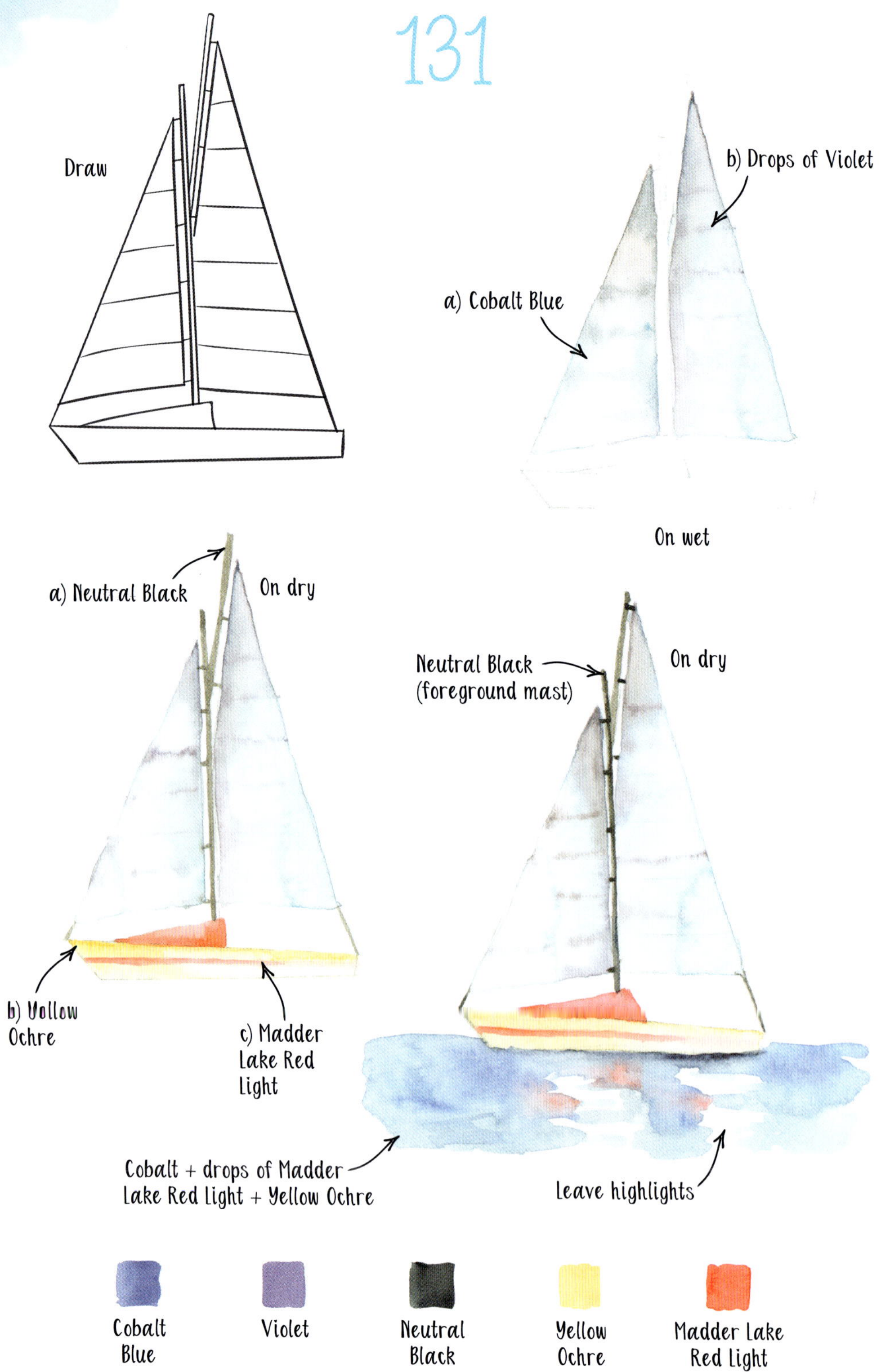
131
Draw
a) Cobalt Blue
b) Drops of Violet
On wet
a) Neutral Black
On dry
b) Yellow Ochre
c) Madder Lake Red Light
Neutral Black (foreground mast)
On dry
Cobalt + drops of Madder Lake Red Light + Yellow Ochre
Leave highlights
Cobalt Blue
Violet
Neutral Black
Yellow Ochre
Madder Lake Red light

132

Draw
a) Titian Red around inner + outer edges of circle, then water around centre
b) Indigo on dry (all four sections, in varying dilutions)
a) Raw Sienna on dry
b) Repeat part (a) of previous step, starting on dry
a) Drops of Titian Red on wet (edges)
b) Burnt Sienna on dry
c) Indigo on dry, leaving highlights
Titian Red
Indigo
Raw Sienna
Burnt Sienna

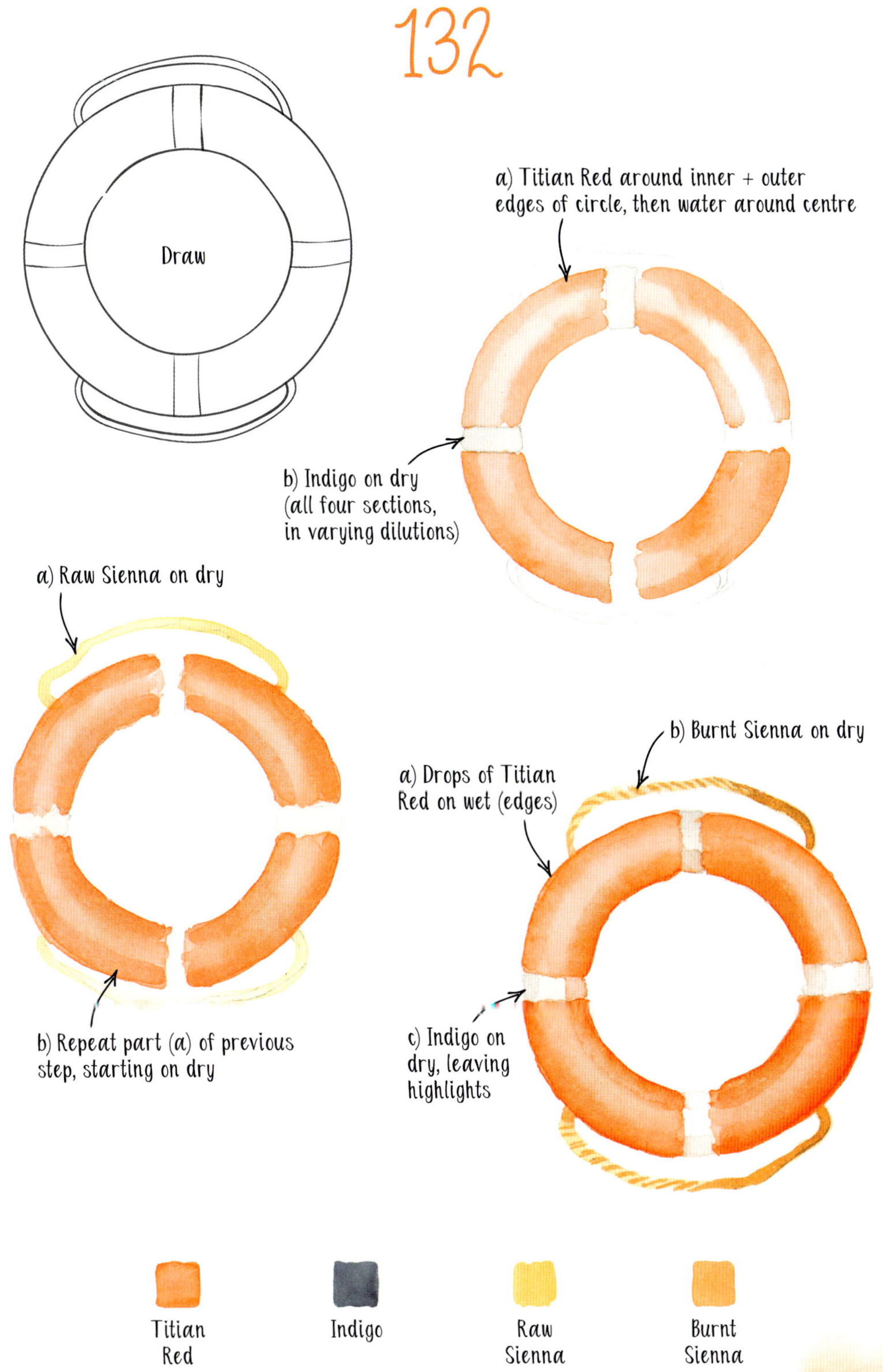

133

Draw
Scarlet
Throughout project, use drops of water to cause granulation (see page 14)
Indigo
Leave highlights
Neutral Black
On dry
Yellow Ochre
Cadmium Yellow
Neutral Black
On dry
Scarlet
Indigo
Neutral Black
Yellow Ochre
Cadmium Yellow

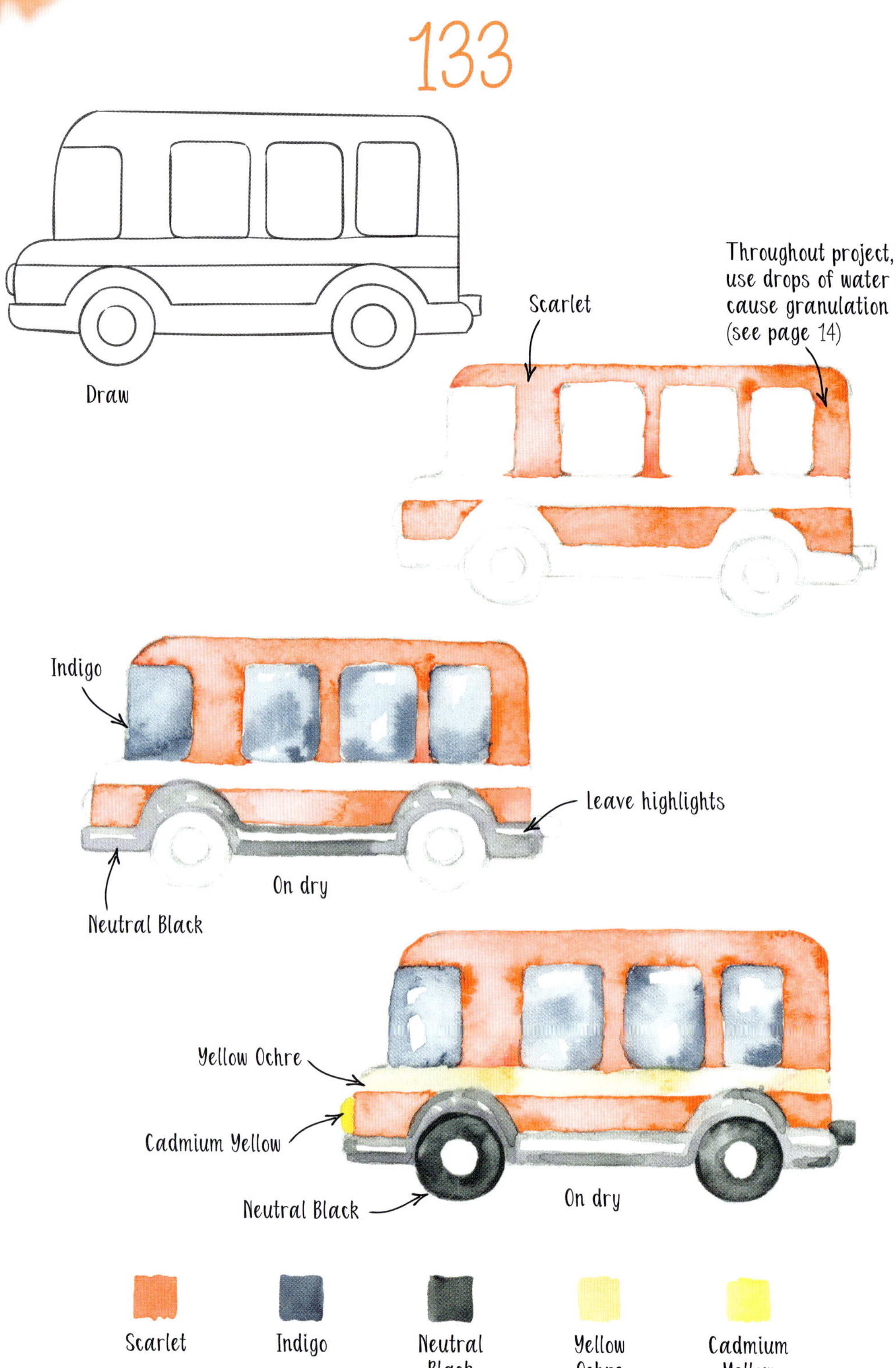

134

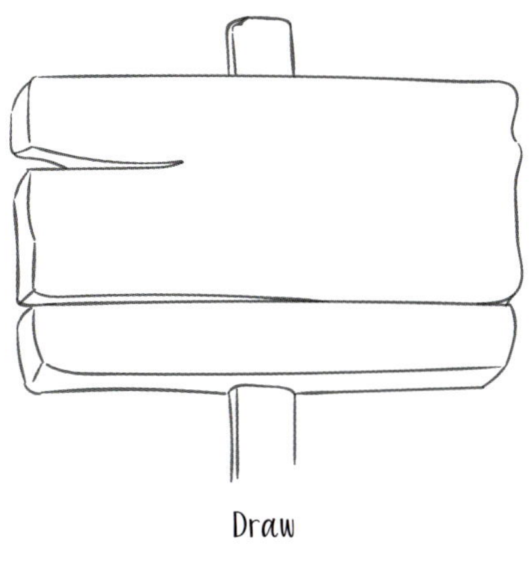

Draw

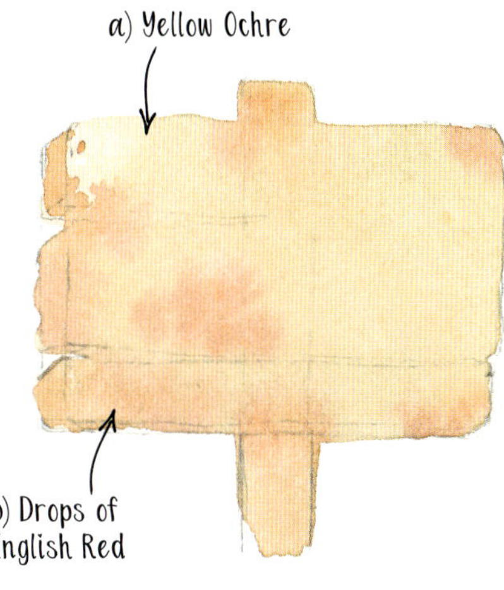

On wet

On half-wet

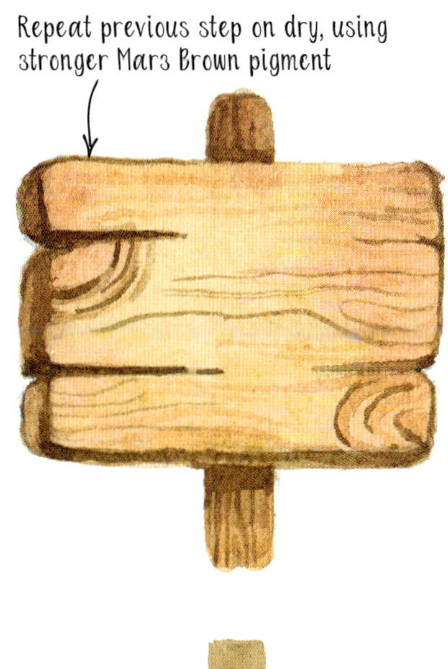

Repeat previous step on dry, using stronger Mars Brown pigment

Yellow Ochre

English Red

Mars Brown

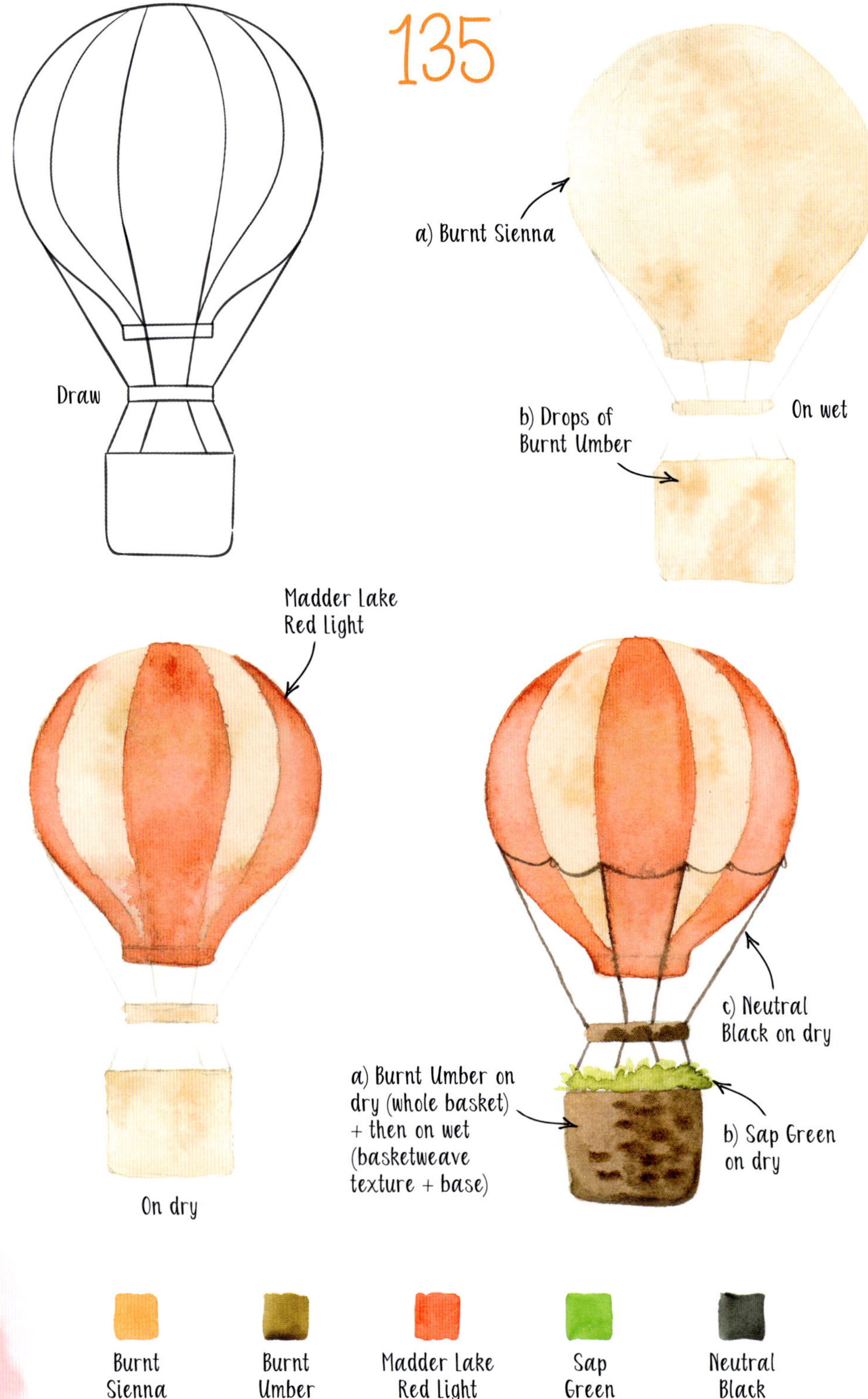
135
Draw
a) Burnt Sienna
On wet
b) Drops of
Burnt Umber
Madder Lake
Red Light
On dry
c) Neutral
Black on dry
a) Burnt Umber on
dry (whole basket)
+ then on wet
(basketweave
texture + base)
b) Sap Green
on dry
Burnt
Sienna
Burnt
Umber
Madder Lake
Red Light
Sap
Green
Neutral
Black

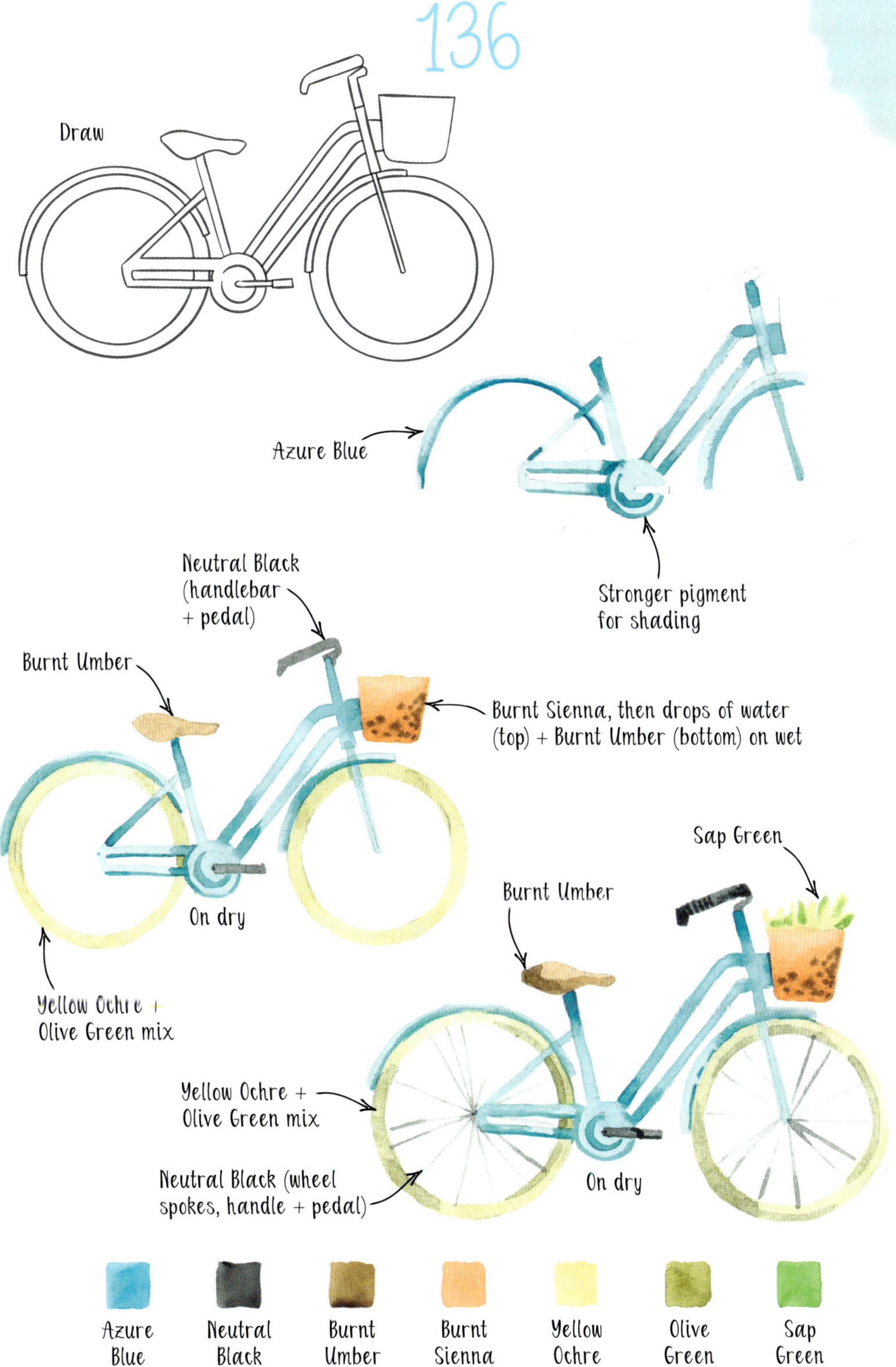
136

Draw

Azure Blue

Stronger pigment
for shading

Neutral Black
(handlebar
+ pedal)

Burnt Umber

Burnt Sienna, then drops of water
(top) + Burnt Umber (bottom) on wet

Sap Green

Burnt Umber

On dry

Yellow Ochre +
Olive Green mix

Yellow Ochre +
Olive Green mix

On dry

Neutral Black (wheel
spokes, handle + pedal)

Azure
Blue

Neutral
Black

Burnt
Umber

Burnt
Sienna

Yellow
Ochre

Olive
Green

Sap
Green

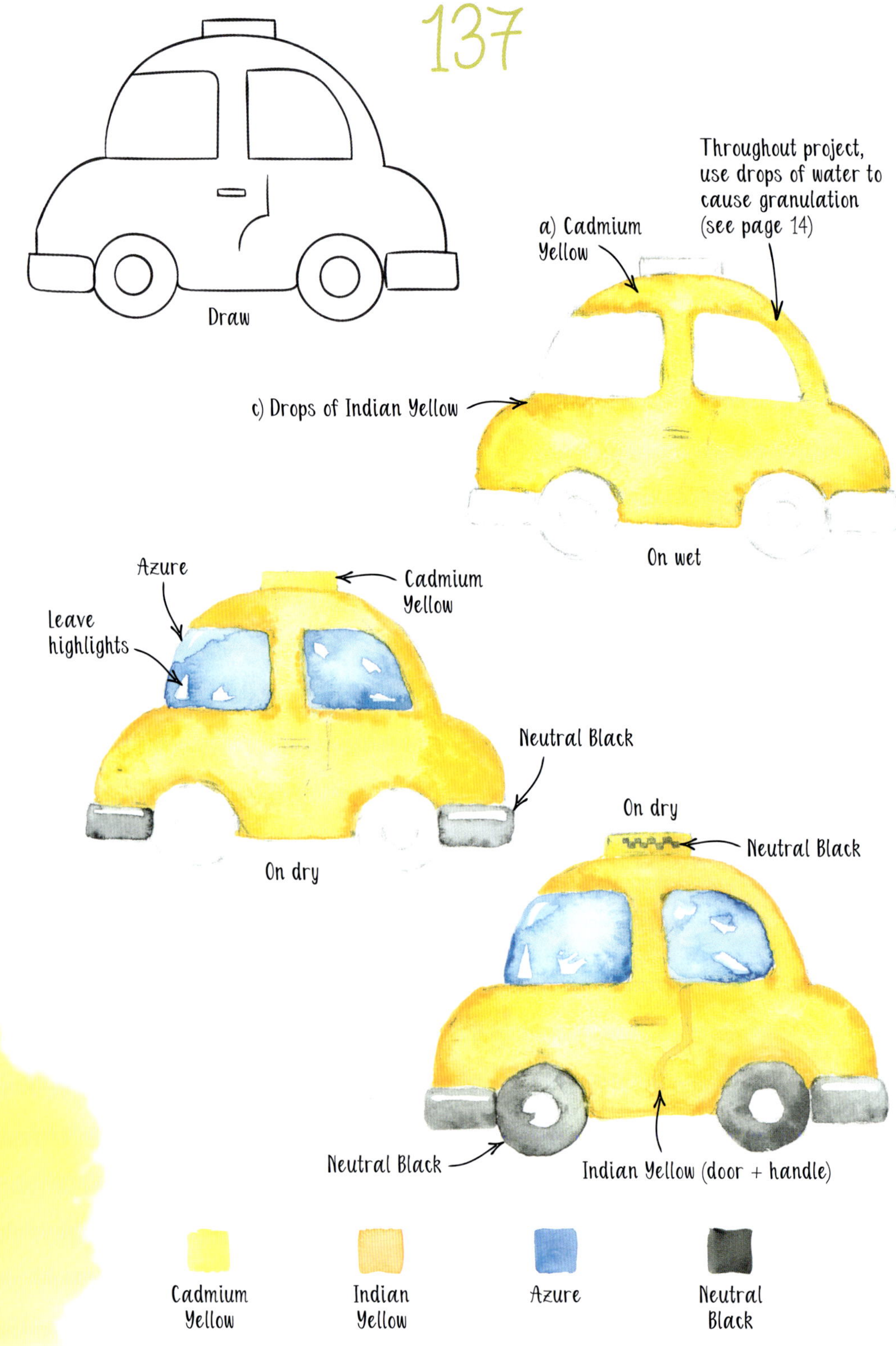
137
Draw
Throughout project, use drops of water to cause granulation (see page 14)
a) Cadmium Yellow
c) Drops of Indian Yellow
On wet
Azure
Cadmium Yellow
leave highlights
Neutral Black
On dry
On dry
Neutral Black
Neutral Black
Indian Yellow (door + handle)
Cadmium Yellow
Indian Yellow
Azure
Neutral Black

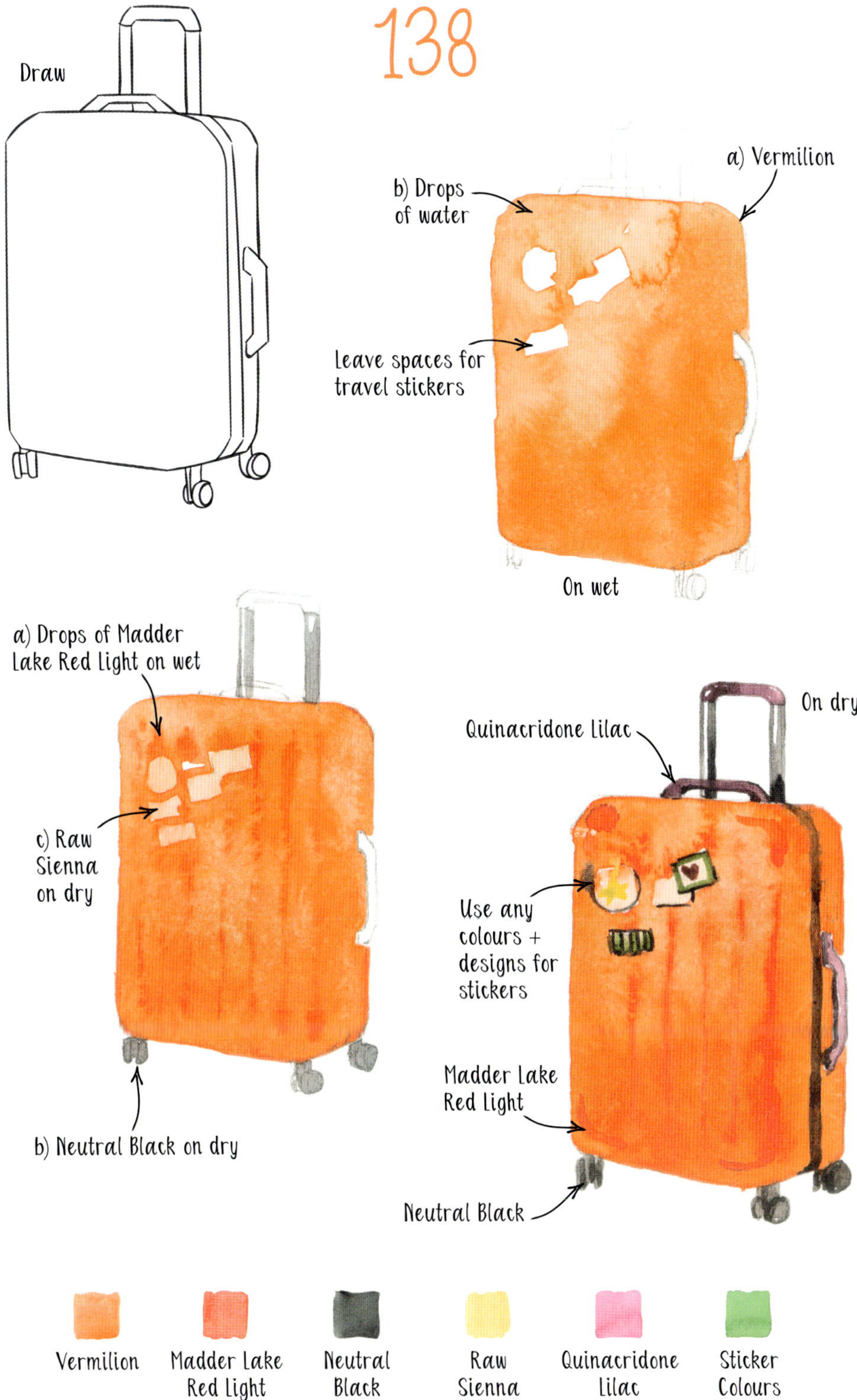
Draw

138

a) Vermilion
b) Drops of water
leave spaces for travel stickers
On wet

a) Drops of Madder Lake Red light on wet
c) Raw Sienna on dry
b) Neutral Black on dry

Quinacridone Lilac
On dry
Use any colours + designs for stickers
Madder Lake Red Light
Neutral Black

Vermilion
Madder Lake Red Light
Neutral Black
Raw Sienna
Quinacridone Lilac
Sticker Colours

139

Draw

On wet
a) Carmine
b) Drops of Carmine
Leave highlights

a) Sap Green on dry
b) Drops of water on wet
leave highlights

On wet
a) Drops of Green
b) Violet (re-wet the berries first)

Carmine
Sap Green
Green
Violet

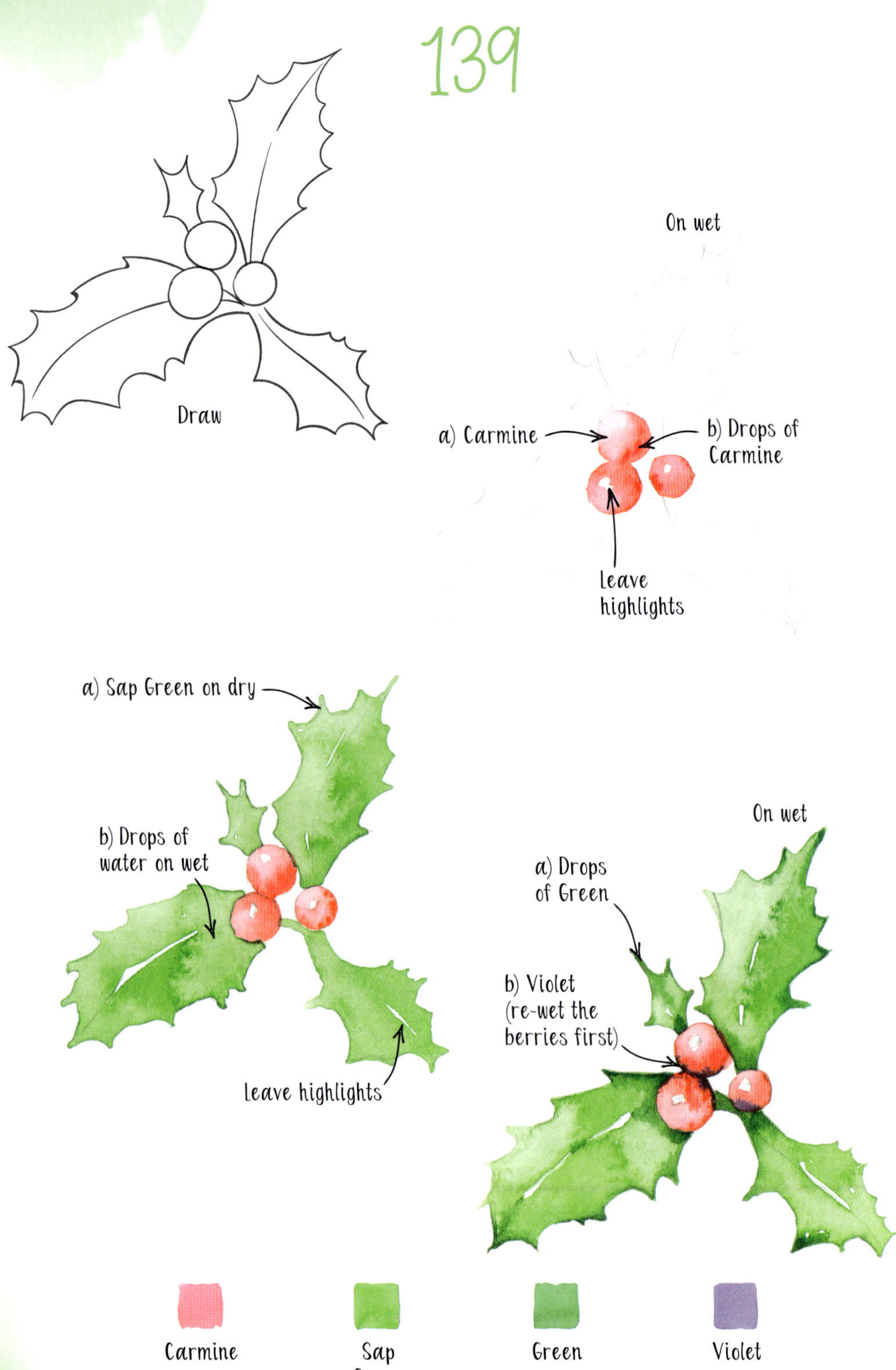

140

Draw

On wet

a) Scarlet

b) Drops
of water

c) Drops of Scarlet

a) Repeat previous
step with Sap Green,
starting on dry

b) Do the same
with Neutral Black
+ Violet mix

b) Scarlet
on dry

a) Neutral Black +
Violet mix on wet

c) Paint knitted texture on dry with
Sap Green, Scarlet + White Ink

Scarlet

Sap
Green

Neutral
Black

Violet

White
Ink

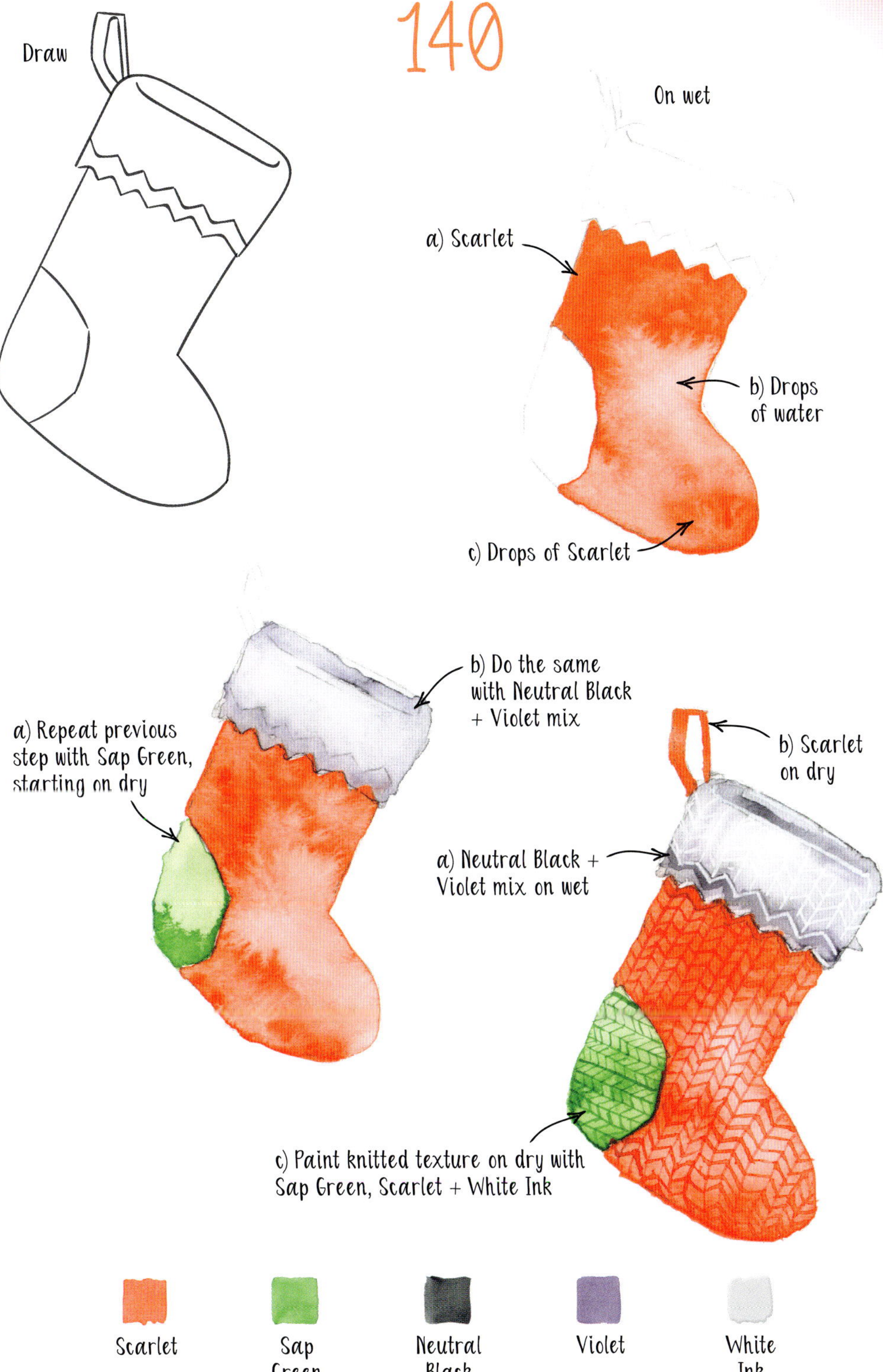

Draw

141

a) Masking fluid
(allow to dry)

b) Sap Green

c) Drops of Azure on wet

On dry

a) Green

b) When paint is dry,
rub off masking fluid

Starting on dry, paint
the decorations like holly
berries (see page 164)

Golden

Claret

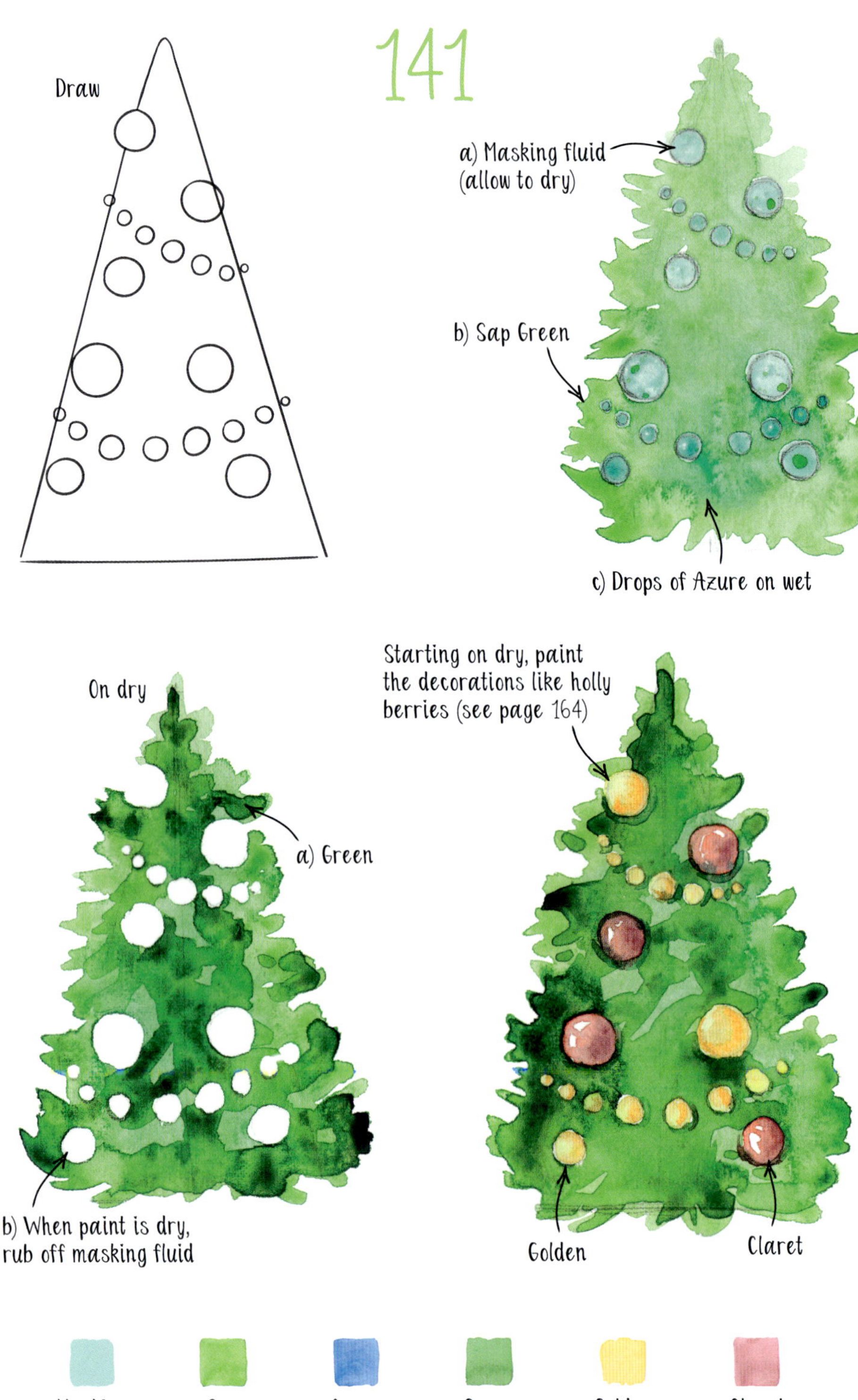

142

Draw

On wet
a) Azure
b) Drops of
Azure + Violet

b) Cadmium
Yellow on dry
c) Drops of Indian
Yellow on wet
a) Drops of Azure on
wet (around edges)

Cadmium Yellow
+ Indian Yellow
On dry

Azure
Violet
Cadmium
Yellow
Indian
Yellow

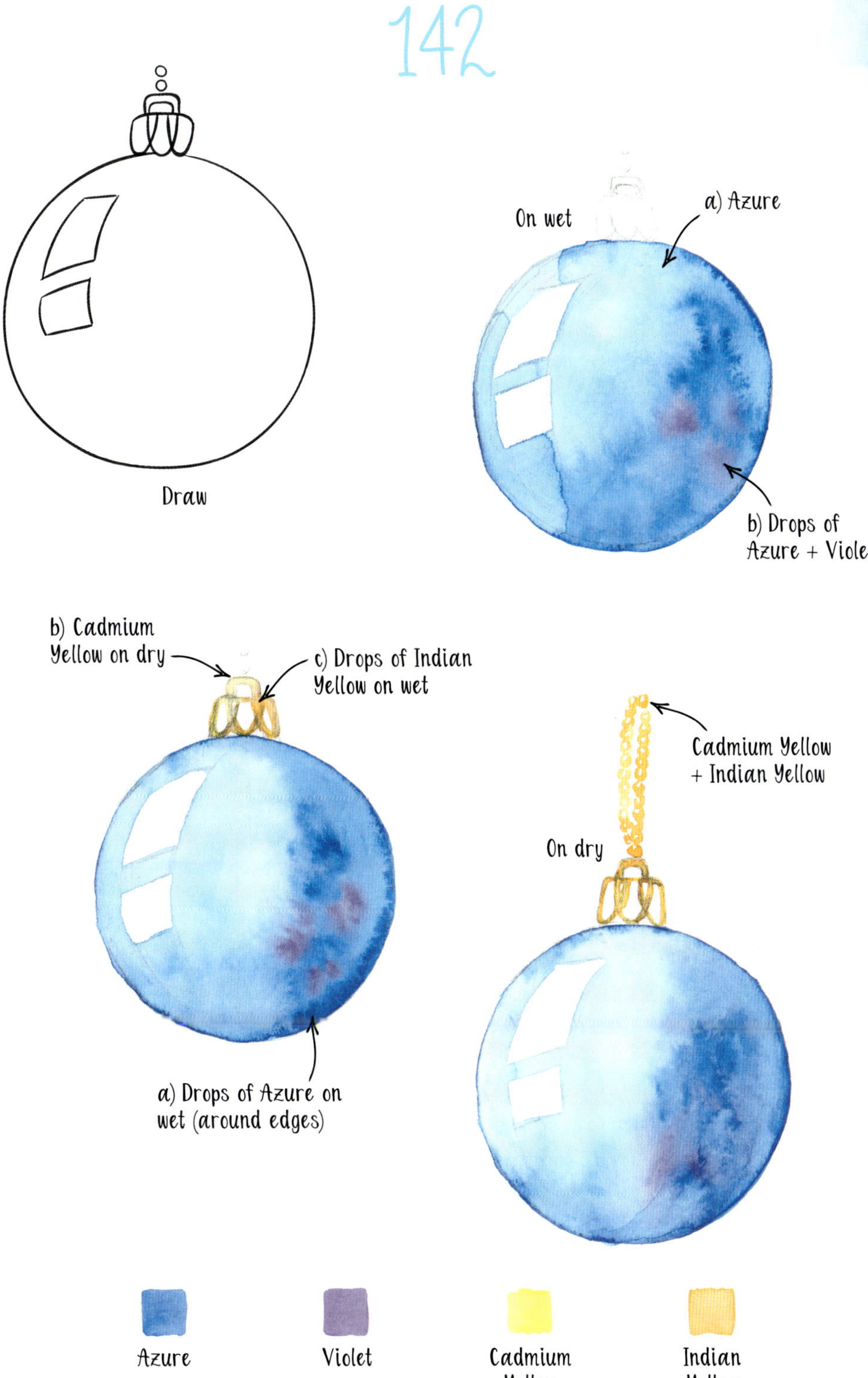

143

Draw
On wet
Azure Blue
leave highlights
Yellowish Green
Drops of
Azure Blue
On dry
On wet
Mars Brown
Azure
Blue
Yellowish
Green
Mars
Brown

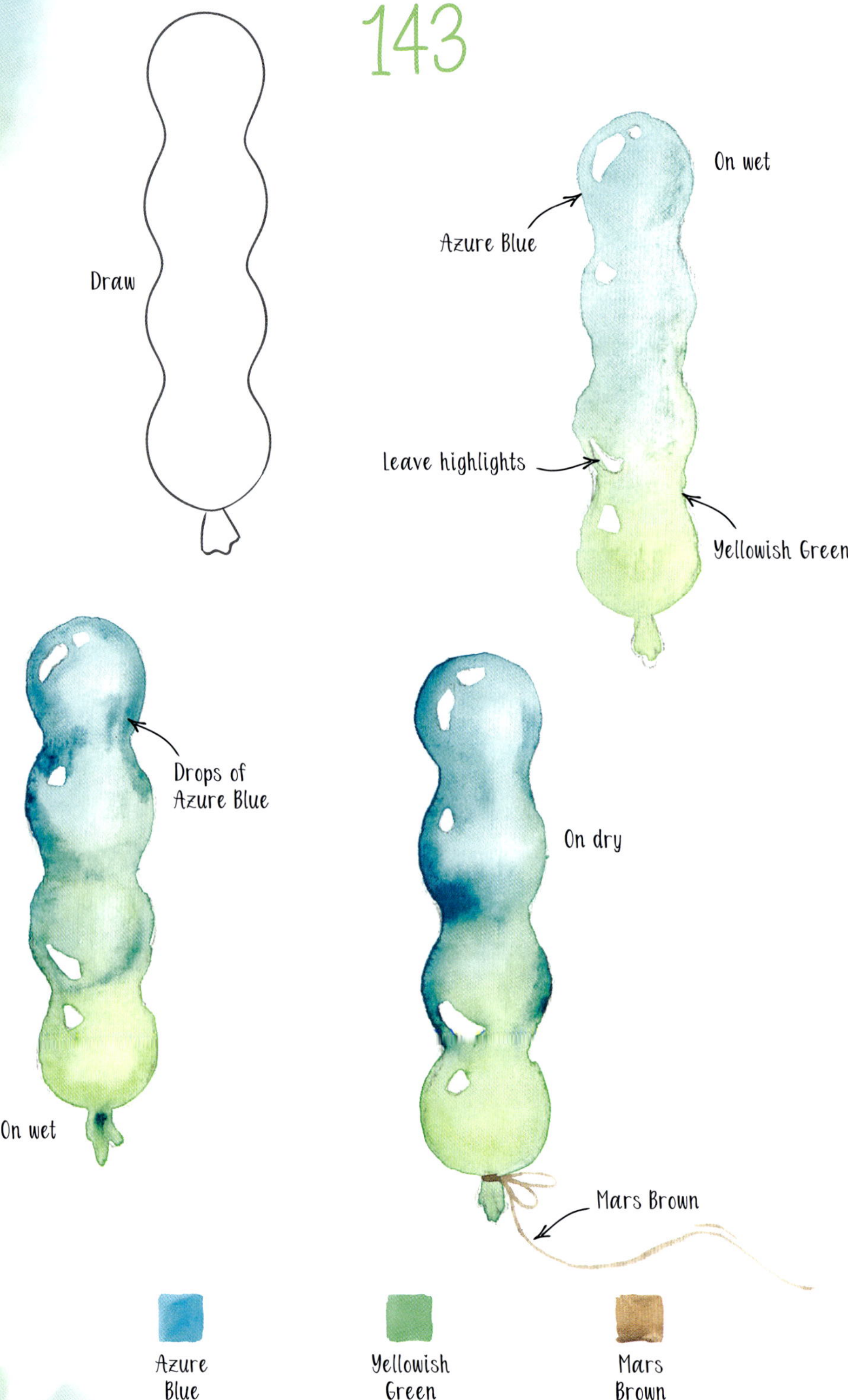

Draw

144

Azure Blue +
Cobalt Blue mix

leave corner edges

a) Cadmium
Yellow on dry

b) Drops of Red
Ochre on wet

b) Repeat
previous step

e) White Ink
on dry

c) Cadmium
Yellow on dry

a) Cobalt
Blue on dry

d) Cobalt Blue (box edges) +
Red Ochre (bow edges) on dry

Azure
Blue

Cobalt
Blue

Cadmium
Yellow

Red
Ochre

White
Ink

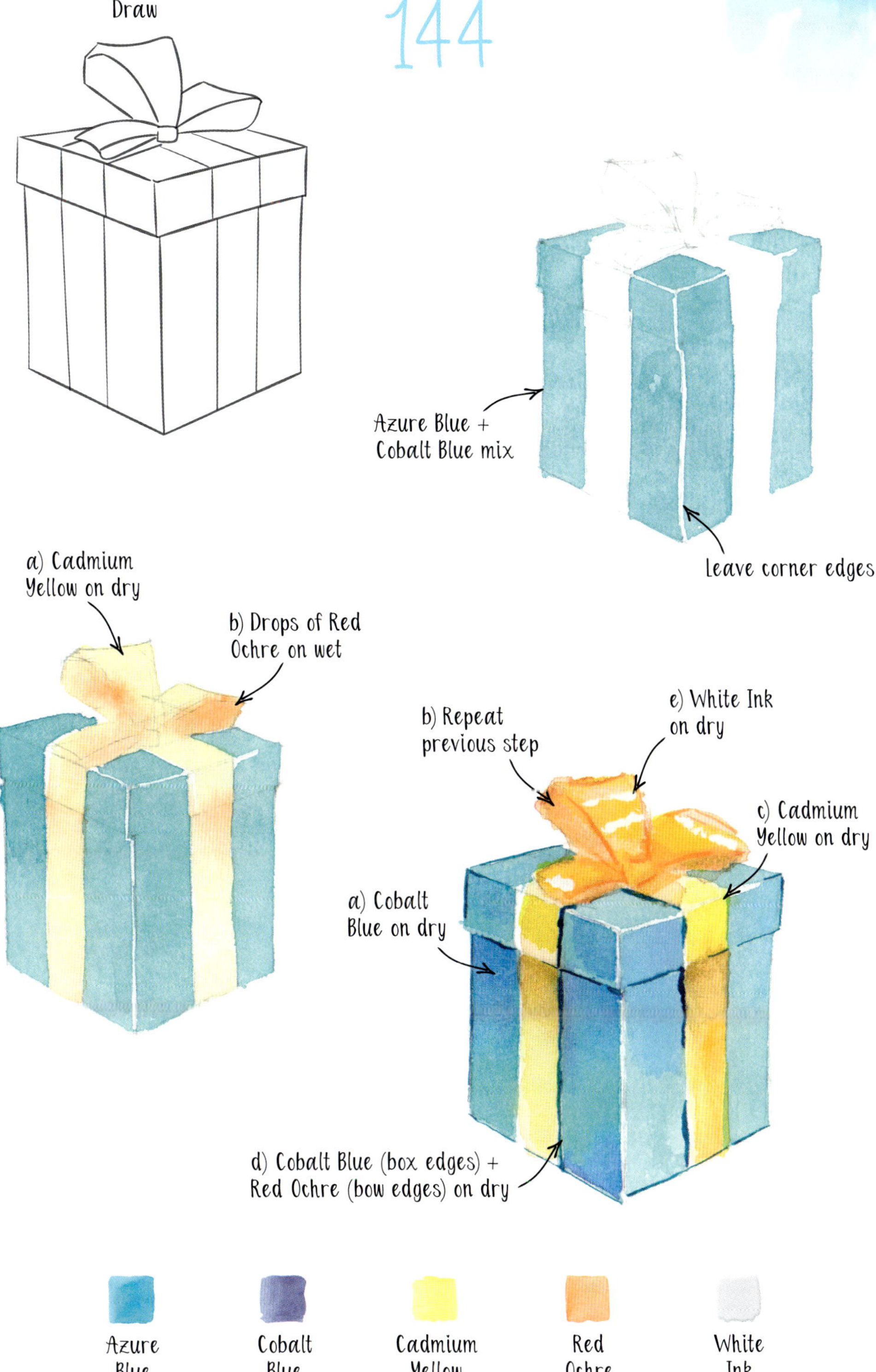

145

Draw
Quinacridone Lilac
a) Cadmium Orange (flame)
+ Burnt Umber (wick)
b) Water, then
Cadmium Yellow
b) Claret
c) Burnt Umber
a) Drops of
Quinacridone
Lilac
On wet
On half-wet
Quinacridone
Lilac
Cadmium
Yellow
Cadmium
Orange
Burnt
Umber
Claret

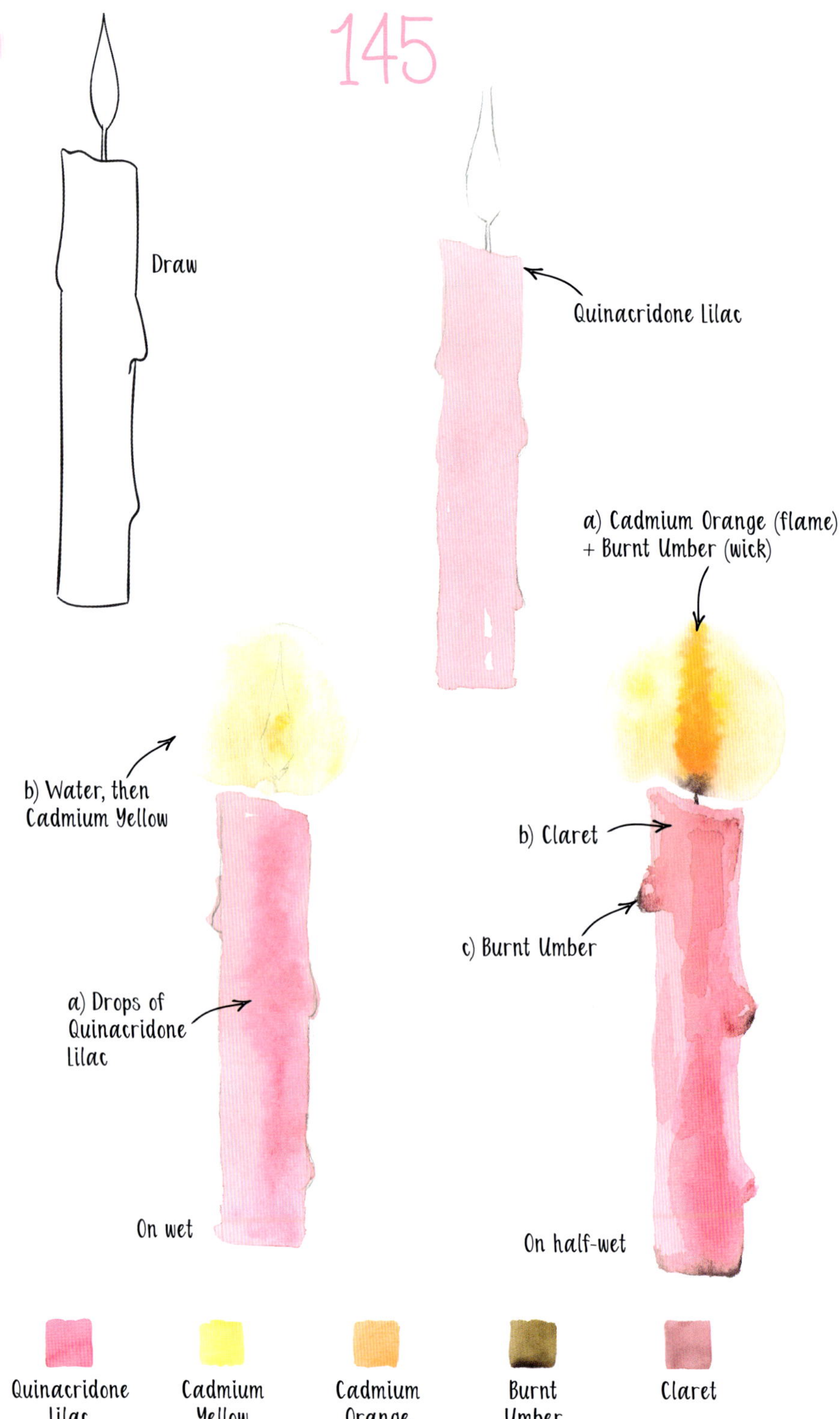

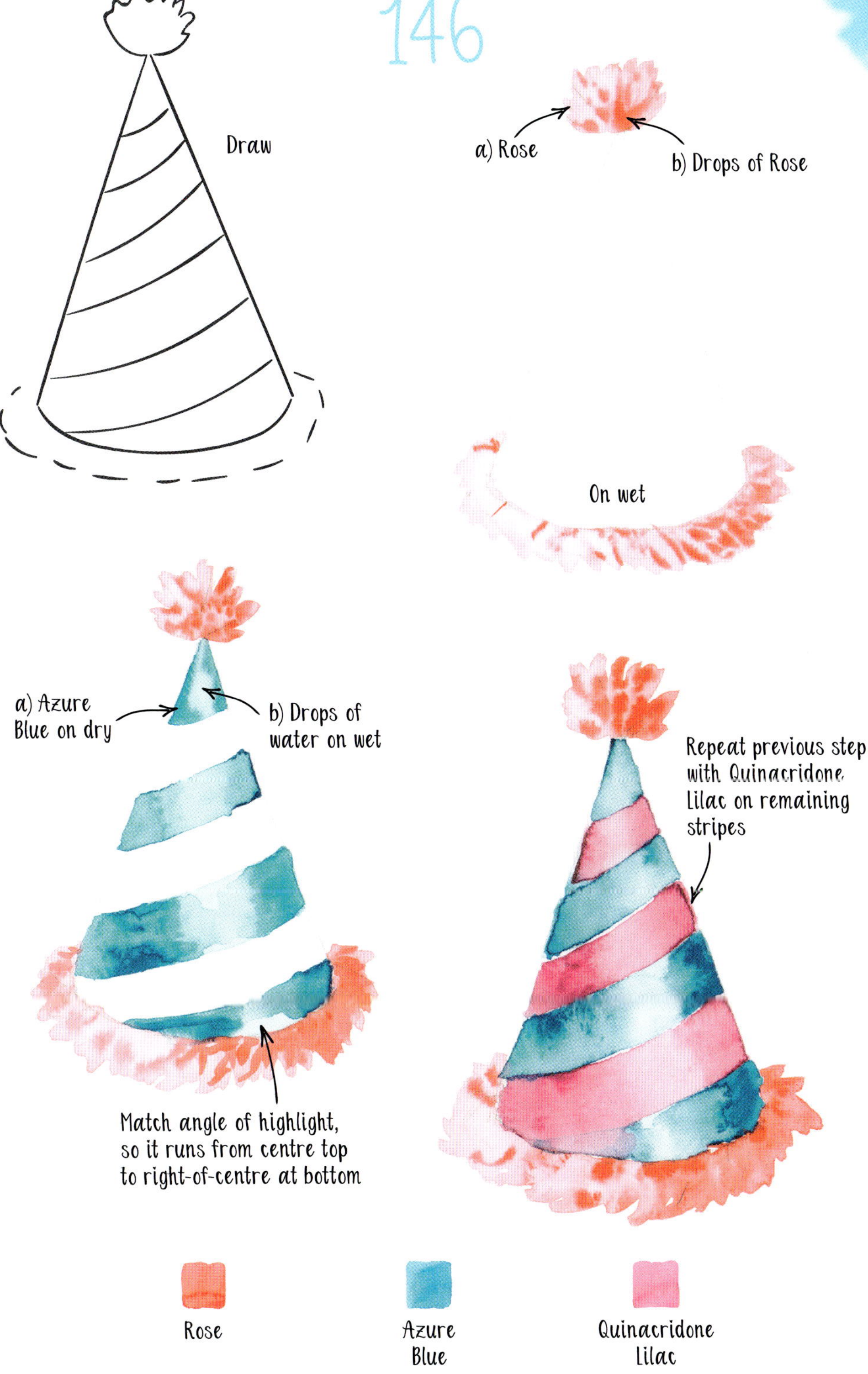
Draw

146

a) Rose
b) Drops of Rose

On wet

a) Azure
Blue on dry
b) Drops of
water on wet

Repeat previous step
with Quinacridone
lilac on remaining
stripes

Match angle of highlight,
so it runs from centre top
to right-of-centre at bottom

Rose

Azure
Blue

Quinacridone
Lilac

147

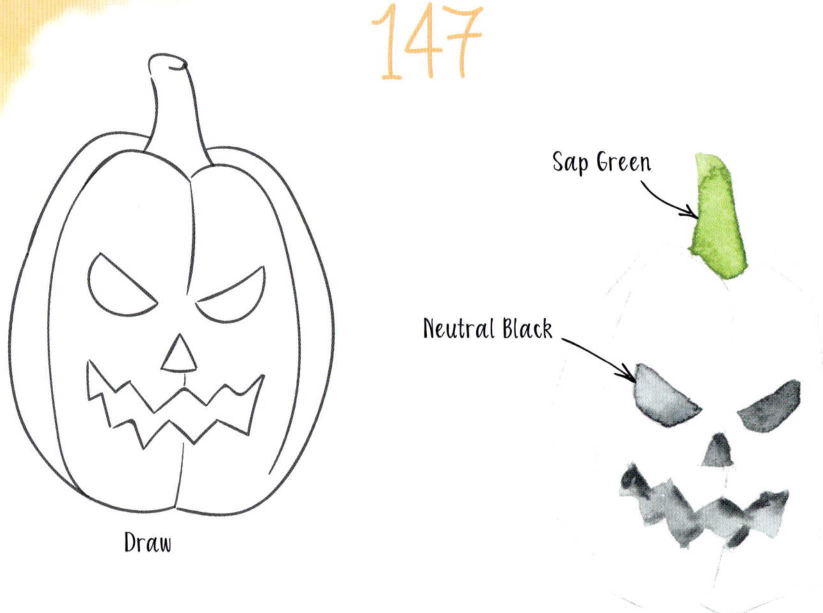

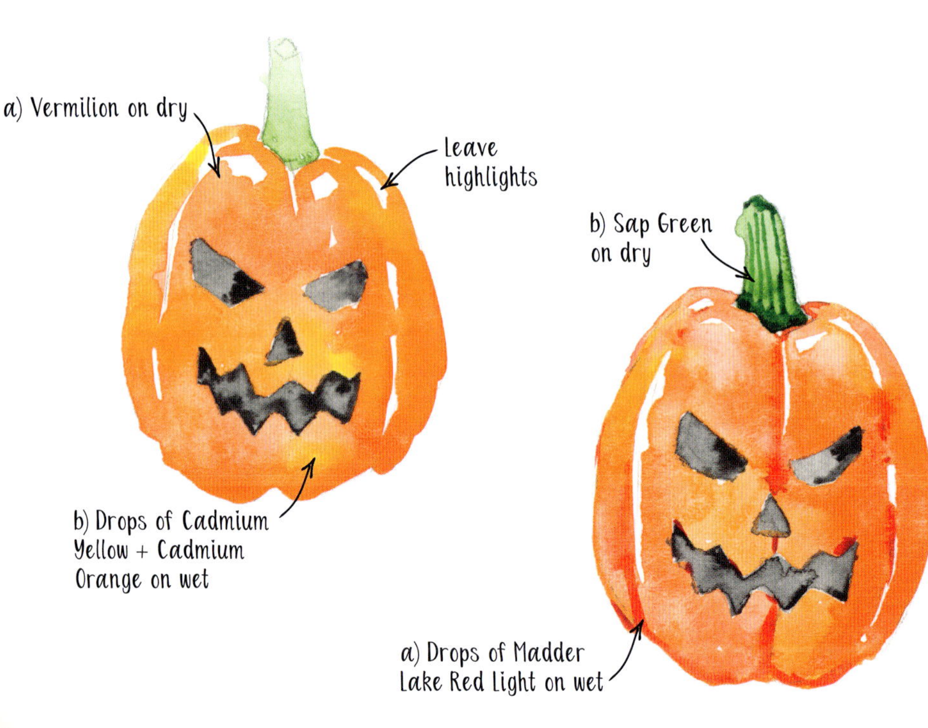

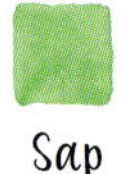 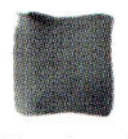  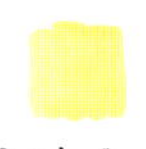  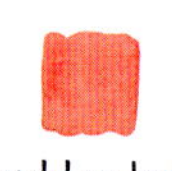

Sap Green	Neutral Black	Vermilion	Cadmium Yellow	Cadmium Orange	Madder Lake Red light

148

Draw
a) Indian Yellow
b) Scarlet
On dry
b) Burnt Sienna on dry
a) Big drop of water on wet
a) Mars Brown
b) Scarlet
c) Madder Lake Red light
On dry
Indian Yellow
Scarlet
Burnt Sienna
Mars Brown
Madder Lake Red light

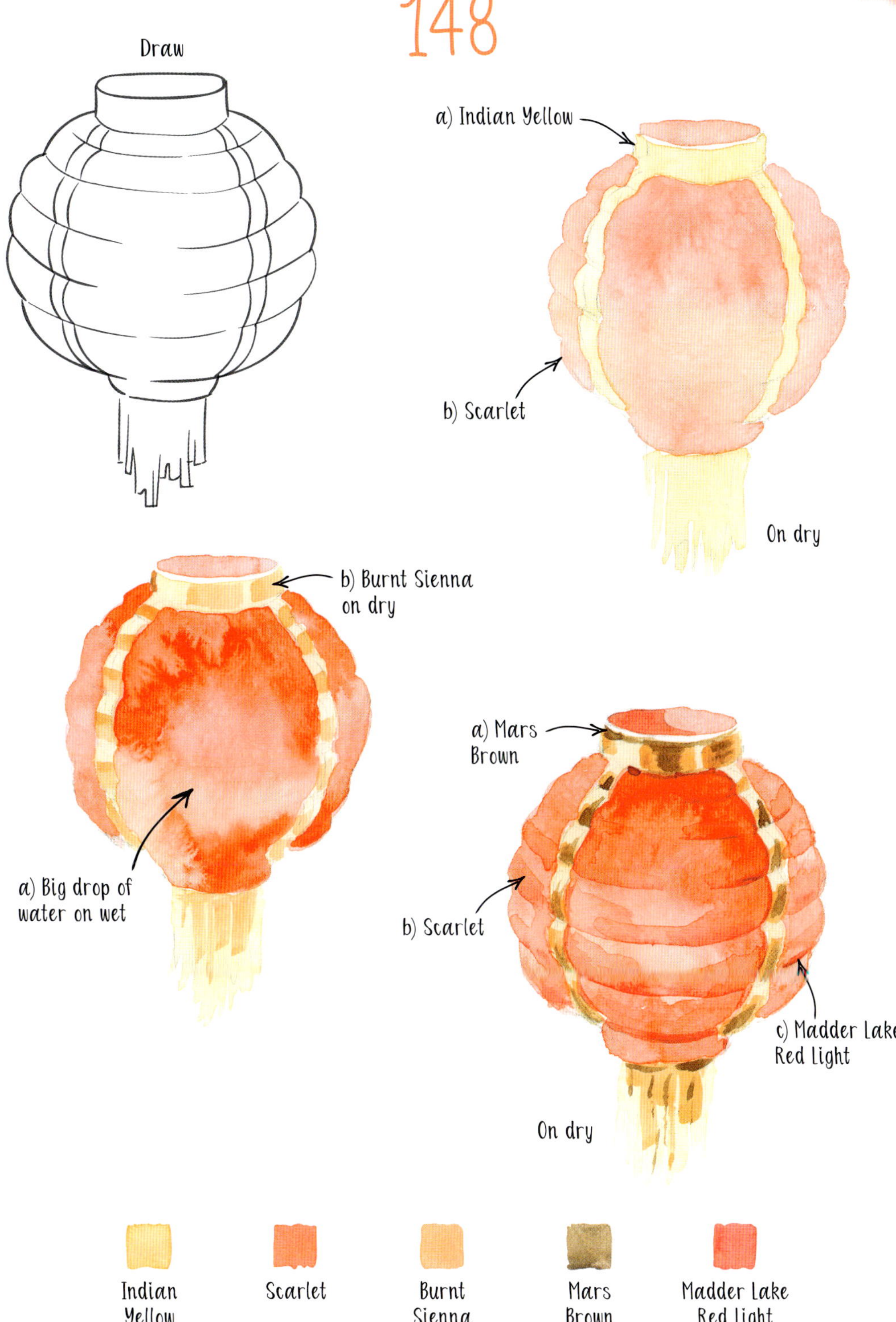

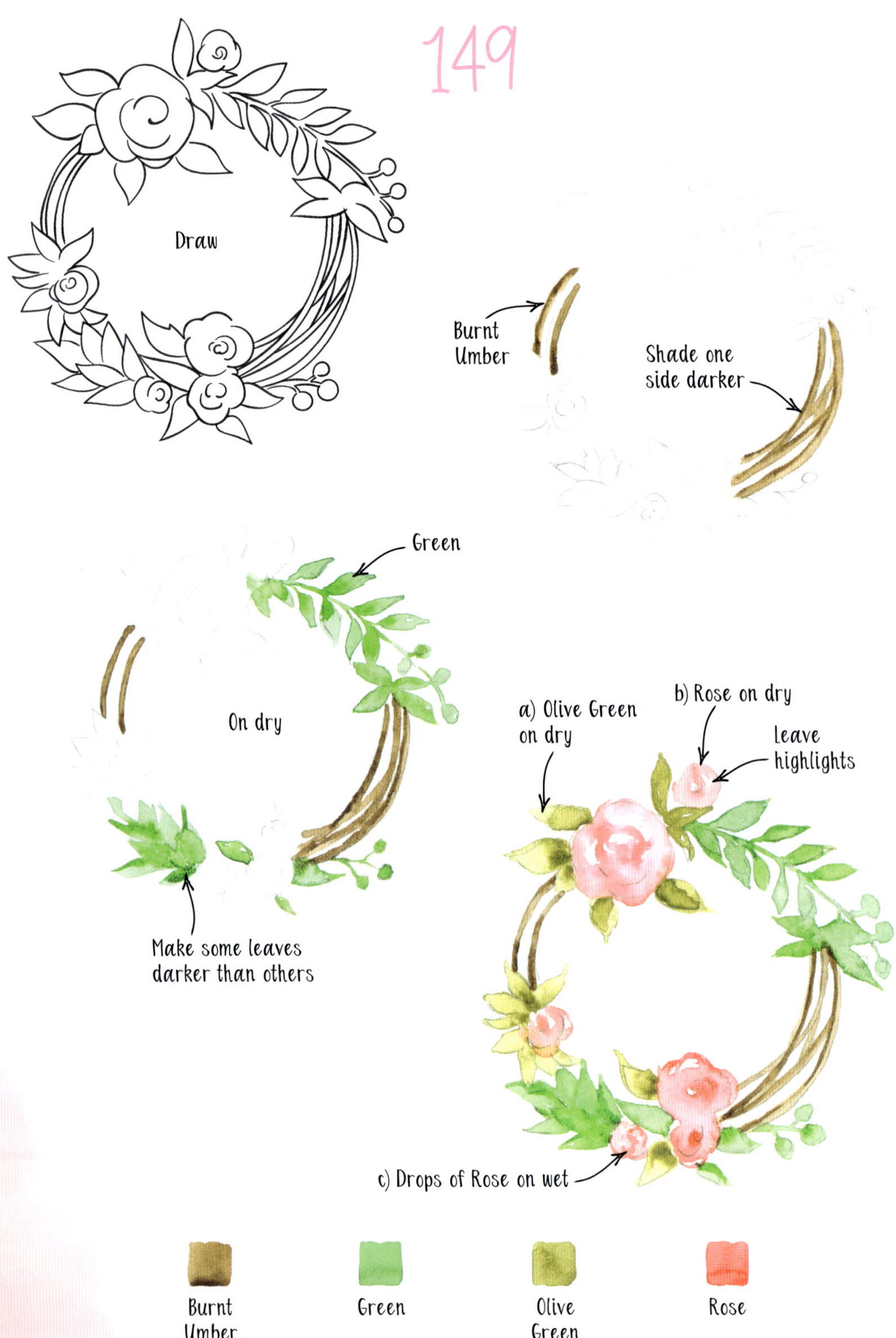
Draw
149
Burnt
Umber
Shade one
side darker
Green
On dry
Make some leaves
darker than others
a) Olive Green
on dry
b) Rose on dry
leave
highlights
c) Drops of Rose on wet
Burnt
Umber
Green
Olive
Green
Rose

150

Draw

a) Cobalt Blue

Leave
highlights

On wet

b) Drops of
Burnt Sienna

Sap Green

Turquoise Blue

Start on dry,
then work on wet

Carmine

On dry

Graduate from one colour to
the other around the wreath
+ add drops of pigment
along edges of leaves

Cobalt
Blue

Burnt
Sienna

Sap
Green

Turquoise
Blue

Carmine

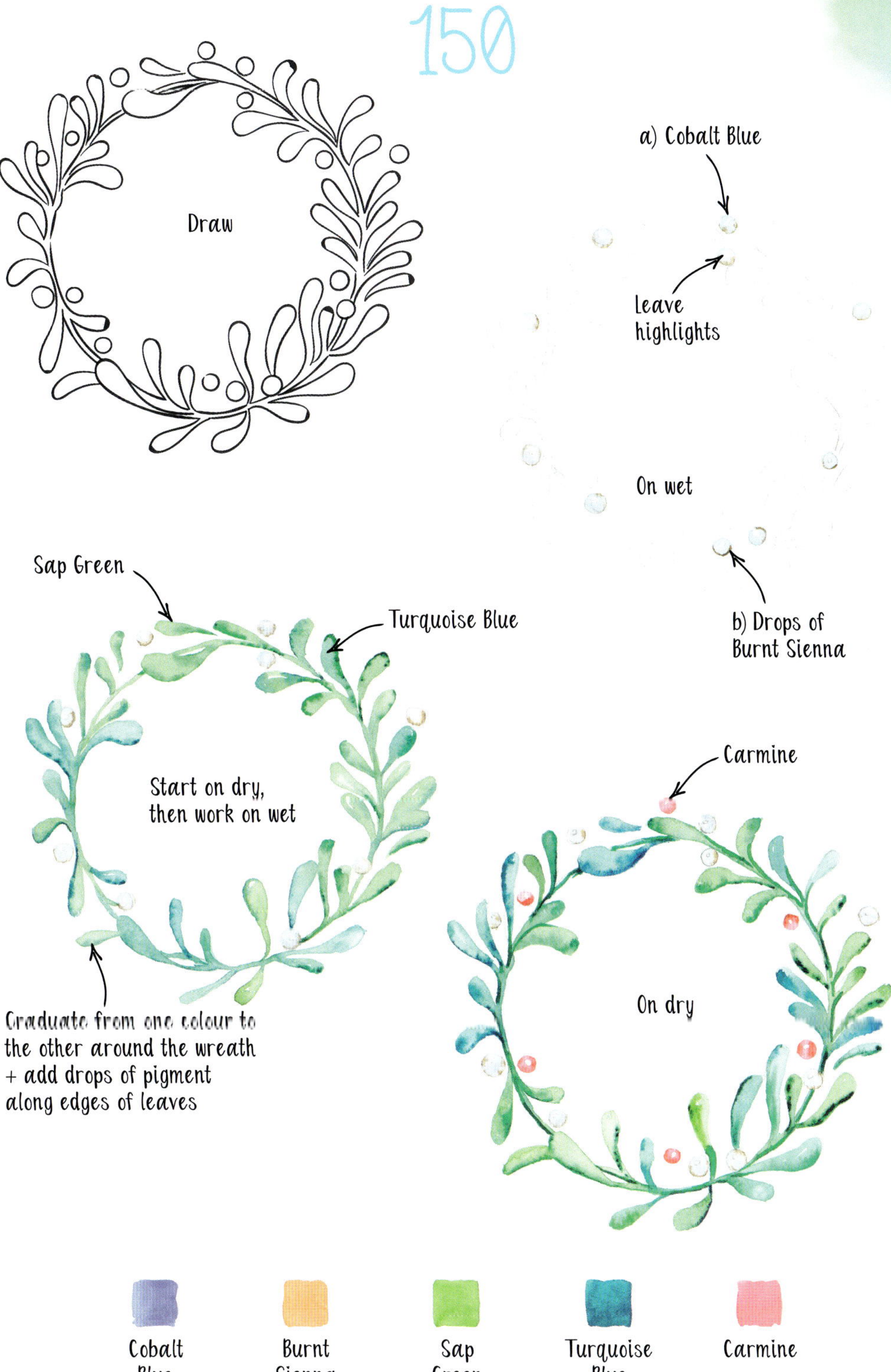

INDEX + CREDITS

Picture credits

The digital drawings for the projects are based on original freehand sketches by the author.

All photographs and illustrations are the copyright of Quarto Publishing plc. While every effort has been made to credit contributors, Quarto would like to apologize should there have been any omissions or errors – and would be pleased to make the appropriate correction for future editions of the book.

Author's acknowledgements

I am really proud of having the opportunity and responsibility to be both the author and illustrator of this book. I am grateful for working with Quarto and its team of professional people, who were always ready to help with any difficulties I faced.

I also thank my supportive family. My mum, who always believes in my strength. My dad, who hasn't understood for a while why I have been drawing 'all those bananas'. My grandparents, who always wait for news from me. The beloved man, who overcomes all the problems with me each day.

I am just grateful to my destiny that gives me a chance to share my art with lots of people.